1-30-75

THE IMAGINATION OF MAURICE BARRÈS

PHILIP OUSTON

The Imagination of Maurice Barrès

UNIVERSITY OF TORONTO PRESS

University of Toronto Romance Series 26

Toronto and Buffalo
Printed in Canada
ISBN 0-8020-5274-6
LC 79-190347

TO MY CANADIAN FRIENDS

ACKNOWLEDGMENTS

It is a pleasure to be able to express my thanks to Professor John Cocking, of the University of London King's College, for the guidance and encouragement he has given me at every stage of the planning and preparation of this book, which is a revised version of my doctoral thesis. It has been published with the help of a grant from the Humanities Research Council of Canada, using funds provided by the Canada Council, and the Publications Fund of the University of Toronto Press. I am also much indebted to the Court of the University of St Andrews and to the Cassel Educational Trust for assisting my research financially.

Chapter Ten, 'An Image of France,' was published in *Forum for Modern Language Studies* VI 4 (October 1970), and is reprinted here by permission of the editors of that journal.

I am most grateful for all the help and advice I have been privileged to receive from the editors of the University of Toronto Press, and I should like to record the very special debt of gratitude I owe to Professor Frédéric Grover, of the University of British Columbia, who encouraged me to submit my manuscript to them for publication.

I also wish to thank Monsieur Philippe Barrès for the generously attentive and helpful interest he has taken in this study of his father's work, and for his kind permission to publish the three photographs with which it has been illustrated.

St Andrews, March 1974 PAO

CONTENTS

Acknowledgments / vii
Foreword / xi
Chronological Table / xv

PART I: INTRODUCTION

1 Exemplars / 3
2 The Limits of the Imagination / 7
3 The Development of Barrès's Traditionalism / 15

PART II: IMAGINATION IN BARRÈS'S PHILOSOPHY

4 The Religious Imagination / 81
5 Scientific Imagination / 93
6 The Reconciliation of Science and Religion / 99

PART III: IMAGINATION IN BARRÈS'S RHETORIC

Introductory Note on Propaganda and Education / 121
7 Function and Forms of the Persuasive Image / 123
8 The Cult of Heroes / 136
9 The Rhetoric of Commemoration / 160
10 An Image of France / 176
11 Imagination in Barrès's Theory of Education / 204

PART IV: CONCLUSION

12 Barrès's Unity / 241

Notes / 276 Bibliography / 287 Index / 296

FOREWORD

Many critics have called attention to the predominance in Barrès's work of such forms of imaginative consciousness and expression as image, metaphor, symbol, myth.[1] But the sustained effort he made, throughout three bitterly contentious decades of French political history, from the Dreyfus affair to the Treaty of Versailles, to establish and to defend nationalist and traditionalist positions within the 'area of interest' these 'overlapping' forms may be said to delimit,[2] has not, I claim, been adequately recognized and explored.[3] The purpose of this book is to make good this claim. The word 'imagination' in its title and text has the general and familiar meaning, authorized by the Concise Oxford Dictionary, of 'mental faculty forming images of external objects not present to the senses.'

The semantic difficulties of this field of study, springing from the double reference of such words as imagination, image, and imagery to both psychology and literary criticism, are well known.[4] Psychologists and students of style may avoid many of them by restricting the meaning of 'image' respectively to either 'an experience which reproduces or copies in part, and with some degree of sensory realism, a previous perceptual experience in the absence of the original sensory stimulation,'[5] or 'all those numerous stylistic figures ... in which an

1 *See* p. 276.
2 R. Wellek and A. Warren, *Theory of Literature* 3rd ed. (London Peregrine Books 1963) 186
3 *See* p. 277.
4 R. Wellek and A. Warren, *Theory of Literature,* 186
5 P. McKellar, *Imagination and Thinking: A Psychological Analysis*

element of comparison or identification of two terms appears or is inspired.'[6] No such restriction is desirable in the present study, however, since it is neither exclusively psychological nor stylistic in the technical sense, but historical, an attempt to ascertain the place and the weight in Barrès's thought and art of a 'faculty forming' what he, less exclusively than either psychologists or stylisticians, called *images*, both when referring to experiences of the mind's eye and when referring to figurative expressions.[7] Context and comment will show, as Professors Wellek and Warren recommend they should,[8] whether Barrès is using the word *image* for such psychological experiences as perception, recollection, or association, or whether he is using it to denote word-pictures or their synaesthetic *correspondance* or *transposition*; or, again, whether the psychological and the figurative senses of the word are blurred, as in the following mature example of his self-consciously imaginative philosophy of traditionalism, and where the reference of *images* may be either the experience or the vehicle of an act of secondary perception,[9] or both: i.e. either or both (a) the author's mental image of a traditional way of life, (b) pictures, descriptions, or models representing it in forms that can be handed on from one generation to the next:

> Voilà trente ans que l'idée de tradition m'émerveille et m'émeut, et que je subis, comme on adore les dieux, avec un sentiment de vénération, la puissance des images et des sentiments qui nous viennent du fond des âges, où ils ont formé des hommes, pour qu'à notre tour nous les transmettions à nos petits-fils.
> [*Chronique de la Grande Guerre* (Paris: Plon-Nourrit, 14 vols 1920–4) v 102][10]

(London: Cohen and West 1957) 201, 204. Cf. J. Drever, *A Dictionary of Psychology* (London: Penguin Books 1952) 127.

6 F.W. Leakey, 'Baudelaire's Metaphor in *Les Fleurs du Mal*' (typescript, University of London Library 1951) xii–xiii

7 *See* p. 278.

8 *Theory of Literature*, 186

9 P. McKellar, *Imagination and Thinking*, 204: 'Perception of an object or situation through some intermediary (e.g. a picture of it, a description of it, a model of it).'

10 Henceforth referred to as *Grande Guerre*

Barrès's use of *imagination* ranges (like its English equivalent, which is used to delimit the present study of his work) almost as widely as his use of the word *image*, stopping short of only the most exclusively sensuous or abstract kinds of perception and the most prosaically bald forms of factual description or theoretical discourse.

Some initial idea of the importance to Barrès of this most 'indefinable and contradictory of faculties or forms of expression'[11] may be gained by noting his widespread attribution of a general imaginative capability to the exemplary figures who helped him to discover his vocation, or to understand it better, or to give it fictitious expression. His conception of the imagination can be clarified by some preparatory plotting of the theoretical limits of abstract thought and sensuous experience between which it operates. These preliminaries occupy the first two chapters of the introduction, which is completed by a brief account of the development of Barrès's traditionalism as it took shape from a literary apprenticeship in the Paris of Mallarmé and Zola, from a political initiation amid the tumultuous assemblies and the backstage intrigues of Boulangism, the Panama Scandal, and the Dreyfus Affair, from a grand tour of the dilettante's Europe and a native's return to his *petite patrie* in eastern France; and as it found expression in his essays, novels, articles, speeches, and diaries from *Sous l'œil des barbares* to *La Grande pitié des églises de France*. The tasks appropriately assigned to the imagination in Barrès's mature scheme of ideas and its associated technique of persuasion may thus be understood before his imagination is shown at work specifically on these tasks, in Part II: 'Imagination in Barrès's Philosophy,' which traces the sources and course of his enquiry into the epistemological foundations of religion and science, and explains the effort he made in the decade before the First World War to reconcile their currently conflicting claims on the basis of a theory of imaginative hypothesis;

11 H. Peyre, *Connaissance de Baudelaire* (Paris: Corti 1951) 78

and Part III, 'Imagination in Barrès's Rhetoric,' which examines his systematic use of such vehicles of persuasive expression as *formule, leçon de choses, récit, image, symbole, légende, mythe, cérémonie, musique*, and characterizes the outstanding operative properties of his propagandistic and pedagogical image of France. Part IV, by way of conclusion, follows in a single sequence, from *Le Culte du Moi* to the final volume of *Mes Cahiers*, the part played by imagination in the progressive composition of 'Barrès's Unity.'

CHRONOLOGICAL TABLE

1862	19 August: birth at Charmes-sur-Moselle, in Lorraine, of Auguste-Maurice Barrès
1870–3	Franco-Prussian War. German invasion of France. Charmes occupied
1877–80	Barrès attends the *lycée* at Nancy
1884–5	Publishes a one-man monthly literary gazette in Paris: *Les Taches d'encre* (four issues)
1886	Co-editor, with Charles le Goffic (1863–1932), of *Les Chroniques: Revue littéraire et artistique*
1887–8	Visits Florence, Siena, Rome, and Venice
1888	April: 'M. le général Boulanger et la nouvelle génération,' in *La Revue Indépendante* *Huit jours chez M. Renan* *Sous l'œil des barbares*
1889	6 October: election to Parliament in the third constituency of Nancy (Meurthe-et-Moselle) *Un Homme libre*
1891	*Le Jardin de Bérénice* *Trois Stations de psychothérapie* Suicide of General Boulanger
1892	*Le Culte du Moi: examen des trois romans idéologiques* *Toute licence sauf contre l'amour* Journey to Spain
1893	Panama Scandal

	L'Ennemi des lois
	Parliamentary elections: Barrès is defeated at Nancy
	Marriage to Mlle Paule Couche
1894	*Du Sang, de la volupté et de la mort*
	Dreyfus convicted of treason by court martial
1894–5	Barrès edits *La Cocarde, journal quotidien d'opposition républicaine*
1896	Birth of a son: Philippe Barrès
	Parliamentary elections: Barrès is defeated at Neuilly-Boulogne
1897	*Le Roman de l'énergie nationale:* I *Les Déracinés*
	20 November: 'La Foi dans l'armée,' in *Le Journal*
1898	Zola publishes 'J'accuse!'
	Parliamentary elections: Barrès is defeated at Nancy
	Death of Barrès's father
	9 December: 'La Raison nationale,' in *Le Journal*
1899	Barrès joins La Ligue de la Patrie Française
	La Terre et les morts
	30 October: 'L'Éducation nationale,' in *Le Journal*
1900	*Le Roman de l'énergie nationale:* II *L'Appel au soldat*
	Journey to Greece
1901	Death of Barrès's mother
	Barrès resigns from La Ligue de la Patrie Française
1902	*Scènes et doctrines du nationalisme*
	Le Roman de l'énergie nationale: III *Leurs figures*
	Journeys to Venice and to Toledo
1903	*Amori et dolori sacrum*
	Parliamentary election: Barrès is defeated in the 4th *arrondissement* of Paris
	Les Amitiés françaises
1905	*Les Bastions de l'Est. Au Service de l'Allemagne*
1906	Barrès is elected to the French Academy in succession to J.-M. de Heredia
	Le Voyage de Sparte
	Parliamentary elections: Barrès is elected in the 1st *arrondissement* of Paris (Les Halles)
1907	Journey to Egypt

1909	*Les Bastions de l'Est. Colette Baudoche*
	Suicide of Barrès's nephew Charles Demange
1910	6 January: 'La Démolition des églises,' in *L'Écho de Paris*
	18 January: *Discours sur l'enseignement primaire, prononcé à la Chambre des Députés*
	Parliamentary elections: Barrès is re-elected in his Paris constituency
1911	16 January: *Pour les églises. Discours prononcé à la Chambre des Députés*
	Le Greco (re-edited in 1912 as *Greco ou le secret de Tolède*)
1912	25 November: *Pour les églises de France. Discours prononcé à la Chambre des Députés*
1913	*La Colline inspirée*
1914	*La Grande pitié des églises de France*
	April: parliamentary elections: Barrès is re-elected in his Paris constituency
	May-June: journey to the Levant
	July: elected to the presidency of La Ligue des Patriotes in succession to Paul Déroulède (1846–1914)
	31 July: assassination of Jaurès
	1–4 August: outbreak of First World War
1915–20	*L'Âme française et la guerre* (re-edited with the title of *Chronique de la Grande Guerre*, in 1920–4) [Barrès's collected daily wartime articles in *L'Écho de Paris*]
1917	*Les Diverses familles spirituelles de la France*
1919	July-September: 'La Grande pitié des laboratoires de France,' in *L'Écho de Paris*
	Parliamentary elections: Barrès is re-elected in Paris
1921	*Les Bastions de l'Est. Le Génie du Rhin* [five lectures given at the University of Strasbourg in November 1920]
1922	*La Politique rhénane. Discours parlementaires*
	Un Jardin sur l'Oronte
1923	*Souvenirs d'un officier de la Grande Armée (Jean-Baptiste-Auguste Barrès), publiés par Maurice Barrès, son petit-fils*

	Une Enquête aux pays du Levant
	4 December: death of Maurice Barrès
1926	*Le Mystère en pleine lumière* [collected essays 1921–23]
1927	*Les Maîtres* [essays, articles, and speeches 1900–23]
1929–57	*Mes Cahiers* [notebooks 1896–1923]
1930	*Les Grands problèmes du Rhin* [collected speeches and articles]
	En Provence [collected essays]
1958	*N'Importe où hors du monde* [essays and stories 1895–1923]
1961	*Le Départ pour la vie* [correspondence with L. Sorg and S. de Guaita 1880–7]

PART I: INTRODUCTION

1 Maurice Barrès in the eighteen-nineties
Photo Bibliothèque nationale, Paris

CHAPTER ONE

Exemplars

In 1906, the year of his election to the French Academy, and of his re-election, after thirteen years' absence, to the Chamber of Deputies, Barrès named two contemporaries he 'respected,' and two he 'admired': Déroulède and Mistral, Maurras and Anna de Noailles respectively.[1] He saw all four as models of imagination in action.[2] Later he claimed a fifth sample of the species for his 'haute ménagerie': Jean Jaurès.[3] The cause of 'Sacred Union' was partly responsible for inspiring the nationalist leader's public homage to the socialist martyr on the eve of the Great War,[4] but the long pre-war debate between the two political adversaries, in the Press, in Parliament, and in an occasional private dialogue, had already aroused Barrès's deeper fellow-feeling for the man, and for some features of his political genius. In the political portrait gallery of *Mes Cahiers,* Jaurès from 1906 to 1914 has pride of place. Though Barrès remained mistrustful of what he had earlier decided was naïve and imprecise in the tribune's optimistic humanism,[5] he became fascinated by the power of his 'sacred rhetoric,'[6] and was compelled to grant this 'Bossuet' of a new creed, this 'Mirabeau' of a new Revolution,[7] quali-

1 *Mes Cahiers, Œuvre,* XIV, 288
2 *Œuvre* XII 159; XIV 61; XV 182; XVIII 90; XIX 302; *see* also XX 102–3 [Léon Daudet]
3 *Œuvre* XIX 206
4 *Œuvre* XVIII 201–4; XIX 290
5 *Œuvre* XIII 71–2, 224
6 *Œuvre* XV 369
7 *Œuvre* XVI 289; XVII 335

ties akin to those he prized in Déroulède, Mistral, Maurras, and Madame de Noailles: a flame, a generosity of spirit, an heroic, rich, and religious nature, a 'sovereign imagination':[8]

> Ce Jaurès, ce puissant esprit que je dis, que nous disons absurde, c'est une imagination reine dans les territoires de l'avenir comme d'autres dans les territoires du passé.
> [*Mes Cahiers*, in *L'Œuvre de Maurice Barrès* (Paris: Au Club de l'Honnête Homme 1965–8) XVII 294][9]

Most of Barrès's models from the past were, similarly, men and women moved and moving others by the gift of imagination. Some of these: Loyola, Hasan, Rashid Ad-Din Sinan ('The Old Man of the Mountains'), and Napoleon, attracted him because, like Déroulède, Mistral, Maurras, and Jaurès, they had applied the persuasive force of imagination to the practical field of political or religious leadership.[10] Others stood near them, on the bookshelves lining the long walls of Barrès's first-floor workroom, in his house at Neuilly-sur-Seine, because, as poets, painters, prophets, saints, they had found in imagination a means of accomplishing a more disinterested vocation: Jalal Ad-Din Rumi, the dervish poet of Konya, for instance,[11] and Victor Hugo, whom Barrès revered at a time when it was not fashionable to do so, particularly among nationalists, and in whose vigorous visionary imagination he traced the influence of those marches of eastern France and the Rhineland which had also, he believed, helped to shape the genius of Hugo's (and his own) compatriots: Joan of Arc, 'qui fait voir dans l'ordre religieux la nature des plus grands poètes'; Claude Gelée ('Ces formes, ces cou-

8 *Œuvre* XIII 4; XV 109–10, 120, 372; XVIII 15–16, 223, 237–8
9 This edition will henceforth be referred to as *Œuvre*.
10 'Psychologie des grands hommes,' *Le Journal* 17 November 1893; 'Les conditions de vie d'un dominateur' *Le Figaro*, 5 May 1894; *Œuvre* V 563; X 112; XI 281, 484. *See* I.-M. Frandon, *L'Orient de Maurice Barrès* (Geneva: Droz 1952) and *'Assassins' et 'Danseurs mystiques' dans 'Une Enquête aux pays du Levant' de Maurice Barrès* (Geneva: Droz 1954).
11 *Œuvre* XI 380–445 and I.-M. Frandon, *L'Orient de Maurice Barrès* and *'Assassins' et 'Danseurs Mystiques'*

leurs ... sont sorties lentement de son être ému, accordé, discipliné, nourri par le regard intense avec lequel, de naissance, il sut approfondir tout ce qu'il voyait'); Pierre Fourier, 'plein d'une imagination véhémente, un visionnaire incomparable.'[12] The list of those whom Barrès continued to call 'les maîtres' to the end of his life is completed by the names of Dante, 'tout imagination et ... tout réalité'; Pascal, 'qui ne fait qu'animer, avec sa prodigieuse imagination, des idées religieuses qui sont déposées au fond de chacun de nous'; Lamartine ('sa tendresse d'imagination est divine'), falling silent because his 'images' have 'taken flight' from the wreck of his political hopes and family fortunes; Saint Teresa, translating the mysteries of her faith into the images of worldly love.[13]

There is no hard and fast dividing line between Barrès's historical and contemporary portraits and the creatures of fiction portrayed in his novels. The provocative subjectivism of his *Culte du Moi*, which led him to prefer the 'legend' of Baudelaire or of Marie Bashkirtseff or of Renan to their historical reality, gave way in his later work to more conscientious documentation.[14] But he continued, he said, to 'prefer himself when looking a little above the head of an individual for the type that he or she seemed to symbolize' (*Œuvre* XIII 21). Some of his most successful fictitious characters show a similar inclination. The subtle amalgam of feminine psychology, the spirit of democracy, and the collective unconscious that he invented for the last volume of *Le Culte du Moi*, and christened Bérénice, is imprinted, for a life that is made to appear exemplary, by the 'images,' 'symbols,' and 'figures' of a small Provençal museum and art gallery which is looked after by her parents, and where she spends many

12 *Œuvre* XII 139–47; XVIII 38, 42, 50, 65–7; XIX 8–9, 17–22; 'Chronique parisienne,' *La Vie moderne* 22 August 1885. *Grande Guerre* XIII 383–8. *See* also Barrès's article on 'Izoulet au Collège de France,' *Le Journal* 1 January 1898 (*cit.* Chapter Twelve, note 13) where J.-J. Rousseau is singled out from among the 'poet-legislators' who 'awaken and determine the states of mind from which spring customs and laws': 'Rousseau dont l'imagination est un des grands ressorts de la vie européenne depuis plus de cent ans.'

13 *See* p. 278.

14 *Œuvre* I 226, 378; II 356–68 and 'Un Scandale littéraire,' *Le Journal* 3 March 1893. Cf. Chapter Twelve, note 40.

childhood hours of solitary fantasy.[15] François Sturel, the central figure of Barrès's second trilogy of novels, *Le Roman de l'énergie nationale,* has a 'powerful imagination' which is apt, like his creator's, to discover abundant 'signs and symbols' of French national history in the observed individual behaviour of his contemporaries, caught up in the political dramas of the Third Republic.[16] Léopold Baillard, the principal protagonist of *La Colline inspirée,* the historical novel which crystallizes and orchestrates the religious aspirations of Barrès's maturity, exemplifies his wary sympathy for another mode of imaginative consciousness, by which a supernatural order of reality is apprehended in music, poetry, and myth.[17] Oriante, the heroine of his last novel, *Un Jardin sur l'Oronte,* inspires in her crusader lover the same strongly imaginative kind of adoration as the hero of *Le Culte du Moi,* thirty years before, had found to admire, and to emulate, in the heroine of *Le Jardin de Bérénice.*[18] Bérénice and Oriante, moreover, have political as well as erotic significance. Bérénice, 'petite secousse par où chaque parcelle du monde témoigne l'effort secret de l'inconscient' (*Œuvre* I 375), epitomizes the power and glory of the common people as revealed to a young Boulangist in revolt against the parliamentary Republic of the eighteen-eighties. Oriante, 'née pour être reine' (*Œuvre* XI 81, 89–91) is the portrait of a natural leader, drawn by an established champion of law and order in France and Europe of the nineteen-twenties. Each personifies an aspect of that initially repugnant 'barbarian' outer kingdom, of people, places, and events ('Les Barbares, voilà le non-moi, c'est-à-dire tout ce qui peut nuire ou résister au Moi' [*Œuvre* I 31]) in which, after a brief and debilitating spiritual retreat from the world, recounted in his first two 'ideological novels,' *Sous l'œil des barbares* (1888) and *Un Homme libre* (1889),[19] Barrès learned to find both a field of virile action and a fount of spiritual energy, and in which he would henceforth seek the substance of his philosophy and the destination of his rhetoric.

15 *Le Jardin de Bérénice, Œuvre* I 33–4, 294-311, 375. *See* below, pp. 50–2, 220–1.
16 *Œuvre* III 456; IV 146, 174, 176–7
17 *La Colline inspirée, Œuvre* VI 334–5, 434 447, 474
18 *See* pp. 40–3 J. and J. Tharaud, *Le Roman d'Aïssé* (Paris: SELF 1946) and I.-M. Frandon, *L'Orient de Maurice Barrès.*
19 *See* below, pp. 15–40.

CHAPTER TWO

The Limits of the Imagination

In the *Memoirs* that Barrès planned but never had time to publish, or to complete, he had meant his readers to find at once a 'history of his imagination' and 'the realities' that he had spent his life searching for, 'beneath appearances' (*Mes Cahiers, Œuvre* XVIII 339, 365–6). Among his notes for what would have been an important part of this work, his recollections of parliamentary life in the middle decades of the Third Republic, there is a good example of the way he habitually used his imagination to prospect for a 'reality' which is not present to the senses beneath 'appearances' which are:

> Pourquoi donner à leurs mouvements un sens historique, religieux. Ce sont des gens de la Basoche. Non pas. J'ai raison de les transfigurer.
>
> Quand j'ai l'âme plate, je les regarde. Je pose dessus mon regard et mon imagination...
>
> J'oserai dire que séances mornes, ou ces discussions de bureau, parce qu'elles n'ont pour exprimer leur musique, pour la rendre sensible, aucune des ressources de l'opéra, laissent plus de liberté à l'imagination et nous permettent d'aller plus profond.
>
> Il s'agit de trouver la vérité, d'atteindre ce qui est réel.
>
> [*Mes Cahiers, Œuvre* XV 98–102]

Unchecked, this quest for the reality that a 'spectacle of everyday life'[1] is supposed to yield up to imaginative consciousness tends, at

1 C. Baudelaire, *Fusées* (*Œuvres complètes* (Paris: Pléiade 1961) 1257)

the end of a process of 'unconscious abstraction' [*Œuvre* I 239–40], to produce dissolving views of infinity. Thus the 'Venetian triumph' of *Un Homme libre*:

> Ses splendeurs tangibles, je les poussai jusqu'à l'impalpable beauté des idées; car les formes les plus parfaites ne sont que des symboles pour ma curiosité d'idéologue.
> [*Œuvre* I 238][2]

About ten years later, analysing, in *La Mort de Venise*, the *rêverie* that inspired Wagner's *Tristan and Isolde*, Barrès describes the same process with more detachment:

> Il n'a fallu que deux temps pour que cet Allemand substituât à cette ville latine sa Germanie intérieure. Dès la première pause, cette Venise magnifique par son manque de symétrie, par sa diversité même, il la réduit à l'unité. Sur la seconde reprise, il la renie, la dit inutile. Elle est la barque qu'il repousse après qu'il a touché la rive. Efface-toi, Venise *ondoyante et bariolée*. Par toi nous avons atteint le point de vue infiniment fécond ... Dès lors, Venise, tu nous deviens inutile; tu n'es que conséquence et nous sommes l'essentiel, le principe. Tu nous gênes, tu nous retiens dans un monde inférieur et qu'il faut dépasser. Effondre-toi sous la lagune...
> [*Amori et dolori sacrum, Œuvre* VII 52]

And his conclusion offers a more guarded appreciation of the cognitive value of an act of imagination which so far forgets its tangible starting point in the actual data of perception:

> C'est ici que nous aurions touché les points extrêmes de la sensibilité, quand le rare s'élargit et se défait dans l'universel

2 *See* J.E. Blanche, 'Maurice Barrès,' *Le Gaulois* 22 February 1913: '[Barrès] déclarait qu'il n'avait guère d'yeux ... pour aucune forme d'art plastique, si ce n'est les œuvres que l'histoire ou la légende magnifiaient pour la nourriture de son imagination.' One probable source of this 'ideologist's' view of art is Stendhal's *Histoire de la peinture en Italie*

et que notre imagination, à poursuivre le but sans cesse reculé de nos désirs, s'abîme dans une lassitude ineffable.
[*Œuvre* VII 53][3]

'La musique seule,' he adds, '– car nous sommes convaincu qu'il n'y a point de discontinuité entre les arts divers – peut intervenir à cet instant où la littérature et la peinture depuis longtemps confessent leur échec.' The belief that music can suggest the impalpable visions of human sensibility in its privileged moments of ecstatic communion with the universal (which the more realistic media of the writer and the painter fail to communicate),[4] never left him. He brought it most confidently into play (with safeguards, however) in his religious meditations of later years.[5] But in the less rarified atmosphere of politics, where he was chiefly active in the decades preceding and following *La Mort de Venise*, the 'musical' indetermination of, for example, a Rousseau or a Jaurès, impressed him chiefly as both foolish and dangerous.[6] What he mistrusted in such political visionaries, however, was not the imaginative character of their genius, which was similar to his own, but the tendency of their imagination, by hypertrophy of one of its constituents, abstraction, at the expense of the other, sensation, to lose contact altogether with the world of concrete and particular facts.[7] Likewise the hero of *Un Homme libre*, finding that his unbridled imagination has carried

which he took with him on his first visit to Italy ['L'Éducation par l'Italie,' *Le Journal* 22 September 1893].

3 *See* pp. 278–9.

4 An Idealist and Wagnerian notion that was very much in the air when Barrès first came to Paris, and not confined to Symbolist circles. *See*, for example, Renan's preface to *Drames philosophiques* (Paris: Calmann Lévy 1888) iii.

5 *See* Chapter Eleven *'In hymnis et canticis'* and *'Transpositions d'art.'*

6 *Œuvre* XII 93: 'Pour moi, je l'écoute [Rousseau] comme un enchanteur dans ses grandes symphonies, mais je ne demanderai pas de conseil de vie à cet extravagant Musicien.' *Œuvre* XV 126: 'Jaurès se plaît dans ces formations indécises, dans cet indéterminé, dans ces formes musicales si j'ose dire.'

7 But cf. *Œuvre* XII 252–3: 'Mirabeau ... ce puissant esprit, père des Danton, des Gambetta et des Jaurès, modèle de ceux qui possèdent à la fois, d'une manière redoutable, le don des formules creuses et une connaissance profonde des moyens réalistes de l'action politique!'

him into a finally uninhabitable void of pure subjectivity – '...j'y étais allé d'une telle chevauchée d'imagination qu'en me retournant, je me trouvais seul. De la même manière, sous le cloître, mes saints, – à Venise, Venise, – et en amour, l'amante, se dissipaient pour me laisser manger du vide, face à face de mon désir' – concludes that it is the intensity rather than the tendency of his excitement that is blameworthy (*Œuvre* I 258–9). Even when Barrès uses the word *image* in its most concrete sense of percept, the 'landscape,' 'panorama,' or 'spectacle' in question nearly always diffuses some aura of symbolic significance by which it is immediately distinguishable from raw sense-data, and which at once invites the dissolving action of 'unconscious abstraction.'[8] The Lotharingian patriotism which was at the heart of his political and religious traditionalism was particularly marked by this action. What started as an 'object lesson,' designed to demonstrate 'the realities' which should govern national self-consciousness, 'des réalités et non des mots,'[9] he later described as 'une belle image que nous nous formons de nous-mêmes.'[10] To assert, however, like Henri Franck, that his Lorraine was imaginary, 'valid only for himself,'[11] is to underestimate, in its 'symbolic' composition ('le sens largement représentatif je dirai même symbolique que je donne au mot de Lorraine' [*En Provence*, Paris: Cadran 1930, 77]), what the natural, monumental, iconographical, and ritual imagery of Lorraine, together with the historical relics and present signs of its actual character, culture, conquest, and resistance, brought to Barrès's 'marriage' with his native province:

8 E.g. *Œuvre* VI 182; VII 17; XVI 358–9. On the other hand, Barrès often gives to images of the mind's eye some of the exteriority of percepts; they lie, or rise, like objects, in the path of introspection or recollection, e.g. *Œuvre* VI 167; XI 132; XVII 177.

9 *Œuvre* IV 20; V 121 and 'Le *Journal* et ses collaborateurs.' *Le Journal* 7 April 1900. *See* pp. 124–5.

10 *Œuvre* XVII 60. Barrès occasionally expressed stronger doubts about the reality of his Lorraine, e.g. preface to L. Madelin, *Croquis lorrains* (Paris: Berger-Levrault 1907): 'Qu'importe si cette Lorraine éternelle est un fantôme créé par notre conscience poétique,' and *Œuvre* XV 392–3: 'Souvent j'ai senti jusqu'à la misère le peu de réalité historique de ma Lorraine et qu'elle était un Eldorado de ma pensée.'

11 *La Danse devant l'arche* (Paris: Gallimard 1921) 194–7, *cit.* Foreword, note 1, p. 276

Mon imagination avait été nourrie et orientée par Strasbourg, Sainte-Odile, Sion, le château d'Andlau et je ne cesse pas de construire avec ces beaux éléments une idée dont j'étais à la fois l'auteur et le disciple. *Mes rapports avec la Lorraine sont d'un mariage, je la crée et je me crée.*
[*Mes Cahiers, Œuvre* XIII 28]

To convey what he meant by 'the word Lorraine,' Barrès normally preferred to draw on such symbols of patriotic self-consciousness as he could find ready-made in the collective imagination of his people. He may not, as he hoped, by checking an individual tendency to 'unconscious abstraction' with such time-tested expressions of national experience, have avoided the charge of solipsism to which all closed circuits of the imagination lend themselves, but the traditionalistic image of a Lorraine incorporated in the greater fatherland of France, which was his most important contribution to the literature of French nationalism, gains thereby a breadth and substance that distinguish it from personal fantasy.[12]

An 'aptitude for expressing the things of the mind by images' came early to Barrès,[13] and experience of public life led him to regard

12 Cf. J.-P. Sartre, *Psychology of Imagination* (London: Rider 1950) 16–18: 'The object of the perception overflows consciousness constantly; the object of the image is never more than the consciousness one has ... Our attitude towards the object of the image could be called "quasi-observation" ... an observation which teaches nothing.' Also R. Ruyer's interesting 'parallel' between perception and belief in 'Perception, croyance, monde symbolique,' *Revue de métaphysique et de morale*, January-March 1962, 10: 'Scientifiquement, toute mythologie est fausse, de même que tout langage est conventionnel. Mais il faut faire une différence entre le langage fabriqué ou la mythologie individuelle d'un dément et le langage ou la mythologie d'une culture originale ou d'un grand créateur génial.'

13 *See*, for example, *Un Homme libre, Œuvre* I 211: 'Alors ... je matérialisai les formes habituelles de ma sensibilité ... devant moi comme une carte de géographie.' The embodiment of the immaterial in representative persons, and in places associated with them, is a strong feature of *Le Culte du Moi.* Bérénice, for example, is 'l'image la plus complète ... des forces de la nature,' posed in a symbolic landscape which is dominated 'à la façon des cartes du Tendre,' by La Tour Constance at Aigues-Mortes (*Œuvre* I 323, 329). Having chosen Marie Bashkirtseff to 'represent' the sensibility of his generation, Barrès found an 'ideal place' for her also: cosmopolitan Rome (*Œuvre* II 361–8).

it as the most valuable of his rhetorical gifts. When a critic was shocked by it, as by a kind of materialism, he professed not to understand, though he was affected sufficiently to note the criticism in his diary (*Œuvre* xv 139). And, in fact, just as his attempt to 'read' appearances imaginatively threatens constantly to end up as fanciful abstraction, so a mechanistic technique of persuasion, which he associated very early with Ignatius de Loyola's art of self-persuasion by 'composition of place,' with the scientist's use of hypothetical models, and with the prodigies of ancient Oriental fanaticism and the findings of modern European psycho-physiology, and which is latently, where not blatantly, indifferent to spirit and truth, develops at the point where his imaginative rhetoric reaches its sensuous limit:

> Il ne s'agit pas d'user de raisonnements, mais d'une méthode mécanique; nous nous envelopperons d'images appropriées et d'un effet puissant...
> [*Une Homme libre, Œuvre* I 169]

> C'est aux *Exercices spirituels* d'Ignace de Loyola, au plus surprenant des psychologues, que nous empruntons cette méthode, dont je me suis toujours bien trouvé....
> Réduisons l'abstrait en images sensibles. C'est ainsi que l'apprenti mécanicien trace sur le tableau noir des signes conventionnels pour fixer la figure idéale qu'il calcule et qui toujours est près de lui échapper.
> [*Un Homme libre, Œuvre* I 178]

> Pourquoi, philosophes, vous indigner contre le mécanisme de Loyola? Michelet, Quinet, Taine qui voudriez le flétrir, n'utilisez-vous pas l'archéologie et l'histoire pour émouvoir votre âme, n'avez-vous pas fait de l'univers tout entier une vaste machine qui fait jouer les ressorts de la mécanique humaine.
> [*Bibliothèque Nationale. Manuscrits. Nouvelles Acquisitions Françaises* no. 11728 fol. 46 (*Un homme libre*)][14]

14 Cf. *Œuvre* I 181.

– D'où juges-tu qu'on puisse ainsi mécaniser les hommes?
– Qui donc l'a jamais contesté? C'est dans l'Orient que tu en vois les plus fréquents, les plus fameux exemples. Espaces sacrés de l'Orient! ... Le don de suggestionner la personnalité des autres et sa propre personnalité se manifeste de différentes manières, selon le génie particulier des époques. Prenons en exemple Loyola...
[*Les Déracinés, Œuvre* III 160]

J'ai 'appliqué à mes propres émotions la dialectique morale enseignée par les grands religieux, par les François de Sales et les Ignace de Loyola, et c'est toute la genèse de l'*Homme libre*'... Ces méditations, ces analyses, c'est une méthode intérieure à laquelle je suis resté fidèle jusque dans la propagande politique (par exemple quand je fondais le nationalisme sur *la Terre et les Morts*)...
[*Amori et dolori sacrum, Œuvre* VII 125, 143]

Est-il des moyens mécaniques pour multiplier en nous l'enthousiasme? C'est un problème que depuis sept siècles on prétend résoudre à Konia ... Peut-on ouvrir au *Codex* un chapitre supplémentaire et dresser une nomenclature d'agents matériels propres à exalter l'âme?
[*Une Enquête aux pays du Levant, Œuvre* XI 379]

Mechanical indoctrination, like fanciful abstraction, marks a danger limit in Barrès's theory of imagination. Normally he used *imagination* and related words to denote the product of coefficient and limited propensities for, on the one hand, abstracting the spirit of things from their material appearance, and, on the other, embodying the things of the spirit in material forms. Both coefficients were essential to his 'poet's' vocation, each inhibiting the tendency of the other to take over and thereby ruin a faculty which he thought of as composite, the token of man's mixed condition. Where neither is reduced to zero to feed the other, Barrès's imagination typically tends towards but stops short of the high but cloudy mysteries and the positive but arid definitions and directives which lie beyond what he saw as the 'musical' and the 'scientific' 'limits' of his 'domain'.[15]

15 *Mes Cahiers, Œuvre* XIX 116. *See* pp. 229–30, 267–75.

CHAPTER THREE

The Development of Barrès's Traditionalism

LE CULTE DU MOI

Alienation: 'J'ai failli être fou.'

A reading of George Sand's *Impressions et souvenirs* (suggested to him by Jean Jaurès, in a conversation at the Palais Bourbon in April 1911) prompted one of Barrès's most successful attempts to illuminate retrospectively the path which had brought him in twenty-five years from the cultivated 'Egotism' of his first trilogy of 'ideological novels,' written in the eighteen-eighties and early eighteen-nineties and retrospectively entitled *Le Culte du Moi*, *via* the combative, partisan nationalism inspired by the Boulangist Movement, the Panama Scandal, and the Dreyfus Affair, to the expansive socio-religious traditionalism of his maturity. He fastens characteristically on Sand's use of imagination, contrasting it, in respect of three crucial stages in the development of his own ideas – represented by *Le Culte du Moi*, 'L'arbre de M. Taine' (a key philosophical dialogue from the first volume of *Le Roman de l'énergie nationale* [1897–1902]), and his current publicity campaign for the preservation of France's historic parish churches: *Pour les Églises* (1911) – with various forms of alienation which she had specified as: 'Madness, fanaticism, atheism, the hatred of God or our fellow men, inordinate pride that is nothing less than a loss of contact with universal life' (*Mes Cahiers*, *Œuvre* XVII 37–8, 43–4). 'This,' he adds, 'must be thought about, for my own improvement.' The entry is headed simply: 'Politics.'

> Le rôle de la politique à un instant donné dans ma vie et dans l'effort que je fis pour saisir mon moi.
>
> Oui, j'ai failli être fou. Je ne sais plus ce qui me sauva. Si, je le sais: la politique.
>
> *Pourquoi j'aime la politique?* D'abord je lui dois la vie. [*Mes Cahiers, Œuvre* XVII 43–4]

Barrès was saved by politics, as Gide would be saved by 'gourmandise,' from the same epidemic of 'fainting fever' and 'cerebral erethism' that George Moore diagnosed in *fin-de-siècle* Paris, where all three writers served their literary apprenticeship and where, as Gide put it many years later: 'Some whispered word of command ... seemed to have compelled us all ... to turn our backs on reality.'[1] By 1896 he was already aware of the 'incalculable' debt he owed to 'public life':

> Personnellement, pour mon développement propre, je crois avoir trouvé un bénéfice incalculable dans la vie publique (la Chambre n'étant qu'un point dans un ensemble). Elle m'a donné le sens des réalités, des vérités, le sentiment de ce qui est commun à tous les hommes, hors de la mode, la compréhension de l'Histoire aussi. [Letter to É. Zola, 6 June 1896, *cit. Mercure de France* CCXXXL no. 800 (15 October 1931) 459–61]

The size of the debt was already obvious both in the recently completed *Culte du Moi*, which depicts Barrès's 'années d'apprentissage' in the allegorical form of Symbolist fiction (*Œuvre* I 41–3) and also in the first volume of *Le Roman de l'énergie nationale: Les Déracinés*, on which he was now embarked, and where the same adolescent experiences and observations are chronicled and explained from the objective point of view, in the full documentary detail, within the

1 G. Moore, *Confessions of a young man* (London: Heinemann 1917) 94 and A. Gide, *Si le grain ne meurt. Œuvres complètes* X 321

broad historical framework, and in the plain language of the post-Naturalist novel. Both works, both perspectives, give impressions of a mind at times so cut off from reality as to be very close indeed to the 'madness' Barrès will recollect so vividly a quarter of a century later:

> J'avais rêvé d'être un homme libre (p. 43, *Impressions et Souvenirs* de George Sand) par orgueil de jeunesse, par réaction contre les Burdeau,[2] contre les basses tâches.
>
> Taine, après avoir lu l'*Homme libre*, me prédisait la folie...
>
> J'ai tout fait d'abord pour ne pas me laisser encombrer, fausser, bref dénaturer par des influences fâcheuses ... Mais il ne faut pas que cela m'amène à 'vouloir rompre absolument avec l'influence de ce qui n'est pas nous-même. Ce serait un essai insensé qui nous conduirait à la *folie*, au fanatisme ou à l'athéisme, à la haine de Dieu ou de nos semblables, à l'orgueil démesuré qui n'est autre chose qu'une privation de nos rapports avec la vie universelle, par conséquent une étroitesse de conception' (George Sand).
>
> Ceci pour mon perfectionnement doit être médité. Car je vois bien ses excès à elle. Je vois bien que d'instinct j'ai suivi la voie de conservation où elle m'invite. En ai-je assez fait? Ne suis-je pas demeuré trop loin de cet universel?
>
> Ceci se raccorde à l'*Arbre de Monsieur Taine.*
>
> La conception que j'accueille du rôle de l'imagination s'accorde avec le sentiment, quasi une obsession, que j'ai des églises.
>
> Il ne faut pas que nous prétendions gouverner absolument notre pensée. Nous entrerions dans quelque chose d'anormal, de monstrueux; cette puissance nous ferait sortir de l'humanité. Nous n'avons pas avantage à nous soustraire aux fugues et aux langueurs de notre pensée. 'Dans les âmes saines, l'imagination est une amie délicate qu'il ne faut pas traiter inconsidérément de folle du logis et qui, triste ou riante, nous parle des choses divines et nous dédommage ainsi du temps qu'elle enlève aux études positives.'
>
> [*Mes Cahiers, Œuvre* XVII 43–4]

2 Auguste Burdeau (1851–94) was Barrès's philosophy master at the Nancy *lycée. See Mes Cahiers, Œuvre* XVII 123 and *Les Déracinés,* Chapter One.

Sous l'œil des barbares, the first volume of *Le Culte du Moi*, 'l'histoire des années d'apprentissage d'un *moi*' (*Œuvre* I 41), describes three varieties of estrangement from what Barrès called in 1892: 'le non-moi, c'est-à-dire tout ce qui peut nuire ou résister au Moi,' and, in 1911, quoting George Sand, 'l'influence de ce qui n'est pas nous-même.' There is first of all the renunciation of young love, palely loitering in the twilit Symbolist landscapes of 'Tendresse,' in the first section of the novel, entitled 'Avec ses livres':

> Alors, soudain, à pleine main, il repousse les petits seins stériles de cette femme. Elle chancelle, presque nue, ses bras ronds et fermes battent l'air; et dans le bruit triomphal de la sagesse sauvée, au travers du temple acclamant le héros, sous les bras indignés, rapide et courbée, elle sortit. Jamais elle ne lui fut plus délicieuse qu'à cette heure, vaincue et sous ses longs cheveux.
> [*Œuvre* I 68–9]

This episode also suggests a high degree of cultural alienation; the 'wisdom of the ages' has no power to ease the pain of the hero's fashionably Schopenhaueresque renunciation of woman: 'Suprême fleur de toutes ces cultures, l'héritier d'une telle sagesse, étendu sur le dos, bâillait' (*Œuvre* I 66). 'Tendresse' is followed by a Parnassian allegory of the collapse of culture, entitled 'Désintéressement' (originally: 'Les Héroïsmes superflus'), which depicts the destruction of the Serapeum in fourth-century Alexandria, by Christian barbarians.

Finally, there is the hero's self-conscious *social* isolation, in the contemporary Parisian sketches and the fragment of *roman d'analyse* which constitute the second half of the novel:

> Durant trente jours et davantage, il gonfla son âme jusqu'à l'héroïsme. De sa tour d'ivoire – comme Athéné, du Sérapis – son imagination voyait la vie grouillante de fanatiques grossiers. Il s'instituait victime de mille bourreaux, pour la joie de les mépriser. Et cet enfant isolé, vaniteux et meurtri, vécut son rêve d'une telle énergie que sa souffrance égalait son orgueil.
> [*Œuvre* I 90]

This 'heroic' posture brings brief solipsistic 'ecstasies,' but these give way regularly to long bouts of nervous prostration ('de longs affaissements'), which lead in turn to the plangent, unanswered prayer addressed to an unknown Master: 'si tu existes quelque part, axiome, religion ou prince des hommes,' with which the novel is concluded.

The dream, shadow, and caricature of some external authority masterful enough to *dictate* a course of action to the alienated self ('qui ferra que je veuille') already haunt many pages of Barrès's intense, complicated, and modish first autobiographical 'novel of the inner life,' in which the bullied mother's boy in the school yard, and the ambitious, vulnerable provincial student in the pavement and printing-press jungle of *fin-de-siècle* Paris, grows perceptibly towards the passionately committed political partisan who will declare for General Boulanger, le Général Revanche, in an article for *La Revue Indépendante*: 'M. le général Boulanger et la nouvelle génération,' dated April 1888, the publication year of *Barbares*.[3] But it was the contrary experience of self-directed, inward 'ecstasy' that led to the next published stage of *Le Culte du Moi: Un Homme libre* (1889). This second volume of the trilogy begins as the 'diary' of a deliberately prolonged period of contemplative withdrawal from the world, the inspiration of which almost certainly precedes Barrès's Boulangist activities, and the publication of *Sous l'œil des barbares*. The 'retreat' of *Un Homme libre* is modelled, ironically, on the disciplines of the Catholic cloister.

The most successful of the brief Parisian ecstasies of Barrès's first novel had been triggered off by precipitate flight from the everyday world of the 'barbarians,' and its spontaneous ritual relegation to outer darkness behind a triple veil of clothes, shutters, and lamplight:

> Harassé, affaibli de sueurs, il monte l'escalier presque en courant. Il ferme les persiennes, allume sa lampe et rapidement jette dans un coin ses vêtements pour enfiler un large pantalon, un veston de velours, puis rentré dans son cabinet, dans son fauteuil, dans l'atmosphère familière:

3 *Œuvre* I 40, 44, 50–6, 74–85, 92–9, 131–2

– Enfin, dit-il, je vais m'embêter à mon saoul, tranquillement.
Un petit rire nerveux de soulagement le secoue, tant il avait besoin de cette solitude.
[*Œuvre* I 113]

Thus unburdened of the *non-moi*, the hero of *Le Culte du Moi*, 'abandoning himself to his imaginations,' and inspired no doubt by some heady cocktail of Fichte's *Doctrine of Science* and Balzac's *Peau de Chagrin*,[4] feels the freed self within him leap forward to the infinite horizon of absolute truth:

Déjà les murs avec leur tapisserie de livres secs ... ont disparu ... Il halète de tout embrasser, s'assimiler, harmoniser ... Il aspire à l'absolu. Il se sent devenir l'idée de l'idée; ainsi dans le monde sentimental le moment suprême est l'amour de l'amour: aimer sans objet, aimer à aimer...

...

Alors dans la fumée, loin du bruit de la vie, quittant les événements et toutes ces mortifications, le jeune homme sortit du sensible. Devant lui fuyait cette vie étroite pour laquelle on a pu créer un vocabulaire. Un amas de rêves, de nuances, de délicatesses sans nom et qui s'enfoncent à l'infini tourbillonnent autour de lui: monde nouveau ... où sont tranchés ces mille liens qui nous rattachent pour souffrir aux hommes et aux choses...
...Cette nuit célèbre la résurrection de son âme ... Qu'elle soit bondissante. J'avais hâte de cette nuit ... ô moi, pour redevenir un dieu.
[*Œuvre* I 114–17]

Unfortunately, the resurrection and the apotheosis do not last after three o'clock in the morning. The next volume of *Le Culte du Moi*

4 *Œuvre* I 31, 241 (*cit.* above Chapter Two, note 3); *Le Départ pour la Vie* (Paris: Plon 1961) 46. Cf. J.-G. Fichte, *Doctrine de la science de la connaissance*, 151: 'l'idée ... de l'unité suprême' and H. de Balzac, *La Comédie humaine* (Paris: Bibliothèque de la Pléiade, Gallimard 1965) IX 41: 'tout embrasser ... tout voir.'

describes the hero's attempt to discover a method of prolonging the 'state of grace' he had known for a few exciting hours in his rooms in Paris: 'Déjà la grâce m'avait visité,' he will write, 'J'avais déjà entrevu mon Dieu intérieur, mais aussitôt son émouvante image s'emplissait d'ombre' (*Œuvre* I 156–7). To remove the shadows, the Self must learn to keep the objective world firmly at arm's length, to become pure subjectivity: 'L'homme idéal résumerait en soi l'univers' (*Œuvre* I 169). That is the 'program' envisaged in *Un Homme libre*, which takes the apprentice Egotist, with an old friend, Simon, who shares his 'prejudices, vocabulary and contempts,' away from Paris to a small country house rented in a secluded part of their native Lorraine:

> Nous sortîmes de la grande ville avec la joie un peu nerveuse du portefaix qui vient délivrer ses épaules d'une charge très lourde. Nous nous étions débarrassés du siècle.
> [*Œuvre* I 155]

A Retreat and Some Excursions

The pervasive irony, and the forward movement, of Barrès's second ideological novel stem from its heroes' inability to prolong the ecstasy of absolute subjectivity except by drawing sustenance for it from the world outside the Self.

The scenery round Saint-Germain, par Bayon (Meurthe-et-Moselle) is, superficially at least, uninteresting; the walls of all the rooms of the house selected for the retreat are whitewashed; silence is observed every day until supper time, and all letters are burnt on arrival. On the other hand, secular disengagement does not extend to the beneficial comfort of the meditative armchair, nor to the tonic pleasures of ceremony, dress, table, and bed (a village girl – 'trop honnête fille pour que j'en fasse des anecdotes' – is hired as a concubine, since the two young men have 'unfortunately lost the habit of chastity'). Balzac alone, representing the world of action at its most dangerously fascinating, is banned from the library. The rule of this curious cloister is inspired by what Barrès had celebrated in his first published work: *Anatole France* (1883), as 'dilettantisme': 'Une discipline [qui] voile les passions sans les supprimer.'[5] Barrès's two self-directed noviciates belong in spirit with those Renaissance painters of the School of Bologna, with whom François Sturel, that other semi-autobiographical hero of a Barresian *bildungsroman, L'Appel au soldat,* also feels some sympathy, and who called themselves the *desiderosi* and *incamminati*: 'ceux qui regrettent la perfection des anciens,' 'ceux qui s'acheminent vers cette perfection,'[6] but who were unable to create for themselves, and by themselves, like a Michelangelo, for instance, the ideal world of 'heroic' energy and enthusiasm that they longed to inhabit.[7] Appropriately, help is sought from a contemporary of the Bologna painters, Saint Ignatius de Loyola:

> Précisément, le siècle venait d'imaginer une méthode pour introduire dans le monde supérieur du mysticisme ceux qui, désireux d'y pénétrer, manquent cependant de la force spontanée des Thérèse, des Loyola, des Catherine de Sienne. On connaît les *Exercices spirituels,* qui pour de brefs instants haussent des médiocres jusqu'à l'état d'âme des héros. Cette extase ne modifie pas la qualité naturelle des êtres, mais les sort momentanément de la réalité ambiante. Ainsi les peintres de Bologne, ne pouvant pas donner à leurs creatures la vie supérieure et divine dont disposait Michel-Ange, du moins les placent dans des conditions telles que leurs facultés prennent leur pleine intensité.
>
> L'art bolonais recherche systématiquement quelles situations extrêmes il pourrait combiner pour mettre des êtres dans un état supérieur à l'ordinaire de la vie.
>
> [*Du sang, de la volupté et de la mort* (1894), *Œuvre* II 164]

These lines from 'L'évolution de l'individu dans les musées de Toscane' were published in 1894, but their retrospective relevance to Barrès's own *Cult of the Self* (as well as forward to his life-long preoccupation with imaginative techniques for 'multiplying' enthusiasm, 'les forces

5 *Œuvre* II 443
6 *Œuvre* III 383
7 *Œuvre* II 158–67; III 383

de l'âme': 'La Chapelle des Medicis, la Sixtine,' he writes, 'sont des réservoirs d'énergie probablement immortels'[8]) is evident, and they explain in particular the paradoxical dependence evinced by his two would-be contemplatives upon that very world of external things, persons, events, and situations from which they had intended to withdraw, a paradox of which they become increasingly aware as their experience of meditation proceeds, and from which Barrès derives the characteristically self-deprecating, and fashionably decadent, humour of the novel (recalling Laforgue in particular), and also its enduring demonstration, through such pseudo-ascetic symptoms as *acedia* and *ariditas*, of the '*folie* ... de vouloir rompre absolument avec l'influence de ce qui n'est pas nous-même.'[9]

The dependence of the spirit upon material *things* is implied and investigated both in the bland misappropriation by Barrès's heroes of such Loyolan exercises as 'colloquy,' 'application of the senses,' and 'composition of place' ('videre visu imaginationis locum corporeum, ubi reperitur ea res, quam volo contemplari'), and in the facetious solemnity of their preliminary 'Installation matérielle' and 'Examen physique,' inspired by the psycho-physiology of Cabanis (whom Barrès seems to have approached by way of Stendhal's *Histoire de la peinture en Italie*[10]):

> Pour parvenir délibérément à l'enthousiasme, je me félicite d'avoir restauré la puissante méthode de Loyola. Ah! que cette mécanique morale, complétée par une bonne connaissance des rapports du physique et du moral (où j'ai suivi Cabanis, quelque autre demain utilisera nos hypnotiseurs), saurait rendre des services à un amateur des mouvements de l'âme!
> [*Examen des trois romans idéologiques, Œuvre* I 32]

Dependence upon *persons* (other than Simon, the convenient inter-

8 *Œuvre* I 157, 169, 242–3; II 162; III 160; XI 379; XIX 200
9 *Œuvre* XVII 43, *cit.* above, p. 17
10 Chapters 92-100, which are strongly marked by the sixth *mémoire* of *Les Rapports du physique et du moral: de l'influence des tempéraments.* Barrès follows Stendhal as closely in places as to reproduce him word for word.

locutor and alter ego of *l'Homme libre*) appears at a second stage of the retreat. The subjects chosen initially for the series of Loyolan exercises the two young men embark on (after it has become apparent that bare walls, simplified sex and food, silent, undirected meditation in the garden and armchair, an occasional cigar and, daily, at two o'clock 'une partie de volant dans le cloître, comme faisaient pour se délaisser, Jansenius et M. de Saint-Cyran,' do not suffice to give them the energy necessary to 'résumer en soi l'univers' [*Œuvre* I 169]), are abstract notions: humiliation, love, mortality, intended to provoke *immediately* the emotions they propose to 'amass,' with a view to godlike omniscience and omnisentience. Almost at once, however, faced with the 'immense labour' of such a 'programme of love,' the spirit of Egotism falters and is driven back a further pace into the world of others, to search for *mediators*: 'Comment, sans m'égarer, amasser cette somme des émotions possibles? Il faut qu'on me secoure, j'appelle des *intercesseurs*' (*Œuvre* I 182).

But the cult of individual intercessors: Baudelaire of course (omitted from the published version of *Un Homme libre*),[11] Benjamin Constant, Sainte-Beuve, and others not named ('nous nous attachions surtout aux personnes fameuses qui eurent de la spiritualité' [*Œuvre* I 194]) also fails to ward off spiritual 'aridity' for very long. Their objectivity is too suspect:

> Vous n'existez qu'en moi. Quel rapport entre vos âmes telles que je les possède et telles que les dépeignent vos meilleurs amis! ... Nous pressions une partie de nous-mêmes déjà épuisée ... L'imitation des hommes les meilleurs échouait à me hausser jusqu'à toi, Esprit. Total des émotions!
> [*Œuvre* I 195, 212]

The third stage of the Egotist's unplanned recovery from the recurrent frustrations of planned spiritual independence results from an actual excursion into the countryside surrounding the hermitage of Saint-Germain. In the spectacle of a peasantry labouring in immemorial fields and, more especially, 'in the echo of his footsteps on

11 'Méditation spirituelle sur Charles Baudelaire,' *L'Aube* (June 1896).

the stone floor of country churches where the *gisants* are his ancestors,' he discovers his dependence upon *events*. The next fifty pages of *Un Homme libre*, nearly half the book, are devoted to two prolonged exploratory sorties into the outside world of history, conceived, in the Hegelian manner of his master Taine,[12] as Spirit manifesting itself generally in time and space, and, particularly, in the evolving styles of art and architecture peculiar to national groups. After Lorraine, Venice:

> Je n'abandonne pas le service de Dieu; je continuerai à vivre dans la contemplation de ses perfections pour les dégager en moi et pour que j'approche le plus possible de mon absolu. Mais je donne congé aux petits scribes passionnés et analystes, qui furent jusqu'alors nos intercesseurs ... je veux me modeler sur des groupes humains, qui me feront toucher en un fort relief tous les caractères dont mon être a le presentiment. Les individus, si parfaits qu'on les imagine, ne sont que des fragments du système plus complet qu'est la race, fragment elle-même de Dieu.
> [*Œuvre* I 222]

The Egotist's discovery in the civilization of Venice of a 'group soul' in harmony with his 'nobler, essential Being' ('un pays qui lui ressemble,' to add the Baudelairian reference to the Hegelian one – Barrès's philosophical and poetical influences are constantly intertwined), was, he claimed, 'the best result' he had achieved so far:

> Enfin, je connus Venise. Je possédais tous mes documents pour dégager la loi de cette cité et m'y conformer...
> Dès lors je ne quittais plus mon appartement, où, sans phrases, un enfant m'apportait des repas sommaires.
> Vêtu d'étoffes faciles, dédaigneux de tous soins de toilette, mais

12 Goetheian 'naturalism,' and the visual arts of Italy directly observed, exerted parallel influences; *see Œuvre* I 40 and III 381–6, 390–3, and *Bibliothèque Nationale, Manuscrits, Nouvelles Acquisitions Françaises*, no. 11728, fol. 2: 'Italie, reine, j'ai touché à la folie, tes musées m'ont relevé.'

> seulement poudré d'insecticide, je demeurais le jour et la nuit parmi mes cigares, étendu sur mon vaste lit.
>
> J'avais enfin divorcé avec ma guenille, avec celle qui doit mourir. [*Œuvre* I 237]

Venice is the 'Church Triumphant,' in the pseudo-theological terminology of *Un Homme libre* (after the 'Church Militant' of Saint-Germain in Lorraine). Yet the seeds of its decay, as a power to sustain the Egotist's 'enthusiasm,' to overcome his 'anæmia' with borrowed 'vigour,' for much longer than his previous spiritual exercises with individual objects and persons had done, soon appear in the very process of 'unconscious abstraction,' by which he sets about disengaging from the outward beauty of Venice a 'law,' 'soul,' or 'being' in which to mirror his better Self: 'mon Être agrandi et plus proche de Dieu' (*Œuvre* I 237–40).

The 'abstract city' that *l'Homme libre* has built (like Michelangelo and Wagner[13]) for his 'personal use' has no more independent an existence than his individual intercessors in the library of Saint-Germain: 'Mes souvenirs, rapidement déformés par mon instinct, me présentèrent une Venise qui n'existe nulle part.' The dissolution of another promised bond between the Self and a fragment of its universal environment is not far off. To overcome a relapse into apathy ('je glissais peu à peu dans la torpeur' [246]), the hero of *Le Culte du Moi* completes the circle of his search for absolute Selfhood by returning to Paris in order to create deliberately, like the *incamminati* of the School of Bologna, one of those 'extreme situations which can raise people above their ordinary level of existence' (*Œuvre* II 164).

> Je jugeai opportun de me vivifier par la souffrance et dans l'humiliation, qui seules peuvent me rendre un sentiment exquis de l'amour de Dieu. Nulle part je ne pouvais mieux trouver qu'à Paris.
>
> (Il est juste d'ajouter qu'à ces nobles motifs se joignait un désir d'agitation: désir médiocre, mais après tout n'est-ce pas un

13 *See* above, pp. 8 and 22.

synonyme intéressant des mes beaux appétits d'idéal? Il faut que je respecte tout ce qui est en moi; il ne convient pas que rien avorte. Or ma santé s'était fort consolidée, et des parties de moi-même, s'éveillant peu à peu, ne se satisfaisaient pas de la vie de Venise.)

Pour me maintenir dans l'Église Triomphante, il faut sans cesse que je mérite, il faut que j'ennoblisse les parties de péché qui subsistent probablement en moi. Je ne les connaîtrai que dans la vie; j'y retourne.
[*Œuvre* I 246]

The idea of creating a suitably tonic and ennobling experience of humiliation and suffering from the reviving animal instincts of convalescence proves to be an extremely productive one for the development of Barrès's traditionalism. But in other respects, the Egotist's last lesson in the awkward but unavoidable dependence of the inwardly spiritual life on the outward and visible world, a lesson entitled 'Excursion dans la vie: Une anecdote d'amour,' follows a now familiar sequence of disenchantment.

Not, of course, that Barrès's protagonist expected anything but Schopenhauerian suffering from the transient delirium of a love affair, the crudest of all manifestations of the will to live: 'Je m'étais proposé pour mes fins idéales de prendre là quelque chagrin, un peu d'amertume qui me restituât le désir de Dieu,' he writes, echoing Villiers de l'Isle-Adam's *Ève future* (which had appeared in serial form in *La Vie Moderne* in 1885 at the same time as a regular column by Barrès): 'Regardez les femmes en examinant à froid *ce qui produit* cette illusion (l'amour), elle se dissipera pour faire place à cette invincible dégoût dont aucune excitation ne tirera un désir.' 'En 1890,' recalled the Tharaud brothers, 'les femmes au Quartier Latin du moins chez les littérateurs, n'étaient pas en odeur de sainteté. Je pense, et j'espère pour eux, que leur dédain n'était que littéraire et mode tout intellectuelle. Mais le certain c'est qu'ils étaient tous plus ou moins empoisonnés par Schopenhauer.'[14] The young Barrès's

14 J. and J. Tharaud, *Sons nouveaux 1900: Maurice Barrès* (Paris: Conferencia, 15 June 1933)

pride and timidity doubtless rendered him particularly susceptible to the current vogue of misogyny.[15] The stereotyped progress of the Egotist's *chagrin d'amour* was planned in advance; though the 'demented' intensity of his jealousy when the girl, having been understandably put off by his defensive affectation of superiority, fails to respond to a repentent letter, comes as an unpleasant surprise, though a perfectly satisfactory one, so long as it lasts, for his ulterior purpose, as well as constituting the most convincingly life-like piece of fiction Barrès had yet composed, and curiously pre-Proustian.[16] The intellectually shocking disproportion between such a passion of jealousy and its 'Object' (which is, appropriately, the only name the girl is ever given by her bizarre lover) is also intrinsic to the theory of love which inspires 'Une Anecdote d'amour,' and its sources in Stendhal, Baudelaire, Schopenhauer – and Renan, whose version of the legend of Krishnu and the shepherdesses had graced the 1887 New Year number of the *Journal des Débats*: 'chacun crée son danseur divin.' 'J'ai habillé selon ma convenance,' recalls the hero of *Le Culte du Moi*, 'le premier Objet à qui j'ai plu. Elle n'est qu'un instinct dansant que je voulus adorer.'

A more original feature of Barrès's portrait of the jealous lover than either the inevitability of his jealousy or the insignificance of its object, is the swift decay of the latter's even apparent objectivity in the solvent of 'unreflecting, mechanical ... unconscious abstraction' which had already eaten its way through the Egotist's individual and collective intercessors at Saint-Germain and in Venice. 'Seule, elle a pu me faire prendre quelque intérêt à la vie extérieure,' Barrès's hero will recollect complacently on the sea-front at Cannes out of season, where he has gone into voluntary 'exile,' in order to 'profit from his emotions': 'Elle était pour moi, habitué des grandes tentures nues, un petit joujou précieux, un bibelot vivant' (*Œuvre* I 254–6). But a few days later, at the intense but brief crisis of his jealous despair, she is no longer even to be patronized as insignificant, the dull, common or

15 *See* 'Chronique parisienne,' *La Vie moderne* 11 July 1885; *Le Quartier Latin* [*Œuvre* II 455–6]; and Rachilde, *Portraits d'hommes* (Paris: Mercure de France 1930) 41–2; also P. Dufay, 'Maurice Barrès au Quartier Latin,' *Mercure de France* 1 January 1924.
16 *See* p. 279.

garden branch on which the lustrous crystals of her lover's fond illusions have fastened themselves; she has ceased to exist in the outside world at all, and so, like the similarly evanescent intercessors of Saint-Germain and the fair outward forms of Venice, rapidly loses value as a remedy for the recurrent fainting sickness of the isolated ego:

> Dès l'aube, je lui télégraphiai à son ancienne adresse. Journée déplorable! À travers Cannes, perdu d'humidité, je ne cessais d'aller de l'hôtel au télégraphe, où les employés agacés me secouaient leurs têtes, et mon cœur s'arrêtait de battre, sans que mon attitude perdît rien de sa dignité ... Vers cinq heures, seul dans le salon humide de l'hôtel, je n'avais encore rien reçu; la totalité des choses me parurent sinistres puis je fus dément.
>
> Comme elle était oublié, la fille des premiers instants de cette aventure, – celle à qui je voulus bien prêter un sourire doux et maniéré! J'avais à propos d'elle conçu un si violent désir d'être heureux, j'y étais allé d'une telle chevauchée d'imagination qu'en me retournant, je me trouvais seul. De la même manière, sous le cloître, mes saints, – à Venise, Venise, – et en amour, l'amante, se dissipaient pour me laisser manger du vide, face à face de mon désir.
>
> [*Œuvre* I 258]

As *Un Homme libre* draws to a close, the hero of *Le Culte du Moi* appears to be returning to the point from which he had set out 'under the eyes of the barbarians': 'essence immuable et insaisissable, derrière ce corps, derrière ces pensées, derrière ces actes que vous me reprochez: je forme et déforme l'univers, et rien n'existe que je sois tenté d'adorer' (*Barbares, Œuvre* I 117–8).[17] Yet his experiments have taught him something new. A dilettante retreat and some informative excursions have incontrovertibly demonstrated his dependence upon things, persons, events, and situations existing *in*dependently of him, however superficial, fragmentary, and transient may appear the rele-

17 *See* Hegel, *Cours d'esthétique* (translated by Ch. Bénard, Paris: Joubert 1843) II 386–7: 'l'esprit ... n'apparaît en harmonie avec son essence que quand il est replié sur lui-même.'

vance of such things, persons, events, and situations to the inner world in which his essential, nobler Self has its being.

The 'rule of life' that the Egotist adopts at the end of the novel (and expounds in a letter to Simon) is to accept the paradoxical interdependence and incongruity of essence and existence in a spirit of irony, and as moral justification for a life of systematic alienation, in time as in all else. By a combination of distancing and discontinuity, all those contacts with the Not-Self that the Self has found to be regrettably necessary for the continuing vitality of its inner life shall be rendered inoffensive:

> Vraiment quand j'étais très jeune ... je me méfiais avec excès du monde extérieur. Il est repoussant, mais presque inoffensif ... L'évidente insignifiance de toutes les postures que prend l'élite à travers l'ordre immuable des événements m'obsède. Je ne vois partout que gymnastique. Quoi que je fasse désormais, mon ami, jugez-moi d'après ce parti pris qui domine mes moindres actes.
>
> Il est impossible que nous cessions de nous intéresser l'un à l'autre; il est probable cependant que nous cesserons de nous écrire. Cela ne vous blessera pas, mon cher Simon. Vous savez que je vous aime ... nous avons une partie de notre moi qui nous est commune à l'un et à l'autre; eh bien! c'est parce que je veux être étranger à moi que je veux m'éloigner de vous. *Alienus!* Étranger au monde extérieur, étranger même à mon passé, étranger à mes instincts, connaissant seulement des émotions rapides que j'aurai choisies: véritablement Homme libre!
>
> [*Œuvre* I 265–8]

The modern reader, reacting to 'Lettre à Simon' in the light of Barrès's future career as the champion of popular patriotic instinct and traditional continuity in Nation, State, and Church, is likely to feel that the hero of *Le Culte du Moi* protests rather too much at this point in his 'apprenticeship.' Indeed this view is justified by more than hindsight. The letter was written, so its author informs his readers of 1889, simply to tie up the loose ends of his life so far: 'pour fermer la boucle de la première partie de ma vie,' and it is backdated two years before publication. The immediate sources and parallels of the Egotist's provisional morality are typical of Barrès's reading and reflections over an only slightly longer period, extending from 1880 to the end of 1888: Anatole France (*see* above, p. 22); Baudelaire (*see* 'Stanislas de Guaita (1861–1898)' [*Amori et Dolori Sacrum, Œuvre* VII 62], and 'Le caractère de Baudelaire,' in *La Jeune France*, August 1887, where Barrès quotes approvingly: 'Glorifier le vagabondage et ce qu'on peut appeler le bohémianisme: culte de la sensation multipliée']; Renan (*see* 'La sensibilité d'Henri Chambige,' *Le Figaro*, 11 November 1888: 'C'est M. Renan qui a le mieux exprimé *La Dispersion du cœur* ... jouir en même temps des voluptés du voluptueux et de l'austérité de l'ascète' and *Dialogues et fragments philosophiques*, 133); Amiel (*see Les Taches d'encre*, 1884 [*Œuvre* I 418] and P. Bourget, *Essais de psychologie contemporaine* II chapter 10); Marie Bashkirtseff (*see* 'La société cosmopolite,' *La Revue Illustrée*, 15 March 1888 and *Œuvre* I 224–6; II 356–8). But even before the diary of *l'Homme libre* is concluded (in April 1887, according to the last page of the novel), the hero of *Le Culte du Moi* has been tempted on more than one occasion to lower the guard of his defensive irony: 'Deux ou trois fois,' he remembers, of his affair with *l'Objet*, 'dans notre jeu sentimental, nous nous sommes touchés à fond, et soudain presque sincères, nous cessions notre intrigue pour vouloir nous aimer bonnement ... tels étaient ses yeux cerclés de fatigue charmante, quand elle se soulevait d'entre mes bras, que je cédais à mon goût pour cet Objet, plus qu'il n'était marqué dans mon programme' (*Œuvre* I 253). Of course, this *fin-de-siècle* lover cannot allow himself to believe that, even so, they could have enjoyed together more than a 'few weeks of true satisfaction.' But no comparable reservation affects the Egotist's certainty, impervious for once to his habit of abstraction, of having discovered on his earlier excursion to the 'heart of Lorraine' the very bed-rock of his true Self: 'À suivre comment [mes ancêtres] ont bâti leur pays, je retrouverai l'ordre suivant lequel furent posées mes propres assises' (*Œuvre* I 196). The sixth evening of his Lorraine pilgrimage finds him in a characteristic stock-taking attitude: 'stretched out on his bed,' in the wretched, candle-lit inn of the melancholy little eastern French town of Haroué, just as, some months later, after spending a number of weeks in the palaces, galleries, churches, and squares of Venice judged necessary for the assimilation of its outward beauty, he will retire to his rooms in order to lose himself in the soul of the city: 'le jour et la nuit parmi mes cigares, étendu sur mon vaste lit.' But whereas his 'Venetian Triumph' will depend upon the reduction of the historical Venice to the status of 'an abstract city existing nowhere,' the 'heart of Lorraine' is more resistant, and what threatens to 'dissolve' in the Egotist's solitary evening meditation in Haroué is not historical objectivity but his own professed independence of time and place:

> ...J'eus raison de rechercher où se poussait l'instinct de mes ancêtres; l'individu est mené par la même loi que sa race. À ce titre, Lorraine, tu me fus un miroir plus puissant qu'aucun des analystes où je me contemplai. Mais, Lorraine, j'ai touché ta limite, tu n'as pas abouti, tu t'es desséchée ... tu m'as montré que j'appartenais à une race incapable de se réaliser ... Il faut que je me dissolve comme ma race.
> [*Œuvre* I 212–13]

In these two comparatively unguarded moments, the hero of *Un Homme libre* gets a glimpse of irrational certainties which contrast strongly with the dilettante 'exercises' out of which most of the rest of the book is composed, and with the 'gymnastic' theory of human existence which constitutes its ostensible conclusion. Such natural appetites and instincts as sensual love and love of country (*Œuvre* I 213, 252–3) seem, from 'Lettre à Simon,' to be precisely what he is determined in future to avoid: 'Celui qui se laisse empoigner par ses instincts naturels est perdu,' 'rien n'est plus dangereux que nos appétits naturels et notre instinct,' 'je me refuse à mes instincts ... Que mes vertus naturels soient en moi un jardin fermé, une terre inculte! Je crains trop ces forces vives qui nous entraînent dans l'imprévu, et, pour des buts cachés, nous font participer à tous les chagrins vulgaires' (*Œuvre* I 260, 266–7). But by the time these precepts were published their author was already a stage ahead in the development of his ideas. A vigorous force of nature, quickening in sympathy for the French people's patriotic and democratic enthusiasm for General Boulanger in 1887–9, had broken out of the Egotist's walled wild garden: 'Cette période électorale me laissera un fécond souvenir ...

C'est là que je me pris à aimer la vie, l'instinct tout nu' ['Notes d'un nouvel élu,' *La Presse*, 31 October 1889]; 'L'âme des foules est fortifiante comme la montagne, les forêts, les fleuves ... Adorons toutes ces grandes forces de la nature pour mieux nous en pénétrer ... ['Un mois au Palais-Bourbon,' *Le Figaro*, 8 December 1889].

The chance that Boulangism had given Barrès of escaping from the almost intolerable tensions of 'dilettante' and 'gymnastic' Self-Culture described in *Sous l'œil des barbares* and *Un Homme libre*, by committing himself for once single-mindedly and wholeheartedly to a course of action shaped in some measure at least by the apparently 'immutable order of events' (*Œuvre* I 266, *cit.* above, p. 30) was not lost along with the General's famous failure of nerve. After the movement had collapsed, Barrès's nationalism continued to evolve as a willing surrender to dynamic natural and historical forces which he felt were beyond his control. 'Le nationalisme,' he will declare in 1902, 'est l'acceptation d'un déterminisme' (*Œuvre* v 23), an act prefigured throughout *Le Culte du Moi* in the form of 'two simultaneous postulations,'[18] to intellect and to instinct, which are fundamental to the development of his philosophy.

Intellect and Instinct

In the depths of spiritual acedia (after his excursion into the depressed 'heart of Lorraine' and before his brief Venetian triumph), the hero of *Un Homme libre* is obsessed by the thought that one day, perhaps on his death-bed, he may come to regret bitterly that he had never let himself be ruled by unreflecting natural instinct: 'je regretterai de n'avoir pas joui de moi-même ... en laissant mon instinct s'imposer à mon âme en irréfléchi' (*Œuvre* I 218). And he imagines the again very Proustian situation of 'une maîtresse jeune et impure, vivant au dehors, tandis que moi je ne bougerais jamais, jamais. Elle viendrait me voir avec ardeur ... mais perpétuellement j'aurais vingt-quatre heures d'angoisse entre chacun de nos rendez-vous, avec le coup de massue de l'abandon suspendu sur ma tête.' That would be

18 C. Baudelaire, *Mon Cœur mis à nu, Œuvres complètes* 1277.

happiness, perhaps, for his life would be 'unified' and 'systematized' by an uncontrollable force acting on him from the outside.

The attractive prospect of surrendering to instinct embodied in a young woman ruled by her senses ('elle serait jeune, belle fille, avec des genoux fins, un corps ayant une ligne franche et un sourire imprévu infiniment touchant de sensualité triste') comes to the surface of the Egotist's consciousness again after his return from Venice, saturated with 'the beauty of ideas,' and inspires his final 'Excursion dans la vie': 'Ah! l'attrait de l'irréparable, où toujours je voulus trouver un perpétuel repos: au cloître ... au soir d'Haroué ... sur les canaux éclatants de Venise ... C'est encore ce morne irréparable que ma fièvre cherche à Paris, tandis que je veux me remettre tout entier entre des mains ornées de trop de bagues (*Œuvre* I 251). The temptation of 'irreparable' commitment to an overwhelmingly ascendent external force takes a second form in his dream of submission under the rough authority of a male *maître à penser*: 'Je ne voudrais pas être mené avec douceur, car je me méfie de mes défaillances. C'est peut-être que mon âme s'effémine; mais elle voudrait être roudoyée. Sous un cloître, dans ma cellule, je serais heureux si je savais qu'un maître terrible ne me laisse pas d'autre ressource que de subir une discipline.'[19]

The point about excursions, said D.H. Lawrence, is that you come back. Barrès's *homme libre* succeeds, if only just, in getting his dangerously exposed sexual instincts back from their sortie in the zone of 'objective' emotional entanglements, and safely inside his 'walled garden' again (*Œuvre* I 267; II 374). The desired spiritual director fails to materialize. But the simultaneous, or alternating, attractions of wild instinct and intellectual discipline have settled for good in the heart of Barrès's philosophy and rhetoric: joint agents of his

19 It was at this period of Barrès's development that he told J.E. Jeanès: 'Je ne trouve que des désirs, et qui ne sont pas tous d'accord. Un grand besoin de liberté touchant à la licence ... mais cette liberté, je la possède. Il est des jours où je regrette d'en jouir car il me serait agréable de violer ou de duper les lois ou les mœurs oppressives. En même temps j'aime le pouvoir, autant pour le subir que pour l'exercer, cela tient au fond bonapartiste dont j'ai hérité.' (J.E. Jeanès, *D'Après Nature* (Besançon: Granvelle 1946) 80–1)

evolving traditionalism, equal and opposite aspects of the typically triadic structure of discourse, allegory and characterization by which he seeks to give it persuasive literary form. The apprentice hero of *Le Culte du Moi* is from the beginning repeatedly drawn out of himself by attraction to people who seem to command one or other of these 'two postulations.'

To the first category belongs the cynical *maître* of chapter one of *Sous l'œil des barbares*: 'Départ inquiet,' who reappears in chapter five: 'Paris à vingt ans,' as the venerable Renanian Monsieur X, a properly rebuffed caricature of the *true* Master: 'axiom, religion or prince of men,' to whom the final 'Orison' of the novel is addressed. In *Un Homme libre*, besides the imagined *directeur de conscience* of chapter seven: 'Acédia. Séparation dans le monastère,' there are the more fraternal 'intercessors' of French Romantic literature, and the master-spirits of Italian painting, in particular Leonardo, whose Brera Christ impresses the Egotist by his comprehensive understanding of men's hearts ('celui qui lit dans les cœurs, le plus compréhensif des hommes' [*Œuvre* I 230]), and Tiepolo ('la conscience de Venise'). Another group of intellectual luminaries is examined in *L'Ennemi des lois* (1892): the French and German social reformers of the nineteenth century – Saint-Simon, Fourier, Lassalle, and Marx. In the preface to the final volume of *Le Culte du Moi: Le Jardin de Bérénice*, Ernest Renan appears in person to give a sophisticated and somewhat sceptical account of the transient success of Boulangism, and the novel itself contains the author's most hostile portrait so far of a representative of the Opportunist Republic's intellectual establishment: Charles Martin, engineer and regional planner of the valley of the lower Rhône, a dedicated technocrat whom Barrès's hero designates simply as 'The Adversary,' but into whose arms he clumsily pushes Bérénice, the instinctively loving Child of Nature. Other early Barresian variations on the master-apprentice relation are to be found in the ascendency of Athéné, priestess of Hellenistic Alexandria over both Amaryllis, the spiritually starved and restless woman of pleasure, and the young Lucius, the sceptical man of the world, whom Barrès has dressed for *Le Culte du Moi* in the mantle of Renan and Anatole France: 'Lucius songeait: "Hélas! Athéné, vous voulez nous élever jusqu'à l'intelligence pure et nous défendre toutes les illusions...''' (*Œuvre* I 79); in the sentimental education of Pia by her half-brother, half-lover, Delrio, 'un amateur d'âmes' (*Du Sang, de la volupté et de la mort, Œuvre* II 23–49); in the socialist education that Mlle Pichon-Picard, 'avec cette soif de s'instruire particulière aux jeunes filles de ce temps qui ont, toutes, la passion des professeurs,' demands of André Maltère, intellectual radical, and hero of *L'Ennemi des lois.*

But intellectual discipleship represents one side only of the characteristically triangular structure of personal relations in Barrès's early fictions. His first published story: 'Nouvelle pour rêveurs' (*Les Taches d'encre*, November 1884, *Œuvre* I 405–17), had been about a young intellectual seeking the secret of happiness, in a rather improbable country house, from, on the one hand an august, dying teacher who has spent his life in the world of ideas, and who recommends philosophical detachment, and on the other a hypersentient young beauty, recently widowed, who follows only her heart; and this pattern was repeated, with variations, between 1888 and 1894, throughout *Le Culte du Moi* and all its *marginalia* and *addenda,* giving evidence incidentally of what Barrès's early work owes to three corresponding literary sources: Romantic discontents from *René* to *Sagesse*, German Idealist philosophy, and Baudelairean eroticism.

Retrospectively, Barrès pointed out that the female characters of the three volumes of *Le Culte du Moi* were one and the same woman 'accommodée simplement au milieu.' The narrator hero of the trilogy, who acquires a first name, Philippe, in the last volume, has a similarly sustained single identity, though the relations that he and his brothers in ideology, Delrio and André Maltère, establish with various Barresian avatars of the eternal feminine are as diverse and intermittent as the corresponding magnetic currents attracting and repelling Barrès's youthful protagonists (of both sexes) within the fields of force that radiate from various incarnations of the Master. Thus the Egotist's first mistress, a frail figure by Gustave Moreau in a grove by Puvis de Chavannes, is as dependent upon the 'Bon-Vouloir créateur' of her lover as Villiers de l'Isle-Adam's plaintive Hadaly had been, and is easily dissolved in the white light of philosophical idealism: 'Je désire que vous cessiez d'exister,' he says in chapter five, 'Dandyisme,' 'et je retire de dessous vous mon désir, qui vous soutenait sur le néant.' Theoretically, the desired Object of *Un Homme libre* can be similarly disposed of: 'En réalité, les traits séduisants que j'assemble autour de son baiser ne furent jamais réunis' (*Œuvre* I 250). But, as we have seen, like an apprentice in the sorcery of love, the young proto-Philippe nearly gets swept away, if not for good, then at least for a longer and more disturbing excursion into life than he has bargained for. Bérénice, the last in this series of Barresian heroines, is married off to the Adversary and, as an almost immediate consequence of this unfortunate shock to her delicately tuned sensibility, dies. But she returns to haunt Philippe more movingly and permanently than the abandoned Object of his earlier 'Anecdote d'amour.' Between 1885 and 1895, the women of Barrès's imagination exist with ever greater independent force and density of character, in contrast to the continuing desultory, transient, lack-lustre or caricatural appearance of his representative types of male magisterial authority.

Feminine intuition appears at first in *Le Culte du Moi* as a value exactly equal to intellectual understanding. For instance, the opinions of Monsieur X, according to Philippe's first love, 'are the exact formula for what my smiling seems to counsel': 'Il est le dictionnaire du langage que tiennent mes gestes à l'univers,' and the great courtesans, according to Philippe himself at a slightly later date, are 'moved by the same god' as the intellectual 'analyst' (*Œuvre* I 104, 252). But as the Egotist's apprenticeship advances, women gain ever increasing authority over him, against fading counter-claims by the advocates of intellectual discipline, and as they do so, feminine intuition is ever more explicitly equated with animal instinct. Marie Bashkirtseff, 'Notre-Dame du Sleeping-Car,' 'Notre-Dame qui n'êtes jamais satisfaite,' is no doubt much nearer to the divine discontent of the Romantic heroine than to the female animality of Baudelairean typology: 'je veux aller jusqu'à croire que jamais tu ne ressentis le moindre trouble ... Tu n'aurais connu que déception à chercher ta part de femme' (*Œuvre* I 226; II 356–68). Mlle Claire Pichon-Picard, another 'cerebral' idealist, who is the fiancée and, later, the wife of André Maltère, is pitted against a complementary rival: the exotic Princess Marina, a creature of pure instinct, with whom Maltère discovers his darker, irrational powers of universal sympathy, in one of those semi-erotic, pseudo-sibling triangles that seem to have attracted Barrès particularly at this period of his life.[20] She holds her own, but only just, at the price of a 'sublime' act of unconventional magnanimity, which will enable all three to move forward to the achievement of a new, libertarian style of existence, by cohabiting passionately in a rural utopia that is to be the model of the future open society, 'une société aux portes ouvertes.' The fourth founder member of this commune, moreover, is a dog named Velu (after Michelet's lines: 'dans la pensée chrétienne, l'animal est suspect, la bête semble un masque. Les velus! Nom sinistre que le juif donne aux animaux!' [*Œuvre* II 219]), whose important educative function Maltère explains as follows:

> Ils décidèrent de s'installer tous les quatre à la campagne, où ils grouperaient autour de Velu beaucoup de bêtes et puis des tas de petits enfants.
> – Ah! dit Marina, en s'interrompant de baiser l'animal, il y aura des enfants! Je les aime moins que les chiens, mais je comprends, notre ami serait trop malheureux s'il n'avait personne devant qui parler.
> – Non, répondit gravement André, ce n'est pas moi qui les enseignerai, c'est Velu...
> Déclaration essentielle! Nul ne doit être un maître, sinon celui qui ne parle pas ... celui qui a des opinions, qu'il se garde bien d'enseigner et s'en tienne à renseigner qui l'interroge.
> Elle est excellente, en effet, l'éducation que donne un chien ... Nos collégiens surchargés d'acquisitions intellectuelles qui demeurent en eux des notions, non des façons de sentir ... réapprendraient du chien la belle aisance, le don d'écouter l'instinct de leur moi...
> Toute bête, c'est près de nous, dans une outre agréable à voir, un peu de vie pure de mélange pédant.
> [*Œuvre* II 289–90]

20 Real or imagined sibling relationships between lovers are to be found besides *L'Ennemi des lois* (*Œuvre* II 239, 244, 262), in 'Un amateur d'âmes' (*Œuvre* II 23–49), 'Les deux femmes du bourgeois de Bruges' (*Œuvre* II 52) and 'Un Amour de Thulé' (*Œuvre* II 57–9).

The Princess Marina is the first of a line of Barresian heroines whose mysterious oriental origins are supposed to account for the energy and fascination of their animal instincts: 'Claire Pichon-Picard ... merveilleusement intelligente, voyait moins net dans la vie que la frivole Marina guidée seulement, pour trancher les questions, par une sensualité qui est exactement le sens de la vie' (*Œuvre* II 228).[21] Bérénice, on the other hand, has nothing exotic about her, except perhaps the brilliant colours she likes to wear (304), but more emphatically still than André Maltère's aristocratic *orientale*, or her shadowy prototypes from *Sous l'œil des barbares* ('fontaine de vie, figure mystérieuse de petit animal nubile') and *Un Homme libre* ('leur corps si souple, leur sourire de petit animal'), and her Andalusian sisters from *Du sang, de la volupté et de la mort* ('une petite mule comme elles sont toutes,' 'frémissement de jeune bête'),[22] this humble French night-club dancer, portrayed against the doubly ordinary background of peaceful provincial childhood and adolescent Parisian corruption, embodies instinctive wisdom. 'Petite bête à la peau tiède,' 'jeune animal,' 'petit animal entêté,' she vibrates in sympathy not just with the donkey and domestic ducks she keeps in her narrow cottage garden 'qui ne voit pas la mer,' but also, 'frémissante à toutes les solidarités de la nature,' with all the wild flood-plain of the Camargue beyond, which, together with the mediaeval citadel of Aigues-Mortes, constitutes her 'garden' in the allegorical sense Barrès gives to the word:[23]

> ...C'est en effet l'idée de tradition, d'unité dans la succession qui domine cette petite sentimentale et cette plaine; c'est leur constance commune qui fait cette analogie si forte que, pour désigner l'âme de cette contrée et l'âme de cette enfant, pour

21 *See*, in particular, Astiné Aravian, the Armenian mistress of François Sturel, in *Les Déracinés* (*Œuvre* III 76–97), and Oriante, in *Un Jardin sur l'Oronte* (*Œuvre* XI); also *N'Importe où hors du monde* (*Œuvre* XII 352–77 and 412–61). Cf. I.-M. Frandon, *L'Orient de Maurice Barrès*.

22 *Œuvre* I 91, 252; II 95–6, 354–5

23 Cf. *Œuvre* I 304–6, 316, 326–7, 330, 341, 359 and II 122: 'Les jardins de Lombardie': 'C'est toute la région qui nous est un jardin, au sens magique que reçoit ce mot quand il désigne les liens [lieux?] mystérieux de la légende...'

indiquer la culture dont elles sont le type, je me sers d'un même mot: *Le Jardin de Bérénice.*

...

Ton rôle, ma Bérénice, est de faire songer aux mystères de la reproduction et de la mort, ou, plus exactement, il faut qu'en toi tout crie l'instinct et que tu sois l'image la plus complète que nous puissions concevoir des forces de la nature.

...

Ton plaisir, ma chère Bérénice, c'est d'être enveloppée par la caresse, l'effusion et l'enseignement d'Aigues-Mortes, de sa campagne et de la tour Constance ... Tu te mêles à Aigues-Mortes; tes sensations, tu les as répandues sur toutes ces pierres, sur cette lande desséchée, c'est toi-même qui te restitue la brise qui souffle de la mer contre ta petite maison, c'est ta propre fièvre qui te monte le soir de ces étangs.

[*Œuvre* I 323, 329–30]

L'ÉNERGIE NATIONALE

Towards participation: 'la bonne méthode'

Barrès's heroines of 1891 and 1892 afford a greatly extended field of view into both the maturing nationalist's sense of his country's particular genius, in contrast to civilizations at once alien and complementary, and the would-be democrat's first revelation of the popular will in action. The individual origins and life-styles of the Princess Marina and Bérénice point specifically to the two great collective reserves of instinctive wisdom that inspired the next, predominantly political, stage of his development, following *Le Culte du Moi:* one is situated, in allegorical space, to the east of France's 'Cartesian' frontier; the other lies below the *lycée-* or college-educated level of contemporary French society in the mass mind of the common people, or what Barrès tried to read as such: 'les femmes adoucissent ... notre individualisme excessif; elles nous font rentrer dans la race ... Ah! c'est bien elle, la chère petite fille, qui m'a aidé à comprendre la méthode créatrice des masses, de l'homme spontané.'

(*Œuvre* I 343). But these are not the only growing points of Barrès's traditionalism in *Le Jardin de Bérénice* and *L'Ennemi des lois.* In both novels feminine intuition is observed from a fresh point of view, which corresponds with an important change of perspective not only in the author's system of expression but also in his scheme of thought.

In 'Une anecdote d'amour,' Philippe had sought self-knowledge by means of the planned, temporary, possession of a rather common female Object. In *L'Ennemi des lois,* Marina is one of two intrinsically much more precious objects of Maltère's affections: 'Tout homme passionné fut servi par des femmes de cœur et des femmes de nerfs. Deux beautés de cette qualité allaient prendre dans la vie du jeune homme une grande importance' (*Œuvre* II 213). But, together with Claire Pichon-Picard, the Princess also contributes very positively to her lover's education, as much by what she tells him, in long hours of reminiscent pillow-talk of life in the East (which has a very authentic quality, reappearing in the confessions of both Astiné Arivian and the unnamed heroine of one of Barrès's late, unfinished *nouvelles, Le Frein couvert d'écume*[24]), as by the act of love itself. As for Bérénice, she is not even part-object of the narrator-hero's possessive lust; she is a beauty to be studied rather than possessed:

> 'Quel sentiment avez-vous pour moi?,' me demanda-t-elle, un jour, avec son sourire un peu triste, dont elle avait assurément remarqué qu'il accompagnait toujours avec avantage ce genre de question. 'De l'inclination,' lui-répondis-je, étonné moi-même de trouver sans hésitation le mot exact, celui qui convient tout à fait au sentiment qui m'incline sur elle, pour y saisir les lois mystérieuses de la vie, la bonne méthode.
> [*Œuvre* I 333]

From Philippe's new point of view on the eternal feminine, as an object lesson rather than as an object of possession, the light no longer falls on an intellectual narrator-hero's complicated and generally unsatisfactory ways with a maid, semi-maid, courtesan, New Woman, or libertine Princess, but instead on the way a child of

24 *Œuvre* III 83–93; XII 412–61

nature and of the common people herself finds the 'continuity' with the past and the 'harmony' with the universe that Philippe longs for, through perfectly instinctive fidelity to the object of *her* affections – François de Transe, the nice, if unremarkable, young hero of a briefly shared idyll cut short by his death in a 'stupid accident':

> Bérénice ... est harmonique à ce pays. C'est qu'elle a comme lui de profondes assises; j'en avais eu tout d'abord une perception confuse. Un sentiment très vif des humbles droits de sa race au bonheur et un secret fait de souvenirs et d'imaginations, voilà toute son âme. Combien j'envie à cette enfant et à cette vieille plaine cette continuité dans leur développement, moi qui ne sais pas même accorder mes émotions d'hier et d'aujourd'hui! [*Œuvre* I 316]

What Philippe calls the 'method' of Bérénice is spontaneous and unconscious ('une passion dont tressaille votre petit corps vous a fait vivre parallèlement à l'univers' [329]), but the detached observer and the ambitious man of action that Philippe is becoming (to the point even of acknowledging certain distantly kindred features in his technocratic Adversary, Charles Martin) means to adopt it deliberately and consciously, in the wider, public context of democratic politics, to which it appears to him to be equally relevant:

> le fond de ma préoccupation n'était ni Bérénice ni la campagne d'Aigues-Mortes; je ne pensais qu'à l'action électorale que je venais d'entreprendre à Arles; je ne pensais qu'au peuple. 'Quelle est son âme? me demandais-je, je veux frissonner avec elle, la comprendre par l'analyse du détail, comme l'Adversaire, et par amour, comme Bérénice; arriver enfin à en être la conscience.' [*Œuvre* I 324]

In the scheme of representative types on which *Le Culte du Moi* is based, Bérénice has taken over the function, if not of the Master, at least of a very persuasive, though unsystematic and inarticulate teacher, a cousin, only once removed, as it were, to the wise, dumb Velu of André Maltère's *ménage à quatre* in *L'Ennemi des lois*.

Thus a chapter of *Le Jardin de Bérénice* is devoted to her 'Pédagogie.' Philippe is her disciple, not her lover. When she dies of a broken heart and is reborn in spirit, then he even falls to worshipping her – the Beatrice, Isis, Madonna, and Child Redeemer of a 'New Life' indeed:

> – Tu étais, ma Bérénice, le petit enfant sauveur. La sagesse de ton instinct dépassait toutes nos sagesses et ces petites idées où notre logique voudrait réduire la raison ... Ah! ... que tu étais fortifiante dans le triste jardin d'Aigues-Mortes!
> – J'étais là; mais je suis partout. Reconnais en moi la petite secousse par où chaque parcelle du monde témoigne l'effort secret de l'inconscient.
> ['Petite–Secousse n'est pas morte,' *Le Jardin de Bérénice*, *Œuvre* I 374–5]

Philippe's proposed new life of action, founded on conscious personal identification with the collective, unconscious wisdom of the people, foreshadows the mature development of Barrès's vocation as the poet-propagandist and image-maker of twentieth-century French traditionalism:

> ce n'était plus Bérénice que je voyais, mais l'âme populaire, âme religieuse, instinctive et, comme cette petite fille, pleine d'un passé dont elle n'a pas conscience; pour Charles Martin, c'était la médiocrité moderne, la demi-réflexion, le manque de compréhension, des notions sans amour.
> [*Œuvre* I 322–3]

For the time being, however, he would find participatory political action on this basis easier to envisage, and to allegorize, than to achieve in the world of facts and events: 'Petite-Secousse, je crois en vérité que tu existes partout, mais il était plus aisé de te constater dans le cœur d'un léger oiseau de passage que de distinguer nettement comment bat le cœur des simples' (*Œuvre* I 376).

Le Jardin de Bérénice was written at a time of slack water in French political history, when the exciting tide of popular patriotic and anti-parliamentary enthusiasm for the Boulangist Movement had already turned. The middle eighteen-nineties gave France 'a brief period of political calm between the subsidence of the Right and the ascension of the Left.'[25] To Barrès, who at the end of this period would move decisively away from dilettantism, against the prevailing political winds of change, from the Left to the Right, it seemed to offer meanwhile nothing but discouragement. Like the philosopher Seneca, similarly becalmed between the decline of Roman virtue and the rise of the Christian religion, whom Philippe, on a night ride back across the Camargue from a pilgrimage to Les Saintes-Maries, imagines at once envious and sceptical of the newly minted missionary zeal that his young friend Lazarus is showing for some 'marvellous agitator' who has apparently raised him from the dead, Barrès might well feel that he had been born at the wrong time or in the wrong place:

> 'J'ai voulu ne rien nier, être comme la nature qui accepte tous les contrastes pour en faire une noble et féconde unité. J'avais compté sans ma condition d'homme. Impossible d'avoir plusieurs passions à la fois. J'ai senti jusqu'au plus profond découragement le malheur de notre sensibilité qui est d'être successive et fragmentaire ... La sensation d'aujourd'hui se substitue à la sensation précédente. Un état de conscience ne peut naître en nous que par la mort de l'individu que nous étions hier...
>
> Cette mort perpétuelle, ce manque de continuité de nos émotions, voilà ce qui désole l'égotiste et marque l'échec de sa prétention. Notre âme est un terrain trop limité pour y faire fleurir dans une même saison tout l'univers. Réduits à la traiter par des cultures successives, nous la verrons toujours fragmentaire.
>
> J'ai donc senti, mon cher Lazare, et jusqu'à l'angoisse, les entraves décisives de ma méthode; aussi j'eusse été fanatique si j'avais su de quoi le devenir. Après quelques années de la plus intense culture intérieure, j'ai rêvé de sortir des volontés particulières pour me confondre dans les volontés générales. Au lieu

25 G. Chapman, *The Third Republic of France: The First Phase 1871–1894* (London: Macmillan 1962) 368

de m'individuer, j'eusse été ravi de me plonger dans le courant de mon époque. Seulement il n'y en avait pas. J'aurais voulu me plonger dans l'inconscient mais, dans le monde où je vivais, tout inconscient semblait avoir disparu.'
[*Le Jardin de Bérénice, Œuvre* I 365–6]

In 1895, now an established Parisian man of letters, a former deputy, a persistent, though for some time yet unsuccessful, candidate for re-election, an attacking nationalist and federal-socialist journalist and pamphleteer, and briefly but memorably, the editor of an opposition newspaper, *La Cocarde*, Barrès was claiming somewhat ambiguously on the one hand that 'action' was not 'drawing up political programmes' but 'transforming the sensibility of two or of a thousand of one's contemporaries by a work of art' and, on the other, that action meant 'grouping together men with the will to act, aiding and precipitating events' ('La Leçon des scandales,' *La Cocarde*, 17 February 1895).[26] When the following year Émile Zola declared that his brief parliamentary career had been a total failure, Barrès insisted in a private reply that 'certain ideas' he had put into circulation had already taken root in an intelligentsia 'now ready for political action,' but he also showed sufficient discouragement to declare that his own *raison d'être* might very well turn out to be 'more that of an observer and an annalist than that of a man of action,' asking his illustrious critic to suspend judgment, moreover, pending the appearance of his next book.[27] This was *Le Roman de l'énergie nationale*, the second of Barrès's major publications, and his first 'encyclopedic' work (in the terminology of Professor Northrop Frye). It does indeed attempt the 'annals' of France from 1879 to 1893, as he had hinted to Zola in advance that it would, though its inspiration was deliberately 'popular' (*Œuvre* III 5), and undisguisedly partisan (as was its considerable influence on more than one generation of active French regionalists, caesarists, and nationalists). The general subject of its three volumes: *Les Déracinés*

26 *See* p. 279.
27 Letter to Zola, 6 June 1896, *cit. Mercure de France* CCXXXI no. 800 (15 October 1931) 459–61

(1897), *L'Appel au soldat* (1900), and *Leurs figures* (1902), is *wasted* energy, through discontinuity and fragmentation no longer simply, as in *Le Culte du Moi*, within an individual (*Œuvre* I 365 *cit.* above, p. 44), but in an entire nation: 'la France dissociée et décérébrée' (*Œuvre* III 179–84). Specifically it relates a multiple failure to act effectively against wastage caused by the accidents of birth and of history, whether these accidents produce privilege doomed to futility, or need answered with callous indifference, and ranging at the two extremes from moral 'liquidation' to judicial and mob 'executions.'[28] The public failures, or alleged failures of the Third Republic's newly established educational, administrative, and parliamentary systems, and also the two great fiascos of protest mounted against the Republican establishment between 1887 and 1893: Boulangism and the Panama Scandal, constitute the historical setting of a variety of fictitious private failures which, with rare exceptions, make up the young lives of seven former pupils of the state *lycée* in Nancy, and of their acquaintances, associates, and mistresses in Paris. In the most important of these interwoven imaginary biographies Barrès again invites his readers to consider the problem of 'participation' that the rising generation of French intellectuals was, in his view, finding so hard to solve:

> Ces analystes, ces égotistes, ces dilettanti, ces sceptiques enfin que vous querellez, loin de mépriser aucun ordre d'activité, se piquent d'être compréhensifs. S'ils demeurent à l'écart ... s'ils sont fort empêchés de prendre un parti, ce n'est point qu'ils les repoussent tous, mais qu'ils les agréent tous ... Pour rompre leur indécision, il faudrait qu'on leur proposât un groupe d'où l'on vît les choses sous un aspect d'éternité.
>
> La pensée, l'usage de la raison isolent...
>
> [*Toute licence sauf contre l'amour, Œuvre* II 387–8]

The problem that Barrès had transposed once already into fiction in the subjective and allegorical mode of *Le Culte du Moi* was now to be viewed from the objective standpoint that the hero of *Le Culte du Moi* had reached in the last pages of the trilogy.

28 *See* p. 279.

The action of Barrès's new novel turns, as in *Le Culte du Moi*, on a variety of master-pupil relations. Between the philosopher master of a provincial *lycée*, Paul Bouteiller (partly modelled on Barrès's own teacher Auguste Burdeau) and the outstanding seven members of his *baccalauréat* class of 1879, in all of whom he inspires some ambition to seek further education, fame, and fortune in Paris, the relationship proves to be a predominantly destructive one. Between François Sturel, the rich, romantic adventurer of the group, and his various 'intercessors' from the world of books and the walls of art galleries, and his 'heroes' from history or contemporary France, it creates the familiar Barresian 'antinomies of thought and action.' Maurice Roemerspacher, on the other hand, Sturel's intellectual peer and closest friend, in the relationships he establishes with his *maître à penser*, Taine, and with his teachers at the École des Hautes Études and Heidelberg University, finds a theoretical solution to the problems of intellectual alienation and social participation: the doctrine of natural and historical evolution, a doctrine that, in the less philosophically sophisticated form of social traditionalism, modelled notably on Mistral and Le Play, inspires the third of the socially privileged members of Bouteiller's *classe de philo*, Henri Gallant de Saint-Phlin, the son of a Lorraine landowner, who alone of *les déracinés* abandons all Parisian ambitions and goes voluntarily home to cultivate the garden he is lucky enough to own in his native province. The four socially or genetically underprivileged members of the group, on the other hand, have nothing to live by except the connections they struggle to establish with various equally rootless *patrons* in Parisian politics, journalism, finance, and police, all of which eventually prove degrading in some way or other, where not actually lethal:

> Le lycée de Nancy avait coupé leur lien social naturel; l'Université ne sut pas à Paris leur créer les attaches qui eussent le mieux convenu à leurs idées innées, ou plus exactement aux dispositions de leur organisme ... ils vaguent dans le quartier Latin ... libres comme la bête dans les bois.
> [*Les Déracinés, Œuvres* III 98–9]

> En haussant les sept jeunes Lorrains de leur petite patrie à

la France, et même à l'humanité, on pensait les rapprocher de la Raison ... Ceux qui avaient dirigé cette émigration avaient-ils senti qu'ils avaient charge d'âmes? Avaient-ils vu la périlleuse gravité de leur acte? À ces déracinés, ils ne surent pas offrir un bon terrain de 'replantement.'
[*Les Déracinés, Œuvre* III 345]

Ces jeunes gens, ces déracinés, le problème est maintenant de savoir s'ils prendront racine.
C'est un livre où l'on doit voir un esprit qui a la tradition, non un esprit réactionnaire...
On me dit, mais la terre lorraine diffère-t-elle de la terre de Touraine? Je ne vous dis pas: vous les avez déracinés de la terre lorraine. Je vous dis: vous les avez déracinés, enlevés de toute terre.
[*Mes Cahiers, Œuvre* XIII 139]

Three of the principal fictitious characters of *Le Roman de l'énergie nationale* also express, by deed and word, the two 'postulations' that intellect and instinct had inspired in Philippe the Egotist and the anarchist André Maltère. Like Maltère for instance, François Sturel is simultaneously attracted by an exotic *femme de nerfs*, Astiné Aravian, and a French *femme de cœur*, Thérèse Alison, whose own affections turn gradually from the highly-strung Sturel ('joli type de nerveux,' 'un enthousiaste qui a trois mille francs de rente' [*Œuvre* III 271, 417]) to the self-reliant and patient pragmatist, Maurice Roemerspacher, who finds serenity in science *and* in marriage to Thérèse (*Œuvre* IV 427). Sturel eventually discovers in the collective animal magnetism of crowds and assemblies a more powerfully attractive force than either intellectual authority or feminine fascination. Like his creator, he becomes a deeply stirred witness to the creative release of popular instinct in the mass demonstrations of Parisian Hugo-worship in 1885 and Boulangist street politics in 1887–9 (*Œuvre* III 325–55, 400–35). He is equally fascinated by its destructive power in the anarchist and criminal underworlds inhabited by Fanfournot, Racadot, and Mouchefrin, the chief victims and drop-outs of Bouteiller's philosophy class (*Œuvre* III 98–114, 293–305; IV 355–61, 429–31) and in the parliamentary bull-ring and politico-financial sewers of power that Barrès imagines running with blood and streaming with corruption during the Panama Scandal of 1892–3 (*Leurs Figures, Œuvre* IV *see* below, p. 200).

As Barrès advanced into the second half of his multi-volume *Roman de l'énergie nationale*, the raw drama of contemporary French political action seemed to excite his imagination more creatively and certainly more violently than the fictitious group portrait of a botched Parisian apprenticeship on which he had embarked in the middle eighteen-nineties. The real life scenes and the political doctrines of his nascent nationalism (*see Scènes et doctrines du nationalisme, Œuvre* v) break assertively through the mask of fiction, and the private lives of his invented characters are relegated for whole chapters at a time to the background of the novel. This change of emphasis reflects a change of political weather in France between 1898 and 1902, brought about by the Dreyfus Affair, which revived Barrès's interest in public events as a field of direct action.

Commitment achieved: 'le choc opératoire'

The rather plaintive letter Barrès had written to Zola in 1896 suggests a decidedly reluctant resignation to the passive role of 'observer and annalist.' The times seemed to be against his greater ambition to 'precipitate events.' For the present, he had written, what 'tangible' success could he hope for when, 'attached to a vanquished party [the Boulangists] and in that party an *isolé*,' he believed in the permanence of the patriotic ideal yet looked forward to the collectivization of private property, holding moreover that this could be achieved only by the dictatorship of a man or of an assembly:

> et que me voilà socialiste, nationaliste et dictatorial, que puis-je faire sinon de m'employer au développement de mes idées et d'être un vaincu, tant qu'une nouvelle génération ne se substitutera pas au personnel parlementaire?
> [Letter to É. Zola, 6 June 1896, *cit. Mercure de France*, CCXXXI no. 800 (15 October 1931) 459–61]

The eclectic national-socialism which was Barrès's contribution towards filling the gap left by the failure of the Boulangist Movement looks even more eccentric and unviable in the light of French history after 1896 because the multiform opposition to the Opportunist Republic of the middle-nineties was blown to pieces in the next great political crisis of the Third Republic, the gravest so far. But if the Dreyfus Affair, that 'limit-situation,'[29] by driving a wedge between nationalism and socialism and between caesarism and democracy, ruined Barrès's programme, not just for the 'new generation' he looked to, but for several more to come, it also, by forcing him, together with most of his contemporaries, to take sides in an ideological civil war, gave him at last the opportunity, for which he had looked in vain among the unimpressive and shifting 'axioms, creeds and leaders of men' of pre-Dreyfus France, of committing himself wholly and out of a sense of imperious necessity to the rough discipline of an embattled cause which would admit no ifs and buts.

The nature of Barrès's commitment to anti-Dreyfusard nationalism and of the lead he was soon to take in defining and disseminating its ideology are foreshadowed in his allegory of the Boulangist experience, *Le Jardin de Bérénice*, written nearly ten years before. The imaginary letter it contains, from 'Seneca the Philosopher' to 'Lazarus raised from the grave,' is a 'Renanian' dialogue, between the 'brain-lobes' of a divided self, such as Barrès will use to mark several further stages in the development of his traditionalism.[30] It represents Barrès as he then was, in two minds as yet whether he should,

29 M. Merleau-Ponty, *Humanisme et Terreur* (Paris: Gallimard 1947) 86–7: 'pour Trotsky comme pour tous les marxistes, la politique n'est pas seulement affaire de conscience, la simple occasion pour la subjectivité d'exprimer au-dehors des idées ou des valeurs, mais l'engagement du sujet moral abstrait dans des événements ambigus. Il savait bien que dans certaines situations-limites on n'a le choix que d'être pour où contre.'

30 *Œuvre* 362–6. *See* E. Renan, *Dialogues et fragments philosophiques* (Paris: Calmann Lévy 1876) viii: 'ce sont les pacifiques dialogues auxquels ont coutume de se livrer entre eux les différents lobes de mon cerveau quand je les laisse divaguer en liberté. Le temps des systèmes élaborés est passé.' Cf. *Œuvre* III 156–7; IV 18–20 445–7; V 47–51; VI 221–2, 499–500 XII 464–5; and preface to M. Beaubourg, *Contes pour les assassins* (Paris: Perrin 1890): 'n'ayant jamais su comprendre quel intérêt on peut trouver à un récit quel qu'il soit, et estimant que les dialogues philosophiques de Platon, de Fichte ou de M. Renan sont les plus comiques et les plus tragiques de tous les récits.'

or could in the prevailing circumstances, become a 'fanatic,' committed to some great and generous public cause, like Lazarus and his fellow missionaries to heathen Gaul, or whether he must remain detached from public affairs, like Seneca, the reluctant, but too clear-sighted 'egotist' at the court of Nero. The heroine of the novel, on the other hand, represents Barrès as he wanted to be: 'Telle que j'ai imaginé cette fille, elle est l'expression complète des conditions où s'épanouirait mon bonheur; elle est le moi que je voudrais devenir' (*Œuvre* I 374). And Bérénice has learned how to 'participate,' in the complicated public activities of adult Parisian society to which her sheltered provincial innocence has been sacrificed, by 'natural' submission to the commanding authority of an idealized father, successively embodied, iconographically and then materially, in the paintings of King René of Provence at the museum in Aigues-Mortes, and a live ballet master at the Eden in Paris:

> Quand, de son musée, Bérénice, orpheline, vint à Paris pour être ballerine à l'Éden, elle ne s'étonna pas un instant, car l'ordonnance des tableaux où elle figura autour des déesses d'opérette lui rappelait assez les compositions du roi René. Elle trouva naturel d'y participer, ayant pris, comme tous les enfants, l'habitude de se reconnaître dans quelques-unes des figures de ces vieux panneaux. Elle accepta l'autorité du maître de danse, comme les simples se soumettent aux forces de la nature. C'est un instinct commun à toutes les jeunes civilisations, à toutes les créatures naissantes, et fortifié en Bérénice par les panneaux religieux du roi René, de croire qu'une intelligence supérieure, généralement un homme âgé, ordonne le monde.
>
> Son acceptation, d'ailleurs, avait toute l'aisance des choses naturelles, sans le moindre servilisme. Ce sentiment avait été développé en elle par l'image familière et bonhomme que la légende lui donnait du roi René, fondateur du château et patron de cet art. Elle savait mille anecdotes où ce prince accueille avec bonté les humbles. L'imagination qu'elle se fit de ce personnage contribua pour une bonne part à lui former cette petite âme qui n'eut jamais de platitude. Bérénice considérait qu'il est de puissants seigneurs à qui l'on ne peut rien refuser,

mais elle ne perdit jamais le sentiment, de ce qu'elle valait elle-même.
[*Œuvre* I 297–8]

The elegance of Bérénice's solution of the problem of participation that Barrès was currently finding so intractable is a particularly interesting aspect of what he called her 'method' and her 'pedagogy.' Her acceptance of paternalistic direction on a public stage accurately prefigures his eventual commitment to the anti-Dreyfusard cause. 'Petite Secousse' is more significant as the exemplary prototype of the Barresian nationalist than as the object of her creator's current, modish, neo-Christian, and anarchistic mood of philanthropy,[31] which the Dreyfus Affair would presently sweep away.

The Affair produced no living leader, like Bérénice's Parisian dancing master, or Lazarus's 'marvellous agitator,' to whom Barrès might have transferred the authority that so many historical and imaginary figures had already embodied for him. But the threat of revolutionary change that seemed imminent in 'the symbol Dreyfus',[32] together with what Charles Maurras described as 'the most violent event of Barrès's private life and perhaps the principal event of his public life,' i.e. the death of his mother,[33] created in him a climate of necessity that functioned very like the commanding presence of the missing personal leader. Paternal authority in its collective form, the ancestral voices that Barrès had begun to make out amid the babel of ideologies promising positive 'religious' unanimity to his generation, and in the murmur and roar of hero-worshipping crowds,

31 *See*, for example, *Toute licence sauf contre l'amour* (*Œuvre* II 389, 395–6) and 'Notes d'un nouvel élu,' *La Presse* 31 October 1889: 'Ne pouvait-on trouver une variante de l'Évangile où se trouverait le mot *socialisme*. Précisément ce livre est divin parce qu'à toutes les époques, les déshérités y trouvent des phrases consolantes ... Cette réconciliation de tous les hommes d'étude pour l'amour de l'âme populaire, voilà ce qui passionne la nouvelle génération.' Cf. J.–M. Guyau, *Esquisse d'une morale sans obligation ni sanction* (Paris: Alcan 1885) and *L'Irréligion de l'avenir* (Paris: Alcan 1887).

32 *Œuvre* V 42–7

33 C. Maurras, *Pour un jeune Français* (Paris: Amiot-Dumont 1949) 234

and behind the silence of the French countryside,[34] spoke to him at last, following the double post-operative shock of 1898–1901, with unanswerable clarity and force:

> Dans cet excès d'humiliation, une magnifique douleur nous apaise, nous persuade d'accepter nos esclavages: c'est, si l'on veut bien comprendre, – et non pas seulement dire du bout des lèvres, mais se représenter d'une manière sensible, – que nous sommes le prolongement et la continuité de nos pères et mères.
>
> ...
>
> '*Je dis au sépulcre: Vous serez mon père.*' Parole abondante en sens magnifique. Je la recueille de l'Église dans son sublime Office des Morts. Toutes mes pensées, tous mes actes essaimeront d'une telle prière, – effusion et méditation, – sur la terre de mes morts. ['Le 2 novembre en Lorraine,' *Amori et dolori sacrum, Œuvre* VII 127]

> Si je faisais le roman traditionaliste, la première scène montre un individu ayant de grandes passions, eh bien, on ne vit qu'une fois, il faut les épanouir.
>
> Vient un choc. Échec politique. Mort de ma mère. Après de tels chocs, on se rallie à la thèse catholique: il faut dompter, soumettre nos passions. Nous avons vu que nous ne sommes pas maîtres absolus de nous-mêmes; nous acceptons nos fatalismes.
>
> Sous la violence du choc opératoire (la mort d'un être cher, un désastre), crise mystique. Il s'humilie, reconnaît ses misères, les misères de l'homme. Phrase du *Mystère de Jésus*: 'Si Dieu nous donnait des maîtres de sa main, oh! qu'il leur faudrait obéir de bon cœur! La nécessité et les événements en sont infailliblement.' [*Mes Cahiers, Œuvre* XV 157]

> État mystique où je me trouvai après la mort de mes parents. Comment je connus la plaine de Sion.
>
> Je ne puis dire que j'aie pensé, senti que je n'étais pas seul. J'ai

34 *See* p. 280.

> su que j'étais eux et que c'était me destinée, ma nécessité de les maintenir aussi longtemps que je pourrais ... De là les *Amitiés françaises* et mon nationalisme. Je me foutais de l'univers dès l'instant que j'étais d'accord avec cette mémoire, et bien sûr d'être dans notre sentiment tel que je l'interprétais.
> ['Mes Mémoires,' *Mes Cahiers, Œuvre* XIII 26]

Meanwhile, in the next of Barrès's imaginary, stock-taking, philosophical dialogues, written some five or six years after Seneca's consolation to Lazarus, Maurice Roemerspacher (who represents in the group of *déracinés* the best of contemporary French philosophy and, especially, its debt to the great universities of nineteenth-century Germany) had justified a Barresian Egotist's eventual surrender to nationalist determinism, in advance, like Bérénice, but from an intellectual's point of view.

'LE PASSAGE DE L'ABSOLU AU RELATIF'

Idealism and Historicism

About half way through the first volume of *Le Roman de l'énergie nationale*, Maurice Roemerspacher, having just published an article on Taine, is privileged to receive a personal visit from the great man, who is curious to know the guiding principles and special problems of the rising generation, which the apprentice philosopher appears to have spoken for. Invited to come for a walk, and to explain his views on the way, Roemerspacher sums up his position in two brief sentences: 'The great thing for your generation will have been the shift from the absolute to the relative ... Allow me to say, sir, that this stage has now been left behind.' The context of these words refers explicitly to some of the sources of Barrès's own similar position as a young man, and implicitly to others:

> Il faut vous dire que nous avions pour professeur de philosophie un kantien: il nous a exposé avec une force admirable la critique de toute certitude. Dès lors, comment parler des propriétés de la

> substance universelle? Ses qualités ne sont rien de plus que des états de notre sensibilité; nous ne connaissons en soi ni les corps, ni les esprits, mais seulement nos rapports avec les mouvements d'une réalité inconnue et à jamais inconnaissable. Le matérialisme est devenu pour nous une doctrine absolument incompréhensible... [*Œuvre* III 147–8]

Kant's criticism was a comparatively remote and misunderstood source of Barrès's relativism. A more immediate one was the epistemological commonplace of his fellow *littérateurs* in the 1880s: 'L'univers n'est qu'une fresque que [le Moi] fait belle ou laide ... la réalité varie avec chacun de nous' (*Œuvre* I 38, 41). A *cliché* which bore the august stamp of Kant, Fichte, and Schopenhauer,[35] but revised by French writers like Renan, Bourget, Taine, and Amiel[36] to express a narrower personal subjectivism, and made more radically world-denying, with the help of Wagner, by literary philosophers of the Symbolist generation like Villiers de l'Isle-Adam, Téodor de Wyzewa, and Jean Moréas.[37] This relativism of idealist origins was linked in the formation of Barrès's traditionalism to the historical relativism which (after what he called the 'sublime' intuitions of Burke and Goethe, the cutting aphorisms of Joseph de Maistre and Hegel's 'admirable dialectic') Comte, Renan, Taine, Proudhon, Fustel de Coulanges, and Marcel Thévenin had recently employed

35 'Les philosophes allemands m'avaient donné le plus profond sentiment de l'énergie humaine, de l'individu, du *Moi*' ('L'Éducation par l'Italie,' *Le Journal* 22 September 1893). *See* Chapter Two, note 3.

36 *See* E. Renan, *L'Avenir de la Science* (Paris: Calmann Lévy 1890) 57; *Feuilles détachées*, 354–400; H. Taine, *Les philosophes classiques du dix-neuvième siècle en France* (Paris: Hachette 1876) 276; P. Bourget, *Essais de psychologie contemporaine* (Paris: Plon 1901) I 130.

37 J. Moréas, *Le Symboliste* 7 October 1886: 'Monsieur Vonderwotteimitties, reprit Fortunato, l'objectif n'est que pur semblant, qu'apparence vaine qu'il dépend de moi de varier, de transmuer et d'anéantir à mon gré.' T. de Wyzewa, *Nos Maîtres* (Paris: Perrin 1895) 6: 'Seul vit le moi et seule est sa tâche éternelle: créer. ... Nous projetons au néant extérieur l'image de notre essence intime; puis, la croyant véritable nous continuons à la créer pareille.' And, *cit.* Jeanès, *D'Après nature,* 83: '[Barrès] ... est un homme que vous arrache le pain de la bouche pour le jeter aux chiens. Les trois idées qui meublent sa tête d'oiseau, il me les doit, et il ne les a pas encore comprises.'

to demonstrate the endless and inevitable innovations and divergencies of the Idea manifesting itself in time and space:

> Rien n'est faux, rien n'est complètement vrai: tout est un élément du vrai, une phase d'un développement indéfini dont l'ensemble serait la vérité ... tout ce qui a été nécessaire a été vrai et ... la place de chaque chose constitue sa vérité.
> [*De Hegel aux cantines du Nord, Œuvre* v 462, 457][38]

> la génération qui a été vaincue en 1870 ... risquait de laisser dans l'histoire une réputation de frivolité. Taine et Renan ont sauvé l'honneur des intellectuels français. Ils comprenaient le devoir: aider à l'élaboration d'une conscience nationale ... Les plus graves divergences n'empêchent pas que nous gardions notre gratitude à celui [Renan] qui a tant fait pour donner à notre nation le sens du relatif. Et jamais mieux on n'a senti la nécessité du relativisme qu'au cours de cette affaire Dreyfus, qui est profondément une orgie de métaphysiciens. Ils jugent tout par l'abstrait. Nous jugerons chaque chose par rapport à la France.
> [*Scènes et doctrines du nationalisme, Œuvre* v 84–5][39]

In his sequel to *Les Déracinés, L'Appel au soldat*, Barrès sends Roemerspacher to Germany, to study, in its native place, the philosophy of 'development in nature and in history' that he had met in the classroom at the Nancy *lycée* and *l'École des hautes études*, where Jules Soury and Thévenin taught. It was Thévenin, as a matter of fact, who in 1896, prompted by an article of Barrès on Renan, gave Barrès the formula later used in *Les Déracinés* to characterize mid-

38 Cf. *Œuvre* III 157.

39 Cf. 'La Raison nationale,' *Le Journal* 9 December 1898 (published with variations in *Œuvre* v 47–51): 'Le conseil de guerre nous fournira une vérité, enfin! Entendons-nous bien, ce ne sera pas *la vérité absolue*. Celle-là aucune institution ne la fournit et personne ne la possède; elle n'est pas de ce monde. Il faut le grossier optimisme religieux de certains orateurs politiques et la surexcitation puérile de certains "intellectuels" pour nous la promettre. Le conseil de guerre, comme toute juridiction, nous fournira *une vérité judiciaire* et nous aurons à la respecter.'

nineteenth-century French thought: 'le passage de l'absolu au relatif.'[40]

Associationist Psychology and Sociology

Jules Soury's influence was much more intimate, precise, and comprehensive.[41] Barrès met him during his first months in Paris at the home of Madame Ackermann.[42] From the beginning, Soury seems to have established a considerable intellectual ascendency over the young provincial. He later claimed Barrès as, intellectually speaking, his adoptive son. In the spring of 1896, while Barrès was writing *Les Déracinés*, Soury delivered a series of lectures on the physiology of the central nervous system and, on leaving the lecture room, he would join Barrès, who had been in his audience, in one of those promenade discussions both men enjoyed. The record of these conversations, between the squat middle-aged Soury, with his sickly complexion, tiny bird-like eyes, black tie, frock-coat, gigantic umbrella, and monumental top-hat, and the sleek, corvine Barrès of thirty-three, checking his stride to the child's steps of his companion, is one of the best of the 'Things seen,' and heard, in all the fourteen volumes of *Mes Cahiers*. Soury had recently lost the mother who had been 'his mistress and his child,' and he was passing through an emotional crisis which heightened his talk with crazy colours that fascinated the 'amateur d'âmes' in Barrès as deeply as the harsh and tonic thesis of the scientist impressed the nascent doctrinaire of nationalism:

> 1er *mai* 1896. – J'ai assisté au cours de Soury. Je fus frappé, jusqu'à en éprouver un malaise physique et l'horreur comme en face d'un dément, de sa pâleur terreuse. Je sortis. Par hasard, un quart d'heure après, je le croisai.

40 *Œuvre* III 20, 147–8; XIII 53, 296

41 *See* J. and J. Tharaud, *Pour les fidèles de Barrès* (Paris: Plon 1944) 123; C. Vettard, 'Jules Soury et Maurice Barrès,' *Mercure de France* 15 November 1924; I.–M. Frandon, *L'Orient de Maurice Barrès*; Z. Sternhell, *Maurice Barrès et le nationalisme français*, 254–67.

42 Letter to P. Campaux, November 1881, published in *La Revue hebdomadaire* 8 January 1927

Ce qui frappe d'abord c'est son petit pas d'enfant quand il court à moi, et puis son sourire si clair par instant dans cette figure jaune flétrie.

Il m'offrit de me reconduire.

'J'aime la locomotion, oh! oui, j'aime beaucoup la locomotion. Je vais à Versailles, à huit heures, quand il n'y a plus de bourgeois dans le parc. Mais surtout j'aime la grande cour avec ses pavés gris.

'La cour janséniste comme les froides chambres de Saint-Sulpice.

'J'ai mon lit à la place du lit où mon grand-père est mort, où ma mère est morte. Les tableaux qui les ont entourés. Je demeure ainsi.

'Je suis la conscience de ma mère, de mon grand-père. Quand je serai mort, il ne restera rien d'eux.'

Il me parle longuement d'un rêve, d'une affreuse angoisse qu'il a eue.

'Je n'aime plus la science. Qu'est-ce que cela me fait tout cela. Ah! oui, Pascal a raison. Divertissement. Le chercheur n'est rien de plus que celui qui tire des lapins.

'Moi aussi, quand ma mère vivait, j'ai été aimé. Je vivais enfin, je jouissais de la vie. Je mangeais trois francs de viande par jour, des choux de Bruxelles, de tout enfin.

'Aujourd'hui trois sous de pain et de l'eau. En vain veux-je manger une orange, une pomme. Je ne peux pas. Une contraction, une angoisse.

'Mais pendant tant d'années, ma mère m'a si bien nourri que je ne peux pas mourir. Je suis encore vigoureux.

'Je me suis procuré des crachats de phtisiques; je les ai fait sécher, je les ai respirés. Je ne suis pas tuberculeux...'

[*Mes Cahiers, Œuvre* XIII 43]

Some of the utterances of this 'sublime madman' found their way textually into Barrès's own work.[43] It was Soury's theory of knowledge, however, that provoked his immediate enthusiasm and a public

43 E.g. 'Les Allemands ne disent pas *je pense*, mais *il* pense en moi,' 'L'intelligence, quelle très petite chose à la surface de nous-même.' (*Œuvre* III 239, 377; XIII 46–7, 250)

recognition of the debt he owed the author of *Les fonctions du cerveau*:

> Mais ce qui fait le grand ressort, les plus belles couleurs, les feux et les nuits de son œuvre, c'est sa théorie de la connaissance. Ce savant, cet artiste affamé de vérité, ressent chaque jour, comme une découverte nouvelle et avec la plus sombre indignation, notre déplorable condition qui est de ne jamais enregistrer que des symboles et des images. L'homme n'est pas un animal qui puisse jamais connaître. Qu'est-ce que la vérité? et qu'est-ce que la science? ... Elle est une vue sur laquelle s'accordent les hommes. Elle n'est rien qu'une entente des esprits ... Son désespoir de connaître que l'homme, prisonnier de ses sensations, est irrémédiablement condamné au relatif, l'élève au rang de Pascal ... Byron: le premier dans l'hiérarchie des esprits.
> ['Notes sur Jules Soury,' *Le Journal* 24 November 1899]

La Cocarde, which was under Barrès's direction from September 1894 to March 1895, counted Jules Soury among its contributors; and Barrès's editorial statement: 'Dans la *Cocarde* ... nous traitons de la vie des relations,' is in sympathy with Soury's teaching:

> Comprendre ce n'est jamais que saisir des rapports. La vérité, les vérités, il n'y en a pas. Il y en a une pour chaque homme. Et il n'en sera jamais autrement.
> [*cit. Mes Cahiers, Œuvre* XIII 56]

It was as a particularly compelling teacher rather than as an original thinker that Soury helped to 'establish' Barrès 'in the relative.'[44] His specialist contribution was to demonstrate current associationist ortho-

44 Cf. *Œuvre* XVII 265–6. André Berthelot, whom Barrès considered 'the most intelligent of the friends of my youth' (*Œuvre* XVII 350) supplied a note to pages 27 and 125 of *Mes Cahiers, Œuvre* XVII, which reveals a further scientifically qualified source of Barrès's relativistic epistemology: 'La note de Maurice Barrès doit se référer à une remarque que je lui ai faite plusieurs fois et que je tenais de mon père. Dès qu'on y réfléchit on est frappé de la faiblesse de l'esprit humain qui ne connaît clairement que les rapports de proportion.' (*Œuvre* XVII 396)

doxy at the laboratory bench (*Œuvre* XIII 52, 57), while his 'definition of science' as the symbolization of the relations between phenomena was orthodox positivism, laying particular stress, important for Barrès,[45] on the linguistic basis of man's secondary signalling system:

> Belle définition de la science par Soury (15 *février*, 1896).
>
> 'Ce qui fait l'homme, ce qui le rend capable d'abstraire le monde, de se le représenter sous forme de symbole, de créer la science: c'est le mot. Il fallait le mot pour créer le monde des abstractions, le monde des symboles où nous vivons presque uniquement.
>
> 'Nous représenter les différents états dans le temps et l'espace des rouages et des mécanismes intervenant dans la production des phénomènes. Voilà l'astronomie, la physique, la chimie. Il n'y a rien de plus dans la science.'
>
> Je le félicite de cette définition.
>
> 'Oui, il nous faut renoncer à savoir. Nous avons tous espéré savoir. Au reste, je ne fais pas fi de ce peu. C'est déjà bien beau pour ce pauvre mammifère simien de connaître les rapports ... Le cerveau n'était point fait pour penser. C'est un grand abus que nous en faisons. Il servait à produire les réflexes protecteurs, les réflexes qui doivent nous permettre d'éviter un obstacle, d'écarter un danger. C'est le langage qui nous a mené si loin. Créer des métaphysiques, des théologies. Le cerveau ne devait point servir à cela!'
>
> [*Œuvre* XIII 50]

Barrès's use of Soury's teaching was most marked in the polemic he conducted, between 1898 and 1901, against the "Kantian' intellectuals – 'ou logiciens de l'absolu' – who spoke for Dreyfus in the name of universal justice and truth.[46] In *Les Déracinés*, Roemerspacher had accounted for his mistrust of such 'universal legislation' by pointing to the discontinuity he had observed, in the philosophy class at

45 *See* Chapters Six and Seven.

46 *See* above, note 39, and *Scènes et doctrines du nationalisme* (*Œuvre* V 52–128); 'L'Université et l'esprit national,' *Le Journal* 25 November 1898.

the Nancy *lycée*, between Kant's critical epistemology and universalist ethics.[47] But the author of *Scènes et doctrines du nationalisme* persisted in justifying his distaste for the latter[48] by a misunderstanding of the former, which Roemerspacher had already betrayed by substituting for Kant's 'forms of the sensibility,' common to all men, what he, Roemerspacher, called 'states of our sensibility,' varying with historical and geographical position this side or that of Pascal's 'Pyrenees.'[49] It was Soury who coloured Roemerspacher's 'Kantian' criticism with the non-Kantian brand of relativism drawn from modern psycho-physiology that is offered in tribute to Taine, as master and disciple make their way together from Le Quartier Latin to Les Invalides. 'Nous ne pouvons pas plus être matérialistes que spiritualistes ... Le matérialisme est devenu pour nous une doctrine absolument incompréhensible' (*Œuvre* III 147–8) echoes a remark made by Soury when Barrès had congratulated him on his 'definition of science' (*Œuvre* XIII 51).[50] And the same peripatetic discussion, after Soury's lecture at the *Hautes Études* in February 1896 (*Œuvre* XIII 53, 57), inspired the unambiguously associationist declaration against universal laws of truth and justice with which Barrès justified his opposition to Dreyfusard humanism four years later:

> Tous les maîtres qui nous ont précédés et que j'ai tant aimés, et non seulement les Hugo, les Michelet, mais ceux qui font transition, les Taine, les Renan, croyaient à une raison indépendante existant dans chacun de nous et qui nous permet d'approcher la vérité. Voilà une notion à laquelle pour ma part je me suis attaché passionnément. L'individu! son intelligence, sa faculté de saisir les lois de l'univers! Il faut en rebattre. Nous ne sommes pas les maîtres des pensées qui naissent en nous. Elles ne viennent pas de notre intelligence; elles sont des façons de réagir où se traduisent de très anciennes dispositions physiologiques. Selon le milieu où nous sommes plongés, nous élaborons des jugements et des raison-

47 *Œuvre* III 149, 152
48 *Œuvre* III 20; V 66
49 *Œuvre* III 149
50 *See*, however, Chapter Twelve, note 9, for what was possibly an earlier source: Claude Bernard, quoted by Zola in *Le Roman expérimental.*

> nements. La raison humaine est enchaînée de telle sorte que nous repassons tous dans les pas de nos prédecesseurs. Il n'y a pas d'idées personnelles; les idées les plus rares, les jugements les plus abstraits, les sophismes de la métaphysique la plus infatuée sont des façons de sentir générales et se retrouvent chez tous les êtres de même organisme assiégés par les mêmes images.
>
> Dans cet excès d'humiliation, une magnifique douceur nous apaise, nous invite à accepter tous nos esclavages et la mort: c'est si l'on veut bien comprendre – et non pas seulement du bout des lèvres, mais se représenter d'une façon sensible – que nous sommes la continuité de nos parents. Cela est vrai anatomiquement.
> [*Nationalisme, Œuvre* v 31]

When, in *Le Journal* of the 8 December 1899, Barrès claimed that his instinctive nationalism had the blessing of science ['L'Œuvre des Ligues'], he was almost certainly thinking in particular of the neurophysiologist who had told him that the brain 'servait à produire les réflexes protecteurs, les réflexes qui doivent nous permettre d'éviter un obstacle, d'écarter un danger' (*Œuvre* XIII 50), whose work he had recently praised in the same newspaper,[51] and whose own nationalism, he believed, was derived from scientifically authorized love of country:

> Soury ... c'est un Français qui pour l'amour de l'idée de patrie, par besoin de connaître le milieu où héréditairement il a baigné, se préoccupe des éléments encore vivants et organisés dans notre pays. Il a le sens national.
> ['Lavisse et Jules Soury,' *Le Journal* 12 October 1899]

Soury's ideas served the most intolerant and narrow phase of Barrès's nationalism, which coincided with the crisis of ideological fanaticism brought on by the Affair, firstly, and negatively, by implying that the standards of absolute truth and justice held by the Dreyfusards were no more universal and disinterested than his own 'French point of view,' but merely the reflexes of organisms formed in a different his-

51 'Note sur Jules Soury,' *Le Journal* 24 November 1899

torical *milieu* and/or reacting to different present stimuli: *déracinés* and/or *désorientés* [*Nationalisme, Œuvre* v 31, *cit.* above p. 62]; and, secondly, and positively, by suggesting that the nationalistic bias of the anti-Dreyfusards was the only position a Frenchman true to himself could possibly adopt:

> *Long travail de forage*! Après une analyse aigüe et profonde je trouvai dans mon petit jardin la source jaillissante. Elle vient de la vaste nappe qui fournit toutes les fontaines de ma cité.
>
> Ceux qui n'atteignent point à ces réservoirs sous-jacents, ceux qui ne se connaissent pas avec respect, avec amour et avec crainte comme la continuité de leurs parents, comment trouveront-ils leur direction?
>
> C'est ma filiation qui me donne l'axe autour duquel tourne ma conception totale, sphérique de la vie.
>
> ...
>
> Ainsi je possède mes points fixés, mes repérages dans le passé et dans la postérité. Si je les relie, j'obtiens une des grandes lignes du classicisme français. Comment ne serais-je point prêt à tous les sacrifices pour la protection de ce classicisme qui fait mon épine dorsale?
>
> *Je parle d'épine dorsale* et ce n'est point une métaphore, mais la plus puissante analogie. Une suite d'exercices multipliés à travers les siècles antérieurs ont fait l'éducation de nos réflexes.
> [*Œuvre* v 26]

The analogy to which Barrès alludes here in the exordium of *Scènes et doctrines du nationalisme*, was a commonplace of nineteenth-century sociology, but it had recently been developed in explicitly associationist terms by another teacher who shares with Jules Soury the leading rôle in the provision of Barrès's nascent traditionalism with a backing of popular contemporary science: Jean Izoulet, appointed professor of social philosophy at the Collège de France in 1897, and whose *Cité moderne* (1894) Barrès hailed enthusiastically for its corroboration of a thesis evolving in his own work since *Le Culte du Moi*, namely that ideas are points of view originating in the collective consciousness of society:

> Si les cellules isolées ont, chacune, une conscience dont l'association forme le 'moi,' c'est également un fait d'observation qu'un grand nombre de 'moi' rassemblés par une salle, dans une ville, forment à leur tour un 'moi' supérieur. Une race, une nation ont une conscience distincte de la conscience individuelle de ceux qui la composent.
>
> Quel sera le rapport entre le 'moi' humain et le 'moi' social, entre l'individu et la collectivité?
>
> Eh! nous dit M. Izoulet, le rapport des unités dans le corps politique est analogue au rapport des unités dans le corps physique... ['Un philosophe du "Moi",' *La Cocarde* 20 January 1895]

The organic unity of society was no more than an analogy for Barrès.[52] But as such, it helped him to clarify and justify and qualify that exciting but rather hazily mysterious notion, the 'soul of the masses,' which had been much in the air of France since the importation of Hartmann's philosophy of the unconscious and the Russian novelists,[53] and which Barrès and his fellow Boulangist Paul Adam had used in *Le Jardin de Bérénice* and *Le Mystère des foules* respectively, to explain the popular upsurge of democratic and patriotic enthusiasm for General Boulanger.[54] Izoulet's formulae: 'L'âme est fille de la cité,' and '*l'"individu"* est *principe et fin*, mais *l'"association" est moyen*'; and their rider: that the City's substance was a civilisation 'capitalized' and 'transmitted' by an *élite* of *savants* and poets as well as by legislators and statesmen, became a permanent part of Barrès's traditionalism, forming a built-in counter-weight, as it were, to the unbridled democratic unanimism he had celebrated in *Le Jardin de Bérénice*.[55] They also helped to warn him off the doctrine of 'politics first and foremost' that was beginning to absorb the systematic single-mindedness of his friend Charles Maurras. And, in the end, they out-

52 *See* his note of a conversation with André Berthelot in 1897: 'La seule objection et il n'y a rien a lui répondre, mais aussi elle ne laisse rien *établir*, c'est qu'il n'y a être que là où il y a conscience. Seul l'individu a conscience.' (*Œuvre* XIII 82)

53 *See* also G. le Bon, *Psychologie des foules* (Paris: Alcan 1895).

54 Cf. *Œuvre* III 412: 'l'âme des foules immédiatement les posséda.'

55 *Œuvre* I 348

stayed the rigorously physiological determinism of his anti-Dreyfusard articles, taught him by Jules Soury. He borrowed Soury's racialist anti-semitism for the polemics of the Affair, but without much conviction,[56] and he soon reverted to his earlier non-ethnic concept of nationality:

> On entend par nation un groupe d'hommes réunis par des légendes communes, une tradition, des habitudes prises, dans un même milieu durant une suite plus ou moins longue d'ancêtres.
> ['Lettre à M. Edwards,' *La Cocarde* 22 October 1894]

As Camille Vettard pointed out, Barrès followed Soury in declaring himself a traditionalist because anatomically the individual is the 'continuity' of his parents. Nevertheless, he tended to stress the importance of environmental, and especially of educational influences, equally with, and eventually more than inherited characteristics.[57]

'LE PASSAGE DU LOCAL À L'UNIVERSEL'

'Le nationalisme manque d'infini'

An extended comparison in the introductory chapter of *Scènes et doctrines du nationalisme*, with which Barrès attempts characteristically to 'render tangible' his concept of nationality, suggests, like his reference a few pages before to the 'spherical'[58] completeness of his 'anatomical' traditionalism, the exclusive and defensive nature of his outlook in 1902:

> Je comparerais volontiers une nation à ces puddings de pierres qui

56 *Œuvre* v 33; xiii 263 and *La Terre et les morts* (Paris: La Patrie Française 1899): 'Hélas il n'y a point de race française, mais un peuple français, c'est-à-dire une collectivité de formation politique ... la nôtre n'est point arrivée à se définir.'
57 E.g. *Œuvre* xiii 98–9: 'L'esprit humain ne peut se dégager de certaines habitudes de penser qui ne sont pas ancestrales au sens d'hérédité psychologique, mais qui sont transmises par l'éducation qui modèle notre intelligence à l'époque où elle est aussi malléable que la cire molle.'
58 *Œuvre* v 26, *cit.* above, p. 63

se forment le plus souvent dans les eaux vives et que l'on nomme conglomérats. Le mortier qui lie ces pierres est dû en partie à leur usure même et à leur mouvement. Quand cet amas est entraîné, des pierres s'y attachent et s'y soudent. Les couches se superposent. Mais si chaque élément de la couche externe garde à l'œil sa personnalité, il est pourtant solidaire, relativement aux actions physiques, de toutes les couches et de tous les éléments, aujourd'hui recouverts, qui se sont attachés à son premier noyau. Et cette solidarité crée sa résistance contre les forces naturelles. [*Œuvre* v 33]

Only a year later, he was privately substituting for his closed figures of sphere and pudding-stone the image of an 'angle' opening out indefinitely (*Œuvre* xiv 98), and publicly 'humanizing and refining' the 'brute fact' of an 'affinity' between Frenchmen, determined by race and family, so as to encourage what he preferred to call a state of 'amity'[59] between the French and their homeland. *Les Amitiés françaises* celebrate a national tradition that is still heavily determinative,[60] but which is indefinable enough to permit a diversity of spiritual families, and the individual's right to free interpretation of their various creeds.[61] At the end of the book, moreover, in the 'abrupt and elliptic' lyricism of 'Notre visite à Lourdes' and 'Chant de confiance dans la vie,' the doctrinaire patriot can barely contain an effusive and exasperated yearning for yet wider horizons:

Extrémités du désir, pointe vers l'impossible, brûlants appels, sanglots, regrets? Voici derrière des grillages une jeune force irritée; voici le fils sur la tombe, le proscrit à qui l'on rapporte le détachement de ses amis, le jaloux qui n'ignore pas combien elle

59 *Œuvre* v 30, 480. Barrès's source is probably Michelet, though he nowhere says so. *See L'Étudiant* (Paris: Calmann Lévy 1899) 235: 'Que sera la loi? L'alliance, le fraternel sacrifice des intérêts opposés, la justice du riche, la modération du pauvre, la voix de cette patrie, que nos aïeux nommaient si bien *l'Amitié*.' Cf. *Le Peuple* (Paris: Calmann Lévy 1877) 219–20.

60 *Œuvre* v 487: 'cet immense brouillard de la Nécessité qui nous opprime... l'intelligence de notre prédestination.'

61 *Œuvre* v 475–6, 479

est charmante dans l'amour. Des images qui ne peuvent plus vivre sollicitent tous mes sens, et c'est à les parfaire, démence! que j'occupe mon énergie. Il est des Lourdes sur toute la terre; il y a pour les plus incrédules d'absurdes promesses de bonheur. De telles minutes où l'on s'enfonce plus avant que l'espérance nous maintiennent sur le fil de notre mince et pure destinée. Je me croyais si loin! Bien au contraire, j'ai tant reculé! Nos voix de désirs font un écho de nos vies antérieures. Ma chanson heurtée, elliptique, c'est le haut chant de mes profondeurs, c'est un oiseau de mes ténèbres qui volette dans mon plein jour. Quel scandale! Mon cri, qui m'étonne, m'oblige tôt à m'interrompre ... O terre mangée de caresses, ô belles grottes de l'espoir, conseillères de toute confiance, combien vous êtes douloureuses!

...

Au sortir de la gare de Lourdes et depuis notre wagon, qui roulait d'abord lentement, nous revîmes au passage, dans la demi-nuit, la grotte divine au-dessous de l'église. Les cierges brûlaient par milliers; je croyais entendre les litanies suppliantes. Quelle fatigue! Quel dégoût de la vie! Quelle délectation! Des larmes de volupté montaient du cœur jusque dans les yeux. L'avenir semblait une plaine stérile.

[*Œuvre* v 551–2]

Barrès was forty-six before he faced squarely the fact that his genius was suffocating within the political system he had built up, amid the 'tumults' of Boulangism, Panama, and the Dreyfus Affair, against the temptations and threats of anarchism and cosmopolitanism; and before the yearning to possess the whole truth, which had known solitary and brief 'ecstasies' and 'triumphs' in *Le Culte du Moi*, and which his nationalism had so far striven to suppress or alienate,[62] began to work in him freely again, towards a final, long, unsure passage out into Littré's 'ocean of the unknowable':[63]

Aujourd'hui, jour où j'achève ma quarante-sixième, année, j'ai

62 *See* p. 280.
63 *Œuvre* xvi 319. Cf. P. Bourget, *Le Disciple* (Paris: Plon 1901) 15.

senti comme un ennui de penser à moi-même, voire à mes doctrines, et de plus en plus je caresse le désir de vivre une vie nouvelle sous un nom nouveau: m'enfoncer dans le taillis pour y mourir. Cela parallèlement à l'idée qu'il faut passer à l'universel et que mes premières étapes, mes premières vérités sont faciles à ruiner, qu'après mon stade individualiste, puis nationaliste, il n'y a plus pour me faire de musique que la religion. La définir.
[*Mes Cahiers, Œuvre* XVI 41]

Je tournais dans le même cercle, j'allais me trouver à l'étroit.
Je sens depuis des mois que je glisse du nationalisme au catholicisme. C'est que le nationalisme manque d'infini. S'il m'employait à faire la guerre (ne fût-ce que la guerre civile de Rennes), il pourrait me captiver tout entier, mais si je m'occupe, comme il le faut bien, à dresser son rituel, à rédiger ses prières, sa liturgie, je m'aperçois que mon souci de ma destinée dépasse le mot France, que je voudrais me donner à quelque chose de plus large et de plus prolongé, d'universel.
[*Mes Cahiers, Œuvre* XVI 263]

A sense of confinement, within the secular, partisan French nationalism which had survived the rout of the anti-Dreyfusard movement,[64] appears more than once, however, in earlier notebooks, dated 1903, 1905, 1906. While the most dynamic part of this movement was narrowing and hardening into the party of counter-revolutionary monarchism by which Maurras hoped to restore the fortunes and consolidate the future of nationalism in France, Barrès was beginning to doubt the present chances of any such violent political surgery,[65] to assert that political changes probably depend on the prior 'education' of public opinion;[66] and to propose as the substance of this

64 *Œuvre* XIV 106, 275; XV 158
65 'la mode est passée de ces violentes persécutions' (*La Terre et les morts*, 30)
66 *Œuvre* V 97–101, 119–23. *See* the rough draft of a preface to *Scènes et doctrines du nationalisme* (which he had originally thought of entitling 'L'Éducation nationaliste' [*Œuvre* XIII 249]) in *Mes Cahiers* (*Œuvre* XIII 332). Cf. 'L'Éducation nationale,' *Le Journal*, 30 October 1899 and Michelet, *L'Étudiant*, 217: 'le XVIIIe siècle ne sut pas assez que ce n'est rien d'écrire des lois, si l'on ne prend pas les moyens de les faire

educational program the conciliatory image of 'flesh and blood France' in its totality as against the 'hypothetical' conceptions of what French history, in the eyes of partisan ideologists, should have made her:

> Chacun refait l'histoire de France. Laissons ces romans. Pourquoi nous enfoncer dans les voies hypothétiques où la France aurait dû passer? Nous trouverons un profit plus certain à nous confondre avec toutes les heures de l'histoire de France, à vivre avec tous ses morts, à ne nous mettre en dehors d'aucune de ses expériences...
>
> Les gens à système sont puérils et malsains; ils s'obstinent à maudire ce qui ne plaît pas à leur imagination. Nulle conception de la France ne peut prévaloir, dans nos décisions, contre la France de chair et d'os.
>
> [*Nationalisme, Œuvre* v 88–90]

> La Ligue a employé un beau mot, et c'est ici que l'emploi de ce mot s'impose (et non dans l'étroite Affaire Dreyfus) : Conciliation.
>
> Nous ne sommes pas des dogmatiques, nous sommes disposés à faire quelque chose avec ce qui est ... Quelles que soient les objections que nous puissons faire contre la Révolution, nous sommes disposés à accepter les choses au point où elles sont, et précisément parce que nous ne sommes pas des révolutionnaires, nous voulons tirer parti des choses.
>
> [*Mes Cahiers, Œuvre* XIII 228]

> Mes amis (M ... et B ... surtout) sont plus amis de leurs systèmes que de la France.
>
> Je me suis toujours arrêté de donner mon adhésion expresse au mouvement de Maurras et de Bourget contre la Révolution, parce que je considère qu'on ne peut pas se dispenser quand on est traditionaliste, quand on est soumis à la loi de la continuité, de prendre les choses dans l'état où on les trouve.
>
> [*Mes Cahiers, Œuvre* XIV 113]

accepter, de les assurer dans l'avenir. – Le premier de ces moyens, c'est l'éducation, celle des enfants, celle des hommes.' Also the title of Michelet's tenth lesson: 'L'éducation nationale.'

This totally inclusive traditionalism, which J.-M. Domenach aptly calls 'integrative,'[67] in contrast to Maurras's Integral Nationalism, formed by pruning away the unwanted parts of French history and literature, was most vulnerable to the charge of ambiguity: 'Fort bien, nous disait-on, vous invoquez la tradition, mais quelle tradition?' (*Œuvre* VII 212). Hence the importance of Catholicism, 'religion nationale, faiseuse d'ordre, faiseuse de paix,'[68] to its survival as a viable political philosophy. For Barrès saw in Catholicism, stretching back into the past by its Christian 'mobilization' of the pagan spirits of the French countryside and forward into the future by the inspiration and fellowship it would, he believed, continue to give the science and socialism of the future, the one as yet unbroken part of French 'continuity':

> Quel est le poème que se crée ce Parlement pour se représenter l'idéal? Son Dieu? Sa vertu? sa morale? ...
> Nous n'avons rien ici de vivant qui soit antérieur à la Révolution, mais le dix-huitiéme, et le dix-septième n'avaient rien eux-mêmes qui fût antérieur à Louis XIII. Nous avons d'époque en époque renoncé à nos sources. Une seule chose dure, le Catholicisme.
> [*Mes Cahiers, Œuvre* XV 48]

> Quand je dis, 'favoriser la poussée des ancêtres,' si nous n'avons pas les mêmes ancêtres...
> Mais tout homme a un cœur religieux. Que puis-je dire à ce cœur ou entendre de ce cœur?
> [*Mes Cahiers, Œuvres* XV 157]

But this does not mean that Barrès's Catholicism can be reduced to M. Madaule's opinion of it, namely: 'the most efficient means of lifting Frenchmen up to a mood of vaguely religious feeling on which to found the cult of the fatherland';[69] or to the mere 'instrument of culture' that François Mauriac said it was.[70] Barrès's long struggle,

67 J.-M. Domenach, *Barrès par lui-même* (Paris: Aux Éditions du Seuil 1954) 54
68 Ibid., 82
69 *Le Nationalisme de Barrès*, 158
70 *Cit.* Domenach, *Barrès par lui-même*, 82

between the Dreyfus Affair and the Great War, to deflect and disarm the self-assured attack mounted against the established position of the Church in France by the party of scientific humanism was inspired by the will to maintain as an essential part of the French tradition a 'reserve' of spiritual nourishment whose properly mystical and individual purposes he never confused with the aspirations and requirements of secular nationalism: a 'civilisation' to be preserved by rather than existing to preserve the nation;[71] 'a life of the soul' distinct from culture,[72] recognizably if never 'totally' Catholic,[73] and transcending rather than subservient to the love of country from which it had grown, in response to a series of poignant personal experiences. The most important of these experiences, which are reflected in, rather than reflections of the patriotic traditionalism of his maturity, were the death of his father in 1898, the deeper shock of his mother's death in 1901, the birth and boyhood of his son, the 'peopled solitudes' and the normal religious crisis of middle age.[74]

'Une formule religieuse acceptable'

Roemerspacher, in *Les Déracinés*, had told Taine that he took the proper object of philosophy to be the relation between the sentient individual and his universal environment, since the total sum of things in themselves (which the hero of *Le Culte du Moi* had sought to embrace: 'Son regard n'est tendu vers rien de relatif ... il aspire à l'absolu,' 'Résumer en soi l'univers' [*Œuvre* I 114, 169]), was unknow-

71 F. Duhourcau, *La Voix intérieure de Maurice Barrès* (Paris: Grasset 1929) 213 and R. Launay, *Mercure de France*, 1 February 1924

72 *Œuvre* XV 382–3

73 As those whom J.-M. Domenach calls 'les convertisseurs' would have it, e.g. F. Duhourcau, *La Voix intérieure de Maurice Barrès*, 226. The 'lame' Christianity of Barrès is examined strictly but charitably from an orthodox Roman Catholic point of view by J. Godfrin, *Barrès mystique* (Neuchâtel, À la Baconnière 1962).

74 *See* above, pp. 52–4 and *Œuvre* XIV 24–5, 80; XV 177–8. The shock that Barrès received when his nephew and disciple committed suicide, in August 1909, an event for which he held Anna de Noailles responsible, 'froze' his soul with horror, paralysing temporarily his capacity even to 'feel' religion: 'Même la religion dont j'éprouve mes limites à la sentir. Les cérémonies religieuses me laissent ce sentiment de mon insuffisance à percevoir, à vivre le divin.' (*Œuvre* XVI 168–71, 182)

able (*Œuvre* III 148). Barrès's comment on Roemerspacher's position, namely that he was ripe for 'an acceptable religious formula' (*Œuvre* III 152), approximately predicts his own return from both the runaway idealism of *Un Homme libre* and the dead-end of political realism which would only provisionally suppress its depressing consequences (*acedia, torpeur, démence*) by shutting him up in an airless system which proved in the end, for opposite reasons, equally uninhabitable: 'le nationalisme manque d'infini ... mon souci de ma destinée dépasse le mot France' (*Œuvre* XVI 263). Barrès's resurgent desire and pursuit of the whole would lead him ultimately to a supranational 'religious formula' of mankind's 'kinship with the stars'[75] that could nevertheless be effectively expressed, he thought, in terms as concrete and familiar as the 'courte solidité' of his particular national tradition.[76]

He did not abandon his French point of view. He spoke in *Les Amitiés françaises* (1903) for an education appropriate to the heirs of Lorraine farmers and soldiers, of Joan of Arc, Bernadette – and the treaty of Frankfort. He called for national unity, spiritual, linguistic, and territorial, behind *Les Bastions de l'Est* (1905–21); and for the integration of parish priest, *instituteur*, scientist, trade unionist, and provincial notable, in a spiritual, regional, and corporative national order, in *Pour les Églises* (1911), *La Grande pitié des églises de France* (1914), *Les Diverses familles spirituelles de la France* (1917), and *Pour la haute intelligence française* (1925).[77] But in the foreground of the still close-bordered image of France that emerges from all this patriotic literature, the highlight falls, ever more brightly, on those features of French civilisation which open the patriot's mind to his wider destiny as a man: firstly, and pre-eminently, though not exclusively, its village churches.[78]

75 *Œuvre* VI 497–8; VIII 64–5; XIV 279, 289; XV 70, 238, 241, 252, 284, 344, 372; XVI 117; XVII 5–6, 37; XX 145

76 *Œuvre* I 142, *cit.* note 62, p. 280

77 Cf. 'Le problème de l'ordre,' *Le Gaulois* 9 July 1905; 'Les groupements professionnels en face du Parlement,' *L'Écho de Paris* 3 May 1909; 'Lettre ouverte à M. Gabriel Hanotaux sur les instituteurs,' *L'Écho de Paris* 11 April 1911, etc.

78 *See* below, Chapter Ten, 'An Image of France.'

Thus, without shifting or abandoning his relativistic point of view, Barrès made what he called 'Le passage du local à l'universel' (*Œuvre* XV 239). Like the 'French justice and truth' he had defended in 1902 against the Dreyfusard 'intellectuals or logicians of the absolute,'[79] his Catholicism was not a statement of objective truth ('des choses à savoir') but the expression of a relationship between an historically conditioned individual and certain given 'objects' ('L'ensemble des rapports justes et vrais entre des objets donnés et un homme déterminé, le Français' [*Œuvre* V 27]). His shift to the universal brought new objets into his angle of vision; it did not substantially alter his way of looking at things:

> S'accorder avec les étoiles.
> Quelle que fût mon admiration de Mireille qui est l'âme de la vie provençale, je trouvais cela plébéien et local, c'est-à-dire que je voulais passer à un étage supérieur. Passer à l'universel. Il ne me suffit pas de me retrouver dans le local, humblement; il ne me suffit pas d'être dans la terre humide, de vivre dans l'obscurité, de mettre tout mon esprit dans mes racines; je tends vers la lumière, le ciel, je tends à certaines minutes à réaliser un plus haut degré d'activité et de liberté...
> [*Mes Cahiers, Œuvre* XV 238]

> J'ai besoin d'unité dans l'univers et dans mon cœur. J'ai besoin de sentir mes rapports avec toutes choses et que toutes les parentés éclatent; j'ai besoin qu'un dialogue, long ou court selon les espèces, s'établisse entre moi, toutes les choses et tous les êtres. Si mon regard était assez fort, je voudrais n'avoir pas de limite; je veux du moins, aussi loin qu'il se porte, comprendre, accepter mes rapports avec tout ce qui survient dans mon horizon. La terre est enserrée dans un réseau divin dont je ne voudrais rompre aucune des mailles innombrables.
> [*La Grande pitié des églises, Œuvre* VIII 172]

This extension of Barrès's relativistic angle of vision did react in one

79 *Œuvre* V 73–128

respect, however, on the nature of his relativism, by softening the point of the angle. With the revival of his youthful desire to embrace the whole universe, something of his earliest unconditional individualism reappears, and with it a broader tolerance than his nationalism had hitherto allowed, a tolerance which is the mature form of that ironical way of looking at things that *Un Homme libre* and *L'Ennemi des lois* had prized, before their creator's submission to the siege discipline of the Affair, as a guarantee of liberty 'pour les personnes d'une vie intérieure un peu intense ... qui parfois sont tentées d'accueillir des solutions mal vérifiées' (*Œuvre* I 39):

> *Ma religion. – Sur le mot catholique-athée.* – Toutes les hypothèses sur l'origine des choses sont également absurdes. *Ignoramus et ignorabimus.* Cependant sur un point de notre planète, en France, le catholicisme a présidé à notre formation. Je respire seulement dans cette atmosphère catholique.
>
> Je le subventionnerai et veux le maintenir.
>
> Mais si je crois qu'il est à maintenir, pourquoi me proclamer catholique-athée? Il m'est loisible de donner en secret un plus riche sens aux formules.
>
> [*Mes Cahiers, Œuvre* XIV 294]

Barrès's relativism was ineradicable,[80] and this made it difficult for him to resolve what appeared to him as the 'paradox' of Catholic 'cosmopolitanism.' For this seemed to be a 'centrifugal force,' tending always to detach itself from the intensive media of his own religious experience: national, local, personal; and, in its most concentrated and direct form, sensuous:

> Nous touchons là au paradoxe qui est le propre de la religion catholique.
>
> Une religion c'est avant tout le lien qui relie les vivants aux morts.

80 His last recorded profession of faith, which F. Duhourcau places 'a few days before his death' (*La Voix intérieure de Maurice Barrès,* 225), is an excellent example of this enduring relativism: 'Le christianisme a fourni à l'Occident la plus belle et la plus saine des formules pour quelque chose d'éternel qu'il y a dans nos êtres. J'aime l'Église et je suis du Christ.'

C'est une tradition. Qui dit tradition dit chose locale, nationale. La terre et les morts, voilà ce qu'il y a dans la religion.
Mais le catholicisme, c'est (le mot le dit) un cosmopolitanisme.
Il y a donc là une double force de vie, force centripète, force centrifuge. L'une et l'autre doivent exister. Il y a un équilibre.
[*Mes Cahiers*, *Œuvre* XVII 308]

(Noël ... *La Messe sur le Nil*) Toutes ces idées associées me font une peau de plus, une douce chaleur, c'est le plasme où je dois baigner. S'il me manque, je me dessèche, m'enfièvre, m'écorche.
Et qu'est-ce que tout cela prouve? Rien. Je vous dis une émotion profonde. Je suis devenu une nappe d'émotions.
[*Mes Cahiers* XV 334–5, 343][81]

So he was, consciously and resignedly for a time, and later, in spite of himself and less ready to admit it, torn between Chateaubriand, whose 'sensuous' and 'aesthetic' Christianity appealed strongly to him, but which he knew he must subordinate to the inner way of conviction in heart and mind, and Pascal, whose leap from scientific scepticism to the experimental proof of a God sensible to the hearts of all men alike he held ardently and humbly to be his supreme example,[82] but which he failed to follow all the way, largely because the scientific method applied to psychology and epistemology in his own time had convinced him of the inevitable variations of the heart's reasons and of philosophers' systems alike. Only where particular

81 *Cit.* H.-L. Miéville, *La Pensée de Maurice Barrès* (Paris: Édition de la Nouvelle Revue Critique 1934) in a perceptive chapter on 'Le Nationalisme élargi et l'aspiration religieuse de Barrès,' which, however, rather too lightly takes Barrès's relativism for indifference ('La question de la vérité ne se pose pas pour ce raffiné à l'affût de ce qui peut lui causer de beaux émois') and ignores the imaginative faculty which Barrès used consciously to mediate between 'l'intelligence et la rêverie,' and between 'la sensation' et 'l'idée,' not only for general rhetorical purposes but for the solution of the special 'problème de la religion et de la société moderne,' in a poetry of great creeds (both scientific and religious) conceived as something more than mindless 'jouissance.'

82 *Œuvre* XIV 277; XV 141, 210; XVI 254 and, especially XVI 22: 'Le numéro 483 de la petite édition Brunschvicg est un nationalisme qui va à l'universalisme.' See H. Franck, *La Danse devant l'arche*, 189–91.

sensations and general principles meet and are 'balanced' ('force centripète, force centrifuge')[83] in, at poorest, a hypothetical 'formula,' at richest a persuasive 'image' of the whole shape of things as it appears in perspective, from a viewpoint embedded in material time and space, did Barrès succeed in passing from the 'local' ('la terre humide ... mes racines') to the 'universal' ('la lumière, le ciel'):

> Pascal a fait la critique de nos facultés. Il a reconnu leurs limites et notre impuissance. Cet éternel *ignorabimus*, qui fait encore aujourd'hui souffrir les hommes prédisposés à la grande curiosité, c'est proprement le mal de Pascal.
>
> Pour en avoir l'idée, il faudrait participer de la puissance intellectuelle et sentimentale de ce grand homme, il faudrait être capable de former des images, égales en force et en netteté à celles que son génie se formait du clair-obscur de l'univers et de la vie ... Cependant, une âme moyenne, pourvu que la sensibilité chrétienne soit vivace en elle, peut s'émouvoir auprès de Pascal ... L'auteur des *Pensées* ne fait qu'animer, avec sa prodigieuse imagination, des idées religieuses qui sont déposées au fond de chacun de nous. Quand nous croyons admirer son génie dans ce qu'il a de plus personnel, nous admirons, en même temps, toute l'architecture chrétienne.
>
> [*Les Maîtres*, *Œuvre* XII 61–2]

> J'aime la paix, le silence, la tristesse de ce village [Gugney-aux-Aulx] où bruissent les noyers sous le vent. Je puis prier les images de son église. Il n'est pas nécessaire de posséder une foi parfaite pour prendre un plaisir de vénération devant l'image sereine de la foi. ... La sainte Claire de Gugney me ramène dans un étroit horizon, le mien, et mon esprit refoulé s'élève d'autant mieux vers le ciel.
>
> [*La Grande pitié des églises de France*, *Œuvre* VIII 14[84]]

In an article entitled 'Pas de veau gras!' (*Le Journal* 8 February

83 *Œuvre* XVII 308, *cit.* above, p. 75
84 *See* p. 280.

1900), Barrès had maintained, justly, that the *method* by which
1900), Barrès had maintained, justly, that the *method* by which the *Moi* and *barbares* are distinguished in *Un Homme libre* is the same as that by which the Lorrainer, etc., distinguishes himself from the foreigner. But in trying to use this as a defence against the charge (laid by René Doumic) of adoring as a nationalist the idols that the egotist tried to break, he tendentiously altered the original meaning he had given to *barbares*, i.e. 'le non-moi, c'est-à-dire tout ce qui peut nuire ou résister au Moi' (*Œuvre* I 31):

> *Un homme libre*, pauvre petit livre où ma jeunesse se vantait de son isolement! J'échappais à l'étouffement du collège, je me libérais, me délivrais l'âme, je prenais conscience de ma volonté ... Je me suis étendu, mais il demeure mon expression centrale. Si ma vue embrasse plus de choses, c'est pourtant du même point que je regarde. Et si l'*Homme libre* incita bien des jeunes gens à se différencier des *Barbares* (c'est-à-dire des étrangers), à reconnaître leur véritable nature ... c'est encore la même méthode que je leur propose quand je leur dis: 'Constatez que vous êtes faits pour sentir en Lorrains, en Alsaciens, en Bretons, en Belges, en Juifs.' [*Œuvre* V 29]

This bit of special pleading reveals inadvertently an important truth about the development of Barrès's ideology. His individualism was laid aside for the duration of and in the exigencies of anti-Dreyfusard polemics. It was not abandoned. What was superficial, and temporary, was not, as Doumic had suggested, Barrès's individualism, but his partisan use of a loosely defined behaviourist terminology of groups: 'organism,' 'family,' 'race,' 'reflex,' to invest nationalist unanimity with the rigour of a simple biological law. The Affair behind him, *un homme libre* reappears at the centre of a broader and looser traditionalism which recognizes the unpredictable complexity of ancestral and environmental influences:

> Les hymnes et les cantiques dont je voudrais nourrir un enfant favorisent en lui toutes les influences familiales, régionales, historiques et corporatives; mais l'on me comprend bien mal si l'on attend que j'énumère les avantages de ce racinement. Sa véritable

efficace sera dans une activité profonde et inexprimable, dans une piété infiniment riche et vibrante, dans une orientation qui sans contraindre un jeune être, lui suggérera de quoi exercer sa virilité.
Les aptitudes d'une famille et d'une région comportent simultanément plus de puissances qu'il n'y en a dans les paroles par où elles se définissent, ou dans les biographies que les signifient. C'est pourquoi des enfants à qui nous transmettons les formules originaires et les mélodies premières de leur race gardent toute liberté d'interprétation.
[*Les Amitiés françaises, Œuvre* v 479]

Le romantique voulait vivre des existences du passé ou ailleurs, moi j'aspire à faire des connaissances, à renouer des liens rompus, à retrouver des cousinages, des parentés, à élargir mon être, à conquérir toute l'humanité dont je suis capable. Je n'entends nullement me défaire de mon personnage, mais devenir le centre d'un être plus vaste.
[*Mes Cahiers, Œuvre* xviii 109]

PART II : IMAGINATION IN BARRÈS'S PHILOSOPHY

2 Maurice Barrès c1903

Collection Philippe Barrès; cliché Roger Viollet

CHAPTER FOUR

The Religious Imagination

POETIC INSIGHT

The essential fact about any religion, Barrès remarked in 1906, is that it 'produces a new and more perfect relation between man and his surroundings, between man and God' (*Mes Cahiers* xv 128). That this was a relation best expressed imaginatively was one of his fundamental convictions, grounded in personal experience and wide reading both before and after his illuminating encounter with the same belief in the pages of George Sand's *Impressions et Souvenirs*.[1] Among its earliest sources in Barrès must be those 'strong and subtle pages' of Louis Ménard's *Rêveries d'un païen mystique* that Auguste Burdeau had read to his class at Nancy in 1879 and which 'conquered' his pupil's 'astonished soul' (*Œuvre* VII 161). 'Je ne puis regarder sans attendrissement,' Barrès wrote twenty-five years later, 'la position qu'a prise Ménard dans l'équipe des Burnouf, des Taine et des Littré':

> Ces grands travailleurs attristés, attristants, nous font voir les dieux incessament créés et puis détruits par nous autres, misérables hommes imaginatifs. La conséquence immédiate de cette vue sur la mutabilité des formes du divin devrait être de nous désabuser des dieux. Mais, par une magnifique ressource de son âme de poète, Louis Ménard y trouve un argument de plus en leur faveur.

1 *See* above, p. 17.

Ils sont tous vrais, puisqu'on doit voir en eux les affirmations successives d'un besoin éternel.
[*Le Voyage de Sparte*, *Œuvre* VII 170][2]

Barrès's emotion is sympathetic. He may, in 1906, suspect that there is an element of literary dilettantism in this poet's interpretation of symbols, but this is preserved from frivolity, he says, by an exquisite tact, and justified because it is a means of reconciling faith, doubt, and negation in a sense of traditional order. Moreover, when, in the next few years, he was driven to define his own religious position with regard to the faith of his fathers, his personal doubts, and the negations of radical-socialist rationalism on the rampage, it was to a familiar and forceful poetry of the supernatural that he rallied:

Ces *Ave Maria*, ces louanges, tout se déploie, ondoie dans une clarté simple et enchanterait la douleur ... Le monde devient plus léger, plus diaphane; les laideurs et les brutalités s'éloignent; une nostalgie s'éveille dans notre âme, mais adoucie, recouverte, effacée; nous éprouvons un surplus de sympathie, de reconnaissance ... J'ai entendu *Parsifal* à Bayreuth; tout y est lourd, grossier, volontaire, près de cette fête de la pureté...

J'ai vu passer la poésie dont je suis un fils reconnaissant et privilégié.
[*La Grande pitié des églises de France*, *Œuvre* VIII 81–2]

The displacement towards Catholicism which characterized the evolution of Barrès's thought between the Dreyfus Affair and the Great War took place in the hostile historical context of the victorious Dreyfusards' attempt to secularize the French state and nation, as throughly as was in their power, in the name of free enquiry and scientific

2 Next to Ménard Barrès placed 'certaines *Méditations* de Lamartine, le *Port-Royal* de Sainte-Beuve, l'œuvre de Renan et la poésie de Leconte de Lisle.' (*Œuvre* VII 175) Other acknowledged sources of religious symbolism were Philippe Berthelot ('Quelques notes sur Louis Ménard,' *La Revue Bleue* 12 July 1902), Rio and Ozanam (*Œuvre* XIX 396). *See* also Dr P. Hartenberg's remarks on Stanislas de Guaita quoted in *Amori et Dolori Sacrum* (*Œuvre* VII 72).

reason. His defence of religion as poetic insight was shaped to meet this philosophical assault on the French Catholic tradition with as impressive an intellectual counter-force as he could muster. He found one group of authorities to speak, like George Sand, for the rehabilitation of 'la folle du logis ... qui nous parle des choses divines' in that Anglo-Saxon culture which, he declared, would give so enthusiastic a welcome to a translation of Louis Ménard (*Le Voyage de Sparte*, *Œuvre* VII 175). In 1905 he opened the long familiar pages of *Histoire de la littérature anglaise* to quote Taine on the philosopher of Fantasy as the organ of the Godlike:

> Prenez le monde tel que le montrent les sciences: c'est un groupe régulier, ou, si vous voulez, une série qui a sa loi; selon les sciences ce n'est rien davantage. Comme de la loi on déduit la série vous pouvez dire qu'elle l'engendre, et considérer cette loi comme une force. Si vous êtes artiste, vous saisirez d'ensemble la force, la série des effects et la belle façon régulière dont la force produit la série; à mon gré cette représentation sympathique est la plus exacte et la plus complète...'
> [*Mes Cahiers*, *Œuvre* XV 86]

Barrès got to know Carlyle (and Emerson) through Taine and Izoulet, who both turned their English lessons to their own account. On page 654 of the latter's *Cité moderne*, from which Barrès quoted in an article on Izoulet for *Le Journal*, 1 January 1898, there is the following statement: 'il faut voir dans l'*imagination* non pas une simple ouvrière de fictions, mais la révélatrice de l'idéal.'[3] In the former's *Essais de critique et d'histoire* (Paris: Hachette 1874, 399–400), parts of which are quoted in Barrès's *Au service de l'Allemagne* (*Œuvre* VI 60–1), the 'exact language' of primitive religions is contrasted favourably with the 'abstract' languages of sophisticated metaphysics:

> Quand nous dégageons notre fond intérieur enseveli sous la parole apprise, nous retrouvons involontairement les conceptions

3 Cf. Fichte, *Doctrine de la science*, *cit.* below p. 85.

antiques ... Le mythe éclôt dans notre âme, et, si nous étions des poètes, il épanouirait en nous toute sa fleur.[4]

In 1906 Barrès read his friend Henri Bremond's book on Cardinal Newman and was struck by the similarity between his own and the Englishman's poetical, irrational, and autobiographical kind of apologetics; after two pages of transposition and commentary he concluded as follows:

> C'est que l'imagination chez Newman n'est pas une maîtresse d'erreurs, comme le dit Malebranche, 'elle est cette claire, directe et vive intuition des réalités qui fait les poètes.'
> [*Mes Cahiers*, *Œuvre* XIV 294][5]

In 1910 he read André Chevrillon's *Nouvelles études anglaises*, and made a note in his diary of page 244, which contrasts the abstract cast of the French mind and language with the English 'concrete imagination,' illustrated by Burke, Ruskin, and Chesterton;[6] and he copied down part of Chevrillon's essay on the latter's 'Christian apologia,' including the following lines:

> 'Comme le savent d'intuition les artistes et les poètes, cette vie qui fait lever la matière et l'ordonne spontanément en formes de beauté, participe du divin. Donc, sans doute, un tel système est d'espèce et d'origine divines puisqu'il est si bien d'accord avec elle. Et qu'il soit inintelligible en même temps qu'efficace, qu'il ne se laisse pas réduire aux exigences de notre raison, c'est une preuve de plus de cet accord. La vie aussi est mystérieuse et ses procédés ne sont pas ceux de la raison.'
> [*Mes Cahiers*, *Œuvre* XVI 280]

A copy of Darmesteter's *Essais de littérature anglaise* in Barrès's library has the following passages about Wordsworth marked:

4 *See Œuvre* XVII 227: 'Une religion, dit Taine, c'est un poème auquel on croit' and VI 497: 'Nous avons besoin d'harmonie, d'un poème qui se fasse croire.'

5 Cf. *Œuvre* XIII 300

6 *Œuvre* XVI 376

> La nature ... médiateur entre notre monde et quelque monde au-delà, de qui elle prend sa splendeur et dont la pompe, à travers elle, se glisse et se mêle à notre terre...

> la poésie ne fait qu'ajouter la cadence du mètre au *langage réel* de l'homme parlant dans un état de vive émotion.

These jottings do not prove that Barrès was really familiar with the English writers he cited; they were cited, for what Barrès has learnt, from a critic's essay, quotation, or anecdote, about certain relevant details of their work, experience, or personality, as witnesses for the defence of the poet's claim to have sympathetic and imaginative access to the secrets of life in a rationally impenetrable universe, just as, elsewhere, Burke and Oswald John Simon were called upon to speak for secular traditionalism.[7] Many years before, he had also caught a 'hazy' glimpse, in Fichte ('eagerly devoured in a student's cramped bedroom overlooking Paris' [*Œuvre* I 31, 241]), of the original source of this claim, lying upstream of English Romanticism, in the idealist philosophy of eighteenth-century Germany: 'L'imagination ne trompe pas; elle donne la vérité et la seule vérité possible' (*Doctrine de la science de la connaissance* [Paris: Ladrange 1843], 141).

Barrès also scanned *Hamlet*, *King Lear*, and *The Tempest* for the same poetic insight that he loved in the visionary poems of the aging Victor Hugo. About the time he was composing *La Colline inspirée* he began to cast about for further evidence of that power of the poet to bring the mysterious into the full light of day, which was to become a major theme of his own last years, pushed aside by the exigencies of war-time journalism, but reappearing in the post-war *Cahiers*, and providing the title of his last completed volume of essays: *Le Mystère en pleine lumière*. He found this power in Hamlet and Prospero as in Victor Hugo and in 'Louis Lambert-Balzac':

> Oui, Shakespeare, c'est Hamlet. Mais Hamlet, c'est 'un homme trop clairvoyant et qui par là pour le public paraît énigmatique. Il

7 *Œuvre* V 32; XV 89–90

y a une apparente folie comme celle de Hamlet, qui n'est que l'expression forte et crue, hors des conventions banales de la pénétrante raison' (Blondel).

Ces gens-là, un Hamlet-Shakespeare, un Louis Lambert-Balzac, ils font voir du mystère où les autres voient de la clarté. 'À qui sait l'entendre, le mystère est une illumination nouvelle, parce qu'il propose comme obscur ce qu'on sait justement qui dépasse la force d'un regard borné.'

Ils rejoignent Hugo sur les frontières de la gnose.

Ils s'avancent dans les ténèbres, comme tous, mais avec une clarté qui élargit pour eux le cercle de la lumière de leurs visions et de leurs pressentiments. Alors ils semblent fous.

Leur activité diffère de l'activité des autres hommes. Ils voient du mystère (de la demi-lumière) là où les autres voient des ténèbres (rien).

[*Mes Cahiers, Œuvre* XVIII 16–17]

In 1919 the preparation of a lecture: 'Hugo sur le Rhin,' aided by the recent biographical studies of Guimbaud and Barthou, improved Barrès's understanding of the connections between the 'old prophet's' imagination and 'reality' (*Mes Cahiers, Œuvre* XIX 33). The religious quality of Hugo's and Lamartine's last years ('Il faudra qu'un jour j'étudie les conclusions religieuses de tous ces grands prêtres, les songes et les intuitions de leur vieillesse' [*Mes Cahiers, Œuvre* XVIII 4]) has become by now part of a broader enquiry embracing Tasso's voices, Luis de Leon, St John of the Cross, Jamblicus, Matter's *Le Mysticisme en France au temps de Fénélon*, the Abbé Migne's *Dictionnaire de mystique chrétienne*, the poetry, dancing, and music of the Konia dervishes (*Une Enquête aux pays du Levant, Œuvre* XI 380–455)[8]; while Jaurès himself enters the company of visionaries, 'all sons of the spirit, brothers and collaborators' (*Mes Cahiers, Œuvre* XIX 182), with their sisters, the sibyl of Auxerre cathedral, 'cette fille-poème, où chante-pleurent toutes les strophes, et qui dépasse la clairvoyance normale' (*Le Mystère en*

8 *See* I.-M. Frandon, *'Assassins' et 'Danseurs mystiques' dans 'Une Enquête aux pays du Levant' de Maurice Barrès.*

pleine lumière, Œuvre XII 189), Joan of Arc (*Mes Cahiers, Œuvre* XVII 127), and a 'vivante' of the twentieth century, Anna de Noailles.[9]

The preparatory notes of 'La Sybille d'Auxerre' refer to the scientific interest of the 'voyant':

> Ne pourraient-ils pas donner à la science, qui enregistre en hésitant leurs facultés, un nouveau et prodigieux moyen de connaissance? Le moyen de savoir les choses autrement que par l'expérience et par le raisonnement? ... Convertir la divination en science expérimentale.
> [*Mes Cahiers, Œuvre* XIX 147]

This passage, written in 1919, relates obliquely to the historical background of Barrès's reiterated witness to the authenticity of the poet's religious insight, namely the controversy into which he had entered in his middle forties with the chief critics of religion in twentieth-century France: the 'militants of Truth through Science' (Alphonse Aulard, *cit. Mes Cahiers, Œuvre* XVI 236).

'LE FAIT RELIGIEUX'

The zealots of the scientific method, which, when Barrès first came to Paris seemed 'to have invaded the entire realm of thought' (*Les Taches d'encre, Œuvre* I 451), succeeded, twenty years later, in registering their contempt for the established religion of France in the statute books of the nation. Barrès questioned the anti-Catholic party's exclusive claim to be called scientific; he did not contest the validity of the scientific method itself. On the contrary when, in January 1910, he was first challenged in Parliament to justify his stand against the disestablishment of the French Catholic Church and the secularization of French education, he spoke as a 'positivist,' defending in Catholicism a system of moral laws in accord with the natural laws of individuals and nations, and a proved source of magnanimous actions and spiritual vigour:

9 *See* I.-M. Frandon, *L'Orient de Maurice Barrès.*

> *La Chambre. Séance du 24 janvier 1910. Suite de la discussion sur l'Instruction publique.*
>
> ...
>
> Je suis de ceux qui se détournent de la recherche des causes. Je suis de ceux qui substituent à cette recherche la recherche plus immédiate des lois. Ma connaissance de l'histoire, si insuffisante qu'elle soit, et mon expérience de la vie me prouvent que les lois de la santé, pour la société comme pour l'individu, sont d'accord avec le décalogue que nous apporte l'Église...
>
> ...Je vois dans le catholicisme l'atmosphère où se développe le mieux les plus magnanimes sentiments de notre nation...
>
> Santé sociale, exaltation des plus hautes puissances de l'âme, telle est le double vertu que je constate à travers notre histoire dans le catholicisme. Voilà de quoi il est générateur. Voilà pourquoi je le défends avec un respect filial.
>
> [*Mes Cahiers, Œuvre* XVI 252–3]

Two years later he tried to counter-demonstrate his historical proof of the two virtues of Catholicism by showing that Rousseau's revolutionary ideology was extravagant and harmful because it proceeded from an imagination that was ignorant of the scientific disciplines of observation and experiment (*Les maîtres, Œuvre* XII 93). This use of his adversaries' shibboleth was not just a debating point. The pious angelism which gave him some pleasure, though meagre and distant, in the Catholic literature of Jammes, Le Cardonnel, and Pomairols, seemed to him out of place at the rostrum of the Palais Bourbon, where the debate between clerical and anti-clerical turned primarily on the nature and effect of the Catholic religion as a part of French civilisation: what he called 'le fait religieux,' and which he tried to deal with in appropriately empirical terms.[10] With Maurras, disciple of Auguste Comte, he asked:

> 'Quelle sera, en attendant que la science soit complète, notre conception du cercle entier des choses? N'y pas rêver est impossible, s'il est déjà assez malaisé de n'y pas penser. De quels mythes

10 *Œuvre* VIII 200–1; XV 241–2; XVI 139–40, 149–50

> repaîtrons-nous l'imagination? Quels seront les objets de ce sens religieux qui est inétouffable chez l'homme? Comte se demandait si l'antique Église romaine ne pourrait pas fournir à l'homme une enceinte de mythologie protectrice' (Maurras).
> [*Mes Cahiers, Œuvre* XVI 305][11]

A 'son of the University' himself, he thought it both 'honest' and 'useful' to conduct his defence of the Church as counsel for the 'sociologists' rather than for the 'believers'[12] and, in particular, to stress the contrast between the shallow anti-religious rationalism of his opponents ('Un rationalisme indigne de son nom veut ignorer les collines éternelles. Comme si la raison pouvait mépriser aucun fait d'expérience')[13] and the pragmatic caution with which a Taine, a Renan,[14] the Sorbonne of yesterday and even its present Grand Master, viewed the destruction by science of the 'current illusions' of religious imagination:

> Oui, la religion est une indestructible force de cohésion qui, sous quelque forme qu'elle se présente, selon les climats et selon les

11 Cf. 'Les nouvelles religions,' *Le Voltaire* 1 December 1887: 'une religion est un ensemble de notions ... sur l'existence de puissances surnaturelles. Or ces notions, qu'on nomme des mythes, l'intelligence humaine à cette heure semble incapable d'en créer.' Also L. Ménard, *Rêveries d'un païen mystique* (Paris: Durel 1909) 72: 'Les questions d'origine échappent à l'observateur et à la science; cependant l'esprit humain ne peut pas se désintéresser de ces grands problèmes; il faut donc qu'il se contente des solutions mythologiques, puisqu'il ne s'en présente pas d'autres.'

12 *Œuvre* XVII 10–11

13 *Œuvre* XVIII 8–9

14 Cf. Taine on 'le christianisme ... la grande paire d'ailes indispensables pour soulever l'homme au-dessus de lui-même' [*Les Origines de la France contemporaine: Le Régime moderne* (Paris: Hachette 1926), 146–7] and Renan's articles on Amiel, enthusiastically greeted in the first number of Barrès's *Les Taches d'encre* (*Œuvre* I 418): 'Notre monade en tant que pensant, s'affranchit des limites ... du milieu historique; mais en tant qu'individuelle et pour faire quelque chose, elle s'adapte aux illusions courantes et se propose un but déterminé.' (*Feuilles détachées* [Paris: Calmann Lévy 1876) xix: 'À force de chimères, on avait réussi à obtenir du bon gorille un effort moral surprenant.'

époques, est indispensable pour sauvegarder les sociétés et la civilisation. (*Applaudissements à droite. Interruptions à gauche.*)

Ne protestez pas. Ce n'est pas moi, c'est l'un des vôtres, c'est M. Durkheim qui dans son livre sur les suicides vous dit: 'La religion a incontestablement sur le suicide une action prophylactique.'

Notre vieille Université le savait bien, elle qui respectait, sauvegardait, présentait aux enfants la force de toutes les disciplines du passé.

[*Mes Cahiers, Œuvre* XVI 140][15]

Vous me rendrez cette justice que je ne vous ai apporté aucune considération tirée de la politique de parti, ou de l'apologétique dogmatique. Je me suis placé devant les faits, devant le fait religieux. Il n'est pas permis à des législateurs de ne pas tenir compte d'une réalité. Le sentiment religieux existe; l'église du village est ce sentiment rendu visible. Ces églises sont idéologiques, les seuls édifices idéologiques qu'ait le peuple, c'est-à-dire chargés uniquement d'idées qui ne représentent pas de la besogne. Respectez donc ces pierres nécessaires au plein épanouissement de l'individu.

Monsieur le Ministre ... il ne faut pas compromettre quelque chose de séculaire et qui joue un tel rôle dans l'histoire de notre pays et de la civilisation. (*Très bien! très bien! au centre et à droite.*) Eh bien! que pensez-vous faire pour protéger ces hautes expressions de la spiritualité française?...

Pour ma part, je suis venu défendre à cette tribune l'église de village au même titre que je défendrais le Collège de France. (*Très bien! très bien! au centre et à droite.*)

[*La Grande pitié des églises de France, Œuvre* VIII 57][16]

Barrès denied that these pratical considerations made him a social

15 'Séance de la Chambre, 21 juin, 1909: Question adressé à M. le Ministre de l'Instruction publique sur le suicide d'un élève d'un lycée de Clermont-Ferrand.' *Journal Officiel* 22 June 1909, 1541.

16 'Discussion du budget du ministère de l'Intérieur.' *Journal Officiel* 17 January 1911, 85

'utilitarian' in religion, however: 'La religion n'est pas pour moi un simple moyen d'ordre public' (*Mes Cahiers, Œuvre* XVI 254–5) ; 'Je ne viens pas pour parler en utilitaire social ... je viens vous dire, parce que cela me touche plus, vous dire qu'elle est utile pour la vie de l'individu ... qu'il faut ... augmenter le degré de vie de chacun' (*Mes Cahiers, Œuvre* XVII 14). Barrès specifically wanted the Church preserved for his own good, not simply for the good of the greatest number:

> j'ai horreur de cette conception sèche d'une religion pour le peuple. Je ne suis pas de ceux qui aiment dans le catholicisme une gendarmerie spirituelle! C'est pour moi-même que je me bats.
> [*La Grande pitié des églises de France, Œuvre* VIII 91]

The religion that Barrès wished the positivists in the *hémicycle* of the Palais Bourbon to recognize as a 'fact' corresponded exactly with his own experience of Catholicism as the expression of an emotion rather than the dogma of a faith:

> Pour moi ... les églises tirent leur valeur de leur emploi. Je les aime et veux les défendre comme un signe de l'esprit, comme une aide pour l'esprit. J'aime en elles un mouvement de l'esprit, un mouvement rendu visible par ces pierres édifiées.
> [*Mes Cahiers, Œuvre* XVII 10]

> Les lois de notre esprit ne vont pas se modifier pour suivre les caprices des législateurs. En vain, deux équipes s'acharnent sur notre Lorraine; des Prussiens qui détruisent notre langue; des sectaires qui veulent détruire notre religion, c'est-à-dire le langage de notre sensibilité. Ni les uns ni les autres peuvent sous leurs semelles user notre terre: elle produira toujours une aspiration, un enthousiasme qui veut être discipliné. Quand les clochers seront effondrés et les statues saintes exilées auprès des Dianes et des Mercures gallo-romains dans les salles poussiéreuses de nos musées départementaux, une génération surgira, qui voudra relever les temples de l'âme dans nos villages français.
> [*La Grande pitié des églises de France, Œuvre* VIII 14]

Against the anti-Catholics' claim to have 'put out the stars'[17] in the white light of science, the author of *La Grande pitié des églises de France* thus counterclaims for the Church in France not the monopoly of light, the certain revelation of a transcendently Christian universe, but the guardianship of a uniquely precious, clear-obscure 'language,' given to the Frenchman, like a mother tongue, to express imaginatively his trans-ascendent sense of kinship with the stars.[18]

In order to persuade the *scientistes* on the government benches, their supporters in Parliament and the country, and the 'son of the University' in his own mind, to treat this language with respect; and as a basis for comparing the 'two ideals'[19] of contemporary France directly, Barrès utilized a commonplace of nineteenth-century epistemology: the imaginative structure of the hypothesis.[20]

17 Viviani, *cit. Œuvre* XVI 235
18 *See* above, Chapter Three, note 75.
19 *Œuvre* XV 158, *cit.* below, p. 98
20 *La Grande Encyclopédie* and *Larousse du* XIXe *siècle*

CHAPTER FIVE

Scientific Imagination

The 'broad hypotheses' of theosophy, wrote Barrès, in one of his first pieces on the nature of science, philosophy, and religion (a review of his school friend Stanislas de Guaita's *Essais de Sciences maudites*), must be classed with the 'magnificent hypotheses, more fertile than our reflective positivism' of Spinoza, Fichte, Schelling; 'every general philosophical system, ancient or modern' must be seen as a poem: 'la plupart des esprits ne peuvent se satisfaire de ces amas de petits faits ... nous construisons, nous imaginons là où nous ignorons.'[1] The scientific orthodoxy of this imaginative construction of poetic hypotheses, designed to supply the deficiencies of positive knowledge, is stressed in an article on darwinism and collectivism Barrès wrote for *La Cocarde* eight years later:

> Pour toute science on a coutume de bâtir une hypothèse – ainsi à cette heure l'hypothèse darwinienne du transformisme – qui n'a pas la prétention d'être l'expression de la vérité totale (l'esprit humain peut-il l'embrasser?) mais qui est la construction la plus propre à encadrer et à ordonner les faits innombrables laborieusement amassés par les savants.

1 'Les nouveaux kabbalistes,' *Le Voltaire* 31 July 1886; 'Les Mages,' *Le Figaro* 27 June 1890. Guaita called his 'black sciences' a 'general synthesis' – hypothetical but rational – doubly founded, he alleged, on 'positive observation and analogical induction.' (*Essais de sciences maudites* I: *Au seuil du mystère* [Paris: Carré 1886] 'Avant-Propos'). Cf. 'Stanislas de Guaita: 1861–1898' (*Œuvre* VII 60–75). *See* also L. Ménard, *cit.* above, Chapter Four, p. 89, note 11.

> Le darwinisme n'est qu'une vue de l'esprit. De même le collectivisme ... Simplement c'est la fiction qui paraît à quelques-uns de nos contemporains relier de la façon la plus satisfaisante les faits économiques constatés après la transformation industrielle de l'Europe ... C'est un poème plus ou moins séduisant, qui pourra devenir une vérité, mais qui n'est encore qu'une hypothèse sociologiquement lointaine.
> ['L'Idéal et les premières étapes,' *La Cocarde* 18 September 1894][2]

The Christian apologetics of Barrès's forties, like the socialist propaganda of his thirties, seek common ground with science in the hypothetical nature of their assertions. The scientist assumes rightly, supposes Barrès, that the universe is governed by laws the human spirit can understand: 'Notre science rend compte des choses. Sans doute bien des choses échappent à notre esprit, mais nous n'avons jamais vu qu'elles dussent le contredire. Il ne semble pas qu'elles nous soient incompréhensibles par nature. L'univers est dans les ténèbres, il n'est pas un monstre' (*Mes Cahiers, Œuvre* xv 284). Man is right then, he continues, to predict an after-life which alone makes sense of his earthly destiny:

> Mon esprit ... a besoin qu'il y ait autre chose que ce néant.
> Entendez bien, il ne s'agit pas d'un besoin sentimental, du besoin de retrouver dans une autre vie ceux qui nous sont chers, non je veux dire que mon esprit est construit d'une telle manière qu'il ne peut pas admettre que tout cela soit et que tout cela soit un néant. Mon esprit a besoin de, veut, exige autre chose. Et de la même manière que Le Verrier croit qu'il apparaîtra une étoile au bout de sa lunette, je crois à une autre vie.
> Sinon l'homme est un monstre qui n'est pas accordé à la vie et la vie est pour lui un non-sens (mot trop faible), quand je sais déjà, il est vrai, qu'elle est un guet-apens.
> [*Mes Cahiers, Œuvre* xv 284]

2 Cf. É. Zola, in *Le Roman expérimental* (Paris: Charpentier 1890) 41–53: 'Par exemple, le transformisme est actuellement le système le plus rationnel ... Pour nous, romanciers expérimentateurs, l'hypothèse est fatale.'

'All this ... is contained in Pascal and Goethe,' he adds. The analogy of Le Verrier's planet is to be found earlier in the lighter context of *Le Jardin de Bérénice*, with other guarantors, Descartes, Kant, Comte, and Pasteur:

> en admettant la méchanceté et la mauvaise foi de mes adversaires ... je fais une hypothèse très précieuse et bien conforme à la méthode indiquée par Descartes ... par Kant ... et par Auguste Comte, qui vous touche peut-être davantage, dans son *Cours de philosophie positive*. La science, en effet, admet couramment ceci: '*La planète Neptune, n'eût-elle jamais été vue, devrait être affirmée. Fût-elle un astre purement fictif, la concevoir serait un grand service à l'astronomie, car seule elle permet de mettre de l'ordre dans des perturbations jusqu'alors inexplicables.*' De même les vices de mes adversaires, fussent-ils fictifs, me permettent de relier, sans trente-six subtilités de psychologue, un grand nombre de leurs actes fâcheux ... Pour ce procédé je m'en rapporterai à un maître que vous goûtez certainement: personne n'a vu la figure du ferment rabique; personne n'a constaté expressément son existence, et Pasteur guérit de la rage en cultivant ce microbe hypothétique, peut-être absolument fictif.
> [*Œuvre* I 349]

Friedrich Lange, Nietzsche, and Taine may also have suggested to Barrès the importance of imagination in the task he believed science and religion should alike attempt, namely the discovery of the 'laws that govern the world.'[3] He appears to have been struck as well by two pages of Marcel Hébert, on Kant as a forerunner of the pragmatists, which suggest that the hypothetical postulates of practical reason

3 'Toute l'affaire de la science et de la religion, c'est de rechercher et de connaître, chacune dans sa sphère, les lois qui gouvernent le monde.' (*Œuvre* IX 364) *See Œuvre* XIII 226 (Lange); XIV 83 (Nietzsche); XV 86 (*cit.* above, p. 83: Taine). Barrès dismissed Taine's Classical paganism in Alsace (*Essais de critique et d'histoire*, 399–400) as the 'fantasy' of a *normalien* perverted by foreign deities; but he adopted his mythopoetic method of meditation in a landscape in order to find the true *genius loci* of the Ottilienberg (*Œuvre* VI 60–5; XIV 11–12, 22–3). Cf. *Œuvre* XII 241–2, 517.

extend our theoretical knowledge of the 'suprasensible' in as much as reason is forced to admit that there are suprasensible objects, although it cannot define them exactly.[4] Renan's more explicit assimilation of religious and scientific hypotheses certainly made a deep impression on the conciliator of Church and University that Barrès wanted to become. This master of suggestive ambiguity, who never tired of repeating in one way or another that every general philosophy was 'une épopée sur les choses,'[5] was no doubt a main source of Barrès's assimilation of metaphysical with poetic symbolism, and the symbolism of religion with the language of science:

> La religion rentre ainsi dans le cas de ces nombreuses hypothèses telles que l'éther, les fluides électriques, lumineux, caloriques, nerveux, l'atome lui-même, que nous savons bien n'être que des symboles, des moyens commodes pour expliquer les phénomènes et que nous maintenons tout de même.
> [*Feuilles détachées* (Paris: Calmann Lévy 1892) 432]

Twenty-eight years after reading Renan's article on Amiel from which this passage is taken,[6] the same theory of religion, and Renan's second analogy, the electric current, reappear in Barrès's justification of the 'Christian hypothesis':

> *Le raisonnement qui justifie l'hypothèse chrétienne.* Il y a en nous quelque chose qui désire Dieu, un besoin de ceci et de cela. J'ai besoin de Dieu, ce n'est pas une preuve en temps normal,

4 *Œuvre*, XV 392; XVI 330. For Hébert himself intuition yields the certitude of a 'mode of being' beyond demonstration, and 'analogical induction, the hypothesis, intervene when a precise indication of its nature is required.' [*Le Pragmatisme* (Paris: Librairie critique, Émile Nourry 1909), 157–60].

5 *L'Avenir de la science*, 57; *Dialogues et fragments philosophiques* (Paris: Calmann Lévy 1876), 286–8, 323. Cf. *Œuvre* II 162: 'Les grandes métaphysiques, celles de Platon, de Dante, de Hegel et de Fichte, et tous les systèmes du monde ne sont que des images poétiques pour extérioriser et rendre logiques des sensations par elles-mêmes profondes et obscures. Il ne faut pas s'embarrasser des différences de vocabulaire, c'est toujours le même bouillonnement de l'homme qui veut devenir Dieu.'

6 *Œuvre*, I 418

mais vienne la certitude de la mort prochaine, vienne un deuil écrasant, ce besoin de Dieu persuade.

Puis il y a la nature qui n'a pas de réponse pour cet appel.

Elle nous écrase. Mais cela n'est pas une réponse. Cette part qui veut Dieu sera sauvée, obtiendra un autre monde, une autre vie. Sans quoi la vie, l'univers seraient absurdes. Ils ne peuvent pas être absurdes, dénués de sens, car l'absurde, le dénué de sens n'existent pas...

Au-dessus de la nature il y a Dieu qui un jour nous a envoyé son Fils pour nous dire: Je suis là.

Cette autre vie, cette vie spirituelle, nous n'avons pas de sens pour la connaître, pas plus que pour connaître l'électricité. Mais elle est là.

[*Mes Cahiers, Œuvre* XVII 206–7]

The 'marriage of science and religion,' which the 'natural affinity' suggested by Renan's analogy demands, seemed to the Barrès of 1915, reflecting on the destiny of the philosopher who, thirty years before, had been so important an initiator of his own thought, like a piece of unfinished business that it was vital and normal for Renan's successors to complete:

On a discuté souvent pour savoir si le petit Breton Renan s'était diminué en échangeant la foi de ses pères contre l'hégélianisme. Je serais disposé à croire que son vrai péché contre l'esprit fut de s'arrêter en route et de ne pas arriver au bel accord, au puissant mariage que toutes les intelligences attendent de la science et de la religion 'pour mettre fin au dix-huitième siècle qui dure toujours.' Attendez que l'*affinité naturelle de la science et de la religion* les réunisse dans la tête d'un seul homme de génie, s'écriait Joseph de Maistre, et notre grief, notre déception, c'est qu'un Renan, chargé de son double trésor, se soit détourné de cette destinée qu'il avait peut-être entrevue.

[*Grande Guerre* IV 174–5, *cit. Les Grands problèmes du Rhin, Œuvre* X 368]

Barrès himself searched diligently in the philosophical literature of his day for arguments capable of sustaining the conciliatory position he aimed at, and where, conjured by the old Breton magician into the common and amenable shape of symbolic figures, a venerable expression of religious experience and the tentative predictions of modern science might be isolated from the nationally divisive dogmas of the French clerical and the anti-clerical parties, and 'married' together in a 'higher ideal':

> Deux idéaux s'opposent l'un à l'autre dans ce pays. Me suffira-t-il de représenter l'un d'eux? Je suis malheureux et arrêté si je ne me hausse pas à un idéal supérieur qui les puisse concilier.
> [*Mes Cahiers, Œuvre* XV 158]

CHAPTER SIX

The Reconciliation of Science and Religion

PROBABILISM, MODERNISM, PSYCHOLOGY AND ANTHROPOLOGY

Among the Christian writers to whom Barrès turned for support for his parliamentary and press campaign against the secularist militancy of the post-Dreyfusard *Bloc des Gauches*, was Élie de Cyon:

> *À méditer, à rapprocher de Cournot et de Soury.* – 'Il n'a jamais existé la moindre incompatibilité entre la science et la religion. Ces deux plus sublimes manifestations de l'intelligence restent inséparables dans l'esprit des véritables créateurs de la science qui furent en même temps de profonds penseurs ... *L'harmonie entre les sciences naturelles et les enseignements de la religion ne repose nullement sur la diversité de leur origine ou la séparation de leur domaine d'action...*'
> [*Mes Cahiers, Œuvre* XVI 255]

This is the beginning of a long extract from Cyon's *Dieu et Science* that Barrès copied into his notebook in 1910, shortly after Jaurès had challenged him in the Chamber of Deputies to state the principles of his anti-secular speech on the teaching of ethics in the Republic's elementary schools (*Mes Cahiers, Œuvre* XVI 234–48, 252–3). Like Barrès, Cyon based his reconciliation of science and religion on the belief that religious revelation, scientific invention, and artistic and poetic inspiration had the same 'characteristic elements.' He also asserted, as Barrès would, that the test of time had demonstrated the validity of the Christian hypothesis, though Cyon interpreted this more literally and dogmatically than Barrès (*Mes Cahiers, Œuvre* XVI 255–7). The cross-reference in *Mes Cahiers* ('À méditer, à rapprocher de Cournot et de Soury') indicates the growing complexity of Barrès's reflections on the position of the Church in twentieth-century civilisation. Soury's assimilation of the religious and the scientific vocations and his free interpretation of the Church formulary were firmly implanted in Barrès's Catholicism (*Mes Cahiers, Œuvre* XIII 52; XIV 49–50), but the neurotic maceration of the flesh that Soury practised (like Pascal, 'trop mêlé de maladie,' thought Barrès), and the hard logic of his distinction between scientific knowledge and the 'dreamland' of Christianity's poetry of consolation were alien to him. Cournot's probabilism was nearer to the less fanatical, abnormal, and rigorous cast of mind of the author of *La Grande pitié des églises.* He read F. Mentré's *Cournot et la renaissance du probabilisme* in 1909. It contained ideas with which he was already familiar, notably a relativistic epistemology,[1] an analysis of the role of analogy in the framing of hypotheses designed to grasp 'the order and relations of things,' and the evaluation of Christianity by the test of time rather than by the 'trivial' question of the Gospels' historical accuracy.[2] Features of Cournot's thesis that he noted specifically were the origin of religion in the mysterious and fascinating obscurity of the 'supreme questions,' the identity of the miraculous and the mysterious, the primary importance of instinct in social psychology, the uniqueness of the destiny of Rome, and the desirability of a progressively broader interpretation of the Scriptures 'à mesure que l'intelligence de l'homme se fortifierait et qu'il avancerait dans la connaissance des œuvres de Dieu.'[3]

Barrès once judged Loisy and the Modernists harshly:

1 F. Mentré, *Cournot et le renaissance du probabilisme* (Paris: Rivière 1908) 249: '"Il répugne à la raison d'admettre que nous puissions, avec les organes et les facultés dont la nature nous a doués *pour connaître les choses à la faveur des relations qu'elles ont avec nous,* atteindre en quoi que ce soit à l'essence des choses et à la réalité primitive et absolue."'

2 *Cournot,* 243, 539

3 *Œuvre* XVI 218, 227; XIX 172–3

Les modernistes, Loisy. – Cela vient de ce fait qu'ils ont été mêlés à la Sorbonne aux étudiants en licence et craignent la science des Salomon Reinach. C'est le sourire aux professeurs.

Il s'agit d'accorder le christianisme avec la science. Ils définissent la science. La science nous dit que tout ce qui est vivant évolue. Donc si le christianisme est vivant, il évolue. Si Christ est vivant en moi, il évolue, il n'est pas ce qu'il était. Originairement Christ était un pauvre petit juif qui ne savait pas ce qu'il fondait. Il a été chargé de richesses par les générations.

– Mais, pardon, monsieur Loisy, est-il un Dieu?

– Dieu! monsieur Barrès, c'est ce sentiment qui est en vous.

De même que si je dis à Vogüé l'argument perpétuel et, il faut bien le dire, décisif de Renan:

– Croyez-vous aux miracles?

Il me répondra:

– Les miracles! Mais la nature n'est-elle pas un miracle perpétuel.

Ce sont des calembredaines. Et pourquoi ces messieurs prêtres gardent-ils leurs robes, disent-ils la messe. S'ils rougissent de leur prêtrise, qu'ils la jettent aux orties.

[*Mes Cahiers, Œuvre* XVI 11–12]

Barrès's own religious position, however – equally removed from 'Catholic atheism' (*Mes Cahiers, Œuvre* XIV 294) and from the closed and static systems championed by the rival dogmatists of the Vatican and the Sorbonne alike (*Mes Cahiers, Œuvre* XV 242–3) – was very similar, fixed by the open theology of two of his early masters: Renan and Izoulet,[4] and by two recognized Modernists read more recently: Newman,[5] and Blondel, whose *Insuffisance de l'exégèse comme apologétique* is mentioned, together with Bergson's *Introduction à la métaphysique*, in a *cahier* for the summer of 1907 which is almost entirely given up to Barrès's wrestling with the problem of Christian belief (*Mes Cahiers, Œuvre* XV 222).

4 *See* J. Izoulet, *L'Âme française et les universités nouvelles selon l'esprit de la Révolution* (Paris: Colin 1892) 15–17.

5 *See* above, p. 84 and Hébert on Newman in *Le Pragmatisme*, 101.

EXPERIENCE AND EXPERIMENT

Barrès's search for allies against anti-religious rationalism drove him well beyond the limits of the most modern forms of Catholic thought to adduce evidence for his case from the 'vast enquiry' that William James had recently undertaken into the variety of religious experience (*Mes Cahiers, Œuvre* XIV 285; XVI 313), from Sir James Frazer's theory (somewhat distorted in the Barresian sense) of the continuity between magic, religion, and science (*Mes Cahiers, Œuvre* XVII 126), from Émile Durkheim's study of the elementary forms of religion (XV 215, 394; XVII 254–5), from Claude Bernard's theory of the unconscious (XVI 318–19), from Bergson's concept of intuition (and his imaginative philosophical vocabulary).[6] Barrès's habit of reading was always wide-ranging and penetrating, rather than thorough. He practised the *razzia* rather than the methodical conquest and assimilation of new ground, in the manner of Gide, for instance. From his raids into the territory of contemporary anthropology and psychology in the decade before the First World War, he acquired a mixed bag of booty for personal purposes determined in advance, rather than any new philosophical positions. The instinctive and collective forms of experience he studied after 1905, in James, Frazer, Durkheim, Bernard, and Bergson, belong to the same order of 'fact' and 'reality' as that much earlier Barresian 'vision of the divine,' which the hero of *Le Culte du Moi* had 'rediscovered ... under its more up-to-date style of The Unconscious,' in *Le Jardin de Bérénice* ('Hartmann in action' [*Œuvre* I 33, 377]), and which had been the original inspiration of Barrès's always consciously relativistic doctrine of traditionalism:

> Les tenants de la méthode expérimentale, ceux qui ont voulu l'appliquer même aux choses de l'âme et constituer une science psychologique, vous disent que de ces parties profondes de l'être, de ce domaine obscur surgissent toutes les puissances créatrices de l'homme, toutes les intuitions, celles que la raison peut contrôler, aussi bien que celles qui dépassent la raison...

6 *Œuvre* XII 19; XV 214; XVI 306, 374; XVII 126

De plus en plus, les esprits se tournent vers cette région subconsciente de l'âme.

Vous ne pouvez pas ne pas tenir compte de cette grande activité intérieure. Cette vie mystérieuse, cette conscience obscure, ce besoin du divin, c'est un fait et qu'il n'est pas en notre pouvoir d'abolir dans l'homme...

Cette conscience obscure, en effet, c'est elle qui a voulu l'église du village et qui continue à la vouloir...

[*La Grande pitié des églises de France*, *Œuvre* VIII 52–3]

Écoutez les bruits qui nous sont familiers et qui montent du village ... Tout y est vrai, créé par le temps, chargé de sens. C'est une harmonie, c'est la somme des expériences accumulées par les générations ... Je l'accepte dans sa totalité. Mais certains veulent détruire l'église.

Que reprochent-ils à ces hauts murs qui se dressent au-dessus de nos champs? Supposons qu'à une époque bien lointaine leur ombre ait été trop grande sur le village. Aujourd'hui qui, de bonne foi, peut prétendre qu'elle le gêne? Elle contient quelque chose, elle met une réalité à notre disposition.

[*La Grande pitié des églises de France*, *Œuvre* VIII 79–80]

The ambiguity of the French word *expérience*, which led some Modernists to take the religious experience of the many to be much the same as an experimental proof of God's existence,[7] and which tempted a Durkheim to credit group experience with something approaching the objectivity of a scientific demonstration,[8] was resisted by Barrès, in whom his latest scientific sources seem to have confirmed what he had already learnt from the philosophers and psychologists

7 E.g. M. Blondel, *Histoire et dogme* (La Chapelle-Montligeon: Imprimerie Librairie de Montligeon 1904), 54, 72 and Hébert on Newman in *Le Pragmatisme*, 101

8 Barrès cites pages 299, 300, 602, 603, 604, 610 of *Les Formes élémentaires de la vie religieuse* (Paris: Alcan 1912) [*Mes Cahiers, Œuvre* XV 215, 394] but not page 625: 'Une représentation collective parce qu'elle est collective, présente déjà des garanties d'objectivité ... elle peut ... exprimer [son objet] à l'aide de symboles imparfaits: mais les symboles scientifiques ... ne sont jamais qu'approchés.'

of the nineteenth century, namely that human experience has given birth to 'a multitude of solutions to the problem of the universe,' none of which is absolutely satisfactory.[9] For Blondel, pre-Christian religious tradition carries the premonition, and Catholic 'Tradition' embodies the certainty of a divine truth darkly but definitively revealed by Christ.[10] To Barrès, on the other hand, Catholicism appears normally as part of an unbroken chain of natural religious 'premonitions' and 'approximations' reaching back to the earliest forms of paganism and forward to a potentially non-Catholic new order:

> Ah! si je pouvais considérer comme définitif que jamais l'esprit n'a pu arriver et n'arrivera jamais à aucune lueur sur ces questions-là par une autre méthode que la scientifique, je vous dirais moi aussi qu'il est plus digne de l'homme de s'abstenir totalement. Mais en fait, que voyons-nous? nous voyons que depuis l'origine des temps il se trouve tout une tradition dont le lieu est jusqu'à nouvel ordre l'Église et qui a intégré les pressentiments les plus légitimes, les certitudes les plus approchées de chaque génération.
>
> Et voici que maintenant les penseurs n'élèvent plus les objections qu'élevait un Renan ou un Taine contre la possibilité de la chose: Boutroux, philosophe officiel de la République, William James, un protestant, un individualiste tout ce qu'il y a de plus libre. Ainsi l'instinct des simples se trouve justifié par les démarches supérieures de la pensée.
>
> [*Mes Cahiers, Œuvre* XVI 313]

> Ce que je défends et veux sauver, ce n'est pas un catéchisme, mais c'est un ensemble de sentiments qui s'expriment tant bien que mal par ce catéchisme et qui pour ce moment ne s'expriment que par lui.
>
> [*Mes Cahiers, Œuvre* XVII 72]

Or to what his 'integrative' traditionalism led him to prefer, a new order of Catholicism 'enriched' by a meaning that science can admit:

9 *Œuvre* XVI, 214
10 Blondel, *Histoire et dogme*, 47–72

> Mais comment Jaurès, Sembat, Pressensé ont-ils ce courage de détruire. Je ne m'étonne pas qu'ils croient à l'avenir, mais jeter bas le catholicisme...
> N'était-il pas plus beau de donner un sens plus riche à la vieille maison?
> Nul plaisir dans la destruction pour eux. Il suffirait de mettre la solution en rapport avec notre raison. Il suffirait de féconder, de transformer notre catholicisme.
> [*Mes Cahiers, Œuvre* xv 130]

Such transformation is feasible, in Barrès's view, because both science and religion are hypothetical expressions of 'the universal harmony,' the 'laws that govern the world,' composed by imaginative means from the data of 'experience' (*Œuvre* IX 364; XX 37); it is desirable, moreover, because, beside the 'immortal and complete poem of Catholicism' (*Œuvre* XV 238), the transitory general systems invented by the scientific imagination seemed to him, while no different in form, comparatively poor in substance:

> La science! la science! Mais on ne sait rien! On a des recettes pour construire un cuirassé, des canons, des ponts, des ballons. Et puis certaines gens, des artistes en somme, ont une puissante imagination pour inventer, pour créer des systèmes qui relient le plus grand nombre des faits. Ils font accepter leur petit roman durant quelques années, puis des faits nouveaux surviennent qui ne rentrent pas dans leur système, il faut en inventer un autre.
> [*Mes Cahiers, Œuvre* XVI 374]

While maintaining his sceptical aversion to the 'perverted religion' of those French school-teachers who dogmatized in the name of Science (*Mes Cahiers, Œuvre* XIV 106; XVI 246), Barrès was no more able to declare the literal truth of Christian doctrine than he was willing to defend the Church as a mere 'spiritual police force' (*Œuvre* VIII 91). Instead he looked forward to an open-minded Catholicism freed from its fixed dogmas, and enlightened by a 'high conception of the sciences' (*Œuvre* XVIII 36) which, when detached likewise from the narrow-minded anti-religious prejudices of contemporary *scientisme* would appear perfectly compatible with the aims and methods of Christian philosophy:

> Par quel défaut de flamme ou quel scrupule positiviste, l'histoire qui connaît ces lieux souverains n'ose-t-elle pas nous en retracer avec amour les annales? Un rationalisme indigne de son nom veut ignorer les collines éternelles. Comme si la raison pouvait mépriser aucun fait d'expérience! Dans la pleine lumière et dans le grand frémissement de midi, des yeux distraits ou trop faibles pourront ne pas distinguer les feux de ces éternels buissons ardents. Mais nous sentons avec émotion quelque similitude entre ces espaces sacrés de la nature et les parties les plus desséchées de notre âme. Dans notre âme, comme sur la terre, il existe des points nobles que le siècle laisse en léthargie. Ayons le courage de marcher de nouveau hardiment sur cette terre primitive et de cultiver par-dessous les froides apparences le royaume ténébreux de l'enthousiasme. Mais respectons à la fois toutes les clartés et les ombres. Nulle science ne rend inutile l'enthousiasme qui palpite sur certains sommets; celui-ci ne vaut toutefois que pour nous conduire à plus de science.
> [*Mes Cahiers, Œuvre* XVIII 8–9]

THE CHRISTIAN FORMULA: FROM DEFINITION TO INCANTATION

The passage quoted above from Barrès's notebook for the latter half of 1913 closely resembles parts of the philosophical overture, and the Epilogue, of *La Colline Inspirée*, the fullest literary expression of his religious philosophy, published earlier in the same year, an historical novel about the inspired, anarchic, and eventually heretical attempt, in the middle of the last century, of a simple, visionary priest, Léopold Baillard, supported by his two brothers, also priests, and, at first, by considerable local peasant and feminine sympathies, to revive an ancient pilgrimage to the shrine of Sion-Vaudémont in Lorraine, the 'sacred hill' near Barrès's birth-place at Charmes-sur-Moselle. Religious orthodoxy is represented emblematically in this novel by a sustained 'property',[11] which is typical of finished Barrésian rhetoric. This emblem is the hilltop chapel of Vaudémont, and its tenor corresponds to what is designated in the *cahier* version as, plainly, 'la science,' and, metaphorically, 'les clartés':

> rien ne rend inutile, rien ne supplée l'esprit qui palpite sur les cimes. Mais prenons garde que cet esprit émeut toutes nos puissances et qu'un tel ébranlement, précisément parce qu'il est de tout l'être, exige la discipline la plus sévère.
> [*La Colline inspirée, Œuvre* VI 498]

This tangible representation, in 'four stone walls,' of an established Roman and Catholic social and doctrinal order: 'la règle, l'autorité, le lien ... un corps de pensées fixes et la cité ordonnée des âmes,' is proposed as the necessary complement of its natural surroundings: 'vaste ensemble de pierrailles, d'herbages maigres, de boqueteaux, de halliers toujours balayés du vent, tapis barbare où depuis des siècles les songeries viennent danser ... un lieu primitif, une source éternelle ... la prairie,' symbolizing the socially disruptive and intellectually disturbing, unconfined, and inchoate vital force of spontaneous religious experience, 'agitating,' 'exciting' the solitary individual till he seems to 'vibrate' in reckless sympathetic communion with 'the infinite.'[12] That 'la chapelle,' over against 'la prairie,' stands for something that to Barrès's mind is perfectly compatible with the spirit and methods of open-minded scientific enquiry, is strongly suggested, not only by the substitution, from novel to *cahier* of the words 'pour nous conduire à plus de science' for 'exige la discipline la plus sévère,' but also, in the novel itself, by the attitude that the priests who personify what seems best in the Church adopt towards their errant brother in God, who has been led into rebellion against the Church by the wild influences that are abroad on the abandoned 'Acropolis' of Lorraine: 'N'était-ce pas mon rôle de prêtre de reconnaître, au milieu de ses erreurs, le mouvement de Dieu?,' asks the dying Père Aubry, thus inspiring the young Oblate Father who finally succeeds in 'reconciling' the rebel.

11 *See* Chapter Ten, pp. 190–6.
12 *La Colline inspirée, Œuvre* VI 497–500

And Barrès, in the epilogue of the novel: 'Qu'est-ce qu'un enthousiasme qui demeure une fantaisie individuelle? Qu'est-ce qu'un ordre qu'aucun enthousiasme ne vient plus animer? L'église est née de la prairie, et s'en nourrit perpétuellement, – pour nous en sauver' (*Œuvre* VI 500). The last word of *La Colline inspirée* is with the saving order of a particular rule, authority and bond; but the 'eternal dialogue' on the sacred hill has no last word: 'Ah! plutôt qu'elles puissent, ces deux forces antagonistes, s'éprouver éternellement, ne jamais se vaincre et s'amplifier par leur lutte même!'[13]

The 'testing' and 'amplification' of Barrès's own religious experience by an ordered, positive system of theory and precept in which the Catholic tradition and the future of science are reconciled did not altogether remove the suspicion he voiced in 1903 in *Les Amitiés françaises,* that any such 'song of confidence' must be a life-lie contradicted by the 'senseless tumult' of the universe and human existence (*Œuvre* V 559)[14]; but his belief in the truth of what was for him the essence of religious belief, namely the 'mysterious' but not 'monstrous' connexion between man and the stars,[15] while never unassailable, grew increasingly assured, and became increasingly important to him during the last twenty years of his life. His impulse to 'test' and 'amplify' *chapelle* by *prairie,* on the other hand, took him simultaneously into territory that he found powerfully attractive, but which was both non-Catholic and pre-scientific. Thus, for instance, to use Jaurès's apt metaphor, he 'dug down and down to Rosmertha' on the slopes of Sion-Vaudémont (*Mes Cahiers, Œuvre* XVII 294),[16] he put the features of a Celtic prophetess into his loving portrait of Joan of Arc, honoured the pagan sibyl in Auxerre cathedral, and made a special cult of the *genius loci* he found abiding in the meadows, springs, and groves of Lorraine and Provence; and of the Levant too, where, in the early summer of 1914, between the publication of *La Colline inspirée* and the outbreak of the Great War which would claim all his attention and energy for the next four years, he would find time to explore the 'dark life' and the

13 *Œuvre* VI 500. Cf. J.-M. Domenach, *Barrès par lui-même*, 83.
14 *Grande Guerre* IV 178: 'le chapitre *Chant de confiance dans la vie* (vers 1902) ... qui demeure ce qui me définit le mieux.' Cf. *Œuvre* VIII 444–5; IX 253; XVII 396; XVIII 327.
15 *Œuvre* XV 284, *cit.* above, p. 94
16 Cf. *Œuvre* VI 496.

'religious heart' of Asia, teeming with a 'miraculous catch of religious facts.'[17] What most attracted Barrès to the 'multitude of heterodoxies' and the 'pagan survivals' of Syria and the Lebanon, which Louis Ménard, William James, and Henri Bremond had taught him to recognize as various forms of the one 'fluid,' 'spark,' 'electric current,' 'vibration' of 'eternal mysticism,' were, firstly, the 'innumerable techniques' for rousing religious 'enthusiasm' and 'sympathy' he found there, techniques which he saw the Catholic Church skilfully and cautiously borrowing from its predecessors and sharing with its rivals;[18] and, secondly, such ancient prefigurations of Christianity, as the sound and movement of bacchanalia, 'faintly echoed' in Saint Teresa's tambourine and dancing Carmelites, and the 'liturgy' of the Sun God at Baalbek, remotely thrilling the young Racine as he offers up his slender sheaf of hymns to the beneficent dawn of Christ, the Sun of righteousness[19] – Levantine prototypes of the Roman Catholic faith which are akin to those larval 'semi-forms' of Christianity in Europe that he had recently attempted to 'mobilize,' under Catholic command, and together with all the little village churches that official France seemed in danger of forgetting, for a conservation and rescue operation intended to 'redeem and unify the entire realm of the sacred,' for the French of his own and future generations:

> Ces cultes de jadis, ces croyances indigènes, bien antérieurs à l'occupation romaine qui les a déguisés sans pouvoir les abattre – d'où viennent-ils et faut-il l'aller demander aux grottes des Eyzies? – en même temps qu'ils se prolongent jusqu'à nous en vieilles pratiques misérables, demeurent à l'origine de notre plus grande poésie. Ces imaginations, ces rumeurs, si nous en faisions table rase, si elles disparaissaient des sommets, des bois, des vallées et de notre âme, quel appauvrissement!...
>
> Églises du village, nature française, profondes forêts, sources vives, étangs au fond des bois, comme tout cela sonne harmonieusement ensemble! Puissions-nous pieusement recueillir ces parcelles agissantes, organiser nos rapports avec ces vérités de brouillard,

17 *Une Enquête aux pays du Levant, Œuvre* XI 105, 222
18 *See* pp. 165–6.
19 *Une Enquête aux pays du Levant, Œuvre* XI 174–6, 198–205

> assister au retour des pauvres dieux locaux dans l'arche du divin, à leur purification et à leur salut! Puissions-nous les réconcilier avec Celui qui préside notre civilisation et créer en nous la plus riche unité contre les grossiers destructeurs.
>
> Tout le divin, à la rescousse!
>
> ['La mobilisation du divin,' *La Grande pitié des églises de France*, *Œuvre* VIII 172–3]

Barrès set Christ's Church above but not apart from the 'imaginations' of paganism (*Œuvre* VIII 172; XI 126). Its rôle as he saw it was 'to rethink and to regulate the impetuous desire of the imagination for some glimpse of the supernatural,' just as, in the humanist *maison d'en face*, the gift of divination might be 'converted into an experimental science' (*Mes Cahiers, Œuvre* XIX 147). The word *formule* often occurs to Barrès in this context. By general usage it seems to bridge the gap between science and religion much better than *hypothèse*. But Barrès was more wary of its relevance to the conciliatory position he had adopted in the disestablishment controversy of 1904-11 because, no doubt, of its overtones of dogmatism in both spheres. He had long been wary of formulae, in both religious and secular connexions, and the unqualified use of the word in his work generally points to an unattained or a fall-back position:

> Je n'ai pas comme Saint Louis de formule déterminée, mais je cherche ma formule à travers toutes les expériences.
>
> [*Le Jardin de Bérénice*, *Œuvre* I 314]

> Je ne vous ferai pas croire que je possède une formule avec laquelle je tiens la vérité, tel un chevalier de jadis portant sur son écu sa devise ou son cri de guerre. Mais il y a, par périodes, des mots qui me viennent à l'esprit, ou que je recueille, et qui pour un temps me satisfont.
>
> [*Mes Cahiers, Œuvre* XIX 325]

> À mon sens, il faut que le nationalisme soit une formule qu'on retrouvera chaque fois qu'on en aura besoin.
>
> [*Mes Cahiers, Œuvre* XIV 287]

Le christianisme a fourni à l'Occident la plus belle et la plus saine des formules pour quelque chose d'éternel qu'il y a dans nos êtres. J'aime l'Église et je suis du Christ.
[*cit.* F. Duhourcau, *La Voix intérieure de Maurice Barrès* (Paris: Grasset 1929) 225][20]

The mistrust of formulae once displayed by a sceptical *princeps juventutis*[21] – 'Qu'il y ait donc de vigoureux esprits dogmatiques, mais qu'ils permettent pourtant d'exister à ceux qui possèdent la défiance des formules' (*Œuvre* II 386) – reappeared in the 'patriarch'[22] of the post-Dreyfus patriotic and religious revival: 'ne me demandez pas d'enfermer dans une formule ce que j'appelle Lorraine' (*Œuvre* XVII 74); 'La tradition, cette force, cette vertu mystérieuse qui contient le plus précieux trésor de l'humanité, son esprit même, et qui ne se met pas en formule' (*Grande Guerre* V 102–3); 'Nous sommes la vie et nous ne pourrions pas être prisonniers d'une formule' (*Œuvre* X 367). This attitude was very marked *vis-à-vis* the dogmatic Royalists and Catholics of *Action Française* and *La Revue critique des idées et des livres*:

Encore repensé à Maurras.
Vous laissez trop de choses en dehors de vous.
Vous resserrez la doctrine et moi je l'étends.
Vous voulez dominer les esprits, les contraindre dans une formule, les diriger.
Effort pour rompre la prison étroite d'un raisonnement, d'une doctrine (pour la revoir telle qu'elle est, une hypothèse) dans un essor libre et instinctif du sentiment et de la foi...
Je reconnais que l'esprit humain ne peut pas se passer de doctrines

20 Cf. *Les Déracinés*, *Œuvre* III 152: 'À cette âme de bonne volonté il faudrait seulement qu'on proposât une formule religieuse acceptable.' Also 'Maître Aliboron,' *Le Gaulois* 17 March 1907: 'Louis Ménard développe que "l'Église a donné au monde la vraie formule de la prière".'

21 Paul Adam *dixit*, *cit.* P. Moreau, *Maurice Barrès* (Paris: Sagittaire 1946), 59

22 Charles Péguy *dixit*, *cit.* J. and J. Tharaud, *Mes Années chez Barrès* (Paris: Plon 1928) 55: 'Vous êtes notre patriarche!'

> et d'hypothèses et que la raison seule est apte à construire les unes et les autres, mais je n'assujettis pas la vie à des arguments. Je ne veux pas me battre pour un parti, soyons plus clair, je ne veux pas me battre pour des parties. Chaque groupement laisse trop de choses de côté.
> [*Mes Cahiers, Œuvre* XVII 157–8][23]

The kind of formulae that Barrès needed to contain and to communicate his indefinitely 'integrative'[24] and finally religious traditionalism were more like incantations than definitions, closer to the poetry of Baudelaire than to the rival ideologies of Claude Bernard and Thomas Aquinas which currently held the battle-line between thinking Frenchmen. His philosophy tended to resolve naturally and consciously into the rhetoric of 'magical suggestion,' *sorcellerie évocatoire*:

> Si l'on ignore la platitude, l'anarchie et le vague d'une vie d'interne dans un collège français, on ne comprendra pas la puissance que prit, sur l'auteur de cette notice, la beauté lyrique, quand elle lui fut proposée par un de ses camarades du lycée de Nancy, Stanislas de Guaita. En 1877, il avait dix-sept ans et moi seize. Il était externe; il m'apporta en cachette *les Émaux et Camées, les Fleurs du Mal, Salammbo*. Après tant d'années, je ne me suis pas soustrait au prestige de ces pages, sur lesquelles se cristallisa soudain toute une sensibilité que je ne me connaissais pas ... M'inquiétais-je beaucoup d'avoir une intelligence exacte de ces poètes? Leur rythme et leur désolation me parlaient, me perdaient d'ardeur et de dégoût. Une belle messe de minuit bouleverse des fidèles, qui sont loin d'en comprendre le symbolisme. La demi-obscurité de ces œuvres ajoutait, je me le rappelle, à leur plénitude.
> [*Un Rénovateur de l'occultisme. Stanislas de Guaita (1861–1898)* (Paris: Chamuel 1898), *Œuvre* VII 60][25]

23 Cf. *Œuvre* VIII 394; XII 160; XVII 176.
24 *See* p. 70.
25 *See* pp. 232–3 and *Œuvre* VI 334–5 (*cit.* Chapter Eleven, note 41) and XII 241–2 (*cit.* p. 226).

Acknowledging the absolute truth of neither revealed religion nor natural science, though he was much interested towards the end of his life by the 'direct communication' with the supernatural that was claimed by ancient sibyls and modern seers, and he was not always prepared to deny the eventual possibility of a comprehensive science of nature, Barrès believed that he must depend on the synthetic faculty of imagination to combine his feeling and his idea of man's universal destiny, in 'semi-obscure formulae' open to a variety of interpretations, and in musical or visual 'forms' signifying semi-articulate thoughts:

> Que veux-je dire, avec exactitude?
> Simplement que la religion catholique est le poème qui me satisfait le plus, où je trouve le mieux exprimé ce que je sens et qui éveille en moi les plus riches sons. Elle résonne d'accord avec moi et beaucoup plus richement que moi. Elle me formule et m'éveille.
> [*Mes Cahiers, Œuvre* XV 127]

> *Sur les Psaumes.* – Puissance magique des formules demi-obscures, mais très pleines, sur lesquelles on médite longuement, où l'on trouve une succession de sens superposés, concordants et appropriés aux siècles, aux âges, aux circonstances.
> [*Mes Cahiers, Œuvre* XV 200]

LA MESSE SUR LE NIL

> le centre de mes expériences d'Égypte, – c'est cette matinée de Noël où, lassé mais non rassassié, irrité plutôt par des dieux étrangers, j'assiste à une pauvre messe catholique sur le quai.
> ...
> Ce que j'éprouvais alors, comment pourrai-je l'écrire? C'était une merveilleuse exaltation où me plongeait l'idée que nous étions si divers et pourtant réunis. J'éprouvais saisissement et joie qu'un spectacle aussi éternel pût m'être présenté et que j'y participasse. Mais le plus essentiel et le plus original dans nos conceptions les plus étendues et les plus profondes est incommunicable par la

parole, et ce que je ressentais ne pouvait être exprimé précisément que par la liturgie et je n'étais si ému que parce que je voyais exprimé par nous tous ce qui ne peut être exprimé par la parole individuelle.
[*Mes Cahiers, Œuvre* xv 343–4]

La forme de ma pensée, elle se dresse en pierre au milieu de chaque village. Son clocher la signale de loin. J'y entre et parmi ceux qui prient je suis bien pour méditer.
[*Mes Cahiers, Œuvre* xvi 249]

The human condition is a mixed one, as Barrès implies continually by the use of antithetically paired key words such as 'ardent' and 'clairvoyant,' 'musique' and 'science,' 'mystère' and 'lumière,' 'prairie' and 'chapelle,'[26] and by his fondness for philosophical dialogues in the manner of Renan,[27] and as he states from time to time explicitly, for example in the following characteristic defence of the 'material expressions' of the Christian tradition suggested by Émile Boutroux's similar views regarding the purely 'imaginative' and 'symbolic' definition it is desirable and possible to give to religious inspiration:

Ces hommes supérieurs, ces Faust, ils ont leurs rêveries, leurs imaginations, leur esprit, leur religion. Vous l'admettez, vous le

26 *Œuvre* i 40 ('ardente,' 'clairvoyante'), 366 ('enthousiasmes,' 'clairvoyants'); iii 486 ('excitation,' 'clairvoyance'); xix 116 ('science,' 'musique'); i 142 ('musique,' 'géométrie'); xiii 20 ('harmonie,' 'pensée'); xiv 133 ('sentiment,' 'géométrie'); xv 211 ('panthéisme... rythme,' 'ordre ... science'); xviii 8–9 ('enthousiasme,' 'science'); xii 193 ('ténèbres,' 'lumière'); xii 197 ('ciel obscur,' 'lumière'); xii 228 ('profond,' 'clair'); vii 122 ('ombres,' 'pleine lumière'); v 551 ('profondeurs ... ténèbres,' 'plein jour'); x 136 ('mystère,' 'lumière'); xi 101 ('mystères,' 'lumière'); xii 113 ('plein jour ... cœur mystérieux'); xii 141 ('mystère en pleine lumière'); x 522 ('le germanique à la lumière du Rhin'); xv 157 ('Mettre à la clarté du soleil des parties voilées de mon âme'); xviii 284 ('le mystère,' 'le clair'); xix 46 ('lumière,' 'ténèbres'); xix 196 ('ténèbres,' 'lumière'); xii 19; xx 73 ('mystère en pleine lumière'); xx 166 ('traduire en idées claires ... le mystère qui bourdonnent autour des orchestres'); vi 499–500 ('prairie,' 'chapelle'); viii 9 ('rivière,' 'chapelle'); ii 189 ('prairie,' 'cité').

27 *See* above, Chapter Three, p. 50, note 30.

> leur passez. Mais 'vous voulez que cette religion soit exclusivement esprit et vie et vous êtes choqués si elle vient à se manifester dans des conceptions et dans des expressions matérielles.' Pourtant il faut des formules. L'esprit ne peut se réaliser sans s'incarner dans une matière...
> [*Mes Cahiers, Œuvre* XVI 317][28]

'Between man and the invisible,' he wrote after his visit four years later to the Temple of Afaka at the source of the Adonis, 'there is a secret ... harmony.' The human experience is not complete without some quickening 'encounter' with the mysteriously 'other' order with which it is man's destiny to cohabit: 'ce phénomène, nommez-le comme vous voudrez, qui nous fait entrer en relations avec une réalité, un être, une présence, une chose invisible, insaisissable, intraduisible et différente de nous' (*Œuvre* XI 173–4). But the only valid expressions of this strictly speaking 'untranslatable' phenomenon are 'acts' and 'poems.' These are necessarily coloured by the material circumstances of history, place, and temperament under which the flesh-bound spirit of man 'makes contact' with the Absolute Other. They may thus be appropriately shaped by religious conventions which have stood the test of time in a given milieu, just as a purely individual literary inspiration may achieve significant form in the fixed metrical patterns and rhyme-schemes of a familiar verse tradition:

> quand il y a eu en nous cet accroissement de chaleur et que nous avons pris ce contact, fût-ce pour une seconde, nous rendre compte à nous-mêmes de cette rencontre, et la traduire, soit par des actes, soit par des poèmes, c'est le désir héroïque des grands esprits. Mais de vrais poèmes, qui ne soient pas des divagations, mais des

28 Cf. E. Boutroux, *Science et religion dans la philosophie contemporaine*, (Paris: Flammarion 1908) 382–3: 'Telle, l'inspiration religieuse se traduit par des conceptions qui, pour nous, débordent nécessairement l'expérience, puisqu'elles concernent la source même de la vie, et qui se présentent comme des révélations. ... Ces conceptions veulent être définies, fixées dans une formule, c'est-à-dire, en somme, dans une image. Cette image ne peut être qu'un symbole.'

> actes raisonnables, conformes à l'ordre et vraiment féconds! L'expérience laissée à son impulsion unique ne produirait que l'absurde: il faut la régler. C'est l'immense service que l'Église rend à l'humanité, quand elle surveille, modère et canalise l'enthousiasme mystique, quand elle l'entretient et tout ensemble l'apaise, par ses rites stimulants et paisibles, par ses sacrements. Et c'est ainsi que, de leur côté, les poètes soumettent aux heureuses contraintes du rythme et de la rime une inspiration qui, libre de tout contrôle, ne serait que du vent.
> [*Une Enquête aux pays du Levant, Œuvre* XI 174][29]

This reflection on the poetic principle of religions in a pagan setting ('l'idée religieuse d'Afaka, comment la saisir? ... C'est tout le but de mon expédition ... Les femmes ici devenaient bacchantes ... À l'origine de ces brutalités et de ces grandeurs, il y a un principe religieux. Principe très simple, petite source toujours la même' [*Œuvre* XI 172–3]) echoes Barrès's regularly mythopoetic interpretation of Christian worship, for example the following entry in *Mes Cahiers* written about four months after he had suffered the trauma of his nephew Charles Demange's suicide:[30]

> Si je suis dans une église, si je vois la messe, quelle poésie! Comment un simple homme (je ne parle pas d'un Faust, qui peut se créer un système du monde par delà le domaine de la raison et de la science, sans les contredire, avec ses seules forces; d'une âme qui crée Dieu), comment un simple homme est-il insensible? On le guide vers l'invisible, le surnaturel, le divin, on le met se voyant [*sic*] en rapport avec l'ordre universel.
> C'est l'endroit où la curiosité humaine déborde le domaine du rationnel, se demande si l'histoire a un sens, si l'humanité marche vers un but, si nous-même...

29 Cf. *Œuvre* XII 324–5, and XIII 326, *cit.* H. Clouard, *Histoire de la littérature française du Symbolisme à nos jours* (Paris: Albin Michel 1947–9) I 315: 'J'aime cette discipline dont je suis né à travers les siècles pour prendre la forme. Elle me contraint, elle m'assujettit, mais j'y sens mieux ma force. J'y suis comme la pensée dans un poème à forme fixe.'

30 *See* Chapter Four, p. 71, note 74.

> Agitation sans trêve et sans fin.
> 'Rien ne nous donne la clef universelle, la vraie et souveraine formule du divin ouvrier, laquelle surpasse vraisemblablement l'ordre de nos idées, de nos observations et de nos raisonnements.'
> [*Mes Cahiers, Œuvre* XVI 225–6]

Barrès is very close here to the most subtle exponent of post-Baudelairean rhetoric in France:

> La vie intérieure ... on ne saurait la représenter par des images. Mais on la représenterait bien moins encore par des *concepts*, c'est-à-dire par des idées abstraites, ou générales, ou simples ... Or l'image a du moins cet avantage qu'elle nous maintient dans le concret. Nulle image ne remplacera l'intuition de la durée, mais beaucoup d'images diverses ... pourront, par la convergence de leur action, diriger la conscience sur le point précis où il y a une certaine intuition à saisir.
> [H. Bergson, 'Introduction à la métaphysique,' *La Pensée et le mouvant* (Paris: PUF 1962) 185]

No would-be master-formula is transparent to the whole truth. But just as, at a point of intuition to which his consciousness has been guided indirectly by the suggestive power of many convergent images, Bergsonian man makes 'sympathetic' contact with a transcendent 'eternity of life' which, it is alleged, conceptual thought can never grasp,[31] so those 'ordinary' people who cannot, like Faust (or a Michelangelo)[32] 'create their own God' may, according to Barrès, be brought into touch with the 'universal order' by the 'poetry' that has been handed down in the religious tradition of their nation, as an orderly if incomplete system of familiar, oblique pointers to the ultimate meaning of human life and history lying beyond the range of observation and reason.

How Barrès uses his own imagination in the service of tradition in France will be examined in the chapters which follow: 'Imagination in Barrès's Rhetoric.'

31 H. Bergson, *La Pensée et le mouvant*, 188–9, 210–11
32 Chapter Three, p. 22 and *Œuvre* II 162, *cit.* Chapter Five, p. 96, note 5

PART III:

IMAGINATION IN BARRÈS'S RHETORIC

3 Maurice Barrès at Gerbéviller-la-Martyre in 1916
Collection Philippe Barrès

INTRODUCTORY NOTE

ON PROPAGANDA AND EDUCATION

Propaganda and education are generally contrasted: the first defined as a 'systematic' form of persuasion which tends to enclose the mind in prejudice; the second said to be 'informative,' meant to open the mind.[1] It is, however, commonly recognized also that in many circumstances propaganda and education overlap: 'What almost always occurs is a combination of the two, or the influence [of an individual upon his contemporaries] can be variously appraised by observers with different conceptions of science and value ... Propaganda ... operates where there is no science or when people's values are in conflict.'[2] These were the conditions prevailing in the field of political and religious opinion that Barrès chose to cultivate during the middle years of the Third Republic. Thus the kind of 'national education' he advocated for school and after was as mixed with propaganda as the state system to which it was opposed. On the other hand, his propaganda for adults was of the didactic rather than the coercive sort, showing readiness to argue and demonstrate a point of view earnestly and honestly and almost always, in its mature form at any rate, respect for and tolerance of 'many sectional and individual differences,' together with the will to 'plan ahead and for the long view.' These are all features proper to education: 'an attempt to influence

1 C. Morris, *Signs, Language and Behaviour* (New York: Prentice-Hall 1946) 102–4, 123–52; L.W. Doob, *Public Opinion and Propaganda* (London: The Crescent Press 1949) 23–55; F.C. Bartlett, *Political Propaganda* (Cambridge: Cambridge University Press 1940) 5–6.

2 L.W. Doob, *Public Opinion and Propaganda*, 240–2

and control thinking and conduct, but to do so in such a manner that the persons who think and act are stimulated to seek to understand for themselves why they do what they do.'[3] In the pages following, Barrès's views on education will be studied separately from his art of adult persuasion (by journalism, oratory, and literature), not because they are more or less inclined towards propagandistic or educative ends, as defined above (Barrès originally intended to call *Scènes et doctrines du nationalisme*: 'L'Éducation nationaliste' [*Mes Cahiers, Œuvre* XIII 249]), but because they naturally take special account of features and circumstances found mainly, if not exclusively, among the school-children that his pedagogical method was primarily designed for.

3 F.C. Bartlett, *Political Propaganda*, 153

CHAPTER SEVEN

Function and Forms of the Persuasive Image

DIRECTION AND STIMULUS

Barrès's nationalism began as a protest against what he believed to be the disorientation and paralysis of French drive and purpose that the Third Republic had inherited from the declining years of the Second Empire (*Mes Cahiers, Œuvre* XIII 5; XX 155). The first volume of *Le Roman de l'énergie nationale* contains a diagnosis of this French sickness in terms borrowed from Jules Soury and Jean Izoulet:

> nous avons cru reconnaître que la France est dissociée et décérébrée.
>
> Des parties importantes du pays ne reçoivent plus d'impulsion, un cerveau leur manque qui remplisse près d'elles son rôle de protection, qui leur permette d'éviter un obstacle, d'écarter un danger. Il y a en France une non-coordination des efforts. Chez les individus, c'est à de tels signes qu'on diagnostique les prodromes de la paralysie générale.
>
> [*Les Déracinés, Œuvre* III 193]

In the second volume of the trilogy, a dialogue, characteristic of Barrès's moments of crucial stock-taking, between Sturel, the most restless and demanding, and Saint-Phlin, the most settled and practical of the *déracinés,* recapitulates his earlier diagnosis and indicates the lines along which he thought the nationalist cure must be followed:

> – ...Il n'y a plus de coordination entre les efforts des Français; nous ne connaissons pas ce que nous sommes ni par suite ce que nous devenons.
> – Très bien! ... Alors?
> – Alors je sens diminuer, disparaître la nationalité française, c'est-à-dire la substance qui me soutient, et sans laquelle je m'évanouirais. Il faut reprendre, protéger, augmenter cette énergie héritée de nos pères. Et pour cette tâche, sans m'enfermer dans aucun parti, je fais appel à la bonne volonté de tous mes compatriotes...
> – Tu veux donner une direction commune aux énergies françaises, les coordonner; il faudrait d'abord nous rendre compte de ce qu'elles sont dans l'état actuel et puis analyser dans quelles conditions elles seraient unies. Et voici que j'arrive à t'exposer mon projet d'enquête, ce fameux plan de voyage qui va prendre son plein sens dans ton esprit préparé...
> Nous prendrons une leçon de choses.
> [*L'Appel au soldat*, *Œuvre* IV 18–20][1]

Realism, opposed to the 'abstractions,' 'verbalism' or 'idealism' of the Radical and Socialist Left and of the Royalist Right,[2] was a notable and, in regard to the Left, a well-advertised feature of Barrès's nationalism; and Saint-Phlin's plan to make an 'object lesson' ('leçon de choses') out of a cycling tour of the Moselle valley with his former school friend was an early example of it: ' – Voyons, nous faisons ce voyage pour que je prenne contact avec les réalités ... Je ne veux pas me payer de mots... '(*L'Appel au soldat*, *Œuvre* IV 42). But Barrès's

1 'Ce qui fait une force, ce n'est pas seulement l'intensité, c'est encore la direction.' (*Œuvre* IV 307.) 'Oui, mais dans l'énergie il y a l'intensité et la direction. Voilà les deux choses essentielles à considérer.' (*Œuvre* XIII 5–8). Cf. J. Izoulet, *La Cité moderne,* 539: 'pas de mouvement sans direction. Toute force est tendance.'

2 *See* p. 281.

notion of reality was strongly coloured by his epistemological relativism: *objective* knowledge of what 'things in themselves' *actually are* lies beyond the scope of human understanding (*Les Déracinés, Œuvre* III 148 *cit.* above, pp. 54–5). So the purpose of an object lesson cannot be to inculcate realism in this sense. What he believed an object lesson could do in the way of nationalist propaganda was to 'realize' ideas *tangibly*:

> Nous voulons d'une politique qui tienne compte des traditions nationales et qui protège tout ce qu'elles ont encore de vivant au milieu des modifications que le temps apporte chez les êtres vivants, chez des êtres en perpétuelle transformation...
>
> Voilà ce qu'Henri Vaugeois nous a dit d'une façon philosophique, et pour *sentir* ce qu'il nous a *démontré*, nous pourrions prendre des 'leçons de choses.' Ah! si nous pouvions circuler tous ensemble ... à travers les paysages français! si nous prenions connaissance de la figure de notre pays!
>
> ...
>
> Pour ma part, je voudrais être votre cicérone en Lorraine. [*Scènes et doctrines du nationalisme, Œuvre* V 124–5]

Barrès's 'real France' (*Œuvre* V 424; VII 172) was a picture in perspective rather than a matter of objective fact:

> QU'EST-CE QUE LA VÉRITÉ?
>
> Ce n'est point des choses à savoir, c'est de trouver un certain point, un point unique, celui-là, nul autre, d'où toutes choses nous apparaissent avec des proportions vraies.
>
> Précisons davantage. Combien j'aime cette phrase d'un peintre qui disait: 'Corot, c'est un homme qui sait s'asseoir.'
>
> Il me faut m'asseoir au point exact que réclament mes yeux tels que me les firent les siècles, au point d'où toutes choses se disposent à la mesure d'un Français. L'ensemble de ces rapports justes et vrais entre des objets donnés et un homme déterminé, le Français, c'est la vérité et la justice françaises; trouver ces rapports, c'est la raison française. Et le nationalisme net, ce n'est rien autre que

de savoir l'existence de ce point, de le chercher, et l'ayant atteint, de nous y tenir pour prendre de là notre art, notre politique et toutes nos activités.
[*Scènes et doctrines du nationalisme, Œuvre* v 27]

Failure to see where the true interests of France lay in the midst of its Dreyfus Revolution was less characteristic, thought Barrès, of the untutored or misinformed person's ignorance of facts than it was of people whose acquired, often sophisticated opinions, conflicted with their spontaneous convictions, allegedly moulded in depth by heredity and history:

Vous rencontrez beaucoup d'hommes-mensonges dans la vie ... ils disent, et même ils croient penser des choses qui, de l'extérieur, sont tombées au fond de leur conscience ... des individus qui ne se mettent pas d'accord avec eux-mêmes et qui contrarient leur innéité font de détestables éléments sociaux. Au lieu d'être un mot dans une phrase commencée par leurs pères et que continueront leurs fils, ils bégaient, coupent tout le sens.
[*Les Amitiés françaises, Œuvre* v 478]

In order to try to stimulate a nationally unanimous response in the deep patriotic sensibility that he believed all his countrymen must share, beneath the divergencies of their superficially acquired ideologies, Barrès developed a range of imaginative devices, limited by the *formule* at one extreme and the *leçon de choses* at the other, all of which were designed specifically to represent not facts in themselves ('des choses à savoir') but the bearing of facts on the rights and duties of Frenchmen ('l'ensemble de ces rapports justes et vrais entre des objets donnés et un homme déterminé, le Français'), a propaganda program relying for its principle techniques of persuasion on the rough and ready combination of Izoulet's associationist sociology ('Oui, l'association prend un anthropoïde et rend un homme')[3] and the associationist psychology expounded by Soury ('les idées ... les

3 'Izoulet au Collège de France,' *Le Journal* 1 January 1898

jugements ... sont des façons de sentir générales et se retrouvent chez tous les êtres de même organisme assiégés par les mêmes images').[4]

FORMULE, MOT, VERBE

'Formulae' get as mixed a reception in Barrès's theory of persuasion as they receive in his philosophy of tradition. Their value as slogans (*sluaghghairm*, the Gael's warcry) he recognized very early:

> 'À bas les Juifs!' sera-t-il le titre d'un chapitre de notre histoire intérieure? La foule eut toujours besoin d'un mot de guerre pour se rallier, elle veut quelque cri de passion qui fasse tangible les idées abstraites. Jamais cette vérité ne fut plus évidente qu'à l'heure présente où les déshérités sont las des programmes et même des discussions.
>
> ...juif n'est qu'un adjectif désignant les usuriers, les accapareurs, les joueurs de Bourse, tous ceux qui abusent de l'argent...
>
> ...Voilà donc une des plus belles formules de haine.
>
> ['La formule antijuive,' *Le Figaro* 22 February 1890]

Twenty years' experience confirmed this first analysis of the power of formulae to excite and to rally:

> J'écoute, je vois sur la Chambre le pouvoir magique de certains mots. Brisson, c'est le guérisseur du secret. Avec des formules toujours les mêmes et qui semblent quasi dépourvues de sens, on déchaîne dans les êtres des sentiments, on groupe les êtres, on les transforme.
>
> Ces formules servent à rappeler au peuple ses directions. Cohérence et excitation. Ils émeuvent des sentiments antérieurs, les parties affectives et mystiques.
>
> [*Mes Cahiers, Œuvre* XVII 210][5]

4 *Scènes et doctrines du nationalisme, Œuvre* V 31. Cf. *Mes Cahiers, Œuvre* XIII 57 (*Jules Soury*)

5 *See* G. Le Bon, *Psychologie des foules* 40th ed. (Paris: Alcan 1937) 84 ff.: 'Les images, les mots et les formules.'

Nationalism too he believed, 'must be a formula ready at hand for whenever it is needed' (*Mes Cahiers, Œuvre* XIV 287). The nationalist view of Alsace-Lorraine, for instance, could be summed up in a formula that is at once descriptive and directive:

> La romanisation des Germains est la tendance constante de l'Alsacien-Lorrain.
>
> Telle est la formule où j'aboutis dans mes méditations de Sainte-Odile. Elle a l'avantage de réunir un très grand nombre de faits et de satisfaire mon préjugé de Latin vaincu par la Germanie. J'y trouve un motif d'action et une discipline ... Je ... propose un système de direction qui tienne compte des rapports qu'il y eut toujours entre la France, l'Alsace-Lorraine et la Germanie, en même temps qu'elle nous justifie d'agir comme nous tendons naturellement à faire. Ainsi je puis dire que ce système contient de très nombreux faits historiques et tout notre cœur.
> [*Au service de l'Allemagne, Œuvre* VI 64–5]

But simultaneously his mistrust of those who possessed 'the gift of hollow formulae,' 'father of tempests,' 'arming every passion,' increased (though he continued to recognize the redoubtable power of this gift when allied to political realism, in a Mirabeau, a Danton, a Gambetta, a Jaurès) (*Le Mystère en pleine lumière, Œuvre* XII 253); and the words *formule* and *mot*, now usually denoting abstract as opposed to 'tangible' expressions, appear most frequently, after 1900, as terms of abuse for condemning as inoperative or confusing the 'verbalism' of propaganda that is adverse or uncongenial to Barrès's cause:

> Certaines personnes croient avoir atteint un idéal d'autant plus élevé qu'elles ont mieux étouffé en elles la voix du sang et l'instinct du territoire. Elles préfèrent se rallier à des formules, vides le plus souvent, et qui, fussent-elles pleines d'intentions excellentes, seraient comme toutes les formules, incapables d'agir sur nos sentiments et sur notre conduite.
> ['Novembre à la campagne,' *Le Journal* 6 November 1900]

His early, unqualified, enthusiasm for the power of the 'Word' (*'le*

Verbe') to move crowds and assemblies in unison[6] developed, with experience, into a more narrowly defined verbal rhetoric which aims at the excitement and direction of public sentiment by words specially chosen for their power of associating effective tone and mental image:[7]

> Contre l'expression abstraite. (Darmesteter. *Les Prophètes*, p. 379.)
> 'Moïse et les Prophètes ne parlaient guère par abstractions; chez eux plus que nul autre l'idée est image et c'est pour cela que l'idée vit, éclate et rayonne. *Il n'y a dans l'univers, même spirituel, que des mouvements et des couleurs, et, par suite, il n'y a de vivant et de durable dans la parole que le cri et l'éclair.*'
> [*Mes Cahiers, Œuvre* XIV 236]

Barrès's approach to the art of propaganda followed a path parallel to the one he had outwardly taken once and for all after leaving behind him the cerebral 'madness' of *Le Culte du Moi*, but which inwardly he went over again and again; which was for him, in fact, a deeply scored mental track:

> Parfois je suis dans mon cabinet, il n'y a que mon cerveau qui aime ma Lorraine. Je raisonne, j'intellectualise, je suis un déraciné, plongé dans les mots, dans les idées, c'est-à-dire dans un pur néant. Mais voici que je vais à la promenade: l'air doux me baigne, l'horizon rafraîchit mes yeux, de tout mon corps je me conforme à ma Lorraine. Je cesse de penser; je suis maintenant une plante lorraine, heureux, joyeux, intéressé par tous mes sens.
> Des formules ne donnent rien. On ne les comprend pas. On les répète comme une algèbre. On se sert des mêmes mots. C'est qu'aucun des mots des formules ne contient rien. L'ineffable.
> [*Mes Cahiers, Œuvre* XIV 211]

6 'L'Enseignement de Lourdes,' *Le Figaro* 15 September 1894: 'Le Verbe toujours mène le monde ... par le Verbe les foules les plus disparates sont animées d'un même mouvement.'

7 *See* p. 281.

RÉCIT, IMAGE, SYMBOLE, LEÇON DE CHOSES

'Des formules ne donnent rien.' On the other hand, 'leçons de choses' are equally unproductive if things are to be left to speak for themselves:

> Il est impossible d'aimer, voire de comprendre, aucun objet si nous n'avons pas mêlé nos songes à sa réalité, établi un lien entre lui et notre vie.
> [*Colette Baudoche, Œuvre* VI 211]

The most effective way Barrès knew of expressing this necessary 'link' between external objects and personal experience – 'the world outside the artist and the artist himself' (C. Baudelaire, 'L'Art philosophique')[8] was what he called the *récit*:

> Un récit, c'est l'impression reçue par une conscience, par une imagination, par un être humain; c'est une âme qui pense, qui donne de l'émotion, le sentiment qu'elle a reçu d'un fait.
> [*Mes Cahiers, Œuvre* XVII 42]

The imaginative character of the Barresian *récit* is suggested in the notes for a working plan which accompany this definition of its use:

> Des détails reçus par notre esprit doivent s'y marier, se pénétrer, s'accommoder les uns avec les autres, en prenant contact ils prennent des rangs, le plus coloré devant dominer l'autre...
> Moi qui ne sais rien de la musique je sens si bien que ma pensée, que mon thème pourrait se traduire en musique.
> [*Mes Cahiers, Œuvre* XVII 41–2]

The pages headed 'Esthétique' from which these paragraphs are taken refer to the art of the novel in general and to *La Colline inspirée* in particular, and echo the fullest description Barrès left of his experience of literary creation, written the previous summer (1910).[9] He defined

8 C. Baudelaire, *Œuvres complètes,* 1099
9 *Œuvre* XVI 342–4, *cit.* Chapter Twelve, pp. 252–4

late in his career, and practised only in *La Colline inspirée,* and in his relatively uncommitted last novel, *Un Jardin sur l'Oronte*, this complete interpenetration of details in an imaginative whole that is close to music yet tells a story, and which was his idea of what a *récit* should be. But, as he showed in his defence of the completed *Colline inspirée*, even in the inexplicit, leisurely, and indirect art of the *récit* there was room for a sharper and more abbreviated and straightforward means of 'making himself understood,' which was yet opposed to the 'definitions,' 'theories' and 'formulae' he wanted to avoid:[10] the episode of the pagan idol disinterred from the slopes of Sion-Vaudémont, for instance, and meeting the jeers of the vulgar, the rigours of the Church, and the obscure reverence of Barrès's hero:

> Soit la scène de la statue. Elle est clairissime dans ses profondeurs pour le vrai lecteur que je désire. Que j'y ajoute des commentaires, je déchaînerai telles colères et je ne contenterai personne. Les symboles valent infiniment mieux que les théories ... À ces profondeurs-là, toutes les formules sont fausses, irritantes, décevantes. [*Mes Cahiers, Œuvre* XVII 284]

In his earlier novels and essays, and in the necessarily rough, plain, and hasty arts of journalistic, parliamentary, and platform persuasion he had mastered between Boulangism and the Affair, and which he continued to employ for the four great campaigns of his maturity: *La Grande pitié des églises de France, Chronique de la Grande Guerre, Le Génie du Rhin*, and *Une Enquête aux pays du Levant*, such isolated symbols, used as the starting-point or as the culminating synthesis of theoretical argument or an exposition of facts, stand out as one of the most characteristic of Barrès's rhetorical devices.[11] Of these campaigns, *Le Génie du Rhin* (five lectures given at the University of Strasbourg in 1920, and published with a preface the following year) was prepared with the most deliberation, and cost most in rejected notes and repressed lyricism (*Œuvre* X 35–8). It is also the most

10 *Œuvre* XVII 282–4

11 E.g. *Œuvre* I 211–12, 320–3; III 153–4; VIII i, 55, 64, 100–2; X 134–5; XI 121–3, 187, 232, 351–2, 365, 452, 470–2; *Grande Guerre* III 79; VI 58; VII 179; VIII 21–4, 27, 154; X 210, 214, 293; XII 293

methodical and self-conscious example of Barrès's use of imaginative synthesis in unadulterated propaganda, what he calls 'une prédication nationale' [34]. The 'enumeration of individual and precise facts,' heightened and dramatized by passing metaphors, gives way in the last lecture to the abstract formulation of the 'direction' the orator wishes to give his audience:

> Il nous faut une direction des esprits, une pensée commune, un terrain d'entente...
>
> Cette direction, tous les faits que nous venons de recueillir nous permettent de la formuler comme suit: la France sur le Rhin doit agir de telle manière qu'elle incline les Rhénans à concevoir un idéal spirituel, politique et social qui les détourne à tout jamais du germanisme de Berlin et qui les amène à rentrer en contact plus étroit avec la culture latine, avec notre esprit occidental. [*Le Génie du Rhin, Œuvre* X 133–4]

Then, almost immediately, and in conclusion, Barrès selects what he calls elsewhere 'une belle image, propre à fixer les idées' (*Mes Cahiers, Œuvre* XVII 225):

> Messieurs, à ce point de notre cours et quand il va s'achever, me permettrez-vous de synthétiser par une image saisissante et simple l'esprit même de nos analyses? [*Le Génie du Rhin, Œuvre* X 134]

And the whole *prédication*, apart from an exordium directed specially at the Alsatians and Lorrainers in the hall, culminates in the opposition of two representative images: the massive, helmeted figure of Germania ('image d'une certaine Allemagne') erected after 1870 in the Bingen gap, and a statue of Joan of Arc which Barrès wanted on the banks of the Rhine 'comme un signe de l'apostolat français et de la force rayonnante qu'il y eut toujours dans notre nation.'

Straightforward academic exposition of the kind required from Barrès at Strasbourg in 1920 was rare in his work as a propagandist; his characteristic technique of imaginative climax, for instance, had been acquired in the very different atmosphere of partisan politics:

writing to a newspaper editor's deadline or speaking against the storm-waves of an election meeting or a parliamentary debate. For such occasions he had command of a polemical register that was at once more brutal than the tone he considered appropriate to academic discourse, or an address to political friends [*see*, for example, *Discours pour l'Anniversaire de l'Action française* (15 June 1901), *Œuvre* v 123–8], and more immediate in its intention than the interpenetrating colours and the suggestion in depth that he tried to produce for his literary essays and novels (apart, of course, from the 'scenes' of contemporary French political warfare that he transposed directly into such novels as *Leurs figures* and such collected articles, essays, and *croquis* as *Scènes et doctrines du nationalisme* and *Dans le cloaque* (*Œuvre* IV, VI, and VIII), which are, on the contrary, deliberately raw and extremely violent). Two interlocking examples of graded hyperbole in images perfectly judged to produce the emotional shock which can rivet attention and excite controversy in an assembly are to be found in his 'Premier discours pour les églises,' delivered to the Chamber of Deputies on 16 January 1911, amid noisy interruptions:

> *M. Maurice Barrès.* – Il est intéressant de chercher à comprendre les divers étages du sentiment religieux dans la population française...
> *M. Léon Perrier* (Isère). – La religion chrétienne est pleine de ces superstitions. Voyez saint Expédit!
> *M. César Trouin.* – Et saint Antoine de Padoue?
> *M. Maurice Barrès.* – ...sous une épaisseur plus ou moins forte de christianisme, demeurent d'obscures survivances du paganisme, toute une barbarie prête à remonter à la surface, des débris du passé, des détritus de religion, auxquels la civilisation n'a aucun intérêt à laisser la place libre...
> ...
> Je ne veux d'autre preuve de cette barbarie toute prête à réapparaître que les scènes scandaleuses qui se sont passées à Grisy-Suisnes sur les décombres de la vieille église ... des hommes brutaux, excités par les pourboires ... faisant danser le rigodon aux corps qu'ils déterraient, au milieu des petits enfants accourus de l'école (*Exclamations*). Le cœur se soulève de dégoût.

> *M. Jacques-Louis Dumesnil.* – C'est absolument inexact. Comme représentant de Seine-et-Marne, je connais la question...
> *M. Maurice Barrès.* – Quelles mesures de défense prendrez-vous contre ces nouveaux barbares qui, hier, au sortir de l'encan, traînaient dans les ruisseaux de Grisy le drap des morts?
> [*La Grande pitié des églises de France, Œuvre* VIII 55–7]

Such functional variations of tone being understood,[12] Barrès's preparatory notes for *Le Génie du Rhin* may be seen to show a preoccupation with the effects of imaginative discourse that is characteristic of his rhetoric as a whole: 'il faut intéresser l'imagination et le cœur aux Rhénans, sympathiser avec leur secret, donner de l'âme aux documents les plus secs' (*Mes Cahiers, Œuvre* XIX 194).

There is no hard and fast distinction in the terminology of Barrès's art of persuasion between *image* and *symbole*. Both are figurative devices: actual, mental, sense, or word pictures conveying, explicitly or implicitly, an abstract tenor. Both terms may refer to the same picture.[13] Both work on the imagination.[14] *Symbole* is usually found where the stress is laid on the tenor of the expression (normally designated explicitly by a prepositional phrase) and also where Barrès suggests that a distortion or dilution of reality is involved. It tends there-

12 I am indebted for the points made in the last paragraph, and for the examples of Barrès's polemical imagery from *La Grande pitié des églises de France* chosen to illustrate them, to Mme I.-M. Frandon, who has also been kind enough to contribute the following valuable comment: 'Les images de cette dernière séquence ont, chacune prise en elle-même, un caractère conventionnel (les barbares, l'encan, les ruisseaux, le drap des morts). Mais, réunies, elle tendent à traduire et à provoquer le paroxysme du mépris.'

13 E.g. 'J'ai appris à lire dans une *Histoire de France* ... remplie d'images sur bois qui vivent dans mon âme profonde: symboles vénérables autour desquels je classe toutes mes connaissances' (*Œuvre* VI 75). 'L'idée de la Société des Nations ... est pour lui [President Wilson] simplement une image, un symbole destiné à faire comprendre qu'il y a quelque chose au-dessus des nations' (*Grande Guerre* XI 20).

14 E.g. 'la colline de Sion-Vaudémont ... c'est le point où l'imagination peut le mieux se poser pour comprendre le génie propre de la Lorraine. Quel symbole d'une nation ...' (*Œuvre* VI 275–6). '"Un moyen d'agir sur le sentiment par des symboles concrets, par l'imagination." C'est trop peut dire. Konia' (*Œuvre* XX 107).

fore towards the meaning he gave *formule*.[15] *Image*, which he uses more often than *symbole*, usually occurs in contexts, or with an adjective, which direct attention to the living or life-like reality of the vehicle and its natural correspondence with the tenor: its implied synonyms range away from formulae, through metaphors,[16] icons,[17] fictional paragons,[18] land- and town-scapes fashioned by history,[19] exemplary events, and lives from legend and history,[20] to those 'object lessons' that come nearest in Barrès's rhetoric of images to persuasion by fact.[21]

An excellent example of the generally divergent connotations of *symbole* and *image* in Barrès's propaganda is his use of Joan of Arc as the 'symbol' of his patriotic theme, and his use of iconographical, legendary, and biographical 'images' of her to realize this symbol.[22]

15 E.g. 'le drapeau est le symbole de certaines réalités et ces réalités, nous voulons les reconnaître' (*Œuvre* v 121). 'Odile ... le symbole de la plus haute moralité alsacienne' (*Œuvre* vi 63). 'une tête de Christ qu'il a sculptée dans ses loisirs ... je me surprends à voir là un symbole de la force éternelle qui sommeille dans cette terre privilégiée' (*Grande Guerre* viii 154). 'Il est curieux de voir dans Mathiez ... quel effort fit la Révolution pour donner une forme, un corps, des symboles et un culte à cette religion de la patrie, de la raison, de la liberté et de la justice...' (*Œuvre* xvii 293).

16 E.g. 'Je m'attache d'une manière coupable aux images mondaines qu'employe la sainte [Teresa]' (*Œuvre* xii 38). 'Quelles saisissantes images révélatrices de toute une civilisation, dans ce titre espagnol: *El tizon de la Nobleza Española o Maculos y Sambenitos de sus linajes?* Le Tison, le bois brûlé, noirci, fumeux, sans étincelle, la branche quasi morte de l'arbre héraldique' (*Œuvre* vii 364).

17 *See* p. 281.

18 E.g. 'Bérénice ... il faut qu'en toi tout crie l'instinct et que tu sois l'image la plus complète ... des forces de la nature' (*Œuvre* i 329). 'Colette ... une vive image de Metz' (*Œuvre* vi 249).

19 E.g. 'Une chapelle sur le bord d'une rivière rapide, une pierre éternelle dressée auprès d'une eau qui s'écoule, quelle image et quel thème de réflexions infinies' (*Œuvre* viii 9). 'une ville tassée, assoupie, demi-submergée dans la plus jeune verdure, et par-dessus, là-haut, le grand mur sérieux de Byzance et des Croisades; quelle image, dont je me nourris!' (*Œuvre* xi 365).

20 *See* p. 282.

21 *See* p. 282.

22 *See* pp. 282–3.

CHAPTER EIGHT

The Cult of Heroes

LEGEND AS A MEANS OF INTERCESSION

The first kind of propaganda Barrès used systematically was hero-worship. This was a salient feature of his editorial policy for *La Cocarde* from September 1894 to March 1895:

> C'est dans ce souci nationaliste que les rédacteurs de la *Cocarde* affirmèrent à plusieurs reprises, et d'une façon spéciale leur conviction quant à l'utilité des héros et même quant à la nécessité de servir un culte aux grandes figures de l'histoire.
> ['Histoire intérieure d'un Journal,'
> *La Revue encyclopédique* 15 November 1895]

The acknowledged sources of Barrès's nationalist cult of heroes were 'poet-philosophers' nourished by the 'realities' of history: Comte, Mickiewicz, and Barrès's Emersonian and Carlylist contemporary, Jean Izoulet.[1] But Barrès had 'used' the great, as guides and patterns,

1 Cf. 'Discours pour la Pologne,' *La Pologne* 1 April 1923: 'à 20 ans j'allais avec M. A. Chodzo, professeur au Collège de France ... qui ... me racontait les grands jours de Mickiewicz.' And 'La Glorification de l'énergie,' *La Cocarde* 19 December 1894; 'L'Utilité des héros,' *La Cocarde* 20 December 1894; 'Un philosophe du "Moi",' *La Cocarde* 20 January 1895; 'Izoulet au Collège de France,' *Le Journal* 1 January 1898; *Mes Cahiers, Œuvre* XIII 83; also 'Déroulède et Tolstoï,' *Le Journal* 17 August 1894 and 'Pas d'archéologie,' *La Cocarde* 10 February 1895.

before ever assuming a political rôle, and used them with the same characteristic disregard for plain historical objectivity as would later inform his nationalist 'realism' (*see* above, pp. 54–6 and 124–6). What Barrès needed at all times from his heroes was a legend, sublimated from the raw material of their real lives and symbolizing an exemplary ideal. This particular way of using heroes bears the hallmark of French Romantic historiography: 'L'inexactitude c'est Michelet, c'est Lamartine' ('L'esthétique de l'interview,' *Le Journal* 2 December 1892). Though he mistrusted the abstract tendency of Michelet's patriotism ('la haute et abstraite unité de la patrie' [*Tableau de la France*]) : 'Léon Blum et Michelet veulent m'affranchir de ces nécessités. Je hausse les épaules' (*Mes Cahiers, Œuvres* XIV 174), he refused to sacrifice him to the anti-Romanticism of *Action Française*: 'J'ai horreur de l'ingratitude ... Il est un instant de notre passé et demeure une portion de notre vie. Mais il y a la conscience française' (*Mes Cahiers, Œuvre* XIII 249; XIV 96). Michelet's belief in the educative value of 'naïve' patriotic legends, his 'glorification' of the nation's 'saints,' make up a large part of Barrès's 'aesthetic' debt to the author of *L'Étudiant* (a new edition of which was published in 1899, and which Barrès appears to have read and used more than once in the years immediately following) : 'Il faut un système de l'âme, voici la Bible; une morale, voici le Code Napoléon; une esthétique, voici Michelet' (*Mes Cahiers, Œuvre* XIII 168).[2] J. Barbier, in his critical edition of *La Colline inspirée*, has noted an interesting marginal comment in Barrès's copy of Renan's *Life of Jesus*: 'L'histoire est une science'; Barrès corrects: 'Faux: l'histoire est Michelet, l'image.'[3]

2 Two key phrases of Barrès *circa* 1900: 'L'éducation nationale' and 'L'amitié française' occur in *L'Étudiant* (Paris: Calmann Lévy 1899) 235, 261–72. See also *L'Étudiant*, 177: 'l'histoire symbolisée en naïve légende, en sublime poésie'; 217: 'l'éducation'; and 295: 'Le besoin urgent de la France est de se retrouver elle-même, de se redire qui elle est, ce qu'elle fit. La légende ... répondra seule à ce besoin.'
Cf. *Mes Cahiers, Œuvre* XV 34: 'Hugo, Michelet glorifient nos saints français,' and *L'Étudiant*, 66: 'Ceci, c'est la légende (légende vraie, historique) des saints de la patrie.'

3 Maurice Barrès, *La Colline inspirée*, Édition critique par J. Barbier (Nancy: Berger-Levrault 1962) 37, note 3

The 'intercessors' of *Un Homme libre, Trois stations de psychothérapie*, and *Du Sang, de la volupté et de la mort* are instruments of the same kind of therapeutical devotions as the national heroes presented subsequently to the readers of the political *Cocarde*, that is to say, they are great individuals whom legend has made into 'ideas incarnate,' personifications of 'the sum of all possible emotions' to the Egotist (*Un Homme libre, Œuvre* I 182), of 'the sense of the universal' to the cosmopolitan ('La Légende d'une cosmopolite,' *Trois Stations de psychothérapie, Œuvre* II 360), of 'contempt for the established laws' to the anarchist:

> cette masse énorme de filles et de souteneurs qui enserrent nos grandes villes ... peut-elle être rapprochée des courtisanes et des affranchis qui furent un bon terrain pour la première propagande chrétienne? Ceux d'aujourd'hui, comme ceux de jadis, approuveront l'apôtre qui prêchera le mépris des vieilles lois, qui viendra juger les mérites et les démérites d'un nouveau point de vue. Mais pour convaincre de tels êtres, maintenent comme il y a dix-neuf siècles, c'est peu de raisonner, il faut atteindre leur imagination ... Ayez des dogmes par derrière; ayez le *Capital*, de Marx, la 'loi d'airain,' mais poussez quelques fables jusque dans les cœurs.
> ['La fidélité dans le crime et la honte,'
> *Du Sang, de la volupté et de l'amour, Œuvre* II 75–6][4]

The development of Barrès's cult of heroes, from the Egotist's 'walled garden' (*Œuvre* I 267; II 383), to the public platform of French nationalism, is continuous. What is new in *La Cocarde* is not the method but the objects of Barresian hero-worship. The heroes of his youthful libertarian and cosmopolitan phase mediate between individual experience and mankind's boundless possibilities of sensation, sentiment, knowledge, and freedom:

4 The original version of this essay, published in *Le Figaro* 26 December 1893, specifies the legend of the anarchists of Chicago. Cf. *L'Ennemi des lois* (*Œuvre* II 267): 'L'opinion populaire, dans les légendes qu'elle crée, va droit au point essential: elle simplifie l'ensemble, déblaye les détails, exagère la part de singularité, et, en l'isolant des circonstances explicatives, lui donne plus de relief et d'allure.'

Voilà plusieurs mois qu'on annonce la prochaine publication d'une 'Correspondance de Baudelaire' ... C'est un scandale.
...Est-ce dire que nous voulions développer l'argument ordinaire; à savoir que c'est aller contre les volontés du mort que nous admirons! ... Non, chaque époque est à ceux qui la vivent, et les morts, tapis dans les cimetières et dans les dictionnaires, sortiraient de leur véritable rôle s'il prétendaient influencer de quelque façon que ce fût notre manière d'organiser la vie ... Pour protester je me place à un tout autre point de vue.

Charles Baudelaire c'est un des personnages les mieux dessinés devant notre imagination. C'est un des joujous que nous nous sommes confectionnés pour nous distraire. C'est un des héros de cette arche de Noë où nous avons placé les individus que nous voulons exempter du dégoût sous lequel nous noyons tout le reste de l'humanité. C'est un homme beau à voir, et voilà quelqu'un qui va tout abîmer! ... la légende de Charles Baudelaire ... est compromise.
...J'aimerais qu'on créât un poste de 'conservateur de légendes' comme il y a des conservateurs de musée.
['Un Scandale littéraire,' *Le Journal* 3 March 1893]

Une bibliothèque nous offre tous les types de l'humanité. Au milieu d'eux nous nous orientons selon notre instinct profond... nous marchons ... jusqu'à ce que nous ayons trouvé les esprits de notre race.

Les livres sont cosmopolites, ils brisent les cadres des nations, mais ils reconstruisent les familles spirituelles.

Le livre est dans l'humanité la force qui conserve par excellence, en même temps que la force qui éveille; en lui repose l'essence même de l'énergie humaine.

['Le livre seule richesse normale essentielle,' *Le Livre à travers les âges. Numéro unique résumant l'Histoire du Livre depuis les Origines de l'Écriture*, publié sous la direction de Charles Mendel par Georges Brunel (Paris: Charles Mendel 1894)]

The heroes Barrès first called for in *La Cocarde* were to 'intercede' between 'each citizen and the nation' ['Histoire intérieure d'un Journal,' *La Revue Encyclopédique,* 15 November 1895]; they are a way of picturing history, in propaganda designed to whip up the nation's 'reserves of energy':

> Il faut toujours une traduction plastique aux sentiments des Français, qui ne peuvent rien éprouver sans l'incarner dans un homme ... Boulanger ... jeune ministre de la Guerre, chevauchant sur son cheval noir, dispose d'un éclat, qui parle toujours à une nation guerrière; en outre, son autorité constitutionnelle, par tel grand mot, par tel acte qui va jusqu'à l'âme, il saurait bien la multiplier: il convoquerait nos réserves d'énergie.
> [*L'Appel au soldat, Œuvre* III 406–7]

HEROES AND LEADERS

'There are leaders, and heroes, saints,' wrote Barrès in 1897, 'they can be useful in different ways at different times' (*Mes Cahiers, Œuvre* XIII 113). The editor of *La Cocarde,* and his fictitious contributor in *Les Déracinés,* François Sturel, the author of an article for *La Vraie République* entitled 'L'Utilité des hommes-drapeaux,' were scarcely more explicit:

> On accorde que les grands hommes sont les aspects pittoresques de l'histoire, qu'ils ne déterminent pas les événements mais sont déterminés par eux. Distinction futile d'ailleurs dans la suite universelle où tout est à la fois cause et effet. Mais qui pourra nier leur puissance victorieuse.
> Sublimes éducateurs. C'est à chacun de nous de choisir parmi les héros de sa race nationale son guide, son directeur, son chef d'âme.[5]
> ['Histoire intérieure d'un Journal,'
> *La Revue encyclopédique* 15 November 1895]

5 Contrast with the earlier 'L'Utilité des héros,' *La Cocarde* 20 December 1894: 'C'est à chacun de nous de choisir parmi eux son guide, son directeur, le chef de sa race. Ils sont les intercesseurs entre chacun de nous et notre idéal personnel.'

'Très bien! nous sommes d'accord; mon thème n'est pas qu'un individu fait l'histoire, mais c'est comme exaltants et pour leur vertu éducatrice que j'entends vanter les individus. Je crois à l'utilité passagère des hommes-drapeaux à la nécessité de reconnaître systématiquement et de créer, dans des périodes de désarroi moral du pays, un homme national...'
[*Les Déracinés, Œuvre* III 236–7]

But the political experience of the next few years cleared Barrès's mind for him, by confirming his faith in the 'educative' value of the hero as 'standard-bearer,' and convincing him, on the other hand, that the hero as 'leader' was particularly unlikely to make history in the climate of the Third Republic. Barrès's caesarism had been badly shaken by the Boulangist *fiasco*; it hardly survived at all Déroulède's abortive *coup* of 1899. Although Boulanger ('le général Revanche,' 'le pur que le peuple appelle') appeared quite admirable as a national and popular hero, his ineptitude among the political realists of the parliamentary Republic, whom he had to measure swords with if he were to become an effective leader, both shocked and enlightened the young partisan fresh from his meditations in Italy upon the *condottieri* of the Renaissance and the *Risorgimento,* and who, like Sturel of *Les Déracinés,* no doubt, had been in the habit of worshipping heroes without giving enough attention to the particular circumstances which had made them into heroes (*L'Appel au soldat, Œuvre* III 386). Déroulède had Barrès at his side for his pathetic 'acte de la Place de la Nation' eight years after Boulanger's disappearance; but when the 'révolutionnaire pour l'ordre' was bundled into Reuilly barracks with the troops he had hoped to follow to the Presidential Palace, his 'witness,' who had already begun to seek a political alternative to personal dictatorship in the dictatorship of an assembly,[6] was left with apparently conclusive proof of what he had no doubt long suspected:

Peut-être le soldat n'existe-t-il pas tel que nous le concevons. Raison de plus pour lui souhaiter l'existence. Qu'il vive! Ah! oui qu'il vive, enfin!

6 Letter to Zola, 6 June 1896, *cit.* above, p. 49

> Au reste le *vivat* n'implique point nécessairement notre croyance à une réalité tangible. Nous vivons entourés d'ombres. Falstaff, Hamlet, le roi Lear n'ont pas existé; ils agissent sur l'humanité. Le général que nous louons est une créature de notre esprit, un type. Les types finissent par former les êtres, par s'imprimer sur la réalité. Que du moins les types vivent!
> [*Scènes et doctrines du nationalisme, Œuvre* v 230]

Henceforward Barrès preferred to use such men as Déroulède, Marchand, Morès (whose heroic temper he saw stifled or squandered by the Republic) in the useful and possible task of enlightening public opinion as representative heroes, rather than in one that his now conciliatory traditionalism was bound to condemn, of actively, and vainly, leading a violent counter-revolution against the Republic.[7] Thus Marchand, foiled in action, could find a place in *Scènes et doctrines du nationalisme* as a 'stimulus' (*Œuvre* v 344); Morès alive and active had been a 'splendid living banner,' but a dangerous one in the prevailing anarchy of the French state; dead he became a useful 'model of the great national virtues,' with a 'brilliant legend' of 'wasted force': 'Voilà l'utilité à tirer d'un Morès: qu'il nous serve à multiplier les hommes, à les exciter, à élargir l'horizon du possible et à former des petits groupes sensibles aux leçons de choses de l'héroïsme' (*Œuvre* v 294–327). The exemplars Barrès sought were hard to come by, he thought. Looking back on his early years he saw himself hungering for 'high types of civilisation' and not finding any; as late as 1912 he deplored 'le malaise de vivre dans une société sans drapeaux' ('Les Foyers nouveaux,' *L'Écho de Paris*, 15 March 1912). Not until the War did he find, in the soldiers of '"La nation-drapeau"' (*Mes Cahiers, Œuvre* xix 61), and in his old enemy, their chief, *le père la Victoire*, an abundance of contemporary heroes: 'modèles,'

7 According to a note written in 1920 (*Mes Cahiers, Œuvre* xix 248), the Great War finally cured Barrès of his faith in the hero as leader, as Lyautey found out when, the following year, he came to 'enrol' Barrès, and was lectured on the inopportunity of 'caesarism' by the author of *L'Appel au soldat*. Barrès recognized admirable qualities of leadership in the Marshal, and a leader's ambition, but: 'Il est d'avant-guerre' (*Œuvre* xix 283–4).

'hommes exemplaires,' 'hommes-drapeaux,' fit to stock a French Plutarch.[8] Even then he doubted whether, the victory won, 'nous allons décidément trouver notre besogne, notre modèle ici, ou retourner à nos besognes de la veille' (*Mes Cahiers, Œuvre* XVIII 288). Nevertheless, while reminding the Chamber of Deputies in 1920 that it had been easy for public opinion to find its 'direction' during the War, and demanding that the government should now 'create a national consciousness to confront post-war Germany,' he also acknowledged the fact that 'France had not lacked glorious leaders of opinion,' and proposed for his part to honour with gratitude the debt of the French nation to Paul Déroulède (*Les grands problèmes du Rhin, Œuvre* X 197).

FOUR CONTEMPORARY HEROES

Déroulède stands alone among Barrès's contemporaries as a national exemplar consciously and entirely dedicated to a life-long rôle of patriotic representation, 'chef d'opinion' and 'homme-drapeau': 'l'incarnation vivante de notre protestation contre le traité de Francfort'; 'il a été une sorte de Français exceptionnel qui a voulu vivre et mourir bien en vue pour servir de modèle à tout le pays' (*Chronique de la Grande Guerre* I 1–15):

> C'est un modèle, il le sait, il le veut être et dans ses insomnies il songe aux exemples qu'il peut encore donner.
> [*Mes Cahiers, Œuvre* XVIII 95]

> Il y a du Don Quichotte dans Déroulède. Il y a aussi l'homme de théâtre qui dispense les effets de manière qu'ils passent la rampe et émeuvent une salle de spectacle.
> [*Mes Cahiers, Œuvre* XVIII 90]

> Nous devons saisir chaque occasion de ranimer ... la grande figure de Déroulède. Nul ne songe à le recommencer; ses titres et ses

8 *Grande Guerre* I ii, 100, 272; II 180; III 12, 222; IV 184; VII 357, 363; VIII 26–7; IX 66; X 260; XII 311

aptitudes composaient une force unique, et chaque plante humaine produit un fruit selon sa nature propre; mais l'exemple d'une belle vie s'élève au-dessus de la forêt pour servir de repère à nos activités et pour stimuler nos âmes.
[*Grande Guerre* VI 361]

Two other heroes of Barrès who had shown themselves capable in his time of arousing and directing the patriotism of the French people, though less self-consciously and durably than Déroulède, were Victor Hugo and General Boulanger. It was the power of a popular legend to transform a hundred thousand excited individuals into 'a single formidable being' that had impressed the future nationalist in the crowd massed at the Arc de Triomphe, on the night of 31 May 1885, for the lying-in-state of the 'poète-prophète,' 'chef mystique,' 'voyant moderne' (*Les Déracinés*, *Œuvre* III 331–4). And Boulanger's legendary image is identified as the principal agent of an equally thrilling and almost as transient moment of unanimistic French patriotism two years later: 'Sa revue du 14 juillet, reproduite par les dessinateurs, commentée par les journaux et les café-concerts, c'est l'attitude où il se fixe dans les imaginations.' 'Ce qui caractérise et actionne les héros populaires, c'est, bien plus que leur volonté, l'image que se fait d'eux le peuple.' 'Admirable par son instinct à créer la légende, il ne sait pas analyser. Magnifique image d'Épinal, il fait au Palais-Bourbon une médiocre figure' (*L'Appel au soldat*, *Œuvre* III 406–7, 410, 530). 'Quel beau morceau d'histoire pour nous instruire ... Voyez s'y former une légende, croître et décroître une popularité, penser et combattre et souffrir l'être collectif qu'on appelle un parti politique' ('Les enseignements d'une année de Boulangisme,' *Le Figaro*, 3 February 1890). 'Le beau livre qu'il faudrait qu'on écrive, *Histoire de la popularité du Général Boulanger* ...Dans un tel livre deux chapitres entre autres me passionneraient à écrire ... Le premier: *Comment naît une légende* ...' ('De l'épuisement nerveux,' *Le Journal* 19 May 1893).[9]

9 Compare the similar curiosity attributed to Renan in the imaginary dialogue which serves as preface to *Le Jardin de Bérénice*: 'comment naît une légende, comment se cristallise une nouvelle âme populaire' (*Œuvre* I 284).

Clemenceau was nearer than Déroulède, Hugo, and Boulanger to what Barrès called 'un chef,' namely a hero transformed by circumstances into a leader:

> Une des raisons de l'existence des grands hommes c'est qu'il y ait de grandes choses à accomplir. Clemenceau n'est pas un génie, mais il fut apte à agir dans le moment où l'action dont il était capable était d'immense portée dans l'espace et dans le temps. Ce boulevardier fut le bon génie de la France et des Alliés.
> [*Mes Cahiers, Œuvre* XIX 154]

Under the pressure of events, the savagely good-humoured 'tiger,' the frivolously cynical 'Mongol' was 'heroized': 'On aurait soumis du plomb à une pression effroyable et il serait devenu argent' (*Mes Cahiers, Œuvre* XIX 134, 169–70). In the circumstances Clemenceau had no need of the theatrical devices of Déroulède: 'Il nous a donné de ces faits et de ces réflexions qui, sans être mis en musique, d'eux-mêmes, dans leur nudité, émeuvent une intelligence française' (*Mes Cahiers, Œuvre* XIX 123). Nevertheless, it was not as a leader, but as 'incarnation of the invincible hope' of France, as a 'representative man' that Barrès, introducing Clemenceau to Emerson's compatriots after the War, placed him, along with Hugo, Boulanger, Déroulède, Morès, and Marchand, 'dans la série des hommes-drapeaux par lesquels une race se symbolise': 'Autour de lui la France s'est ramassée pour tenir jusqu'au bout ... L'homme d'une telle légende est un homme sacré' (*Œuvre* IV 450–1). The moment of personal leadership having passed, it was time, thought Barrès, with the majority of his colleagues in Parliament, for Clemenceau's metamorphosis from *chef* to *homme-drapeau*. The hero as leader, out of his time and place, was likely to prove a pest if not a failure:

> Car les héros, s'ils ne tombent pas exactement à l'heure et dans le milieu convenables, voilà des fléaux.
> [*Les Déracinés, Œuvre* III 184]

> Ce n'est point dans les livres, c'est tout autour de moi que j'ai appris combien étaient rares les circonstances où le héros est utile

> à l'État. Pour l'ordinaire, ce genre de personnage est un péril public.
> [*Le Voyage de Sparte*, *Œuvre* VII 213]

> Je pense qu'il faut travailler pour créer de grandes figures. Mais que pouvons-nous? Mettre un homme sur le pavois? Peuh! Les morts, oui, on les salue, mais les vivants, dans ce grand jour cru, nul n'y croit. C'est aux événements de désigner et de soulever les hommes. Ainsi ce Clemenceau.
> [*Mes Cahiers*, *Œuvre* XIX 170]

THE FABLED PAST

The imaginative transformation of historic fact into representative legend which governed Barrès's choice and use of contemporary heroes also shaped his cult of heroes from the nation's past, the latter enjoying the additional advantages of the more natural sense of veneration that the dead command, and the greater sense of security that their removal from the ranks of active leadership brings:

> Toutes les nations vaincues et refoulées, l'Irlande comme la Pologne, l'Arménie comme la Roumanie, ont des poètes qui lamentent la destinée de leur patrie; ils enchaînent dans leurs récits les héros fabuleux aux soldats les plus récents de la liberté.
> [*Le Voyage de Sparte*, *Œuvre* VII 222–3]

> La grande Germanie! C'est un ensemble d'idées et de sentiments que nous avons vu prendre forme en moins d'un siècle. Jacob Grimm, en reconstituant et combinant tous les débris plus ou moins authentiques d'une mythologie où préside le vieux dieu Odin, a unifié les dispositions poétiques profondes des Allemands. Il a crée l'âme germanique en tant qu'elle s'oppose à l'âme latine.
> [*Grande Guerre* III 101]

Barrès noted that his old friend Charles Maurras believed it possible to 'invent fables, and get the public to accept them' (*Mes Cahiers*, *Œuvre* XX 44–5). He watched the 'myth' of *Action Française* take shape with interest and qualified sympathy. But he quite soon came to the conclusion that, while something of what the Royalist doctrinaire was trying to put over was in fact passing into public opinion and modifying the balance of political forces in France, nevertheless this 'work of art' generated by Maurras's 'creative imagination' was too narrow, bookish, and 'up in the air' to represent the living substance of the French nation, that it got too near the point where imaginative form is reduced by abstraction to a restrictive formula.[10] Maurras and Barrès were, in fact, looking for different things in the past: Maurras sought the institutions of a counter-revolution, Barrès the inspiration of a patriotic climate of opinion. Less sectarian and less theoretically minded than Maurras, Barrès required from French history not a model form of government likely to divide the nation into rival constitutional factions, but heroic paragons in which all Frenchmen might find the 'incarnate' expression of their underlying community of ideals and interests. This is shown, in terms of hero-worship, by the almost total eclipse of the Napoleonic legend in Barrès's works after about 1900, and its replacement by the cult of Joan of Arc.

A CAESARIST LEGEND: NAPOLEON

Among the heroic legends of French history, the Napoleonic had threefold significance for Barrès. Frenchmen of every political persuasion and social class, from Ségur to Barrès's own grandfather, and from Rastignac to his seven *déracinés*, had helped to make and preserve it;[11] its first author was Napoleon himself, an example of the self-conscious legendary hero;[12] its effect was to 'multiply' and 'con-

10 *Mes Cahiers, Œuvre* XVI 305, 355; XVII 157–8, 184, 226; XIX 301–2. Barrès noted a similar, if less marked tendency for reality and its imaginative perception to part company in Déroulède's 'quixotism' (*Œuvre* XVIII 90).

11 *Œuvre* II 389; III 165–7; VII 126; XX 227–36

12 'Napoléon qui avait une légende à soigner et qui avait le génie plus théatral que l'auteur de *Faust*, ne nous a pas donné *Réalité et Poésie*, mais seulement *Poésie*, c'est-à-dire sa gloire.' ['Psychologie des grands hommes,' *Le Journal* 17 November 1893]. 'Seule sa clairvoyance des moyens par quoi l'on domine les imaginations le décidait à vivre deux

centrate' the nation's reserves of energy: 'il est nécessaire qu'au bout de toutes les transformations de la légende on aboutisse à ceci: NAPOLÉON, PROFESSEUR D'ÉNERGIE' (*Les Déracinés, Œuvre* III 168).

Barrès's cult of Napoleon was at its height during the years between the collapse of Boulangism and the Dreyfus Affair, when he was laying the secular foundations of his traditionalism, and finding the imaginative basis of his rhetoric. It was in 1893 that he first celebrated the abiding power of the Napoleonic legend to unite Frenchmen:

> Une même langue et puis des légendes communes, voilà ce qui constitue les nationalités...
>
> Il est douteux que Roland, Godefroy de Bouillon ou Saint Louis lui-même aient gardé une force légendaire suffisante pour nous grouper. Mais on sera d'accord pour penser que Bonaparte y convient. Les premiers ne sont plus que des héros de cabinet de travail, mais l'autre est vivant dans la rue, dans les casernes, dans les lycées, chez les paysans. L'Empereur! Ah! celui-là est bien capable de servir de centre, de point de contact aux imaginations françaises, aux plus simples comme aux plus cultivées.
> ['Les Femmes de Bonaparte,' *Le Figaro* 6 November 1893]

Four years later he showed his seven *déracinés* deriving a short-lived sense of common purpose from a pilgrimage to the Invalides. The growth of the Napoleonic legend in the medium of nineteenth-century French public opinion was explained as an interaction of objective fact and human sensibility resembling erotic crystallization, an analogy he had already used to describe his youthful Boulangist ardour, and which he would use again to characterize his mature nationalism:[13]

> Depuis cent ans, l'imagination partout dispersée se concentre sur

existences et à descendre de son cabinet où il servait les Français dans des cérémonies par quoi il les impressionnait' ('Les Conditions de vie d'un dominateur,' *Le Figaro* 5 May 1894).

13 *See Œuvre* I 281, 284 (*cit.* above, note 9) and III 406; also XIII 28 *cit.* Chapter Twelve, p. 252.

ce point. Comblez par la pensée cette crypte où du sublime est déposé; nivelez l'histoire, supprimez Napoléon: vous anéantissez l'imagination condensée du siècle...

Ce rapport constant qui s'établit entre la terre et le ciel par les vapeurs qui s'élèvent pour retomber en pluies bienfaisantes, je le retrouve entre l'empereur Napoléon et l'imagination de ce siècle ...Napoléon, notre ciel, par une noble impulsion, nous te créons et tu nous crées! ... Dès l'abord, les regards ardents de son armée lui donnèrent son masque surhumain, comme une amante modifie selon la puissance de son sentiment celui qu'elle caresse. Et depuis un siècle, dans chaque désir qui soulève un jeune homme, il y a une parcelle qui revient à Bonaparte et qui l'augmente, lui, l'Empereur. Dans sa gloire s'engloutissaient des millions d'anonymes qui lui règlent sa beauté. Comme sa force était faite, en juin 1812, au passage du Niémen, des hourras de 475,000 hommes, le plein sens de son nom est déterminé par les plus puissantes paroles du siècle.
[*Les Déracinés*, *Œuvre* III 165–7]

But this same moment in the career of Barrès's young Lorrainers in Paris also reveals the limitations of Barrès's napoleonism, and, incidentally, the difference between his and Maurras's way of using French history. 'On sort du tombeau comme on peut' (*Œuvre* III 185); indeed, all that the group of uprooted French provincials derives in common from the Invalides crypt is a horror of platitudinous routine and common sense, and the complementary ambition to rise energetically above the level of the ordinary in the wake of a 'Professor of Energy' whose caesarist lesson has been torn from its political context. Napoleon's authoritarian state and its laws must be left behind, with his principles of war, where they belong, in the past, since 'all the conditions of social and individual life as he saw them will alter'; his legend remains a stimulus to the individual, a lesson in energy, but can no longer, as it did when the leader was alive to exploit the hero's legend, stimulate and direct the individual to serve the nation:

Quelque chose d'imaginaire, comme la figure de Napoléon en

> 1884, ne peut pas fournir à des unités juxtaposées la faculté d'agir ensemble. Bonne pour donner du ressort à certains individus, cette grande légende ne peut donner de la consistance à leur groupe, ni leur inspirer des résolutions.
> [*Les Déracinés, Œuvre* III 179][14]

A TRADITIONALIST LEGEND: JOAN OF ARC

Following Barrès's disenchantment with caesarism, a legend less encumbered than Napoleon's with superannuated and partisan political theory came to the forefront of his propaganda. Joan of Arc had first appeared in her characteristically Barresian rôle of integral patriot as early as 1890: 'sainte laïque, sainte chrétienne ... le meilleur symbole du patriotisme';[15] but her leading place in his propaganda dates from about 1906, when he was beginning to be preoccupied, 'almost obsessed' with the need to reconcile Catholicism with its primitive precursors and present adversaries as the best hope of maintaining the 'continuity' of the French nation.[16] Now the references to Joan in *Mes Cahiers* start to multiply, and the beauty and the difficulty of the subject begin to challenge his powers of expression insistently:

> Comment fixer dans une œuvre d'art les éléments magnifiques offerts par la réalité ... On s'interroge ainsi des mois, des années; l'imagination ne se lasse pas de tourner autour de Jeanne, et puis un jour on s'aperçoit qu'on a sans doute été la dupe d'un mirage. La vie et la mort de Jeanne telle que nous les connaissons par le

14 Cf. *Mes Cahiers, Œuvre* XVI 9 and 37, inspired by a visit to Rouen eleven years later: 'Dans notre vie moderne, il n'y a pas de prêtres pour tous ces grands hommes. Il faudrait les incorporer à la religion. On a bien essayé pour Napoléon, voire pour Zola. Mais tout est de travers. Je mettrais, je crois, une chapelle dans la maison de Petit-Couronne: Saint-Pierre-Corneille. Napoléon disait: Je l'aurais fait prince. ... Dans ce cahier XX j'ai tous les éléments d'une note sur Rouen qui tend à prouver qu'il faut mettre les héros dans un culte.'

15 'Une Journée à Flavigny,' *Le Courrier de l'Est* 24 August 1890. Cf. 'Jeanne d'Arc ou la République ouverte,' *Le Figaro* 4 July 1890.

16 *Œuvre* XV 48, 157; XVII 43. *See* above, pp. 71–7, 99–106.

mauvais latin des greffiers de Rouen est une œuvre d'art complète, achevée et qui se suffit à elle-même. Que saurions-nous y ajouter? Toute invention paraîtra froide.
[Preface to G. Meunier, *En lisant l'histoire de Jeanne d'Arc* (Paris: Delagrave 1913)][17]

The only possible solution, he concluded, was the one suggested by Schiller and Péguy and which he, Barrès, himself attempted, in the form of a drama, in 1914: 'utiliser la sainte comme un symbole, un support des grandes rêveries' (Preface to *En lisant l'histoire de Jeanne d'Arc*). Barrès's thirty-seventh *cahier* (*Œuvre* XVIII 48–50) contains the rather unpromising outline, headed Charmes, January 1914, of a play about Joan which he had discussed with Rostand with a view to joint authorship. The project was inspired by the same authors as *La Colline inspirée* and *La Grande pitié des églises de France*, recently completed: Shakespeare, Goethe, Scott, Hugo, Frazer; and the three great dramas Barrès admired most: *Antigone, Phèdre, Iphigenie in Tauris*; in form and atmosphere it followed the post-Wagnerian revolution of the French Symbolist theatre, and it recalled, at a time when poetic drama was reviving magnificently in France, Barrès's dream, long before, of a playwright of Aristophanic or Platonic imagination who would put contemporary religious and social problems on the stage in symbolic form.[18] Two recent books, 'les Jeanne

17 'Nul vol n'est assez grand, nulle aile ne suffit, avait déjà pu ... dire... Michelet' (*Grande Guerre* I 226).

18 Barrès, *cit.* W.G.-C. Byvanck, *Un Hollandais à Paris en 1891* (Paris: Didier 1892) 277: 'que la vérité pratique mettrait des vêtements de fantaisie. Oui, la fantaisie devrait venir en aide à ceux qui s'occuperaient de théâtre moderne; j'attends une grande imagination à la façon d'Aristophane, ou plutôt encore de Platon, qui animera d'une vie supérieure les symboles qu'elle voudrait nous représenter sur la scène. Nous devrions aller à l'école de Platon, pour apprendre à formuler nos pensées les plus profondes par des mythes élégants et sublimes.' Maurice Pottecher's 'Théâtre du Peuple' at Bussang also interested Barrès (see M. Pottecher, 'Maurice Barrès,' *Le Monde français*, October 1947). The only play he actually wrote, however (*Une Journée parlementaire*), was a satire in the Naturalist manner. It was produced by Antoine before an invited audience on 23 February 1894, public performance being forbidden by the Censor.

d'Arc du jeune Péguy et du vieil Anatole France (Je dis jeune et je dis vieil pour donner à l'un et à l'autre sa valeur mystique),' had recently led him to wonder whether Joan of Arc was not 'becoming for us a great theme, like certain national legends for the Greeks' (*Mes Cahiers, Œuvre* XVI 264). If so, Barrès was in the forefront of the movement. Though he never wrote the play which was to have been, like its Greek, German, and Symbolist models, 'une cérémonie, une solennité à organiser' (*Mes Cahiers, Œuvre* XVIII 339), yet in the broader public arena of Parliament, the Press, and the Street, he was more successful. He enthusiastically took up the cause of a national Joan of Arc Day, delegated to him by its inventor, Jules Fabre;[19] got himself nominated to the parliamentary committee appointed to investigate the project (to his regret, the office of *rapporteur* eluded him) (*Mes Cahiers, Œuvre* XVI 363–9, 403–4); and became its tireless champion until in 1920, a *projet de loi* having been put to the Chamber of Deputies by Barrès, the 'fête nationale de Jeanne d'Arc' was at last, thirty-six years after Fabre's original proposition, legally recognized. 'Notre joie est complète,' he wrote, 'On demande quelquefois: "Qu'est-ce qui vous fait plaisir dans la vie?" Je réponds: "Rien que le travail." – "Mais encore?" – "Eh bien! d'avoir contribué à donner à la France, hier, la croix de guerre, et aujourd'hui, le patronage de Jeanne d'Arc" (*Grande Guerre* XIV 338).

The 'mythological' significance of Joan of Arc, to which Barrès had been unable to give dramatic form, was eloquently and abundantly expressed in the articles and essays of which he was a past master. The special capacity for breaking down the political divisions of modern France with which he had credited this 'secular and Christian saint' in 1890 ('Une Journée à Flavigny,' *Le Courrier de l'Est* 24 August 1890), reappeared in his arguments for her official nomination as the patron and symbol of the nation after the civil war of the Affair:

> La politique n'aide pas à aimer. Mais si je pouvais conduire mes collègues à Domremy et montrer ce touchant pays à ceux d'entre eux qui le connaissent mal, je crois qu'à l'unanimité ils reconnaîtraient que toutes les puissances morales qui vivent en nous

19 *Grande Guerre* I 135; II 301–5, 309; VIII 208–19; XIV 296–303

> s'harmonisent en Jeanne d'Arc, pour faire d'elle un merveilleux symbole de l'unité française.
> ['Au bord des Fontaines-Fées,' *Le Gaulois* 20 January 1908]

And again, after the victory of the Sacred Union:

> Jeanne d'Arc n'appartient à aucun parti: elle les domine tous, et c'est là son véritable miracle. Si pour les catholiques c'est une sainte, l'ange du sacre pour les royalistes, c'est la fille du peuple pour les républicains. Les jacobins, en 93, décoraient de son nom 'La Bergère,' le canon fondu avec le bronze de la statue du pont d'Orléans ... Pour les rationalistes, elle est le triomphe de l'inspiration individuelle. Jamais Voyante ne fut si clairvoyante...
> ['M. Maurice Barrès commente sa proposition de loi' (interview with J.J. Brousson), *Excelsior* 16 April 1920]

Meanwhile this most characteristic of Barresian intercessors had acquired a further significant dimension: the prehistoric depth of her allegedly part-pagan inspiration, in those Celtic spirits of the corn and wild whom the author of *La Grande pitié des églises de France* had tried to 'mobilize' against the anti-clericalism of the Republic's parliamentary majority between 1910 and 1914:

> À Domremy nous sommes enveloppés dans la vapeur de mystère où Jeanne se forma. Nous voyons agir en elle, à son insu, les vieilles imaginations celtiques. Le paganisme supporte et entoure cette sainte chrétienne. La Pucelle honore les saints: mais d'instinct, elle préfère ceux qui abritent, sous leurs vocables, les fontaines fées. Les diverses puissances religieuses éparses dans cette vallée meusienne, à la fois celtique, latine et catholique, Jeanne les ramasse et les accorde, dût-elle en mourir, par un effet de sa noblesse naturelle...
>
> Ce pays, dont Jeanne rassemblait toutes les puissances, n'est pas un pays simple. De même qu'aujourd'hui l'instituteur est posé dans le village pour contredire le curé, le curé du quinzième siècle contredisait tout un monde ténébreux. Il avait à lutter contre une mythologie qui ne s'avouait pas vaincue. Nulle part cette fidèle terre française n'a mieux cherché à transmettre au

> christianisme sa poésie autochtone ... Certes, Jeanne, par son sublime, échappe à ce paysage ... elle obéit à d'autres voix qu'aux inspirations de cette terre. Mais les forces opposées que l'on voit lutter dans ce paysage n'ont à aucun moment cessé d'exercer sur elle une action.
> [*Le Mystère en pleine lumière, Œuvre* XII 266–72]

In the five years which remained to Barrès after the War, Joan of Arc, now a saint for Rome, the patron of France, and venerated in the capitals of her allies, became the chief vehicle of his triumphant patriotism. Against those who would concentrate French propaganda on facts and figures he asserted that 'Les chiffres reçoivent leur pleine efficacité des valeurs spirituelles et morales qui s'y incorporent. Que la France se personnifie dans la plus noble figure que l'humanité a jamais produite, c'est bien beau et bien utile' (*Grande Guerre* XIV 297–8). And between those who, like René Gillouin, claimed that the mass of Frenchmen in the twentieth century were moved only by abstractions, like Right, Liberty, and Justice, or who, like R. Havard de la Montagne, retorted scornfully to Gillouin that 'on s'est battu pour la France, et le "philosophe" n'y entend rien,' Barrès proposed, as the natural product of a lifetime's 'obsession' with the art of 'multiplying the power of the human spirit,' a characteristically conciliatory synthesis of idealistic abstractions and matter of fact: the embodiment of an ideal in a heroic individual:

> La dernière phrase de *Sous l'œil des Barbares*: 'Toi seul, ô maître, si tu existes quelque part axiome, religion ou prince des hommes,' annonce *L'Appel au soldat* et toute mon obsession, de toute ma vie, pour ce qui multiplie les forces de l'âme.
> Mauvaise découpure que je mets dans *L'Appel au soldat* relié et qui réplique à Gillouin. Je les concilie. Il y a axiome et prince des hommes.
> [*Mes Cahiers, Œuvre* XIX 200][20]

'Notre proposition dit en toutes lettres,' he had assured Gillouin, 'que

20 'La mauvaise découpure' is Havard de la Montagne's article.

la fête de Jeanne d'Arc sera la fête du patriotisme. Ce sera aussi le signe de cette puissance de résurrection qu'il y a dans notre nation comme dans aucun autre peuple' (*Grande Guerre* XIV 298). Abroad also, and particularly in the Rhineland, Joan was to 'signify' a French way of life:

> Cette fille surhumaine toute pleine d'une pitié divine, nous devons l'opposer à l'indigne surhomme, d'une férocité diabolique où se complaît la Germanie prussianisée. Que Jeanne soit un étendard au-dessus des peuples unis pour le triomphe de la civilisation. Et d'abord un étendard sur le Rhin.
> [*Grande Guerre* XIV 354]

FRENCH AND GERMAN HERO-WORSHIP

In Barrès's lectures in the University of Strasbourg on the 'Genius of the Rhine' in November 1920, he characteristically sought out this 'elusive' force where he had already looked for the spirit of Lorraine, and of the Italian city-states, of Spain, of modern Europe, that is to say in a legendry of representative heroes:

> Nous ne mépriserons pas les légendes, dans l'ordre de recherche où nous sommes engagés. Une légende c'est plus qu'un rêve, c'est une persistence qui se protège en s'enveloppant de vapeurs dignes de la faire aimer. Le légendaire du Rhin n'est pas fait de simples jeux de l'imagination effrayée ou séduite. Dans les valeurs épiques et morales qu'il contient, nous saurons discerner un produit de la réflexion populaire et les dispositions mêmes de l'*esprit rhénan.*
>
> Ah! certes, les Rhénans songent à d'autres réalités encore qu'à celles qui s'expriment dans leurs légendes ... mais la connaissance exacte des faits et des personnages qui émeuvent leur imagination, la connaissance du monde d'idées et de sentiments où ils s'exaltent ...nous serait un précieux indice sur leur nature historique...
> [*Le Génie du Rhin, Œuvre* X 57, 60][21]

21 Cf. 'La Mort de Venise,' *Œuvre* VII 33; 'Toute réunion d'hommes...

The thesis of the second of Barrès's Rhineland lectures, entitled 'La vie légendaire du Rhin,' is that 'the heroes of the Scandinavian Edda and the barbarous divinities of the North' had been brought into this region by Grimm and his disciples on the wave of pangermanic expansion which later carried the soldiers and administrators of Bismarck to Strasbourg in 1870 with, in their wake, the all-conquering theogony of Wagner:

> Après les victoires de Sedan et de Bayreuth, la Rhénanie s'ouvre au cortège triomphal d'Odin et de Freya. C'est l'écroulement du Panthéon rhénan et de tout ce qui s'y trouvait adossé et vivifié. La partie semble gagnée au bénéfice des Alberich et des Fafner. L'assombrissement du Rhin et son annexion à la Mythologie du Walhalla sont accomplis.
> [*Le Génie du Rhin, Œuvre* x 80]

And that this invasion called for a counter-mobilization of autochthonous gods and heroes:

> sous l'alluvion du génie d'outre-Rhin subsistent les dieux en exil de la Rhénanie; les figures des musées de Trèves et de Cologne, le peuple des saints et des preux, toutes les formes bienfaisantes que l'imagination rhénane n'a pas cessé d'accueillir attendent avec persistence l'heure propice. Quel symbole émouvant que ces grands albums, où, en pleine guerre, le commandant Espérandieu a rassemblé et publié tout ce qui subsiste d'images des dieux, des héros et des simples mortels de l'époque gallo-romaine dans la Gaule Belgique ... On dirait un livre de mobilisation.
> [80–1]

Barrès also repeatedly asserted the vitality and persistence in the Rhineland of the Napoleonic legend (which recovered for his post-war foreign policy something of the importance it had lost in his

tend à former une tradition. Elle travaille instinctivement à mettre debout un type sur lequel elle se réglera. Nulle société ne peut se passer de modèle; elle se donne toujours une aristocratie.' Also *Œuvre* I 197–246; II 103–67, 356–68; IV 85–7; VII 76–113

domestic propaganda since 1900) and of the legend of Joan of Arc. His commentary on the latest act in the secular struggle between Germany and France for the soul of the Rhineland culminated in the elevation of the Christian Maid 'pour incarner l'action de la France,' against the *Germania* of Niederwald (*Le Génie du Rhin, Œuvre* x 134–5).[22]

History dealt ironically with Barrès's Rhineland propaganda when, confirming his appreciation of the importance of the fabled past in the dynamics of nationalism, the German National-Socialist leaders of the nineteen-thirties and -forties gathered with its help a force which easily toppled the emblems of French civilisation that the author of *Le Génie du Rhin* had tried to raise in the path of pangermanism, along the ancient river-line, as artificially as Grimm and Goebbels, and with less success. Barrès's Rhineland policy would run counter to both the propaganda of the German Third Reich, and his own earlier and more complete definition of nationality, which put the possession of a common language beside or before the inheritance of the same legends.[23] Incidentally, the Nazi propagandists had, in the unanimistic excitability of their audience, one trump card that a French publicist generally lacks, and another of the same suit which Barrès seems sometimes to have been half tempted to take from the Germans' hand, but which, in the belief that he belonged to a more humane and rational civilisation, he always baulked at playing: a mythology of ecstatic self-immolation, in war as in love, which had thrilled him since the eighteen-nineties in the 'magnificent' but 'half-animal' divinities of Wagner's Walhalla: 'Forces presque élémentaires, bien loin qu'elles règlent et ennoblissent notre activité, elles ne peuvent rien nous donner que le délire vers les gouffres, une sombre ardeur au suicide.'[24]

22 But not in its place: 'Nulle clause du traité de Versailles n'a prescrit de l'abolir, et nous avons raison de la respecter, car il ne s'agit pas ici d'anéantir par la force une idée, et pour refouler du sol rhénan la pensée prussienne nous ne voulons que mieux penser que les Prussiens.' (*Œuvre* x 134–5).

23 'Réponse à M. Edwards,' *La Cocarde* 22 October 1894; 'Évolution nationaliste et contre la guerre,' 25 October 1894; *Scènes et doctrines du nationalisme, Œuvre* v 420.

24 *Œuvre* v 562–3; x 392–8, 541–3; xix 290: 'Devant Wagner, je ne me

The French heritage that Barrès tried to revive in the Rhineland under the standard of Joan of Arc was a real and valuable one; but the Rhinelanders preferred legends in their own language; while at home, Barrès's propaganda failed in all but a small minority (most of the French nationalists were soon to be swept into the narrower if more politically dynamic channel of royalism that Barrès mistrusted), to overcome the chronic inability of his compatriots to find a workable link between realism and idealism, the past and the future.[25] He deplored the fact that France was torn in two by a self-styled anti-democratic 'realism' self-intoxicated by its dogmatic formulae, and a habit of parliamentary cynicism sheltering under flimsy notions of Right, Liberty and Justice. But the weakness of his position as a propagandist intending to fill this gap was given away by his lame answer to Gillouin's criticism of his cult of Joan of Arc: 'la fête de Jeanne d'Arc sera la fête du patriotisme' (*Grande Guerre* XIV 298). Gillouin, who believed Frenchmen had fought for abstract notions of Right, Liberty, and Justice, and Havard de la Montagne, who contended that they had fought for France, might well have both asked why Joan of Arc had to be brought in at all, thereby speaking between them for the majority of their countrymen. The cult of heroes from the fabulous past has taken root in modern France only in those Bonapartist, Jacobin, and Royalist political sects that Barrès was anxious to transcend; while the cult of the leader, which has continued to revive in moments of French weakness or disarray, has, since the Bonapartes, generally failed to unite Frenchmen for more than the passage of a temporary crisis.

Barrès's patriotic hero-worship is of similar historical interest to Romain Rolland's contemporary humanist cult of great men. The two authors stand on opposite sides of a common movement of reaction

suis pas trompé. J'ai senti une force puissante, capable de soulever et de lever des foules, une force religieuse. J'ai cru: "Ici naît une religion nouvelle." Quelle religion? C'est là mon erreur singulière. J'avais reçu un *tonus* ... et ces idées dont je vivais alors, du *Culte du Moi,* s'exaltaient, croyaient entendre leur messe. En fait, les Allemands y trouvaient l'exaltation de leur propre personnalité. Ils assistaient à la messe du pangermanisme.'

25 *Œuvre* x 54, 146–7.

against the spiritual depression of the generation before.[26] Barrès's celebration of heroism no doubt helped mould the mood of faith, exhilaration, energy, and national reconciliation in which France met the shock of 1914, though he would come to believe that he had failed to dominate the long ordeal which followed, as he believed Rolland had failed; the one trying to soar 'above the *mêlée*,' with what Barrès reckoned an excess of 'pride,' the other devoting himself perhaps too 'humbly' to morale-building propaganda in the service of his embattled country (*Mes Cahiers, Œuvre* XVIII 278, 378). But the wider influence Barrès exerted on politico-religious opinion and patriotic feeling in France between Boulanger and De Gaulle, and his abiding interest as a propagandist, can be traced to a rhetoric of tonic commemoration which grew out of his cult of heroes towards a more comprehensive image of the nation: a mythopoetic landscape, with signs and figures, where the pageant of great lives has its place, but not the foremost, within a predominantly collective and panoramic representation of France's traditional values and imperatives.

26 Cf. R.A. Wilson, *The Pre-War Biographies of Romain Rolland* (Oxford: Humphrey Milford 1939) 29–33, 155–92; and A. Germain, *Les Croisés modernes* (Paris: Nouvelles Éditions Latines 1958) 206–9.

CHAPTER NINE

The Rhetoric of Commemoration

ICONOGRAPHY

The iconographical interpretation of the visual arts which is characteristic of the many pages of Barrès inspired by the galleries, churches, museums, and architecture of Italy, Lorraine, Provence, Bavaria, and Spain,[1] has its counterpart in his use of pictures as models and auxiliaries of written propaganda.

Two early articles calling for the founding of a French national portrait gallery and, less seriously, for the creation of the post of 'conservateur de légendes' on the analogy of the 'conservateur de musée'[2] point the way to his later systematic exploitation of the persuasive power of the visual image in propaganda generally, and in particular foreshadow his use of the commemorative portrait in words. In 1906, a commission to write a series of articles for *L'Auto* gave him the opportunity of combining in one literary transposition his youthful enthusiasm for a French portrait gallery with a mature admiration for the popular cartoonists of the Épinal tradition:

> De quinzaine en quinzaine nous publierons dans ce journal le portrait d'un grand homme, d'un type, d'un chef de file tel qu'il

1 'Les formes les plus parfaites ne sont que des symboles pour ma curiosité d'idéologue' (*Œuvre* I 238).

2 'Les grandes figures de France,' *La Grande Revue de Paris et de St-Pétersbourg* 15 September 1888; 'Un Scandale littéraire,' *Le Journal* 3 March 1893 (*cit.* above p. 139)

était à vingt ans: un Pasteur, un Hugo, un Brazza ... Ce seront des études sans prétentions, des images simples et naïvement coloriées, dans le goût de celles qu'on fabriquait autrefois à Épinal, non pas des images légendaires et épiques, mais plutôt des sortes de moralités étayées sur une foule de petits faits véridiques.
['À 20 ans,' *L'Auto* 13 April 1906]

In this instance, Taine's 'petits faits' are brought in to give Barrès's imaginative propaganda, always delicately poised between facts and their sentimental distortion, a realistic bias. Elsewhere he stresses, at the expense of their historical accuracy, the Épinal artists' gift for communicating fervour and arousing faith:

Les Images d'Épinal. – Ces grossières images.
C'est simple et franc, plein de caractère.
Produisent plus d'effet que des vignettes habilement dessinées. Rudesse. A bien du charme.
Naïveté rustique parente de la Bibliothèque bleue et des gravures sur bois qui décorent les légendes populaires.
Vaut mieux que toutes les habiletés et virtuosités.
Je suis tenté d'admettre qu'il y a dans les primitives images d'Épinal une sorte de génie, un génie grossier, barbare si l'on veut, mais du génie si le génie c'est la représentation toute directe d'une réalité vivement ressentie, l'expression d'une âme émue...
Dans ce qui touche à l'art, surtout à l'art populaire, on est en plein mystère. Par quel secret ces artisans ont-ils été d'emblée au cœur des enfants et du peuple? De très grands artistes ont essayé de faire des images d'Épinal. Ils ont pitoyablement échoué. Ils n'ont pas su produire, créer la croyance.
Mettre debout des images, des pensées qui imposent la crédibilité, c'est toujours de cela qu'il s'agit pour Homère, pour Napoléon, pour Karl Marx, pour l'artiste, pour quelque maître que ce soit!
[*Mes Cahiers, Œuvre* XVII 166]

The popular iconography which had communicated the spirit of victory to the seven-year-old Barrès at Charmes in July and August 1870, with the French troops moving up through the town against the old enemy from beyond the Rhine, continued to inspire the primary colours and simplified outlines of those 'speaking images' Barrès used in *L'Âme française et la guerre* to sustain French morale during the next round of the Franco-German struggle, forty-four years later. Meanwhile Barrès had come to see, in the 'modest craftsmen' of Épinal, models for his own ambition to 'rouse' and 'direct' the public imagination:

> Avec quelle violence et quelle sûreté, ces puissantes images, vigoureusement coloriées, m'ébranlaient, allaient promouvoir ma plus profonde sensibilité! Elles y ont laissé leurs traces...
>
> Ils furent, ces petits artisans ce que tous nous [illegible] d'être, des éveilleurs et des directeurs de l'imagination.
>
> [preface to René Perrout,
> *Les Images d'Épinal* (Paris: Ollendorff 1912)]

RELICS AND EMBLEMS

While attempting to transfer to his propaganda in words some of the persuasive force of popular and of fine[3] iconography, Barrès also used commemorative relics and emblems as material for and adjuncts to his writing and his oratory.

Like the young Michelet he pictured, very sympathetically, drawing inspiration from the *Musée des monuments français*, Barrès had breathed the poetry of history at the Trocadero Museum and the Louvre Galleries during his first months in the French capital ('Les Grandes figures de France,' *La Grande Revue de Paris et de St-Pétersbourg* 15 September 1888), and he continued always to seek a 'faithful image of life' in every such exhibition he could find; notably, and with special reference to his traditionalist propaganda, in the *Museo Arletan*, which he considered the model of national reliquaries – as unpretentious as an *image d'Épinal* in its choice of the humble workaday costume and utensil, its common or garden herbarium and

3 Colette Baudoche, 'une vive image de Metz' (*Œuvre* VI 249) owes something to Puvis de Chavannes: 'Quand j'écrivais *Colette Baudoche*, j'avais sous les yeux une petite image, une carte postale de la *Sainte-Geneviève*, de Puvis de Chavannes, *veillant sur la Cité*' (*Œuvre* XX 172–3).

its comparative neglect of great art,[4] and the *Musée Alsacien* whose founders he encouraged to follow in Mistral's footsteps (*Au service de l'Allemagne, Œuvre* VI 135–7; *Mes Cahiers, Œuvre* XIV 124).

As mentioned earlier, Barrès, in reply to the question: 'What has given you most pleasure in life?', named his campaign for the nationalization of Saint Joan together with his part in the creation of the *Croix de Guerre* (*Grande Guerre* XIV 338). They were in fact related media of his patriotic propaganda, and analogous instances of his intense interest in the 'multiplication of moral force' by imaginative means (*Grande Guerre* III 236–7). The association of hero-worship and emblematic propaganda in the term *homme-drapeau* gave him a useful neologism,[5] and the discovery of a similar association in the mind of his fifteenth-century heroine delighted him:

> Je trouve cela bien beau, que Jeanne d'Arc quelquefois ait appelé le Dauphin de France, Charles VII, l'Oriflamme...
> [*Mes Cahiers, Œuvre* XIX 249]

> *L'Homme-drapeau.* – Jeanne appelait Charles VII 'oriflambe'...
> Sicille, dans *Blason des couleurs* (cité par Littré, à *oriflamme*) dit: 'La rouge couleur ou vermeille est de grand estat et dignité, et bien nous le démontre l'auriflamme du ciel miraculeusement aux rois gaulois envoyée, qui estoit de cest couleur, affin de les animer à vertu et courage, magnanimité et prouesse...'
> Ainsi, l'expression *homme-drapeau* est dans la nature même de notre esprit.
> [*Mes Cahiers, Œuvre* XX 32]

CEREMONIAL

The persuasive virtues of heroic personifications, icons, relics, and emblems are brought together and enhance each other in the live spectacle of public ceremonial, which occupies a commanding posi-

4 'Des opinions de tout repos,' *Le Journal* 14 October 1898. Cf. *Œuvre* IV 83; XII 258; XIII 257–60; XVI 295–6; XVII 75.

5 *See* also 'Une Mobilisation,' *La Revue Française* 8 December 1912 ('récits-drapeaux'); *Grande Guerre* I 100; IV 284: ('hommes-drapeaux'); II 234 ('phrases-drapeaux'); VI 251 ('idées-drapeaux').

tion in Barrès's arts of imaginative persuasion, secular and religious alike:

> Je dis l'église, l'*église et ses cérémonies.*
> Que des hommes soient employés à célébrer dans des cérémonies symboliques les plus hauts sentiments de l'âme humaine, cela est pratiquement utile, cela sert effectivement la moralité humaine comme les spéculations des hautes mathématiques sont utiles à l'industrie, au commerce, même à notre bien-être matériel.
> [*Mes Cahiers, Œuvre* XVII 73]

After Déroulède's death, on the eve of the Great War, Barrès became the president of *La Ligue des Patriotes.* The League's objective, as he saw it, was to 'enrich and amplify' the emotional patriotism of the French by means, principally, of those ceremonial street demonstrations it had been its founder's particular genius to invent and to lead:

> Elle entraînera ses membres en pleine activité. Des fêtes, des pèlerinages, c'est le monde du sentiment, et des campagnes sur des faits.
> [*Mes Cahiers, Œuvre* XVIII 200]

> Cette conception des fêtes, elle était si naturelle à Déroulède qu'à toute heure, en toute circonstance, il en inventait. Chez lui, aussi bien que dans la rue. Il en improvisait sans cesse de publiques et de privées.
> [*Grande Guerre* II 318–19]

> C'est une grande et féconde idée qu'eut Paul Déroulède de créer ces solennités patriotiques où l'union se resserre, où l'esprit s'émeut et se relève pour tendre au grand.
> [*Grande Guerre* XI 1]

Throughout the War, Barrès continued to emphasize the value of ceremonial as a patriotic cordial: 'Des cérémonies grandioses, célébrant avec gravité le culte de la patrie, contribuent à maintenir et à fortifier les cœurs' (*Grande Guerre* V 203). He was enthusiastic about 'la fête du Poilu,' which he preferred to call, more respectfully, 'journée du Combattant' (*Grande Guerre* v 148–50; vi 102–6); an anniversary commemoration of the sack of Gerbéviller ('de telles cérémonies nous chargent de force') (*Grande Guerre* vi 58); the double procession on the fourteenth of July 1915, Republicans and *Ligueurs* joining forces in front of the Hôtel des Invalides to symbolize the sacred union of all Frenchmen ('J'aurais voulu ce matin plus de drapeaux, plus de musique, plus de haillons glorieux' (*Grande Guerre* v 208–14); the League of Patriots' own 'liturgy' at the statue of Joan of Arc on the Place des Pyramides, and at the monument to the occupied city of Strasbourg on the Place de la Concorde (*Grande Guerre* v 202, 208–9; ix 308; xi 58); a 'solemnity' in honour of captive Metz (*Grande Guerre* viii 67), and the Victory parade in the liberated town (*La Minute sacrée, Œuvre* ix 123–86); the apotheosis of Joan of Arc in Mayence cathedral in 1919 (*Grande Guerre* xiv 353); the ceremony at Sion-Vaudémont the following June to commemorate the return of Lorraine to France, and which Barrès placed under the Maid's patronage (*Grande Guerre* xiv 331–46); and, in May 1921, to shore up France's crumbling position on the Rhine, the twin national festivals of Napoleon and Joan of Arc (*Œuvre* x 296).

The religious vocabulary Barrès used to describe patriotic ceremonial: 'liturgie patriotique,' 'rite symbolique,' 'minute sacrée,' 'lieu sacré,' 'image sainte,' 'ex-veto,' 'autel du patriotisme,' 'Madone de la Patrie,'[6] expresses not simply the substitution, 'DE COELO IN INFERNA,' of patriotism for Christianity (*Scènes et doctrines du nationalisme, Œuvre* v 25–7), a position Barrès had by now left behind, nor merely war hysteria, but a more deeply-rooted conviction, going back to the observed unanimism of Victor Hugo's funeral, Boulangism, and the pre-war leagues,[7] and reinforced by Durkheim's crowd psychology[8] and his own verification in the Levant in 1914 of the unity underlying what William James (whom he had read in 1910) called the 'varieties of Religious Experience': the conviction that spectacular and sonorous ceremonial affects men and women in groups at a level of experi-

6 *Grande Guerre* v 209; ix 308; xi 58; xiv 333; *Œuvre* ix 123
7 *Œuvre* iii 325–45, 404–23; xix 227, 426–7
8 *See* p. 283.

ence that is deeper than any distinction between the sacred and the profane.[9] Not that he judged ceremonies by the standard of 'psychagogic'[10] efficiency alone. In the Levant, for instance, his great interest in what Catholic orders and Dervish dancers have in common, namely the 'mechanical devices,' the 'signs' and 'sensuous aids' essential, in his view, to all religions, does not prevent him distinguishing the 'charitable' mysticism of the former from the 'sterile' ecstasy of the latter, and valuing it more highly; nor does he confuse ends and means when observing, and condemning, the 'unscrupulous' use of similar means of persuasion by ancient and modern politicians.[11]

TENOR AND VEHICLE

By fixing its attention on what proved futile or seems immoral in the tenor of Barrès's traditionalist propaganda, epitomized in the much mocked slogan: 'Debout les morts!,' posterity has very largely missed what is of enduring interest in his life-long study of the techniques and vehicles of political and religious persuasion:

> Celui qui s'écria: 'Debout les morts!' dans la tranchée pleine de ses compagnons écrasés par la mitraille et que les Prussiens en hurlant envahissaient, s'élève au-dessus de lui-même, s'ouvre au génie de la France, tel que Rude l'a sculpté. En lui vibre quelque chose qui est plus que lui. Voilà des hommes transpercés, transfigurés par le frisson de la patrie.

9 'Plus on s'enfonce dans la laïcité, plus tout devient rite. Nous sommes une société rituelle: Le Soldat inconnu, les centenaires (*Œuvre* XIX 302). On the place of music in Barrès's own art of persuasion *see* Chapter Eleven.

10 J.-M. Domenach, *La Propagande politique* (Paris: PUF 1955) 9: 'La psychagogie, autrement dit la direction de l'âme collective.'

11 *Une Enquête aux pays du Levant, Œuvre* XI 287–8, 440–2, 444, 484; *Mes Cahiers, Œuvre* XX 15–17. Cf. I.-M. Frandon, *L'Orient de Maurice Barrès*, 362, and Barrès *cit.* J. Lucas-Dubreton, 'Notes sur Maurice Barrès,' *La Table Ronde* (March 1957) 23: 'La religion orientale, la religion païenne font appel aux mêmes forces de l'être, elles les exaltent, facilitent leur épanchement – mais n'en tirent rien ... Voilà pourquoi Lourdes est, à mes yeux, un plus grand endroit que Konieh, Byblos ou les rives de l'Adonis.'

Cette pénétration de l'individuel par l'universel et de notre conscience éphémère par la société des âmes justifie les grandes cérémonies civiques.
[*Grande Guerre* v 213–14]

The mobilization of ancestors in the service of a nation at war belongs to that 'carniverous'[12] kind of idolatry against which our age has understandably, if with limited success, rebelled. Whether the Rhineland should look east or west for leadership after 1918 was quickly shown to be a decision that France was hardly in a position to influence.[13] The cult of Saint Joan failed to find a place in the hearts of the majority of Frenchmen comparable to the anonymous lay rituals of Bastille Day and the Unknown Soldier. So much may be attributed to misjudgement or to prejudices of time and place to which Barrès resigned himself too readily. But the decay or vice which may be found in the causes Barrès served should not be allowed to detract from the value of much of what he had to say in general about the art of propagating causes, and in particular about the imaginative techniques that he learned from a 'life-time's obsession with ways of multiplying the power of the human spirit' (and of making an individual, whether we like it or not, 'vibrate' in unison with the mass) : an obsession 'announced' in the first volume of *Le Culte du Moi* (*Œuvre* I 132; XIX 200, *cit.* above, p. 154) and still, nearly forty years later, driving the author of *Une Enquête aux pays du Levant* onward along his exhausting and exhilarating pilgrim routes to the castles of Rashid Ad-Din Sinan, the Old Man of the Mountains, whose hold over the imaginations of an utterly devoted band of assassins had fascinated him since his school-days, and to Konya of the whirling dervishes:

12 A. de Saint-Exupéry, *Œuvres* (Paris: Pléiade 1953) 255
13 Barrès's answer to the threat of revived German expansion was, at the very least, tragically prophetic in the short term: 'Il se constitue une sorte de *bloc atlantique*, et l'Angleterre et l'Amérique ne sauraient sans danger pour elles-mêmes se passer de la clairvoyance de la réceptivité françaises... À la France encore une fois, de voir clair et pour elle et pour eux. Une sorte d'union atlantique est l'œuvre évidente et la constellation politique de demain. La France de l'Est qui agit à l'égal d'un filtre sur les valeurs allemandes, peut prétendre à voir son rôle simplifié, pour l'ensemble même du monde latino-britannique dont elle est géographiquement la sentinelle avancée' (*Œuvre* x 411–12).

> La grande, la seule affaire, c'est de se mettre en rapport avec la masse d'où nous viennent le sentiment de l'énergie, avec la réserve de feu, avec le soleil spirituel, avec Dieu, si vous voulez.
>
> Les cultes ont été institués pour nous y aider, et aussi la poésie, la musique et aussi la danse des derviches tourneurs et aussi le pinard. Et les héros aussi servent de modèles et d'exaltateurs. Tous communiquent à l'homme une force.
>
> [*Mes Cahiers, Œuvre* XVIII 355]

> La grande affaire pour celui qui veut agir sur les hommes, c'est de savoir disposer autour des âmes, dans la chambre secrète, dans le sanctuaire profond où vit l'homme [illegible], un jeu de tapisseries qui le rende maître des humeurs, des rêves et des actes où se prolongent les rêves. Les images auxquelles Sinan recourait avec le plus de succès se rapportent à la transmigration des âmes.
>
> – Voulez-vous que demain je danse pour vous?
>
> Je lui saisis la main.
>
> – Monsieur le Supérieur, c'est une telle vision qui donnera son plein sens à mon pèlerinage de Konia ... la cérémonie où je vais vous voir figurer, avec tous vos prestiges de musique, de chant, de danse, de décors, de symbolisme et de vieilles traditions, me promet la sorte de poème en action, la grande œuvre de lyrisme et d'émoi religieux que toute ma vie j'ai pressentie et désirée. C'est la marmite des sorcières, mais où vous ne mettez rien d'immonde, rien que de noble et de spirituel.
>
> [*Une Enquête aux pays du Levant, Œuvre* XI 281, 420]

Barrès's 'pilgrimage'[14] to the Levant was itself an instance of the private use by a self-conscious and methodical persuader of the device in which his public rhetoric of the imagination naturally culminates, at 'places which are patterns,' stamped with the genius of exemplary men, moulded by the discipline of a traditional order, where 'the material and the immaterial' appear to be most clearly and creatively in communication:

14 *Œuvre* XI 174, 356, 358, 420. Cf. XI 379, *cit.* above p. 13.

J'apporte ici une curiosité, un sentiment, non de l'architecture, mais des types créés, non des races animales, mais des groupes d'âmes. J'aime les gens qui modèlent des groupes. J'aime ces grands imaginatifs qui font descendre des dieux du ciel sur la terre. J'aime les gens groupés autour d'un dieu. J'aime ceux qui créent un chevalier, un ordre. Je viens voir des créations d'art (tel le prêtre-soldat). Il s'agit de poétiser la vie, d'en faire une œuvre savante, d'où sont éliminées les vertus médiocres. J'aime les lieux qui sont des moules.
[*Mes Cahiers, Œuvre* xx 86]

PILGRIMAGE

The grandiose funeral rites of Victor Hugo, which Barrès used to counterpoint the final catastrophe of *Les Déracinés* (the execution of the lone wolf Racadot, 'déraciné, décapité'), were already, many years before his journey to the Levant, associated in his mind with a supposed Oriental mastery of the mechanics of group persuasion (*Les Déracinés, Œuvre* III 331). And the same occasion inspired not Barrès's first essay on the spirit of 'high places,'[15] but the first appearance of this most insistent of Barresian themes, fully armed in a piece of patriotic propaganda:

Cette foule où chacun porte en soi, appropriée à sa nature, une image de Hugo, conduit sa cendre de l'Arc de Triomphe au Panthéon. Chemin sans pareil! Qui ne donnerait sa vie pour le parcourir cadavre!...

Certains esprits sont ainsi faits que deux points les émeuvent dans Paris: – L'Arc de Triomphe, qui maintient notre rang devant l'étranger, qui rappelle comment nous donnâmes aux peuples, distribuâmes à domicile les idées françaises, les 'franchises de l'humanité' – et cette colline Sainte-Geneviève, dont les pentes portent la Sorbonne, les vieux collèges, les savantes ruelles des

15 *See*, e.g., *Un Homme libre, Œuvre* I 206 and 'Un Amateur d'âmes,' *Œuvre* II 23–49.

> étudiants. L'Arc de Triomphe, c'est le signe de notre juste orgueil; le Panthéon, le laboratoire de notre bienfaisance: orgueil de la France devant l'univers; bienfaisance de la France envers l'univers. Le même vent qui passe et repasse sous la voûte triomphale court aussi sans trêve le long des murs immenses du Panthéon, c'est l'âme, le souffle des hauts lieux: nul n'approche le mont de l'Étoile, le mont Sainte-Geneviève qui n'en frémisse, et pour les plus dignes, ce sera le moteur d'une grande et durable activité.
>
> De l'Étoile au Panthéon, Victor Hugo, escorté par tous, s'avance. De l'orgueil de la France il va au cœur de la France. C'est le génie de notre race qui se refoule en elle-même: après qu'il s'est répandu dans le monde, il revient à son centre, il va s'ajouter à la masse qui constitue notre tradition. De l'Arc où le poète fut l'hôte du César, nous l'accompagnons à l'Arche insubmersible où toutes les sortes de mérite se transforment en pensée pour devenir un nouvel excitant de l'énergie française.
>
> Hugo gît désormais sur l'Ararat du classicisme national. Il exhausse ce refuge. Il devient un des éléments de la montagne sainte qui nous donnerait le salut, alors même que les parties basses de notre territoire ou de notre esprit seraient envahies par les Barbares. Appliquons-nous à considérer chaque jour la patrie dans les réserves de ses forces, et facilitons-lui de les déployer. Songeons que toute grandeur de la France est due à ces hommes qui sont ensevelis dans sa terre. Rendons-leur un culte qui nous augmentera.
>
> [*Les Déracinés, Œuvre* III 343–4]

Barrès's secularization of the Catholic ceremony of pilgrimage, comparable to and associated with his misappropriation of Loyola's meditational *compositio loci*,[16] with which it is combined in this account of Victor Hugo's funeral, dates also from the period of *Le Culte du Moi*:

> Certains lieux fameux dans l'histoire de la sensibilité humaine portent nos âmes au-delà de nos propres émotions et nous communiquent les fièvres qui les remplirent un jour ... Ce sont là des

16 *See Œuvre* II 34, 361 and, above, pp. 12–13.

> *stations idéologiques* aussi puissantes sur l'imagination que telles stations thermales sur des tempéraments déterminés, et les pèlerinages catholiques font voir merveilleusement que cette méthode d'exaltation intellectuelle réunit toutes les conditions pour tourner en passions la curiosité et le respect.
>
> Mais chaque génération se choisit ses lieux de dévotion préférés, et c'est même dans ces élections que se révèlent les variations de la sensibilité.
>
> [*Trois stations de psychothérapie*, *Œuvre* II 356]

Thus the author of *Trois stations de psychothérapie* in 1890 prefaces his intention of 'organizing the *legend*' of Marie Bashkirtseff, 'in order to perfect this exceptional figure and to bring out all her symbolic value' (*Œuvre* II 358); and with this in mind he elects as shrines for his generation the typical 'stations' of her life and death ('l'hôtel de la rue de Prony, la villa de Nice pleine de roses qu'elle aimait et le tombeau du cimetière de Passy') and the 'sites' which correspond with the spirit she embodied, and which her legend must evoke (the 'sleeping-car,' and the city of Rome, material correlatives of her 'moral bohemianism' and 'cosmopolitanism': *Notre Dame qui n'êtes jamais satisfaite*).

The complicated irony and the restless and rootless fancy of a sensation-seeking and self-conscious 'amateur d'âmes' determine and colour most of Barrès's early pilgrimages, real or imaginary: the 'magic gardens,'[17] and the strenuous cities of Tuscany; cosmopolitan Rome; the Venice of exiled poets, philosophers, painters, and musicians; the antithetical sites of Moorish and Castilian Spain ('ce pays double, ici toute mollesse et là rien que ressort'):[18] Granada ('des eaux vives, sous un soleil africain' [*Du Sang, de la volupté et de la mort*, *Œuvre* II 37]), the Escurial ('le lieu de l'ascétisme et la traduction en granit de la discipline castillane, issue d'une conception catholique de la mort' [34]), Toledo ('moins une ville ... qu'un lieu significatif pour l'âme ... une image de l'exaltation dans la solitude' [23–4]);

17 *See* Chapter Three, p. 39, note 23.

18 'L'Italie est moins simple, plus composée; dans sa douceur tu peux sommeiller; ici tout est brusque et d'un accent qui mord' (*Œuvre* II 33).

the tomb of Wagner ('Allons à Wahnfried, sur la tombe de Wagner, honorer les pressentiments d'une éthique nouvelle' [191]) ; the dream-ridden castles of Louis of Bavaria (*L'Ennemi des lois, Œuvre* II 265–73) ; the 'sacred' plains of Russia, the Caucasian valleys, Armenia and the shrines of Persia, from which, finally, he composed, in the commerce of friends, or the pages of a book, an atlas, an illustrated Bible, a mysterious '*là-bas*,' as yet out of reach, 'sous les brouillards qu'y met notre ignorance': 'Combien j'aimerais accomplir là-bas mon pèlerinage de gratitude!'[19] But already, before Barrès's first journey to Spain, the hero of *Le Culte du Moi* had begun to discern at Laître-sous-Amance and Saint-Mihiel, in the 'heart of Lorraine,' at Aigues-Mortes and at Maillane, in Provence, the lineaments of a deeply and firmly rooted French tradition: while Sturel's Italian *rêveries* alternate with energetic if still disjointed and inconclusive acts of politics at home, inspired by a call to arms he hears at the *Arc de Triomphe*, the *Panthéon*, the tomb of Napoleon and the campaign headquarters of General Boulanger.[20]

The harvest of impressions that Barrès brought in from the sentimental and ideological 'stations' of his formative years was not wasted. The image of France, with which he enriched the literature of French patriotism, and in which the chief devices of his rhetoric of commemoration (*formule, image, symbole, récit*, legend, iconography, relics and emblems, ceremony, pilgrimage) combine most effectively, is set among three great neighbours whose features he had already traced and fixed by 1900: Italy, '*magna parens* ... the eternal educator ...still civilizing young barbarians' (*Les Amitiés françaises, Œuvre* V 494), Spain, a country of violent contrasts and passionate intensity (*Du sang, de la volupté et de la mort, Œuvre* II 23–72; *Greco, Œuvre* VII 373), Germany, primaeval and mysterious, a kind of anti-France, both complement and rival, fascinating and menacing, attractive and repugnant, and in opposition to which Barrès's portrait of his homeland was chiefly posed and drawn (*Les Déracinés, Œuvre* III 21; *L'Appel au soldat, Œuvre* II 389–400). After 1900 he accomplished a

19 *Œuvre* I 167–8; II 179, 361; XX 72–3. *See* I.-M. Frandon, *L'Orient de Maurice Barrès*, 13–86.

20 *Œuvre* I 196–213, 312–24; III 164–78, 325–45, 456–7; IV 79–84

part of his long desired 'pilgrimage of gratitude' to the civilizations of the Near and Middle East, visiting Greece in 1900, Egypt in 1907, Syria and Lebanon in 1914. His informed sympathy for certain aspects of Oriental culture,[21] pushed to one side by the exigences of war-time journalism, broke into his work again after 1918 more freely and, from a literary point of view, more effectively than before, in *Une Enquête aux pays du Levant*, *Un Jardin sur l'Oronte*, and two essays published after his death in *Le Mystère en pleine lumière*: 'Les Turquoises gravées' and 'La Musique de perdition.' Moreover, as his patriotic and religious inspiration grew stronger throughout this same period, the 'method of intellectual exaltation' he had first seen 'marvellously demonstrated' in the pilgrimages of expiation organized by the French Church after the national disasters of 1870 and 1871, while his *Culte du Moi* was taking shape, recovered its original patriotic purpose in the 'Propaganda for a nationalist education' with which he tried to contain and counter the impetus of Dreyfusard humanism,[22] and its original religious one in the campaign he launched nine years later for the preservation of the parish churches of Catholic France, 'les petites églises qui sont les points de repère des paysages français ... ces points de spiritualité' (*Mes Cahiers, Œuvre* xv 26).

As a methodical nationalist and Catholic pilgrim, Barrès consciously exploited the 'hyperaesthesia' he had inherited from the solitary *rêveries* of his Romantic forerunners. He claimed to have subjected their excessive emotionalism to the control of what he called 'positive' knowledge:

> J'ai trouvé une discipline dans les cimetières où nos prédécesseurs divaguaient, et c'est grâce peut-être à l'hyperesthésie que nous transmirent ces grands poètes de la rêverie que nous dégagerons des vérités positives situées dans notre profond sous-conscient.

21 *See* I.-M. Frandon, *L'Orient de Maurice Barrès*, *passim* and, especially pp. 353–71.

22 *See* Chapter Eleven: 'Saint-Phlin and *Les Amitiés françaises*.' A speech for the anniversary of *L'Action Française*, in June 1901, *Œuvre* v 124–6, *cit.* below, pp. 174 and 179, shows Barrès consciously switching the vehicle of his egotist and cosmopolitan *rêveries* on to the track of patriotic propaganda.

> Ce qui fait les dessous de ma pensée, ma nappe inépuisable, c'est ma Lorraine.
> [*Amori et dolori sacrum, Œuvre* VII 9–10]

But the 'subterranean' origin of the Lorraine celebrated in this introduction to *Amori et dolori sacrum* betrays the distance Barrès has already travelled, since the comparatively genuine fact-finding which still inspired Saint-Phlin's and Sturel's first 'object lessons' in the populous and industrialized Moselle Valley (*Œuvre* IV 4–101), along the primrose path which will become so familiar to him, from 'experimental' Naturalism to experiential traditionalism, from the scientific collection of objective data (Taine's 'petits faits vrais') to the sympathetic intuition of collective experience, pictured here as an underground reservoir of sub-conscious wisdom which can only be tapped successfully by an imagination attuned to the 'spirit of place' with which a site has been invested by its association with a representative event or hero from history or legend. Barrès's cult of intercessory heroes and his rhetoric of tonic commemoration combine to give pride of place in his traditionalistic image of France to what he called, with some metaphorical extension of the normal meaning of the word, his 'cemeteries': 'Mes cimetières lorrains. (Certains grands hommes dans leur paysage)' (*Mes Cahiers, Œuvre* XV 393).

> Plus que tout au monde, j'ai aimé le musée du Trocadéro, les marais d'Aigues-Mortes et de Ravenne, les paysages de Tolède et de Sparte; mais à tous ces magnifiques cimetières je préfère maintenant mon modeste cimetière lorrain, la plaine de Sion-Vaudémont qu'un Lorrain seul sait faire parler.
> [*Scènes et doctrines du nationalisme, Œuvre* V 125][23]

> C'est possible qu'en tous lieux la nature révèle un Dieu, mais je ne puis entendre son hymne que sur la tombe des grands hommes.
> [*Le Voyage de Sparte, Œuvre* VII 267]

> Il me faut toujours animer un pays de divinités topiques,

23 Cf. *Œuvre* VII 132.

l'humaniser ... C'est toujours la lutte de l'homme sur la nature. Je l'admire, puis je veux la conquérir, y poser mon esprit. Mais dans ce travail instinctif d'appropriation, dans cet effort à la Robinson Crusoé, que je respecte et connaisse les sources. Sous ces commodités pour vivre, il y a l'immense océan de songerie. Des demi-dieux, mais il y a là-dessous la divinité. Ils ne sont que des intermédiaires, mes compagnons.
[*Mes Cahiers, Œuvre* XV 248]

Jamais je ne suis allé dans un pays sans honorer le génie du lieu.
[*Mes Cahiers, Œuvre* XVIII 226]

CHAPTER TEN

An Image of France

THE SPIRIT OF PLACE

The compelling sense of his country's decline that Charles Maurras acquired from a journey to Greece for the Olympic Games of 1896 is well known: 'Loin de France ... il vit mieux la faiblesse de notre pays, son abandon en face de l'Angleterre et de l'Allemagne. Bouleversé, il revisa son bagage d'histoire et conclut bientôt à la nécessité urgente de restaurer la monarchie.'[1] The lesson for French nationalists that Maurice Barrès drew from a visit to Athens and Sparta four years later was characteristic of a writer whose fundamentally emotional commitment to France depended less than Maurras's 'integral nationalism' on systematic, arguable theory, but whose intellectual side was constantly attracted to the study of universal, demonstrable techniques of persuasion ('une hygiène de l'âme ... un laboratoire de l'enthousiasme,' 'mécaniser les hommes ... suggestionner la personnalité,' 'des moyens mécaniques pour multiplier en nous l'enthousiasme ... une nomenclature d'agents matériels propres à exalter l'âme,' 'mon obsession, de toute ma vie, pour ce qui multiple les forces de l'âme'),[2] Barrès in Greece made progress in the rhetoric rather than in the philosophy of nationalism, bringing back home to France not a new set of political

1 H. Clouard, *Histoire de la littérature française du Symbolisme à nos jours* I 325. Cf. L.S. Roudiez, *Maurras jusqu'à 'L'Action Française'* (Paris: André Bonne 1957) 313.

2 *Œuvre* I 169; III 160; XI 379; XIX 200

convictions but a perfected instrument of political propaganda: evocatory landscape-with-figures.[3]

Genius loci, the Spirit of Place, active at many of the primary sources of Barrès's intellectual and sentimental education – in the Catholic pilgrimages of atonement after the Franco-Prussian War, in the *Spiritual Exercises* of Ignatius de Loyola ('composition of place'), in Ménard's *Rêveries d'un païen mystique*,[4] in Michelet, Renan, and Taine, in the 'hyperaesthesia' of Romantic and post-Romantic poets[5] – had already, before 1900, inspired a variety of pre-nationalist Barresian landscapes in *Le Culte du Moi*,[6] *Trois stations de psychothérapie*, and *Du Sang, de la volupté et de la mort*.[7] The spirit of 'high places' had found conscious expression in a nationalistic context as early as 1897: the penultimate chapter of *Les Déracinés*, entitled 'La vertu social d'un cadavre,' where the republican funeral rites of Victor Hugo are emotionally recollected for the climax of the first part of *Le Roman de l'énergie nationale*.[8] Most of the characteristic features of the Barresian useful art of politico-religious landscape are already present in this chapter, which pictures the twin heights of central Paris as stage-sets for a mass act of patriotic commemoration, in which the

3 The general inspiration and structure of Barrès's landscapes is admirably defined by J.-M. Domenach in *Barrès par lui-même*, 60. *See* also, H. Bremond, *Maurice Barrès: Vingt-cinq années de vie littéraire* (Paris: Bloud 1911) 46–51; A. Thibaudet, *La Vie de Maurice Barrès* (Paris: Gallimard 1921) 30; R. Audibert, 'Idéologies et paysages passionnés,' *La Table Ronde* (March 1957); J.-P. Sartre, *Situations* (Paris: Gallimard 1948) II 209–10; G. Bauër, *cit. Œuvre* VII xi.

4 *Œuvre* II 356 (Catholic pilgrimages); I 178–81; II 361; III 160–1 (Loyola); I 454–5; VII 162–76 (Ménard)

5 *See Bibliothèque Nationale. Manuscrits. Nouvelles acquisitions françaises*, no. 11728, fol. 46 (*Un Homme libre*), *cit.* above, p. 12; *Le Départ pour la vie* (letters to L. Sorg and S. de Guaita) (Paris: Plon 1961) 46; 'Les Grandes figures de France,' *La Grande Revue de Paris et de St-Pétersbourg* 15 September 1888; *Œuvre* VII 187; XI 133 (Renan); II 126; VI 61–3; VII 114–15, 242–3 (Taine); I 390–401, 432–42, 450–63; VII 9, 33–4, 121, 182 (Romantics and post-Romantics).

6 'En Lorraine,' 'Mon Triomphe de Venise,' 'Reconstitution synthétique d'Aigues-Mortes, de Bérénice, de Charles Martin et de moi-même, avec la connaissance que j'ai des parties'

7 'L'Exaltation dans la solitude,' 'Les Jets alternés de l'Espagne,' 'À la pointe extrême de l'Europe,' 'Les Jardins de Lombardie'

8 *Œuvre* III 343–4, *cit.* above, pp. 169–70.

dead 'poet-prophet,' borne from the 'Pride of France' to the 'Heart of France,' is raised to the status of popular mystical leader by the force of his legend, working on the imagination of a great crowd assembled at hilltop monuments and reliquaries that seem to contain and radiate the nation's powerful reserves of enthusiasm and energy. There are also some already typically Barresian fragments of persuasively slanted landscape poetry-in-prose embedded in the sociological and historical 'object lesson' entitled 'La Vallée de la Moselle,' which he first published in *La Quinzaine,* 1 and 16 April 1899, as a 'journey in search of the roots of the nation' (*Œuvre* IV 20–101). But it was Barrès's voyage to Greece, his first foreign 'pilgrimage' as a fully committed nationalist, that made clear to him what the cause stood yet to gain from French landscape imaginatively transfigured in the light and perspective and unity of patriotic sentiment, and that convinced him of his own potential as a landscape word-painter within the common propaganda effort required for the 'nationalist education' of French public opinion:

> Heureux celui qui, de l'Acropole, en face des collines classiques, réjouit pleinement son âme! Quant à moi, je ne viens pas en Grèce pour goûter un paysage. J'ai pu cueillir les gros œillets d'Andalousie et les camélias des lacs italiens, mais, à respirer au pied du Parthénon les violettes de l'Attique, je mésuserais de mon pèlerinage.
>
> Heureux encore qui se satisfait de comprendre tant bien que mal, des parties de beauté! Moi, je ne puis me contenter avec des plaisirs fragmentaires. Où que je sois, je suis mal à l'aise si je n'ai pas un point de vue d'où les détails se subordonnent les uns aux autres et d'où l'ensemble se raccorde à mes acquisitions précédentes.

> Rien de plus beau que le Parthénon, mais il n'est pas l'hymne qui s'échappe naturellement de notre âme; il ne réalise pas l'image que nous nous composons d'une éternité de plaisir. Épictète disait malheureux l'homme qui meurt sans avoir gravi l'Acropole. Ah! s'il existait un pèlerinage que Pascal eût ainsi recommandé comme la fleur du monde! Je rêve d'un temple dressé par un Phidias de notre race dans un beau lieu français, par exemple sur les collines

de la Meuse, à Domremy, où ma vénération s'accorderait avec la nature et l'art, comme celle des anciens Grecs en présence du Parthénon...

Avec quel plaisir, en quittant cette Athènes fameuse, j'ai retrouvé mon aigre Lorraine! C'était le début de l'automne... un doux ciel bleu pommelé de nuages, d'immenses labours que parsèment des bosquets, un horizon de molles côtes viticoles, et des routes qui fuient avec les longs peupliers chantants.
[*Le Voyage de Sparte, Œuvre* VII 187, 299–300]

It was somewhat less than a year after this homecoming, at a first anniversary dinner of *Action Française*, that Barrès introduced to the Nationalist 'party,' as his own, the formula for the composition of persuasive landscapes, specifically emotive in its purpose and explicitly imaginative in its mode of operation, that was to be his most original contribution to the rhetoric of French nationalism between the Dreyfus Affair and the First World War:

Voilà ce qu'Henri Vaugeois nous a dit d'une façon philosophique, et pour *sentir* ce qu'il nous a *démontré*, nous pourrions prendre des 'leçons de choses.' Ah! si nous pouvions circuler tous ensemble, en automobile par exemple, à travers les paysages français! si nous prenions connaissance de la figure de notre pays!...

Pour ma part, je voudrais être votre cicérone en Lorraine...

Dans ce paysage qui n'a guère bougé ... La motte de terre elle-même qui paraît sans âme est pleine du passé, et son témoignage ébranle les cordes de l'imagination!
[*Scènes et doctrines du nationalisme, Œuvre* V 124–6][9]

From All Souls' Day, 1900, through the next three years, Barrès's private notebooks[10] record a varied program of excursions, by train or car and on foot, alone or with friends, or in the company of his young son, Philippe, to such places as Sion-Vaudémont, Sainte-Odile, Brienne, Domremy, Lourdes, and reveal a conscious effort to find a

9 Cf. *Œuvre* VII 128–33.
10 *Œuvre* XIII 294–8, 312–13, 320–4, 337–9; XIV 11–32, 80, 83, 86; XV 214

way of using 'the senses,' 'mimesis,' 'divination,' 'deep memory,' 'sympathy,' 'artist's perspective,' etc., to make landscapes convey patriotic insights and ideals, an effort leading Barrès diametrically away from the properly objective purpose of the *leçon de choses* which he had by and large respected, in the detailed, documentary, 'Naturalist' technique of 'La Vallée de la Moselle.' The new program and method were further publicly illustrated and elaborated in *Leurs figures* (1902), 'Lettre de Saint-Phlin sur une "nourriture" lorraine.' By 1903, the lesson of Greece having been clarified by time and distance (*Œuvre* VII 298–301), he was ready, in the concluding chapter of *Les Amitiés françaises*: 'Chant de confiance dans la vie' ('qui demeure ce qui me définit le mieux' [*Grande Guerre* IV 178]), to set the evocatory magic of landscape at the very centre of his private inspiration and public mission:

> la plus belle, la plus sûre, la plus constante des ... déesses qui donnent un sens à la vie, c'est la Nature en France, je veux dire nos paysages formés par l'Histoire. Je leur dois mes meilleurs moments. Devant eux, la grâce toujours descendit sur moi avec même efficace.
>
> ...
>
> Ces grands états d'émotivité que chacun connut de l'amour, qu'un homme viril reçoit des héros et des chefs de sa race, je voudrais que la terre française chargée de tombes les communiquât au promeneur pensif...
>
> Il est des lyres sur tous les sommets de la France.
>
> [*Les Amitiés françaises, Œuvre* V 556–7]

THE BASTIONS OF FRANCE

In 'Le 2 novembre en Lorraine' (1900–2), Barrès elected three symbolic 'high places' to command a panoramic image of the patriot's France and looked forward to composing a group portrait of their inter-related destinies:

> Ma pensée française a trois sommets, trois refuges: la montagne de Sion-Vaudémont, Sainte-Odile, et le Puy de Dôme. Le Puy de Dôme régnait chez les Arvernes: il fut le maître et le dieu du pays

où j'ai pris mon nom de famille. Sainte-Odile d'Alsace et Sion de Lorraine président la double région où je veux enclore ma vie; ils symbolisent les vicissitudes de la résistance latine à la pensée germanique. Pourquoi ne dirais-je pas un jour les beaux dialogues que font ces trois divinités, quand le massif central français contrôle et redresse la pensée de nos hardis bastions de l'Est? [*Amori et dolori sacrum, Œuvre* VII 129]

By 1913, he could claim to have completed two-thirds of the portrait, though in fragments only: 'J'avais chanté le lieu sacré de l'Alsace' (in *Au service de l'Allemagne* 1905). 'J'ai voulu chanter le lieu sacré de la Lorraine' (*La Colline inspirée* 1913) (*Mes Cahiers, Œuvre* XVII 279–80). His song of Le Puy de Dôme was never published, however, apparently because, although, as he once noted: 'C'est le centre de la France,' he had taken this opinion from books: Lavisse, Vidal de la Blache, Bloch, and it was liable to be contradicted by other books. His own deeply and strongly sympathetic 'coincidence' with the Auvergne landscape either aroused in him a pantheistic mood too indefinite to serve a public partisan cause, or *via* the intercessory figures of Pascal and Saint Odilon, led him to meditative and musical forms of religious mysticism which did not readily lend themselves to location at any particular place in France. Le Puy de Dôme might be at the centre of France, but the inspiration Barrès got from it was not at the centre of his French nationalism; this lay further east, deep in the Lotharingian roots of a frontiersman's sense of insecurity, and high on the 'bastions' built up against the pressure of pangermanism in front, and the breach of meridional French 'anarchy' behind:

En Alsace ... voilà des cadres, des chefs, des compétences, des mœurs; voilà enfin les conditions qui permettent au système républicain de fonctionner. Mais ces solides qualités, notre Midi français, si éloquent, si amusant, ne les a pas. Ses 'hommes à poigne' et ses 'grands orateurs' ont mis la France en anarchie nullement en république, et nous sommes tout prêts pour le démembrement par l'étranger ou pour une dissolution de société réclamée par des actionnaires mécontents.

...

Ces frivoles méridionaux sont ravis que l'Alsace disparaisse du

groupement qui fait la nationalité française, les voilà devenus les maîtres. Mais cette rupture d'équilibre dénature la France et nous perd.
['La Sagesse de l'Est,' *La Patrie* 10 October 1902][11]

For such reasons, the Vosges 'bastion' occupied a key position in Barrès's patriotic image of France. The Ottilienberg, given the 'accumulated virtues of its landscape' (relics of an ancient frontier: 'mur païen,' 'oppidum gaulois,' 'castellum romain,' and the shrine of a patron saint who, as the first abbess of a Roman Catholic convent, could be said to have succeeded Rosmertha, the pagan spirit of the mountain), was particularly precious to him, representing the 'constant tendency' of the Eastern Marches of France, i.e., the 'romanization of the Germans': 'Aujourd'hui encore, sur la riche région où l'Ottilienberg règne, les éléments germaniques et gallo-romains sont en contact; le problème le plus actuel et le plus pressent y est toujours celui qu'incarne Sainte Odile' (*Au service de l'Allemagne, Œuvre* VI 63).

Of the three main 'summits' of Barrès's France, it was of course Sion-Vaudémont, the 'sacred hill,' the 'centre,' the 'Acropolis' of Lorraine,[12] eight miles from his birthplace, that was the most important to him: the first to call home the young cosmopolitan individualist, fleetingly, in 1888 (*Un Homme libre, Œuvre* I 206–7), and the first to which the nationalist would turn deliberately for propagandist inspiration in 1901 (*Scènes et doctrines du nationalisme, Œuvre* V 124–8). It gave him the theme of the book which, while dramatizing the *genius loci* of the frontier between France and Germany and between Rome and Rosmertha round which he had 'prowled' so long (*Mes Cahiers, Œuvre* XX 188), most effectively transcends the aims and devices of political and religious propaganda in the narrow sense of the term. The same 'sacred hill' was, fittingly, the scene of his greatest personal triumph: the ritual mending of the cross of Lorraine, which his compatriots asked him to perform before twenty or thirty thousand people in June 1920 on an altar where, in 1873, it had been

11 *Œuvre* V 98–9, 126; XII 45–88, 137–47; XIII 209–12; XIV 147–8, 325; XX 185–6, 193
12 *Œuvre* V 125–6, 511; VI 259–82; VII 128–33; XIV 264; XVII 282–3

laid, broken, by the representatives of occupied Lorraine, 'avec un cri d'espérance: "Ce n'est pas pour toujours"' (*Grande Guerre* XIV 331–46).

Nothing could be more contrary to Barrès's intentions than to try to compress into a formula the significance he gave the hill which bears his memorial.[13] It evolved with his philosophy. Thus, in 1888, Sion-Vaudémont provided him with an imaginative vehicle for conveying, with a 'nuance of pity,' his sense of the past greatness and the present decadence of a little nation which, having been 'bled white' by the desertion of its artists and hereditary lords, brought with it, on absorption into the greater French nation, its new mentor and protector, specially strong local traditions of military devotion to duty and, in religious affairs, resistance to Protestant Reform (*Un Homme libre, Œuvre* I 206–13); by 1901–2 Barrès is using the same high place to assert this 'double tradition, religious and military' more confidently: the people of Vaudémont are pictured manning the 'great eastern bastions of Latin civilization' (*Œuvre* V 126; VII 129–33); subsequently, between 1902 and 1913, from 'Le 2 novembre en Lorraine' to *La Colline inspirée,* the 'Acropolis' of Lorraine is given ever greater religious import, at the expense of its secular rôle, to correspond with the similar development of Barrès's traditionalism.[14]

During the second half of his career Barrès gave a prominent place to another frontier shrine in which both sides of his nation's double tradition are equally balanced: Domremy.[15] Here, in 1906, at last re-elected to Parliament, he chose, with touching humility and candour, to make a kind of retreat, in preparation for the task of deputation which was to be his again, after a gap of thirteen years:

> Au lendemain de mon élection (la première au 1er arrondissement, 1906) je suis allé passer quelques jours à Domremy. Affreuse installation. C'était pour y chercher une digne énergie vitale. Sorte de démarche grave, me placer sous un signe beau et noble, en secret.
> [*Mes Cahiers, Œuvre* XIII 25]

13 A lantern, erected in 1928

14 *Œuvre* VI 259–500; VII 129–33; XIV 12–13, 28, 30–1; XV 35, 254; XVII 282–4. Cf. J. and J. Tharaud, *Pour les fidèles de Barrès,* 175–97.

15 *Œuvre* V 520–36; XII 262–73; XVI 363–9

And here, ten years later, his country's struggle to hold Verdun roused Barrès's old desire to see a French Acropolis established at the Maid's birthplace above the Meuse.[16] The saint whose 'cult is synonymous with the *Revanche*' could not, he believed, have too much poetry, too many ceremonies and pilgrimages devoted to her:

> Nous réclamons une poésie populaire, spontanée, anonyme, née des événements, jaillie de l'âme du peuple tout entier. Où personne ne suffirait, que tous s'associent. Que les sanctuaires, les théâtres, les pèlerinages, les cortèges, les conférences et les sermons retentissent. Qu'au village sacré de Domremy, à Vaucouleurs, à Saint-Nicolas, à Nancy, la ville de son duc, dans toutes les étapes de son voyage vers Bourges, à Orléans, à Reims, sur tous ses champs de bataille, dans tous les pas de son martyre, elle soit nommée sainte et patronne de la France.
> [*Grande Guerre* VIII 210–11]

Barrès also pointed his pre-war nationalist campaigns with a variety of minor 'eastern bastions,' showing a sure sense of every propagandist's first figure of rhetoric, repetition with variations. Thus he took his readers through the quiet, civilized countryside of occupied Lorraine ('le signe d'une pensée inexprimable,' 'une vive image du devoir'), to the battlefield of Froeschwiller, and to the war memorial at Chambières, in Prussian-occupied Metz ('Une de nos pierres sacrées, un autel et un refuge, le dernier de nos menhirs').[17]

A MYTHICAL GEOGRAPHY OF THE FRANCO-GERMAN BORDER

Barrès's landscapes of eastern France constitute what G. Gusdorf would call 'une géographie mythique [qui] donne au paysage la sanction des présences transcendantes'.[18] His Alsace-Lorraine is ground reserved for a duel of rival spirits: *germanisme* and *latinité*, an histori-

16 *Le Voyage de Sparte, Œuvre* VII 299–300, *cit.* above, p. 178.
17 *Œuvre* V 90–2, 348–366; VI 170, 186–7, 214–18, 230–6
18 'Mythe et philosophie,' *La Revue de Métaphysique et de Morale* (April–June 1951) 180

cal conflict between nations raised to the status of the 'eternal' and the 'elemental':

> Il en va de cette querelle pour la possession du Rhin comme de la lutte entre le soleil et la pluie qui se développe sans atteindre jamais l'état stable.
> ['La Solution est à Paris,' *La Patrie* 12 September 1902]

Thus the German invasion of 1914 is seen as the fatal re-enactment of a high mystery 'established from all eternity' like a force of nature:

> La trouée de Charmes, le passage de la Moselle sur Mirecourt et Neufchâteau, voilà des pays nobles, des pays de grande histoire et qui furent, en tous siècles, la route des invasions ... Nous sommes un des chemins mystérieux du monde, la route de l'esprit, le sentier de guerre où le germanisme toujours a tenté d'assaillir la civilisation de Rome et ses héritiers. Destinée fatale, établie de toute éternité, de même que sur nos têtes, chaque automne, c'est le grand passage des oiseaux qui émigrent.
> [*Grande Guerre* II 41]

The 'change' in the geography of France that Barrès attributed to the Great War was a change in the mythical geography of its Eastern Marches, the consecration of fresh ground on a sacred and eternal frontier already rich in hallowed places:

> Avez-vous remarqué comme la géographie de la France est changée depuis le début de la guerre? Des noms émergent que tout le monde ignorait; les regards du monde entier se tournent vers des mottes de terre qui ne furent jamais nommées d'aucun nom. Elles prennent une personnalité d'importance mondiale et rien qu'un chiffre les désigne.
> [*Grande Guerre* VII 223]

If Barrès's *Chronique de la Grande Guerre* too often echoes the conventional heroics of official wartime propaganda, at other times his long-practised sense of the tragic spirit of the Franco-German frontier goes, with genuine perception and pity, to the heart of a terrible occasion which, while seeming to confirm the value of his mythical map-making, has also removed much that was facile and unreal in his pre-war exaltation of martial valour; for instance, in this 'composition de lieu,' written in February 1916:

> De la mer du Nord à la Suisse, ne perdons jamais de vue la frontière sinueuse formée par nos fils et par les territoriaux. Voyez ces dunes, ces boues marécageuses, les positions sanglantes de Notre-Dame-de-Lorette, la vallée de la Somme, les tranchées argileuses et collantes de l'Aisne, toutes blanchâtres en Champagne, les sombres collines forestières de l'Argonne, la Woëvre toute trempée, le sinistre bois Le Prêtre, la Lorraine en ruines, les Vosges, cimetière de nos Alpins. Sur ce long réseau, à toutes les heures, depuis dix-sept mois, toujours des efforts, toujours des blessés et des morts. [*Grande Guerre* VII 114]

Eastwards of Lorraine Barrès pictured a perpetually resurgent 'flood' beating against a French 'dyke,' an adversative metaphor aptly expressing the defensive stance of his nationalism and the crucial position on his patriotic map of France, of Alsace and Lorraine, first and second lines of defence, destined either to 'stem' or to 'go under to' the 'German spirit,' which, like a 'tempest coming from the depths of Prussia,' 'ceaselessly assails' the spirit of the French nation.[19] After the religious crisis of his middle forties, as his nationalism grew towards belief in the supernatural, within the doctrinal and institutional cadre of Roman Catholicism, the Church too became part of the same defensive system, a bulwark confronting the 'torrential' Idealism of German metaphysics, which had swept him in youth from his native moorings and alienated him, so he now believed, from his true self.[20] French Catholicism, supported by the 'traditions of Athens and of Rome,' he represented as a 'line of stakes' opposed to the 'threatening cavalcade of German gods,' or as a 'dam,' a 'sacred mole' standing

19 'La Solution est à Paris,' *La Patrie* 12 September 1902; *Œuvre* I 140; IV 76, 398; V 474, 560–1; VI 170, 204

20 'Ce sentiment informe qui nous remplit tous, jeunes gens chez qui les torrents de la métaphysique allemande ont brisé les compartiments latins' (*Œuvre* II 361). Cf. III 19–21.

against an 'ocean' whose far eastern horizon, beyond philosophical, deep-thinking Germany, merges with the 'vast flood' of Asiatic nihilism.[21]

The Great War convinced Barrès that the French could rise above this oncoming flood-tide: 'le flot ne les noyera plus' (*Grande Guerre* IV 177). Germany's defeat did not relieve the French nationalist of his duty to protect France's 'intellectual territory,' but it did allow some attenuation of the defensive screen; let there be no longer a 'total' barrier, but rather a 'filter':

> vertu du primitif, du spontané, de l'irrationnel, notion du vague et de l'illimité, musicalité sourde et psychologie rigide, égocentrisme tenace et insocial, métaphysique alimentant les racines souterraines de l'épanouissement artistique – il y a des valeurs à laisser passer quand on ne les trouve pas dans le sol originel.
> [*Les grands problèmes du Rhin, Œuvre* X 406][22]

After 1918, Barrès exulted freely in 'the perfect spiritual climate' of a Rhineland Lotharingia that he optimistically believed could now be detached from the hegemony of Prussia. This 'magic territority,' at 'the limit of two worlds,' where 'France and Germany are for ever being mixed and remade,'[23] became *le pays qui lui ressemble*, the territorial *correspondance* of that creative antithesis of primitive irrationality and civilized order, of mystery and light, which had inspired the epilogue of *La Colline inspirée*, and which would provide the collective title and the dominant theme of his last volume of essays:

> Il existe un génie rhénan, que l'on peut dire à la fois germanique et latin, et qui redonnera quelque jour des fleurs incomparables. C'est, il me semble, une aptitude à traiter le mystère en pleine lumière.
> [*Grande Guerre* XIII 255]

21 *Œuvre* III 21; V 560–3; VII 66; X 377–8; 542; XI 464–7; XII 21; *Grande Guerre* IX 284

22 Cf. *Œuvre* X 262–3, 385, 411–12, 542 and *Grande Guerre* XIII 256; also, for a much earlier and more negative and arrogant use of the same image, *Œuvre* V 283: 'Nous avons filtré les races inférieures.'

23 *Œuvre* X 37; *Grande Guerre* XIII 261–2, 292, 300–7

A SACRED TOPOGRAPHY OF FRANCE AND THE LEVANT

'Il est des lieux où souffle l'esprit'

Barrès's image of the Franco-German frontier was meant to show how France must conduct her relations with a neighbour whose genius is at best complementary, at worst hostile to her own. It was part of the 'direction' of public opinion which was one of the two main objects of Barrès's propaganda. The other, namely the tapping of the French nation's reserves of spiritual energy, allegedly buried by rationalism and internationalism, was also served by topographical images. The dimension of depth here occupies the place that lateral movement (the oncoming wave, and its counterpart: the dam or filter) held in Barrès's imaginative deployment of French nationalism against Germany. The French tradition is pictured as a store of energy deposited, below the surface of the visible present, by generations of past Frenchmen. Like his mythical geography of Franco-German destinies, Barrès's spiritual geology of France (and later also the Levant) was inspired by the 'hyperaesthesia' of a pilgrim to sites associated with representative episodes and types of history and legend, and was especially (but not so exclusively) concerned with the Eastern Marches of France, in his native Lotharingia, its cultural 'humus' enriched by 'layer after layer' of migrants from central Europe.[24] In his pre-war and wartime nationalist propaganda Barrès often used images of his country's 'subterranean streams' of patriotic[25] or religious instinct.[26] The allied victory freed him to explore the origins of such psychical forces (as he continuously explored the means of their multiplication) further, and more independently of partisan expediency, to the point where he saw them merging darkly and deeply in a single 'lake,' 'ocean,' 'sea,' of inspiration, lying below the surface of rational consciousness and explicit doctrine, but demanding scientific investigation, and accessible through a variety of 'beliefs,' 'myths,' and 'lives,'

24 *Œuvre* IV 36; VI 54, 496; *Grande Guerre* XIII 264

25 *Œuvre* III 344; IV 148, 227; V 26, 92; VII 9; *Grande Guerre* II 79, 84, 252; IX 17, 164; X 16

26 *Œuvre* VIII 52–3, 162, 165; XVII 252; *Grande Guerre* III 340

all of which Barrès came to recognize as 'delegations' of the 'divine.'[27] The problem of illuminating and controlling this obscure 'generative ocean' moved to the forefront of his work after the War and inspired a new range of 'mythical' landscapes beyond the limits of French nationalism, such as Mirabeau, in Provence, Baalbek, Daphne, and the valley of the Adonis, and this, depicting Vesuvius on a spring day in 1922:

> Un tel paysage, mieux que la plus sublime musique, est une initiation. Il nous dispose, nous incline, et nous sentons renaître en notre âme un large sentiment mythique. Nous nous croyons prêts à saisir le mystère de cette nature et de toute vie...
>
> Quel signe il porte au front, le volcan! Son grand panache de fumée et de feu donne un sens inépuisable à tout le golfe miraculeux et m'appelle à méditer ses hauts accès, ses ardeurs secrètes et souterraines, ses paroxysmes redoutables et pleins de fécondité. Au commencement de toute grande chose il y eut ainsi, il y aura toujours une humanité pleine encore d'animalité, un débordement de forces indomptées et passionnées ... C'est sur ces ténèbres ignées, sur cette mer de flammes noires que reposent notre raison, nos sciences, nos religions, tous nos actes. Ici je me penche au centre de l'être et je respire profondément, hors du monde des choses claires, la réalité première, l'océan de feu sur lequel reposent toute notre raison et toute notre science qu'il alimente et qu'il menace.
>
> Sans ces laves, aucune haute civilisation. Mais il les faut endiguer. C'est une chaleur magnifique, à redouter et à vénérer, à contenir et à distribuer, bref à régler. Problème des premiers temps et de chaque jour, de toutes les sociétés et de chaque individu.
> [*N'Importe où hors du monde, Œuvre* XII 517–18][28]

Meanwhile he had enriched his image of France with a new motive, repeated over the length and breadth of the country: the 'open-air

27 *Œuvre* VIII 443; XII 40; XIX 280

28 Cf. *Œuvre* IX 328, 364–5; XI 102, 140, 172–3, 203, 358–9; XII 187, 193, 196, 222, 241–2, 385–93; XX 13–14.

temple,' 'elected from all eternity as a place of religious emotion' (*La Colline inspirée, Œuvre* VI 273). In the lyrical overture to *La Colline inspirée*, he picks out briefly a dozen such 'places where the spirit bloweth' before settling on Sion-Vaudémont. Their virtue resides in an analogy between spiritual profundity and physical depth which is characteristic of the mythological imagination, and which Barrès used spontaneously but conciously when inspired by his country's venerable hilltops, wells, springs, groves, and meadows:

> D'où vient la puissance de ces lieux? La doivent-ils au souvenir de quelque grand fait historique, à la beauté d'un site exceptionnel, à l'émotion des foules qui du fond des âges y vinrent s'émouvoir? Leur vertu est plus mystérieuse. Elle précéda leur gloire et saurait y survivre. Que les chênes fatidiques soient coupés, la fontaine remplie de sable et les sentiers recouverts, ces solitudes ne sont pas déchues de pouvoir. La vapeur de leurs oracles s'exhale, même s'il n'est plus de prophétesse pour la respirer. Et n'en doutons pas, il est de par le monde infiniment de ces points spirituels qui ne sont pas encore révélés, pareils à ces âmes voilées dont nul n'a reconnu la grandeur. Combien de fois, au hasard d'une heureuse et profonde journée, n'avons-nous pas rencontré la lisière d'un bois, un sommet, une source, une simple prairie, qui nous commandaient de faire taire nos pensées et d'écouter plus profond que notre cœur! Silence! les dieux sont ici.
> [*La Colline inspirée, Œuvre* VI 274]

Water, Trees, Meadows

Barrès's open-air temples usually consist of more than one of those natural features which, permitting a variety of metaphors for depth, become 'properties'[29] of his traditionalism as characteristic as his 'summits.'

Water in a landscape always excited Barrès's imagination of the deeps subtending the individual and conscious mind: Haroué, in the

29 R. Wellek and A. Warren, *Theory of Literature* (London: Jonathan Cape 1961) 192–3

'heart of Lorraine,' where *un homme libre*, drawn to the flooded defences of the crumbling *château*, senses, with melancholy resignation, the frustrated and sickly power of his native province dormant in his own being (*Œuvre* I 210); the lagoons of Venice and of Aigues-Mortes (*Œuvre* I 40, 342); the *sources-mères* of Lorraine and Provence, Vaucluse, Saint-Vallier, Charmes-sur-Moselle (*Œuvre* XI 170–1; XIV 14; XVII 80, 108, 338). Water beneath trees, or welling up in a meadow, is the object of a great number of Barresian pilgrimages. Domremy was one, whose springs, meadows, and woods seemed to him still 'charged' with the pre-Christian memories which had nourished and supported Joan of Arc's Christian 'compassion' and 'enthusiasm,' at la fontaine Saint-Thiébaut, la fontaine des Groseillers, l'Arbre des Dames Fées, le Beau Mai; and whose hillside showed him, 'like a spring welling up through a fissure in the rock,' the 'mysterious treasure, the reserves of Nature,' the 'resurgent subterranean lake of all life' that the maid had captured (*Œuvre* V 523–6; XII 262–73; XVII 238; XVIII 50, 53–4). At Lourdes also, where 'the cult of a Virgin had been created by a child beside a running stream,' the *gave* rushing between green leaves seemed a 'landscape to lift the heart' (*Œuvre* V 543–52), its ugly commercial superstructure reminding him of another, similar, but unspoiled sanctuary in Greece: 'J'ai vu sur les ruines de Sparte, sous un platane, auprès des fontaines, un rêveur en fustanelle rouler entre ses doigts un "kombolo" dont les grains d'ambre me plaisaient' (*Œuvre* V 543; XIII 336–9). And for Bernadette's landscape he invents an apt variant of his familiar metaphor of spiritual energy surging from below: 'Je vois à Lourdes les plates conditions de notre vie au jour le jour, mais soumises à n'être qu'un terreau, d'où la fleur surgit sans y toucher que par sa mince tige' [*Les Amitiés françaises, Œuvre* V 544].

A district of France which particularly attracted Barrès by its suggestive combination of vegetation, water, and wide horizons, was the country round his friend Stanislas de Guaita's home at Alteville, in occupied Lorraine, 'parmi les vastes paysages de l'étang de Lindre' (*Œuvre* VII 75):

> Bien que j'aie entrevu un grand nombre de pays fameux, nul ne m'attire davantage que cette région des étangs lorrains.

...De grands espaces agricoles, presque toujours des herbages, ondulent sans un arbre, puis, çà et là, sur le renflement d'une douce courbe, surgit un petit bois carré de chênes, ou quelque mince bouquet de bouleaux. Dans les dépressions, l'herbe partout scintille, à cause de l'eau secrète...

La vertu de ce paysage, c'est qu'on n'en peut imaginer qui soit plus désencombré. Les mouvements du terrain, qui ne se brisent jamais, mènent nos sentiments là-bas, au loin, par delà l'horizon; ces étendues uniformes d'herbages apaisent, endorment nos irritations; les arbres clairsemés sur le bas ciel bleu semblent des mots de sympathie qui coupent un demi-sommeil, et les routes absolument droites, dont les grands peupliers courent à travers le plateau, y mettent une légère solennité...

...les étangs sont nombreux ... Leur atmosphère humide ajoute encore une sensation à cette harmonie générale de silence et d'humilité. Leur cuvette n'est point profonde; ça et là, jusque dans le centre de leur miroir, des roseaux et des joncs émergent, qui forment de bas rideaux ou des îlots de verdure. Sur leurs rives peu nettes et mâchées, l'eau affleure des bois de chênes et de hêtres.

[*Au Service de l'Allemagne* VI 19–20]

This haunting landscape is painted as the backcloth of a dramatic story about the German occupation of Alsace-Lorraine: *Au Service de l'Allemagne*. The 'atmosphere of disaster' it was intended to give the novel is that of 'un pays "welche" submergé,' part of Barrès's patriotic geography of the Eastern Bastions. Some years later, Barrès explored a similar landscape in French Lorraine: the headsprings of the Euron. He published these impressions on three occasions,[30] and they communicate exactly the peculiar thrill of veneration and enchantment which this kind of natural scenery gave him. Comparison with his earlier landscape of the Lorraine plateau in *Au Service de l'Allemagne* shows his progress in disengaging the religious

30 Preface to *La Ville enchantée*, by Mrs Oliphant (translated by Henri Bremond) (Paris: Émile-Paul 1911) [*Œuvre* XII 494–5]; *Œuvre* XII 201–2; *Grande Guerre* X 144–6. Cf. *Œuvre*, VIII 166; XVI 373 and J. and J. Tharaud, *Pour les fidèles de Barrès*, 28

nature of this thrill from the patriotic mood which had previously overlaid it. Instead of the rather strained exploitation of the natural 'properties' of upland Lorraine as symbolic representations of France's desertion and Germany's invasion of eastern France, Barrès by 1910 has found overwhelming religious significance in the scene of wide, glistening grassland fed by secret springs. What was latent in the earlier landscape, expressed imperfectly in a vague muted undertone, *solennité, harmonie, humilité*, has came out on top. In 1910 it is the patriotic emotion which has become the undertone of a predominantly religious *rêverie*:

> Le paysage est sans pittoresque, désert, et d'abord ne donne aucune prise à l'imagination. Il me touche d'autant, car n'ayant rien pour étonner, ni pour qu'on en cause, il ne s'adresse qu'à l'âme. C'est toute une prairie qui suinte, une prairie du vert le plus doux, formant une légère et vaste dépression où la nappe d'eau affleure...
> ...Cette eau qui sourd, qui vient mouiller les herbages, puis prend sa course vive, ces pensées qui naissent éternellement du génie de la race pour rafraîcher notre âme et recevoir d'elle une pente, raniment en nous les émotions primitives. D'anciennes forces accourent sans bruit, comme une barque glisse, comme les flocons de neige tombent. Elles nous enveloppent d'un subtil élément. Loin des réalités incomplètes et grossières, à l'abri de ce nuage, nous accueillons avec amour les songes qui redressent l'âme.
> [preface to Oliphant, *La Ville enchantée* (Paris: Émile-Paul 1911) *Œuvre* XII 494–5]

The late Barresian landscapes of *Une Enquête aux pays du Levant* (1923) are dominated by similar religious properties. The sacred groves and springs of Syria and Lebanon regularly body forth that 'perpetual transfiguration of the divine visage' which was the principal object of Barrès's journey to the Middle East in 1914: at Baalbek ('cette eau et ce bosquet ... le dieu les a trouvé agréables'), at Daphne ('Quel bruissement de fontaines! Quelle épaisseur de verdure! ... ce temple ... comme une explication mythique du paysage'), and up from the 'myth-laden' estuary of the river Adonis to its wild headspring in the gorges of Afaka ('C'est un lieu religieux ... je suis ici à cause du temple et des sources sacrées') (*Œuvre* XI 140, 170–3, 203, 358–9).

Trees and, more rarely, other plants, are characteristic vehicles of Barrès's traditionalism, symbolizing autonomous integrity and self-regulating growth by their need to put down roots – not in any particular place (*pace* Gide), but somewhere – the vital movement of their sap, the formation by stages of their head of scented, sounding, and fruitful branches.[31] The 'meadow' is a Barresian property nearer by a shade to the 'lagoon' and the 'spring': the imaginative correlative of undefined primitive religious enthusiasm. It entered Barrès's work by way of *Parsifal*:

> Alors ce fut notre limite: Gundry, remontant au fond de la scène, s'accouda sur la barrière et, sans parler, contempla la prairie. Immortelle minute...
>
> Dans cette prairie, nous ne voyons ni l'olivier mystique des religions, ni l'olivier des légistes. Ni une cité, ni un Dieu qui nous imposent leurs lois. Gundry n'écoute que son instinct. 'Un pur, un simple qui suit son cœur,' c'est le mot essentiel de Parsifal.
>
> Cette prairie, où rien ne pousse qui soit de culture humaine, c'est la table rase des philosophes. Wagner rejette tous les vêtements, toutes les formules dont l'homme civilisé est recouvert, alourdi, déformé. Il réclame le bel être humain primitif, en qui la vie était une sève puissante...
>
> Le philosophe de Bayreuth glorifie l'impulsion naturelle, la force qui nous fait agir avant même que nous l'ayons critiquée. Il exalte la fière créature supérieure à toutes les formules, ne se pliant sur aucune, mais prenant sa loi en soi-même.
>
> ['Le Regard sur la prairie,' *Du Sang, de la volupté et de la mort*, *Œuvre* II 189–90][32]

31 *Œuvre* I 140, 326–7; II 178, 386; III 152–3; IV 9, 75; V 28–9, 69, 116, 124, 142–3, 190, 485–6; VI 61–2; VII 243; VIII 166; XII 257; XIII 137, 200; XIV 211, 280; XV 142, 182; XVIII 106, 241, 269.

32 *See*, however, the slightly earlier text, inspired by the Baudelairean 'moral bohemianism' of Marie Bashkirtseff, in *Trois stations de psychothérapie*: 'tandis qu'elle mène de prairie en prairie l'élégant troupeau de ses curiosités' (*Œuvre* II 361). Also 'Chronique de Paris. Les "Bohémiens"

'Glorified' unreservedly, with Baudelaire and Wagner, from 1887 until 1892, the 'bohemian' spirit of *la prairie* will reappear twenty-one years later, in the rhetoric of Barrès the traditionalist, on the sacred hill of Sion-Vaudémont, together with a countervailing emblem, *la chapelle*: 'la règle, l'autorité, le lien ... un corps de pensées fixes et la cité ordonnée des âmes' (*La Colline inspirée, Œuvre* VI 499).[33]

Churches, Schools, Laboratories

The expansive religious syncretism of Barrès's final phase, like the defensive nationalism it overlaid (and to some extent modified), found expression in certain symbolic 'properties' of the French landscape. Among these, the enduring stone walls of her country churches stand in the same imaginative relation to the 'submerged vegetation' and the 'eternal springs'[34] of primitive religious instinct as the Barresian Bastions of Lotharingia, in their final role, to the dynamism of Germany – they are meant to filter and contain rather than to block or repulse:

> Mais la chapelle nous dit:
> – Visiteurs de la prairie, apportez-moi vos rêves pour que je les épure, vos élans pour que je les oriente ... Je prolonge la prairie, même quand elle me nie. J'ai été construite à force d'y avoir été rêvée ... Je suis la pierre qui dure, l'expérience des siècles, le dépôt du trésor de ta race.
> [*La Colline inspirée, Œuvre* VI 499]

> Une chapelle sur le bord d'une rivière rapide, une pierre éternelle dressée auprès d'une eau qui s'écoule, quelle image et quel thème de réflexions infinies!

de Félicien Champsaur,' *Les Chroniques*, 1 September 1887: 'Si l'auteur a nommé *Bohémiens* son ballet, ce n'est pas seulement que le premier sujet en est *Djina, reine d'une tribu errante*, mais parce que il n'est rien au monde de passionné sans bohémianisme. Ainsi nous disait Baudelaire, qui ne songeait guère à danser: glorifions le bohémianisme!'

33 *See* above pp. 106–8 and 'L'Enfance de Jeanne d'Arc. L'Enfant dans la prairie' (*Œuvre* XII 267–73).

34 *Œuvre* VI 499; VIII 167

Je suis assis dans la prairie. L'eau brille, accourt, enfle sa volute à mes pieds, murmure et disparaît ... Au bord de cet écoulement universel, j'aspire à dresser une affirmation de stabilité et d'identité.

Thème inépuisable de la chapelle sur la rive! Je n'aime rien tant que cette méditation pétrifiée sur le bord de cette eau qui s'enfuit ...C'est ici le lieu sûr où nous déposons pour les sauver nos sentiments les meilleurs, et ceux que cette voûte ne peut pas recueillir, qu'ils aillent au fil de la rivière et se perdent.
[*La Grande pitié des églises de France*, *Œuvre* VIII 9–10]

If by 1912 Barrès had learnt to appreciate the sense of the basilica whose presence in the wooded and watered sanctuary of Domremy had once appeared an 'indiscretion' and a 'sacrilege' (*Œuvre* v 525–6; XII 272–3), he still worshipped best, like his heroine, 'l'enfant dans la prairie,' 'la victime des fées,' at Christian shrines with pre-Christian origins: enduring emblems of a continuous religious tradition in which the spontaneous instinct aroused by Joan's, the sibyl's, Léopold Baillard's, and Bernadette Soubirous's magic springs is 'captured,' 'decanted,' and 'directed':

Les pensées de nos lointains ancêtres exercent toujours de mystérieuses et fortes poussées dans notre vie. Le peuple des fées et des génies qui vivaient dans les eaux, les bois et les retraites a disparu, mais en mourant il a laissé aux lieux qu'il animait des titres de vénération...

Dans le haut moyen-âge, un très grand nombre de ces pauvres esprits s'étaient rapprochés de l'église du village. Je ne puis voir sans émotion, au chevet de certaines de nos églises romanes, la petite fenêtre ronde, l'oculus, où de jour et de nuit, jadis, on exposait le Saint-Sacrement, de telle manière qu'on pût l'honorer du dehors. Pour moi, ce phare du cimetière, ce fanal autour duquel tournoient dans la nuit les ombres, c'est le signe le plus émouvant de l'appel jeté par l'Église au profond des mystères de la lande, la marque de sa bonté.
['La Mobilisation du divin,' *La Grande pitié des églises de France*, *Œuvre* VIII 164–71]

Saisir ces hautes fusées, jusqu'ici dangereuses ou vaines, et qui sauraient illuminer la nuit, capter méthodiquement ces forces, cultiver, diriger ces aptitudes d'exception, obtenir le desserrement de l'étreinte terrestre et la sainte libération des forces les plus intérieures. Ah! le beau programme!...

Au fond du chœur de la cathédrale d'Auxerre, la sybille, loin qu'elle me donne le plaisir triste d'un objet chargé de souvenirs, m'inspire l'attrait de ce qui n'a pas encore développé ses puissances...

L'arche t'a recueillie, quand le monde antique sombrait et t'a menée jusqu'à nous. Ce haut vaisseau, qui ne contient rien qui ne soit dans nos cœurs, mais dont l'inventaire est plus complet que notre conscience, t'a maintenu quand nous t'avions à la légère déposée. Aujourd'hui la science elle-même commence à reconnaître tes titres que l'Église avait entérinés.

[*Le Mystère en pleine lumière, Œuvre* XII 191][35]

The churches of France were a prominent feature of Barrès's sacred topography of France. The great value of every parish church, in its entirety and as part of its landscape, as the expression of that open Catholicism which assured the Barresian 'passage du local à l'universel,'[36] and as opposed to the historical interest of a few, classified national monuments, and to the artistic worth of parts of others removed to museum collections, is a major assertion of *La Grande pitié des églises de France*: 'points de spiritualité,' 'points de repère,' 'grands vaisseaux de spiritualité,' 'inscrite en pierre une conception très importante ... une parole construite ... le registre de plusieurs siècles,' 'un signe de l'esprit ... un mouvement de l'esprit rendu visible par ces pierres édifiées.'[37] All were essential to the traditionalist's 'physical and moral' image of France:

35 Cf. *Œuvre* V 549–52; VI 452; XII 254, 262–73

36 *See* above, Chapter Three, and also the curiously provocative effect on Barrès of Victor Hugo's pantheistic response to the deserted sanctuaries of Christian Europe and of ancient Greece and Egypt: '"Faites-y la solitude, vous y sentez le ciel" ... Quel grand écrivain! J'ajouterai que c'est un penseur solide, un penseur sur qui on peut prendre un point d'appui; il n'est que de penser juste le contraire' (*Œuvre* XV 337).

37 *Œuvre* VIII 12–13; XV 26; XVI 325, 406; XVII 10

J'ai adressé, il y a quelques mois, une lettre publique à M. le Président du Conseil, pour lui signaler les dangers que courent nos églises depuis la loi de Séparation, et pour lui demander quelles mesures il songe à prendre afin de protéger la physionomie architecturale, la figure physique et morale de la terre française.

J'ai déposé sur le bureau de la Chambre une immense pétition vous demandant de protéger l'ensemble de nos églises, de sauvegarder la physionomie architecturale, la figure physique et morale de la terre française.

Ce qui m'intéresse, ce n'est pas que soient entretenues les églises des circonscriptions qui votent bien, ce qui m'intéresse, c'est que la physionomie artistique, morale, spirituelle de notre terre de France, soit maintenue, respectée, encore améliorée.
[*La Grande pitié des églises de France, Œuvre* VIII 37, 105, 145]

A great weakness of Barrès's pre-War portrait of France was his failure to find a place in it, beside the ancient pagan 'open-air temples' and the traditional Catholic 'village temples of the soul' that are magnificently celebrated in *La Colline inspirée, La Grande pitié des églises de France,* and *Le Mystère en pleine lumière*, any equally worthwhile outward and visible signs of the non-Christian ideals of twentieth-century France, and this despite his ambition to 'transcend' the warring Catholic and Humanist ideals of post-Dreyfus France.[38] The centrifugal forces released by the Dreyfus Affair had thrust him out, like his adversaries, on to the periphery of partisan opinion, where, across the gulf that separated them, each side tended to see the other in its meanest form. Thus the outline of a propaganda play sketched in *Mes Cahiers* soon after the parliamentary debate on Church and School of 1910 opposes two symbolic stage properties: a village church and 'Le café de l'Univers' (*Mes Cahiers, Œuvre* XVI 278–9), and four years later, in *La Grande pitié des églises de France*, Barrès contrasts the traditionalist virtues that 'the most wretched village' possesses in its church, with the people's lack of any other kind of

38 *Œuvre* XV 158, *cit.* above, p. 98.

'ideological edifice' and with the degrading apology for one that corrupts the rich each night in Paris: the *boulevard* theatre (*La Grande pitié des églises de France, Œuvre* VIII 57, 193–4). Certainly his best efforts since the Affair had been bent towards reconciling the Church with a nobler rival than the *café* and the *boulevard*, namely *l'école*. In his notebook headed 'Pour la Sorbonne et pour les églises,' dated 1910, the antithesis: *église, école* is posed repeatedly, with the *café* kept in view certainly, as the symbol of the spiritual vacuum waiting for the products of a state education whose 'mediocrity,' according to Barrès, was 'even more sickening than its fanaticism,' but with the main purpose of resolving the opposition between its two terms:

> SORBONNE. ÉGLISE.
> *Voici le plan:*
> a) Dans le village, il y a l'école et l'église.
> b) Vous sacrifiez l'une à l'autre. Moi, pas.
> [*Mes Cahiers, Œuvre* XVI 321]

But the very way he chose to reconcile the opposing principles of the French Catholic Church and the Third Republic's schools, through the historian's exposure of Christianity's pagan and, by implication, eternal roots, and the psychologist's investigation of its irrational ones, led him, despite his many up-to-date authorities (Bergson, Bernard, Blondel, Durkheim, Frazer, James, Soury), backwards in time along what he acknowledged to be the natural bent of his imagination (*Mes Cahiers, Œuvre* XVII 294), to a nostalgic vision of isolated hill-tops, quiet woodlands, and water-meadows, sleepy villages and small country towns, which takes even less account than his defensive geography of eastern France (whose Bastions have, after all, been twice in service since he fixed their tragic line across the literature of modern French patriotism) of what modern nations must live by as much if not more than their 'soil and their ancestors.' Not that he failed altogether to realize this (*Mes Cahiers, Œuvre* XVI 356–7), nor that he could not make a fair guess at the shape of the future: 'Ce qui apparaît: un internationalisme financier en face d'un internationalisme prolétaire' (*Mes Cahiers, Œuvre* XV 418). But he prided himself on speaking for the 'small towns of France' (*Œuvre* I 139; XIII 28;

XX 5, 193), and his churches, schools and cafés are usually village properties (e.g. *Œuvre* VIII 54–5). He 'understood,' he said, about the industrial wealth of Lorraine, but he 'loved' the orderly and prosperous 'old' civilization of its vineyards and orchards, and preferred above all to seek inspiration in its empty upland wildernesses 'unmarked by the modern world' (*Œuvre* VIII 168). He revolted passionately against the spoliation or pollution of natural beauty:

> Connaissez-vous cette sorte d'angoisse et cette protestation qui se forment au fond de notre être (telle est du moins mon expérience) chaque fois que nous voyons souiller une source, avilir un paysage, défricher une forêt ou simplement couper un bel arbre sans lui fournir un successeur? Ce que nous éprouvons alors, je fais appel à votre mémoire, c'est tout autre chose que le regret d'un bien matériel perdu. Nous sentons invinciblement qu'à notre expansion complète il faut du végétal, du libre, du vivant, des bêtes heureuses, des sources non captées, des rivières non mises en tuyaux, des forêts sans réseaux de fils de fer, des espaces hors du temps.
> ...La mise à mort d'une forêt, d'une rivière, d'un haut lieu offense l'univers, nous fait désirer des cérémonies de purification.
> [*La Grande pitié des églises de France, Œuvre* VIII 163–4]

Capitalism fired his imagination mainly as a malignant force, in the polemical bestiary of *Leurs figures,* where corrupt French politicians and stateless financiers appear as vermin battening on the country, fouling their chosen nesting- and hunting-grounds: Paris and the Côte d'Azur.[39] The 'animal' vigour of the masses, and of their champion, Jean Jaurès,[40] had long impressed the 'professeur d'énergie' in Barrès, though they disquieted the champion of law and order.[41] He called upon the trade unions to take their place in a corporate national order, but they were as little part of his imaginative synthesis of the

39 *Œuvre* IV 276, 288, 311, 382, 385

40 *Œuvre* XVI 145: 'Le comparer à un Albert de Mun, par exemple, si élégant, charmant, fier, chantant, c'est sentir combien est forte chez lui la part animale. ... On se lasse de tout excepté de l'animalité.'

41 *Œuvre* VIII 382; XV 391–2

French nation as the *patronat* or the bureaucracy.[42] The only specifically modern vehicle of civilization that he felt spontaneously and enthusiastically to be a part of his France was the scientific laboratory.

In 1920 he launched a campaign of protest against the pitiable state of scientific research and teaching facilities in France which was the conscious counterpart of his pre-war protestations against the official neglect of France's patrimony of parish churches. 'La Grande pitié des laboratoires de France' (*L'Écho de Paris* 7 June 1920), and the other articles, the speeches, and the *marginalia* connected with it, and published posthumously with the title of *Pour la haute intelligence française*, are, generally speaking, more practical and prosaic, written with lower emotional tension and slighter imaginative resources, than Barrès's books on the French Catholic countryside; but, together with accompanying notes and comments in *Mes Cahiers*, they do strengthen his image of France by adding to it a modern 'property,' *le laboratoire*, which would occupy approximately the same position opposite *l'église* that *l'école* had done before the War, but which was less spoiled, in Barrès's view, by 'abstractions' and 'verbalism' (*Pour la haute intelligence française*, *Œuvre* IX 264–5, 287), and promised more surely, he thought, to absorb and organize at the highest level the capitalist and proletarian, materialist, and rationalist drives of the new age, threatened by the wastage of *le dancing* (post-war equivalent of the village 'Café de l'Univers') and the wreck of the 'grand soir anarchiste' ('La Grande pitié des laboratoires de France,' *L'Écho de Paris* 7 June 1920, and *Œuvre* IX 375) – as, so he believed, the crude and disorderly religious enthusiasm of *la prairie* was threatened, but for *la chapelle*, with dissipation in vain fancy or with degradation in the dead-end of superstitious table-turning or shallow counter-dogmatism (*Œuvre* VIII 54; XVI 246–8).

Barrès first used the word 'laboratoire' symbolically for propaganda purposes before the War, in *La Grande pitié des églises de France*:

42 'Maître Aliboron,' *Le Gaulois* 17 March 1907; preface to H. de Noussane, *Des Faits, des hommes, des idées* (Paris: Plon-Nourrit 1907); 'Réponse à une enquête sur les tendances de la jeunesse,' *La Démocratie* 5 December 1910; 'Les Foyers nouveaux,' *L'Écho de Paris* 15 March 1912. *See* Z. Sternhell, *Maurice Barrès et le nationalisme français*, 156–7.

C'est à la civilisation qu'il faut s'intéresser, si l'on n'a pas le sens de Dieu et si l'on est rassasié du moi. Eh bien! la civilisation, où est-elle défendue aujourd'hui?
Dans les conseils d'administration? Je ne suis pas de ceux qui le croient.
Elle est défendue dans les laboratoires et dans les églises.
[*Œuvre* VIII 194][43]

The formula in which it occurs had been written even earlier on a page of Barrès's private notebooks, dated 1908, about the future of the French Right:

Il serait bien malheureux et pénible, effarant, qu'un jour nous eussions à voir nos idées sous une forme banquière et sous cette forme à les reconnaître ou à les désavouer, à les servir toujours, telles quelles, ou bien à les abandonner.
Peut-on admettre cette situation et quelle sera alors notre décision, notre moyen de reconnaître notre vraie direction?
Il faudra que nous cherchions où est défendue la civilisation. Il faudra peut-être qu'un jour nous voyions (ce que l'on voit au hasard des relations, dans les expériences de la vie quotidienne et privée), il faudra que nous voyions que la civilisation n'est pas nécessairement dans les grands conseils d'administration. Elle est dans les églises et les laboratoires.
[*Mes Cahiers, Œuvre* XV 418–19]

An entry in *Mes Cahiers* two years before this one shows Barrès already moving towards both symbol and formula, characteristically through an intercessory representative hero localized in the countryside of Lorraine: 'Deux points de spiritualité et de fixité. Sion-Vaudémont, – le laboratoire de Pasteur. On voit bien où il prend son esprit de sacrifice, ce Pasteur' (*Œuvre* XV 35).

When Barrès after the War pronounces, like a mid-century technocrat, that 'scientific research is the cornerstone of national recovery' (*Œuvre* IX 367), he is partly concerned with practical matters, like

43 Cf. *Œuvre* VIII 379.

the struggle for markets between rival national economies, and raising the material standard of living in a state run efficiently on corporative lines. But his victory campaign for 'a France fairer than any man ever dreamed' (*L'Écho de Paris* 7 June 1920) pressed *le laboratoire* into service like the frontier and rural properties of his pre-war propaganda: hills, fortresses, forests, meadows, springs, shrines, churches, as an evocatory instrument of moral persuasion also, meant to spur and to guide the collective energy of the French people towards new forms of spiritual greatness. His habit of using landscape imagery to carry a patriotic message was by now so ingrained that it seems almost automatically to have produced, for example, the characteristically emotive, but here rather abstract and idiosyncratic metaphor of scientific laboratories as 'summits and sanctuaries.'[44] As typically, but more reasonably, Barrès desired them to be so many 'centres of enthusiasm,' deriving their efficacy from association with 'exemplary spirits... endowed with the radio-activity of genius' (*Œuvre* IX 327–30, 377): secular 'high places' manifesting the presence, and assuring the survival, of an intellectual function that is vital to the nation:

> Je prends ce mot laboratoire dans son sens le plus large: je ne parle pas seulement de chimie et de physique, je songe à l'ensemble des moyens nécessaires pour créer de la science.
>
> Mon livre sur la science, ce n'est pas à quoi le *Matin* réduit ma campagne. Il s'agit de faire passer de l'intelligence dans le peuple, dans une race, dans une nation.
> C'est le problème de l'élite. Renan l'a posé dans *Caliban*. Comment avoir une élite, comment transférer l'héritage. [*Œuvre* IX 211, 333]

44 *Œuvre* IX 368. The flyleaf of *Pour la haute intelligence française* has the less characteristic 'âmes et sanctuaires,' no doubt a misreading of 'cimes et sanctuaires.'

CHAPTER ELEVEN

Imagination in Barrès's Theory of Education

THE UNIVERSITY CENSURED: BOUTEILLER AND LES DÉRACINÉS

The problem of Renan's *Caliban*, 'Comment avoir une élite, comment transférer l'héritage,' which preoccupied Barrès while he was campaigning for better French laboratories between 1919 and 1923, is naturally a crucial one for the traditionalist, and one that Barrès had raised regularly since censuring the Republic's way of educating its future citizens in *Les Déracinés*, nearly a quarter of a century before. How to convey the traditional 'energies' and 'directions' of France to the rising generation had given him quite as much thought as the means of stimulating and orientating patriotic and religious opinion among his contemporaries:

> Le romantisme ... n'est pas avilissant. Mais il est un excitateur sans frein ni orientation, et voilà son défaut. C'est le défaut de toute l'éducation en France. On semble en avoir senti l'inconvénient çà et là, mais ne pouvant pas trouver de frein, ni d'orientation, on se serait borné à supprimer l'excitation. (C'est du moins ce que je crois comprendre de ce fameux problème de la Sorbonne, où l'on semble surtout dénoncer un mortel ennui parmi d'insipides pédanteries.)
> [*Œuvre* XII 156]

The place of imagination in Barrès's educational theory was partly determined by the psychological and sociological authorities and observations that were also behind the development of his art of propaganda, while the slow shift of emphasis which put churches, schools, and laboratories into the composite image of France he had produced for propaganda purposes partly reflected his simultaneously evolving thoughts on the educative value of music and science.[1] But the particular importance he attached to imaginative processes in the sphere of education, and to educational reform in the life of the nation,[2] appears to stem from personal experience, as a senior pupil at the *lycée* in Nancy, in 1877–80. In the hostile interpretation of this experience with which *Le Roman de l'énergie nationale* begins, and which (after some preliminary skirmishing in the *marginalia* of *Le Culte du Moi* and *La Cocarde*) opened Barrès's life-long campaign against the system of centralized and authoritarian state education that the Third Republic had taken over as part of its Napoleonic inheritance, are laid the foundations of all his future charges against the University of France in the twentieth century. Barrès's *lycée* is half barracks, half convent. In the *vase clos* of the *internat*, cut off from their families and the normal social and natural influences of their native environment, controlled by remote administrative dignitaries and hounded by shame-faced *pions*, without privacy, trust, or affection, the length of each drum-regulated day, a future 'prolétariat de bacheliers' absorbs the explosive mixture of bureaucracy (inspired afresh by the principle of Republican indivisibility) and idealism (fostered by a final-year philosophy course based on rationalism and humanism) which will throw them on to the streets of the capital of the Republic 'pitifully ignorant of life, or its conditions and its purpose,' sure only of their need to conquer Paris with all the impact and innocent force of their blinkered, rebellious adolescence. For this single purpose they

1 *See* pp. 220–3: 'Cette éducation par les yeux' and 233–7: 'In hymnis et canticis.'

2 *See* particularly: *Leurs Figures* ('Lettre de Saint-Phlin sur une "nourriture" lorraine'); *Les Amitiés françaises, Les Mauvais instituteurs, Une Enquête aux pays du Levant, Pour la haute intelligence française, Journal Officiel* 22 June 1909; 19 January 1910; 12 June 1920; 13 June 1920; 22 February 1921; 12 December 1921; 30 June 1922; 1 July 1922; 8 December 1922; 10 December 1922; 29 December 1922; *Mes Cahiers, Œuvre* XVI 131–45, 234–48.

are capable of banding together, but only with the 'solidarity of sly and struggling serfs,' not as 'free men organizing themselves according to a rule of law' – a delinquent 'peer group' such as the American sociologist J.R. Pitts will find in 'the traditional French school,' and at the heart of 'the traditional French value system,' more than sixty years after Barrès first described it.[3]

The bad effects of coercion and unreality in France's 'vast *lycées*' were aggravated, in Barrès's view, by the way the state recruited its secondary school-masters, that 'corporation' of successful scholarship boys, as Thibaudet will call the teachers of the Third Republic,[4] and which Barrès caricatures in Paul Bouteiller, the master who influences *les déracinés* most powerfully. He is the very embodiment of abstract idealism and bureaucratic regimentation. An orphan and an exhibitioner, 'réduit pour toute satisfaction sentimentale à l'estime de ses maîtres,' he is 'un produit pédagogique, un fils de la raison, étranger à nos habitudes traditionnelles, locales ou de famille, tout abstrait, et vraiment suspendu dans le vide' (*Les Déracinés, Œuvre* III 24). He tries to bend all the pupils whom he meets on his 'nomadic' career into the same shape of ideal citizen, submissive to the regulations of a wise administration in Paris:

> Il tient son rôle strictement, comme une consigne reçue de l'État. C'est le sergent instructeur qui communique à des recrues la théorie réglée en haut lieu. Exactement il leur distribue de vieux cahiers, rédigés depuis huit ans et qu'il a dictés à Nice, à Brest, comme aujourd'hui à Nancy.
> [*Les Déracinés, Œuvre* III 25]

The unbridled and ambitious individualism produced by the harsh discipline of the *internat* and the remotely controlled administration of the Republic's educational service gets strong support from Bouteiller's lessons, intended to inculcate a practical and positive morality based on reason and humanity. As Thibaudet points out in his charac-

3 *Les Déracinés, Œuvre* III 12–14 and Jesse R. Pitts, 'Continuity and Change in Bourgeois France,' in Stanley Hoffmann and others, *France: Change and Tradition* (London: Victor Gollancz 1963) 235–62

4 A. Thibaudet, *La République des professeurs* (Paris: Grasset 1927) 128

terization of Barrès's 'Figures de Roman,' Bouteiller, because of his political ambition, is less typical of his confraternity (that *demi-clergé* of the Republican faith) than his creator suggests, and this weakens Barrès's case against Bouteiller's (and the University's) master: Kant.[5] But it is an exaggeration to assert that 'Le professeur Bouteiller exerce une action mauvaise sur ses élèves, il les jette au déracinement et à l'individualisme précisément dans la mesure où il se défroque, dans la mesure où il se sent un homme politique.'[6] It implies an indifference to the lasting moral effect of ideas acquired in a *lycée* philosophy class that has no part in the Sorbonne's, Bouteiller's, Barrès's, or Thibaudet's idea of the teacher's calling. Bouteiller, having come to Nancy 'to make men and citizens' and to teach 'patriotism and solidarity,'[7] leaves for Paris seven months later, having failed, partly because of the example he left behind of political *arrivisme*, but partly also because of the philosophy he taught.

The first stage of Bouteiller's course was what Barrès called 'une étape dans le scepticisme absolu' (*Œuvre* III 21), ending up in Kant's *Critique of Pure Reason*, and therefore, strictly speaking, as Thibaudet shows, incorrectly named. The second part was an attempt 'with Kant, and by the appeal to feeling, to reconstitute ... the category of morality and a system of certainties,' an attempt which fails to convince his pupils (21–4). Kant is not responsible for sending the *déracinés* to 'wander on the Paris pavements like Tonkinese in their marshes, without social bonds, a rule of life, or aim in life' (184).[8] Bouteiller's use of Kant's epistemology as the rationale of Pyrrhonism

5 A. Thibaudet, *La Vie de Maurice Barrès* (Paris: Gallimard 1921) III section VI; also *La République des professeurs*, 140–2. Cf. the letter by C. Maurras to Barrès, and the latter's reply in M. Barrès and C. Maurras, *La République ou le Roi* (Paris: Plon 1970) 145–6.

6 *La Vie de Maurice Barrès*, 182

7 *Œuvre* III 14. Barrès acknowledged the patriotic inspiration of Auguste Burdeau, his principal model for the fictitious Paul Bouteiller, in 'La Grèce utile au réveil français,' *Le Journal* 24 April 1897, 'La Sagesse de l'Est,' *La Patrie* 10 October 1902 and *Mes Cahiers*, *Œuvre* XX 188–9.

8 Cf. Michelet, *L'Étudiant*, 40–5: 'Voilà le jeune homme ... sur le pavé de Paris ... tout seul ... comme un Robinson dans son île. Il y a eu un moment de repos entre le collège et les écoles, il s'est un peu réchauffé au foyer, il arrive là ... Rien que la glace et le vide. Cette ville, elle est pleine de vie, de chaleur, de puissance, mais il n'en sait rien; il appelle ça un désert...'

is very largely so (20–1, 27–8). The categorical imperative is a formal concept which Kant applies to particular cases only with the kind of precautions that Thibaudet alleges to prove how little Bouteiller knew his German master. Moreover, it entails treating individuals as free rational agents and as ends in themselves, and involves a radical distinction between the State and the world-wide community of rational beings. But Barrès makes it clear that it was the absence of such precautions, the treatment of individuals as 'instruments,' and the confusion of the general good and the administrative hierarchy that 'distinguished' Bouteiller's crudely utilitarian application of the imperative in his 'conduct as in his teaching' (25–6). Kant's ethics are innocent of caporalism; Bouteiller's 'Kantism' is not:

> Rappelez-vous le principe sur lequel nous fondons toute morale. Combien de fois nous l'avons formulé! C'est d'agir toujours de telle manière que notre action puisse servir de règle. Il faut se conformer aux lois de son pays et aux volontés de ses supérieurs hiérarchiques.
> [*Les Déracinés, Œuvre* III 29]

Like the regimental discipline of the *internat*, Bouteiller's prussianizing of the categorical imperative, with the contempt for the Lorrainer and the individual in his pupils that it implied, had consequences that 'would certainly have stupefied him,' had he not 'disdained' to study the soil beneath his 'broadly sweeping sower's arm' (14–37). The State he exhorted them to serve was an expression of 'administrative verbalism,' a 'disincarnate vision of officialdom and of a few great men for use in the baccalaureate examination' (33–4),[9] which could only excite their insubordination as individuals and against their provincial background:

> Si cette éducation leur a supprimé la conscience nationale, c'est-à-dire le sentiment qu'il y a un passé de leur canton et le goût de se rattacher à ce passé le plus proche, elle a développé en eux

9 Cf. *Mes Cahiers, Œuvre* XIV 209: 'la principale thèse des *Déracinés* ... était de dire les mots sont des choses mortes. Qu'est-ce que l'enseignement verbal de patrie, bientôt on verra que la patrie est morte.' And Michelet, *L'Étudiant*, 183: 'Des choses et non des mots.'

> l'énergie. Elle l'a poussée toute en cérébralité et sans leur donner le sens des réalités, mais enfin elle l'a multipliée. De toute cette énergie multipliée, ces provincaux crient: 'À Paris!'
> Paris! ... le rendezvous des hommes, le rond-point de l'humanité! C'est la patrie de leurs âmes, le lieu marqué pour qu'ils accomplissent leur destinée.
> [*Les Déracinés, Œuvre* III 38]

Thus both parts of Bouteiller's philosophy course tend to deprive his pupils (already detached from reality by the regimentation and seclusion of the *internat*) of all contact with their natural environment: 'race ... soil ... and ... more real still than soil or race, the spirit of each *petite patrie*' (33). Into the vacuum created by the scepticism, the abstraction, and the verbalism of Bouteiller's teaching, rises a more powerful and positive form of persuasion, the chief multiplier of adolescent energies: incarnate images of individual conquest, which the *lycéens* find, not only in their baccalaureate program, but also, more imposing and exciting, in the fiction and biography on the shelves of the form library (18–19, 22) and in Bouteiller himself, manifestly destined for leadership in the capital of the modern Republic:

> On peut se croire à dix-sept ans révolté contre ses maîtres; on n'échappe pas à la vision qu'ils nous proposent des hommes et des circonstances. Notre imagination qu'ils nourissent s'adapte au système qui les subventionne...
> ...M. Bouteiller, dès le début se confondait avec les deux images les plus importantes qui flottaient sur la France: il fut Victor Hugo et la République héroique.
>
> Ses phrases, durant une demi-année avaient conseillé la soumission aux besoins de la patrie, le culte de la loi, mais son image triomphante dominait ces enfants, les faisait à sa ressemblance et obligeait leur volonté.
>
> Dans un âge où l'on a besoin de beaucoup s'assimiler, l'image de ce maître s'enfonçait de plus en plus en eux et devenait une partie de leur chair; elle leur commandait le plus violent désir de Paris.
> [*Les Déracinés, Œuvre* III 18–19, 32, 52]

The predominantly negative effect of Bouteiller's philosophical precepts combined with the positive influence of his personal ascendency and prestige, produces seven examples of rootless individualism ripe for *L'Appel au soldat*: solipsistic and melancholy in the privileged Sturel; cynical and resourceful in Suret-Lefort and Renaudin, recently deprived of middle-class family support and pride; vulnerable and impotent in Racadot and Mouchefrin, who are congenitally wretched and humble; mitigated in Roemerspacher and Saint-Phlin by other kinds of education (respectively by Taine and in a German university, and by Mistral and country life in Lorraine) :

> Cet excitateur qui prétendait pour le plus grand bien de l'État effacer les caractères individuels, quitte Nancy ayant crée des individus dont il fait seul le centre et le lien...
>
> Son image seule, sa domination de César les a groupés et spontanément les forme à sa ressemblance, ces jeunes Césarions. Déliés du sol, de toute société de leurs familles, d'où sentiraient-ils la convenance d'agir pour l'intérêt général? Ils ne valent que pour être des grands hommes, comme le maître dont l'admiration est leur seul sentiment social.
>
> [*Les Déracinés, Œuvre* III 34–6]

Barrès's proposals for reforming French education, which began to appear after his own path from school to egotism to nationalism had been chronicled and analysed in *Le Culte du Moi*, *Les Déracinés*, and *L'Appel au soldat*, can be satisfactorily summarized as an attempt to fasten the child's imaginative capability, which Bouteiller had unwittingly excited, on to those 'most immediately tangible realities' of the child's family, provincial, and natural environments, of which he had appeared to be 'either contemptuous or ignorant' (33).

SAINT-PHLIN AND LES AMITIÉS FRANÇAISES

In the last volume of *Le Roman de l'énergie nationale*, one of Barrès's seven original *déracinés*, Gallant de Saint-Phlin, who has returned home from Paris and become a well-rooted Lorraine landowner, writes a long letter to François Sturel, still the restless anti-parliamentary agitator in Paris, which reflects quite clearly Barrès's own disenchantment with direct political action after the failure of both Boulangist and anti-Dreyfusard attempts at anti-parliamentary caesarism, his consequent conversion from the doctrine of nationalist political 'surgery' to plans for the traditionalist 'education' of public opinion, and his first positive ideas for bringing up the latest French generation in the way and spirit of the 'real France.'[10] *Les Amitiés françaises*, published the following year (1903), is a detailed working drawing, signed and justified by the author, of Saint-Phlin's sketch. Neither the 'Lettre de Saint-Phlin sur une "nourriture" lorraine,' nor *Les Amitiés françaises. Notes sur l'acquisition par un petit lorrain des sentiments qui donnent un prix à la vie*, proposes an alternative to the *lycée*. Saint-Phlin hopes to persuade the authorities to introduce into the training of primary school teachers the regional education he intends personally to give his son. Philippe, the 'little Lorrainer' of *Les Amitiés françaises* (Barrès's own son) is hardly out of the nursery, and his early education by his father is designed to innoculate him in advance against the contagion of the Republic's official educational methods and program. By implication, however, both Saint-Phlin and his creator propose specific medicine for the contagion as Barrès had observed it in the *lycées*: the cloistered isolation and rigid mass discipline of the *internat* are implicitly denounced in the stress both lay on the value of parental guidance (*Œuvre* IV 397–8; V 475, 482); the University's centralized administration is similarly criticized in the proposal to adapt the curricula of schools and training colleges to the region they serve (*Œuvre* IV 395); the oracular dogmatism of a Bouteiller is censured by the importance attached to the particular disposition and potential each child, they believe, is born with (*Œuvre* IV 397; V 475, 479; XIV 112); humanistic, patriotic, and republican abstractions are condemned in a syllabus dominated by 'leçons de choses' demonstrating the diversity of French local traditions:

> Peut-on espérer que dans les chaires des lycées on interrompra des affirmations oratoires, académiques, *rondouillardes*, pour

10 *See* above, pp. 68–70.

> rechercher avec l'historien et le géographe, région par région, les diverses vérités dont la somme fait la vérité française.
> ...Le sens social est susceptible comme tous les autres de recevoir une éducation, et de cette éducation le philosophe de la Quinzaine (Georges Fonesgrive) trace les grandes lignes.
> ['L'Éducation nationale,' *Le Journal* 30 October 1899][11]

Saint-Phlin calls his system of object lessons 'realistic' (*Œuvre* IV 397). But here, as is usual in Barrès, the observation of 'concrete instances' to counteract 'metaphysics and abstract politics' (*Œuvre* IV 392) is meant to lead to an automatically prejudiced metaphorical reading of some particular object's bearing on a patriot's whole duty, rather than to prosaic objectivity. Saint-Phlin wants to train his son to see in the Lorraine landscape 'a line of forts guarding the Rhine':

> Te rappelles-tu, en 1879, au lycée de Nancy, notre classe de philosophie si fiévreuse? Bouteiller nous promenait de systèmes en systèmes, qui, tous, avaient leurs séductions, et il ne nous marquait point dans quelles conditions, pour quelles hommes, ils furent légitimes et vrais. Nous chancelions. Alors il nous proposa comme un terrain solide certaine doctrine mi-parisienne, mi-allemande, élaborée dans les bureaux de l'Instruction publique pour le service d'une politique. 'Je dois toujours agir de telle sorte que je puisse vouloir que mon action serve de règle universelle,'...
> ...Ah! plutôt que des Bouteiller qui nous imposaient éloquemment leurs affirmations, que n'eûmes-nous un promeneur qui, parcourant avec nous le sentier de nos tombeaux, nous éveillât *en profondeur*! Ses leçons de choses locales, suivant une espèce d'ordre naturel et historique, fussent allées ébranler jusque dans notre subconscient tout ce que la suite des générations accumula pour

11 *See* Barrès's campaign for university decentralization in 'L'Année universitaire,' *Le Journal* 2 January 1894, *La Lorraine-Artiste* 25 August 1895, and *Pour la haute intelligence française*. Fonesgrive is cited, with Demolins, Le Bon, Hennebicq, Comte, Le Play, and Renan against 'Kantism and the Rights of Man' in 'L'Université et l'esprit national,' *Le Journal* 25 November 1898, where L'École des Roches, Demolins's 'école d'un nouveau type, "approprié aux exigences de la vie"' is expressly contrasted with the hollow abstractions that Barrès attributed to most French teachers.

nous adoucir, pour nous doter de gravité humaine, pour nous créer une âme. Nos vignes, nos forêts, nos rivières, nos champs chargés de tombes qui nous inclinent à la vénération, quel beau cadre d'une année de philosophie, si la philosophie, c'est, come je le veux, de *s'enfoncer* pour les saisir jusqu'à nos vérités propres!

...Mon petit garçon s'en assurera, un sac d'enfant de troupe sur le dos, sa main dans la main de son père, au cours de belles promenades sur le plateau lorrain, dans la vallée mosellane et meusienne et sous les sapins de nos montagnes. À chaque pas et dans tous les âges, qu'y trouvera-t-il de principal et qui fait toucher la *pensée maîtresse de cette région? Une suite de redoutes doublant la ligne du Rhin...*

Mon fils, si Dieu favorise mes soins ... possédera la tradition lorraine. *Elle ne consiste point en une série d'affirmations décharnées, dont on puisse tenir catalogue, et, plutôt qu'une façon de juger la vie, c'est une façon de la sentir: c'est une manière de réagir commune en toutes circonstances à tous les Lorrains.* Et quand nous avons cette discipline lorraine, – disons le mot, cette épine dorsale lorraine, – oui, quand une suite d'exercices multipliés sur des cas concrets a fait l'éducation de nos réflexes, nous a dressés à l'automatisme pour quoi nous étions prédisposés, nous pouvons alors quitter notre canton et nous inventer une vie. Sortis du sol paternel, nous ne serons pourtant pas des déracinés. Où que nous allions et plongés dans les milieux les plus dévorants, nous demeurerons la continuité de nos pères, nous bénéficierons de *l'apprentissage séculaire que nous fîmes dans leurs veines avant que d'être nés et tandis qu'ils nous méditaient.*
[*Œuvre* IV 393, 397–9]

Saint-Phlin for his son in Lorraine, like *l'homme libre* for himself in Venice, finds the 'tangible' symbol of what a society means to him by eliminating a 'thousand insignificant features' from its visible setting, through an 'associative' process of 'unconscious abstraction.'[12] As a

12 *See Un Homme libre, Œuvre* I 237–40, *cit.* above, p. 8. Cf. G. Le Bon, *Psychologie de l'éducation* (Paris: Flammarion 1902) 177–81: 'Toute éducation consiste dans l'art de faire passer le conscient dans l'insconscient. – On y arrive par la création d'associations, d'abord conscientes, qui deviennent inconscientes ensuite. – La loi des associations et la création

serious educationalist, expounding Barresian nationalist determinism at its most extreme behaviourist stage (the influence of the physiologist Jules Soury on Barrès was particularly strong during the latter's crisis years of bereavement and the Dreyfus Affair, when *Leurs figures* was being written),[13] Saint Phlin is less cavalier and wholesale than the dilettante hero of *Le Culte du Moi* had been in eliminating 'insignificant features' of the actual and historical country in question from the final view of it that he wishes to leave in the mind. Nevertheless, one feature of the Lorraine countryside from which the image of the Line of Eastern Redoubts is to be isolated, namely the factories to be visited by the student-teacher, which Saint-Phlin mentions on the sixth page of his letter, has already disappeared by the time he comes, on the eighth page, to list the principal sites selected for his son's 'leçons de choses locales';[14] and the patriotic itinerary of *Les Amitiés françaises* composed some months later is reduced by further omissions, the most significant being the Republican shrines of Varennes-en-Argonne 'where the French monarchy perished in a road accident,' and 'Baudricourt and Domvallier, humble villages where Victor Hugo's distant forebears were nurtured' (*Œuvre* IV 398; V 521). But it is the character, rather than the extent of Barrès's habit of 'unconscious abstraction' which distinguishes it from the abstractions of a Bouteiller. Saint-Phlin rejects as 'bald assertions,' Barrès scorns as 'fine aphorisms' the rationalist's expression of the complete data of an observation in an abstract formula (*Œuvre* IV 398; V 481). They are after an expression of their native tradition which will depend for its force and coherence on the elimination from a given spectacle of many objects that are judged, irrationally, to be insignificant, and on the retention of others, selected by unconscious predisposition, and promoted, without loss of concreteness, from the status of percepts to that of metaphors: an imaginative way of expressing a sentimental prejudice persuasively.[15]

des réflexes ... L'éducation doit agir sur l'inconscient de l'enfant et non sur sa faible raison.'

13 *See* above, pp. 57–65.

14 Cf. E. Demolins, *L'Éducation nouvelle: L'École des Roches* (Paris: Firmin-Didot 1898) 158–60.

15 Cf. Sturel's and Saint-Phlin's method in 'La Vallée de la Moselle' (*L'Appel*

Saint-Phlin leaves the 'specialists' to choose the 'means' of 'awakening and shaping' their pupils' predispositions; and the imaginative character of his object lessons is not stressed. *Les Amitiés françaises* is much more self-conscious and assertive on this score. The sub-title of the manuscript is 'Notes sur l'acquisition par un petit Lorrain des images qui donnent un sens à la vie.'[16] It is, in fact, an attempt to give the child a 'prejudice in favour of his country' by 'furnishing' his mind with 'national and family images' that will enable him to stand up to the rival 'goddesses' of Germany and to confront (locally and provisionally, since his traditionalism is the reverse of Utopian planning for ever, and for everywhere) the ineluctable absurdity of human existence. In 1903 Barrès was still unconvinced of even the most rudimentary forms of Christian certitude and consolation. *Les Amitiés françaises* dispenses an 'empiric's electuary' against nihilism (*Œuvre* v 486–7), a prescription that is rather rough and ready, but comprehensive and, according to its promoter, proved by long use:

> Nous ne rêvons pas d'un Eldorado. Nous ne sommes pas les éternels émigrants qui dessinent au bord de la mer mystérieuse et sur le sable d'un rivage détesté les épures d'un vaisseau de fuite. Nous sommes des traditionalistes.

au soldat, Œuvre IV 3–101): 'Le courant d'air vivifiant, la rivière, un sport modéré, l'excitation de l'amitié, leur méthode d'éliminer du paysage ce qui ne se rapporte point à leur programme, tout concourt à faire de ces deux jeunes gens non pas des hystériques livrés aux sensations, mais des êtres qui dirigent le travail de leur raison avec une parfaite santé morale' (87) and Roemerspacher the scientist's criticism of it: '"Je n'ai jamais imaginé d'effort plus consciencieux pour rester en arrière de la transformation générale. Il y a sans doute des gens à paradoxe; lui [Saint-Phlin], il reste dans les réalités; seulement, il élimine celles qui le gênent et il collectionne celles qui le servent; ce n'est pas un esprit très vigoureux, mais d'une structure très déterminée' (104).

16 *Bibliothèque Nationale. Manuscrits. Nouvelles Acquisitions Françaises*, no. 22967. In the first and subsequent editions of the book, Barrès replaces the word '*images*,' standing for the principal means of his pedagogical technique, by the word '*sentiments*,' denoting its proximate object. Mme I.-M. Frandon, noting this variant, recalls a similar phrase in the *Mémoires d'outre-tombe*: 'ces nobles sentiments, qui seuls donnent du prix à la vie' (F.-R. de Chateaubriand, *cit.* I.-M. Frandon, *L'Orient de Maurice Barrès*, 395).

Quand toutes les idées entrent en concurrence dans l'âme d'un enfant, je m'applique à favoriser la poussée de ses ancêtres. Je lui donne un dressage tel que jamais il ne se reniera. J'oblige à reculer la stérile, la niaise inquiétude, celle qui n'est point l'exigence des grands cœurs, mais le balancement des êtres acéphales.

Par elle-même, la vie n'a pas de sens. Si nous repoussons la règle, quelle qu'elle soit, qui disciplina nos pères et à quoi nous approprie notre structure mentale, nous n'avons aucune raison de choisir une vérité plutôt qu'une autre dans le riche écrin des systèmes. Il ne nous reste qu'à jouer à pile ou face.

Au berceau d'un orphelin, à l'hôpital, comme pis aller, il faut bien que l'on appelle la froide déesse Raison. Pitoyable nourrice! J'aimerais mieux la mort que cette infatuée. Par contre, un petit enfant chez qui l'on distingue et vénère les émotions héréditaires, que l'on meuble d'images nationales et familiales, tout au cours de sa vie, dans son fond possédera une solidarité plus forte que toutes les dialectiques, un terrain pour résister à toutes les infections, une croyance, c'est-à-dire une santé morale.
[*Les Amitiés françaises, Œuvre* v 478–9][17]

The 'systematic'[18] image of France Barrès seeks to 'imprint' on his son by taking him to the battlefields of Alsace and Lorraine, to the high fortress of the Counts of Vaudémont, to Domremy and its Bois-Chenu, to the convent and church on the sacred hill of Sion-Vaudé-

17 Barrès's empiricism allowed Reason a modest rôle. The 'cold,' 'infatuated' goddess appears as a 'pitifully' inadequate foster-mother even for unfortunate orphans, and those 'scholarship boys,' like Paul Bouteiller, whom Thibaudet, in a famous antithesis (*La République des professeurs*, Chapter x, 'Héritiers et Boursiers'), discovered at the heart of Barrès's social philosophy, implacably opposed by the fortunate 'inheritors.' But the word 'raisonnable,' standing for what is fitting, and associated with Cornelian 'chivalry' ('qui place ... la gloire en dehors du succès'), distinguishes Barresian anti-rationalism from the variety taught in the fascist schools of the next generation: 'Preparatevi i muscoli e il cuore' *Œuvre* v 479, 482 [*Cit.* p. 217], 556). Cf. *Œuvre* xi 174, *cit.* pp. 115–16.

18 Cf. *Œuvre* v 560 and *Mes Cahiers, Œuvre* xiv 80–1: 'Après la septième année, l'imagination de l'enfant a pris de la patrie une première empreinte. Il possède des images ... a déjà réglé le chaos. Il possède un jeu d'images systématiques; il se courbe sous la discipline des patriotes français.'

mont, and to the basilica and grotto at Lourdes, like the one he was beginning to build up at the centre of his propaganda for adults, is the image of a homeland both vulnerable and defiant along its Eastern Bastions, and richly endowed with religious enthusiasm, surging wild from its natural sanctuaries, but disciplined and directed by a double civilization, French and Catholic. Like his adult propaganda also, Barrès's educational method culminates in the act of 'pilgrimage':

> Si nous cherchons le meilleur dressage pour qu'un enfant se fasse de convenables 'amitiés,' il faut d'abord que son imagination se forme en toute confiance auprès de ses parents. Une magnifique condition, c'est ensuite que le pays où il habite, au lieu d'être une chose inanimée, un milieu morose, devienne une influence. Toute région présente une pensée, et cette pensée demande à pénétrer les cœurs. Que l'enfant la respire. Il ne s'agit point de savoir des choses sur un pays, car cela fait une assez vaine curiosité, mais, tandis que l'enfant s'anime au contact d'un horizon, sa mobilité, son plaisir lui amassent des matériaux; et très aisément, avec de petits pèlerinages, l'on peut dégager chez un jeune garçon ses dispositions chevaleresques et raisonnables, le détourner de ce qui est bas, l'orienter vers sa vérité, susciter en lui le sentiment d'un intérêt commun auquel chacun doit concourir, le préparer enfin à se comprendre comme un moment dans un développement, comme un instant d'une chose immortelle.
> [*Les Amitiés françaises, Œuvre* v 482]

But Philippe's lessons are not confined to the spectacle of 'la terre française chargée de tombes' and the 'lieux classiques de la France' (*Œuvre* v 557). Like most children of his class and generation, he had played with lead soldiers and scanned the 'terrible pictures' of a 'History of the War' before seeing a real army (*Œuvre* v 503–7). The iconographical preparation of his visit to Vaudémont was more unusual:

> L'imagination de Philippe, à cinq ans, est nourrie de deux belles histoires. Plusieurs fois par jour il m'apporte l'un ou l'autre des

albums où Boutet de Monvel et Job ont si bien raconté Jeanne d'Arc et Napoléon. Chaque fois ses yeux m'avouent sa crainte de m'importuner et chaque fois il échoue à couvrir son invasion d'une formule ingénieuse. D'habitude il me tend son livre:

– Est-ce que tu le connais?

Puis, très vite, en secouant la tête d'un air qui signifie: 'Suis-je bête! ... quelle étourderie!' il ajoute:

– Ah! oui, c'est vrai que tu le connais. Alors – tu veux que nous le regardions ensemble?

Son sourire étant plus persuasif que son raisonnement, nous commençons à tourner les pages.

Sur chaque image et même sur chaque détail de l'image, il y a une réflexion très judicieuse ou un peu plaisante ... qui, je ne sais comment, est devenue classique, et, si j'y manque, Philippe, écrasant son doigt sur le feuillet, ne permet pas qu'on aille plus avant.

Depuis trois mois pourtant, après quelques échecs (Don Quichotte n'a pas réussi), nous avons trouvé plus beau que Jeanne d'Arc et plus beau que Napoléon, ou du moins qui contient trente Jeanne d'Arc et soixante Napoléon: le livre des livres, une merveille, le *Roland Furieux* d'Arioste...

Philippe ne rêve plus que d'enchantements et de tournois. Notre jardin et les rues de notre petite ville lorraine sont remplis de paladins, de magiciens et de belles aventurières. En vérité, ne serait-il pas dommage que de telles puissances de sentiment se dissipassent, alors que leurs vapeurs peuvent être dirigées et solidifiées sur de dignes objets qu'elles doreront pour toute sa vie? Fixons ce bel émerveillement sur quelque chose de réel et mêlons ces images qui fuiraient à des images qui demeureront.

– Écoute, petit, je veux te montrer le château d'un paladin, le château-forteresse qu'habitait un compagnon de Roland, de Roger et de Mandricard ... C'est près d'ici, dans un magnifique endroit isolé...

[*Les Amitiés françaises, Œuvre* v 508–10]

Philippe's education is here made to follow the roundabout route his father had taken before, and, so Barrès wished, for him: from the sumptuous fantasy of the Romantic's Italy to the spare and anxious realism of the patriot's France. On the exotic chivalry of Ariosto's paladins are grafted the simple home truths of a little nation driven by 'harsh necessity' to choose between the greater nations of Germany and France: traces of fire on the Tour Brunehaut, a knight in armour on a church tapestry, a dismantled hill fortress, the vulnerable villages of Caesar's granary below, with its poplar-lined roads of invasion (to be scanned for the menacing dust-cloud of the eternal attackers) and of evasion (southwards to the 'magic' gardens of Italy, that 'eternal educator, still civilizing young barbarians,' but which Barrès would close to his son until he has learnt to prefer 'a garden in Lorraine in September') (*Œuvre* II 122; V 494 514):

> Si je berce le petit Philippe dans un demi-rêve de vérité et de poésie, c'est pour former en lui une disposition insensible à recevoir mon héritage comme le plus beau des héritages. Les séries d'images qui l'émeuvent ou qui l'amusent par ce doux après-midi passé gaiement en confiance avec moi, qui ne suis pas encore assombri de vieillesse, lui demeureront à jamais aimables et fécondes et, quand je ne respirerai plus, mes meilleures émotions, que je place dans un être tout perméable, seront devenues son âme. Doucement, j'ébranle le vieil âge accumulé dans ce petit garçon.
> [*Les Amitiés françaises, Œuvre* V 515]

On the other hand, the 'half-dream of truth and poetry' whose function is to give Barrès's son a 'prejudice in favour of his country,' tends, when looked at from the formal point of view, to range away from the 'object lessons' prescribed by Saint-Phlin and towards the 'musical' limit of Barrès's rhetoric:

> L'Arioste est ce concert doré que peignit Giorgione et qui, dans une splendeur voluptueuse, développe des sonorités riches et profondes, s'assouplissant du genre bouffe jusqu'à l'héroïque: une âme neuve n'analyse pas des gammes si fondues de nuances, mais sous chaque beau son, rires ou pleurs, elle s'ébranle tout entière. Le petit garçon m'écoute, grave et avide comme une terre sèche sous la pluie.
> Il y a plus: parfois, intéressé moi-même, je lisais sans les modifier

> une suite de stances, et certainement Philippe n'y pouvait rien comprendre, mais la musique d'un grand poète est une magie qui se passe de clarté. Ce qui subsiste en français de l'harmonie italienne et puis mon accent convaincu persuadait Philippe... Je lui ouvrais les paradis de la grande beauté.
> [*Les Amitiés françaises, Œuvre* v 509–10]

The educational method advanced in *Les Amitiés françaises* brings the full scope of Barrès's art of persuasion self-consciously into play for the first time, from the 'systematic choice of images,' meant to 'direct and stabilize' Philippe's inchoate emotive potential, to an education '*in hymnis et canticis*' which will favour his 'innate faculty of expansion' (477, 510, 560).

'CETTE ÉDUCATION PAR LES YEUX'

The first example of a Barresian education by images occurs in *Le Jardin de Bérénice*, whose eponymous heroine is brought up by the custodian of a Provençal folk museum and art gallery, where she is often left alone for hours at a time, in maiden meditation, fancy free:

> Excellente éducation! qui eût fait d'elle la maîtresse déférente mais non intimidée d'un prince, et qui lui laissait tous ses moyens pour donner du plaisir. Qualité trop rare!
>
> En vérité, ce musée convenait pour encadrer cette petite fille, qui en devint visiblement l'âme projetée: d'imagination trop ingénieuse et trop subtile, comme les vieux fonds de complications gothiques de ces tableaux; de sens bien vivant, comme ces essais de paysages et de copies de la nature, où la Renaissance apparaît dans les œuvres du quatorzième siècle.
>
> Cette petite femme traduisait immédiatement en émotions sentimentales toutes les choses d'art qui s'y prêtaient.
> [*Le Jardin de Bérénice, Œuvre* I 298]

Bérénice's 'visual education' ('cette éducation par les yeux' [297]) is primarily an education by artifacts, ranging from the deliberately persuasive or informative embodiment of an abstraction – allegories of the virtues and astronomical models, emblematic figures, and landscapes – through pictorial chronicles of the past to actual historical relics (*Œuvre* I 294–301). But the natural forms of her native countryside (*Œuvre* I 316, 322, 330, 340–1, 360–1, 368) also bring their influence to bear on Bérénice and her Parisian disciple, the hero of the novel:

> J'aimais cette campagne et j'avais la certitude de m'en faire l'image même qui repose dans les beaux yeux et dans le cœur attristé de Bérénice. Comme mon amie, je laissais mon sentiment se conformer à ces étangs mornes et fiévreux, à ce pays lunaire plein de rêves immenses et de tristesses résignées.
> [*Le Jardin de Bérénice, Œuvre* I 321]

Le Musée du Roi René is a fiction composed from Barrès's memories of his own 'visual education' in the landscapes, art galleries, and museums of Europe, in the steps of Michelet, Stendhal, Taine, and Ozanam;[19] and from more recent recollections of Mistral's *Musée Arletan*.[20] Another part of Barrès's *Culte du Moi* to reappear in the educational reforms of his traditionalist period was the technique of 'reducing the abstract to sensuous images' that he had learnt from Loyola (*Œuvre* I 178, *cit.* above, p. 12), and which depends on the same associationist psychology of the imagination as Bérénice's museum education. Saint-Phlin's 'suite d'exercices multipliés sur des cas concrets' (*Œuvre* IV 398, *cit.* above, p. 213), like Barrès's earlier attempt to 'enclose' and 'fix' the vulnerable and errant sensibility of *un homme libre* within a 'sentimental kingdom catalogued and condensed in evocative pictures, lining the walls of a vast inner palace' (*Œuvre* I 178), is a neo-Loyolan 'suite de mécaniques pour donner la paix à l'âme' (*Œuvre* I 144). Barrès's notes for *Les Amitiés françaises* bring Loyola's lesson up to date with the evident help of Jules Soury, though the book itself somewhat attenuates the behaviourist automatism that the notes, like Saint-Phlin's letter, recommend:

19 'Journal de ma vie extérieure,' *La Batte* 17 August 1888 (on which is based 'Mon Triomphe de Venise,' in *Un Homme libre*); 'L'Éducation par l'Italie,' *Le Journal* 22 September 1893; preface to *Correspondance de Stendhal* (Paris: C. Bosse 1908); *Œuvre* V 481–2; XIII 28; XIX 396

20 *See* above, pp. 162–3.

On voudrait qu'un enfant réçût de son éducateur des images qui ébranlassent sa mémoire profonde et fissent surgir ses réminiscences. Autour de ces états ainsi provoqués et ressuscités, on associerait toutes les sensations aimables, propres à le caresser, à le flatter, à le ramener volontiers vers ces répercussions du passé où il trouvera non point des vérités de tout repos, mais une inquiétude de toute santé. La santé, en effet, c'est de vivre la vie de sa race, c'est de reproduire en soi les états d'esprit pour lesquels notre structure nous prépare.
[*Mes Cahiers, Œuvre* XIV 82]

Another of the masters of Barrès's youth, Michelet, reappears in the same *cahier* to lend authority to the critic of the University's abstractions:

Ce qui manque ici, en tout, je le répète: c'est la spécification, tel trait précis, vif et fort, où l'objet sort du tableau, va prendre le spectateur, s'en empare, saisit son imagination et sa mémoire pour toujours.
[Michelet, *l'Étudiant*, 185, *cit. Mes Cahiers, Œuvre* XIV 68]

The bicycle journey of two of Barrès's *déracinés*, Saint-Phlin and Sturel, down the valley of the Moselle, which was first published in *La Quinzaine* in 1899 before appearing as chapter XI of *L'Appel au soldat*, and which is a prototype of the educational excursions of *Les Amitiés françaises*, gets an epigraph from *De la recherche de la vérité*:

Il ne sera pas malaisé de comprendre comment les pères et les mères font des impressions très fortes sur l'imagination de leurs enfants ... ils donnent à l'imagination un certain tour qui les rend tout à fait susceptibles des mêmes sentiments...
[*L'Appel au soldat, Œuvre* IV 3]

He remarked later in *Mes Cahiers* that the faculty Malebranche regarded as a 'mistress of errors' was for Cardinal Newman, on the contrary, 'a clear, lively intuition of realities' (*Œuvre* XIV 291–4).

This was prompted by his recent reading of a 'psychological biography' of the English apologist by Henri Bremond, whose earlier book: *L'enfant et la vie*, had given him the leading text of the first, methodological, chapter of *Les Amitiés françaises*:

> 'Si l'imagination chez les enfants devance la raison, la culture de l'imagination devrait être mise en première ligne; l'enfance et la jeunesse devraient être élevées *in hymnis et canticis*, nourries dans le culte de la plus haute beauté.' (Ravaisson, cité par Bremond.) [*Mes Cahiers, Œuvre* XIV 38–9][21]

But Barrès's use of Malebranche's child psychology precedes Bremond's study of Newman by six years, and he picked out the *abbé*'s quotation of Ravaisson from among a score of assorted texts on education at the beginning of *L'Enfant et la vie*. He supported and clarified his pedagogy of the imagination by quoting the sympathetic opinions of writers in the same field, but it had grown up slowly out of his own experience from adolescence onwards and from the writers he habitually used in every field to intensify and elucidate his experience.

'IN HYMNIS ET CANTICIS'

The 'visual' method of education propounded in *Les Amitiés françaises* is a way of 'orientating' the youngest generation of Lorrainers with a child's version of Barrès's image of France, communicated by father to son in 'little pilgrimages' to Sion-Vaudémont and Froeschwiller, Domremy and Lourdes. His concomitant proposal to 'unleash' the child's 'inner music' (*Œuvre* V 481, 561)[22] by extending imaginative persuasion to its opposite extreme of indefinite, emotional sug-

21 Cf. *Œuvre* V 476 and Bremond's constant rejection of 'formulae' in favour of an education designed to 'pétrir de réalité l'esprit et l'imagination d'un petit enfant' (H. Bremond, *L'Enfant et la vie* [Paris: Victor Retaux 1902] 165).

22 *Bibliothèque Nationale. Manuscrits. Nouvelles Acquisitions françaises*, no. 22967 (*Les Amitiés françaises*) has 'des images ... qui déchaînent la musique intérieure.'

gestion in this, the most effusively lyrical of Barrès's committed works, where the style of what he called his 'abrupt and elliptic song' reached a high pitch of sympathetic musicality,[23] is, on the other hand, recommended with an unreserved confidence which will not recur in his subsequently closer analysis of the action of music on adults and children alike. As early as 1903, however, in the educational context in which music made its first appearance in Barrès's art of persuasion, he recognized that this part of his rhetoric would require delicate handling by a traditionalist:

> Les enfants sont des petits Davids qui dansent et chantent devant l'arche avant de savoir pourquoi leur arche est vénérable. Le problème de l'instruction primaire, c'est de leur donner de la beauté, ou, plus exactement, de favoriser leur faculté innée d'expansion, de les aider pour qu'ils dégagent ce qu'ils possèdent de naissance: un continuel enchantement, le sens épique et lyrique, un hymne, un cantique ininterrompu...
>
> Le délicat, c'est de nourrir cette disposition sans la déformer, et le plus délicat, c'est de faire entrer ce chant individuel dans le chœur social. Il convient que chacun de ces petits innocents garde son accent juste; il faut en outre que toutes ces voix, tous ces corps si frêles se meuvent en cadence. Quels mots, dès lors, quels rythmes proposer à ces nouveaux venus pour que leur ardeur s'accorde avec la communauté des morts et des vivants?
> [*Les Amitiés françaises, Œuvre* v 477–8][24]

The power of music and, by analogy, the music of words,[25] to arouse

23 *See* p. 283.

24 Cf. 'Vœux pour les enfants,' *Le Gaulois* 1 January 1903 (published posthumously in *N'Importe où hors du monde, Œuvre* XII 509–13): '*Dans les hymnes et dans les cantiques.* Cette phrase du philosophe Ravaisson est pour moi une source vive. Elle m'émerveille, elle évoque une ardente vitalité, une aurore ... Je ne saurais pas très bien distinguer entre les hymnes et les cantiques. Il me semble pourtant que ceux-là sont des poèmes en l'honneur des dieux et des héros, et ceux-ci des actions de grâces pour accompagner toutes les circonstances de la vie.'

25 *See* below, pp. 231–7: 'Transpositions d'art.'

emotion fascinated and also troubled Barrès more and more in the years following the publication of *Les Amitiés françaises*. He came to regard it as the strongest, but also as the most dangerous force in the mechanics of persuasion to which he gave so much thought. As a 'mechanism,' a 'material agent' for 'preparing,' 'exalting,' 'multiplying' feeling, and hence as an instrument not only of education, but also of 'government,'[26] he repeatedly noted its effects, in himself, in his contemporaries, and in the recorded experiences and opinions of individuals and groups as diverse as Delacroix, Nietzsche, Saint Teresa of Avila, Saint Paul; Saint Odilon and the monastic orders of the Christian Middle Ages; Jalal Ad-Din Rumi and the dervish dancers of Konya; the musical magicians of ancient China.[27] But what he saw as the teacher's and propagandist's complementary task of 'directing' sentiment made him look ever more askance at the 'magic formulae' of an art whose 'dangerous glamour,' no longer properly understood, threatened to 'dissolve' and 'submerge' the sympathetic listener in the indiscriminate raptures of a 'pantheistic' trance;[28] an effect, 'at once physiological and psychological,' which, like the corresponding 'animal and divine' effect of those open-air temples and natural solitudes which were Barrès's topographical analogues of music,[29] called for an antidote made up of the solid and orderly *corpus* of sytematic doctrine, representative heroes, and commemorative monuments and sanctuaries out of which French civilization, the Catholic Church and, up to a point, Science, have together made so many indispensable breakwaters against the far sweeping

26 *Mes Cahiers, Œuvre* XIX 124: 'les anciens sages faisaient de la musique un moyen pour modeler les grandes actions du peuple, un moyen de gouvernement. Comment ne pas comprendre que nous jouons avec des airs magiques?' Cf. XIX 135, *cit.* below, p. 25 and *Grande Guerre* XIV 183–5.

27 *Œuvre* I 124, 224–6; V 559; VII 53; XI 174, 221, 379; XII 212–23, 228; XIII 12; XIV 50; XV 194, 200 204–5, 208, 213; XVIII 181, 331; XX 8. *See* pp. 283–4.

28 *See* p. 284.

29 E.g. *Œuvre* VIII 91: 'cette musique courte et profonde qu'un Henri Duparc sait écrire, musique pareille à ces rivières lentes et noires qui coulent à ras de terre dans une campagne déserte.' XX 165: 'J'aime le chant des Gluck, des Mozart, des Méhul. C'est un bouleau d'argent sur les grands bois sombres de l'âge et du travail.'

and potentially destructive torrents of religious sentiment that can be released in the human breast by music no less than by spirit-haunted landscapes of field and flood:

> Je ne souhaite à personne de se soumettre aux influences de cette sublime tragédie, car ce qu'elle met dans notre sang, c'est une irritation mortelle, le besoin d'aller au-delà, plus outre que l'humanité ... Vertige, ivresse des hauts lieux et des sentiments extrêmes! À la cime des vagues où nous mène *Tristan,* reconnaissons les fièvres qui, la nuit, montent des lagunes.
> [*Amori et dolori sacrum, Œuvre* VII 50]

> J'arrive toujours et très vite à quelque chose d'inexprimable. Ce matin ... une merveille m'éblouit ... un verger d'amandiers, planté de luzernes, où les coquelicots fleurissent si nombreux qu'à vingt mètres du regard ils semblent couvrir tout le champ ... Tout l'ensemble légèrement frissonne. Pourquoi donc est-ce si beau? Ou plutôt, devant ce tapis flamboyant, de quoi est faite mon émotion? Ici l'analyse s'arrête. Quel est le chant magique, l'incantation qui couvrit cette prairie d'une vaine pourpre? Ovide nous dit que Cérès blessée par un chant de perdition ne donne qu'une herbe inutile. Je crois entendre cet air enchanté, cette musique sublime et nuisible. A vivre ici, n'acquerrait-on pas la faculté de créer des mythes? ... Mais n'essayons pas d'analyser des heures animales et divines qui atteignent les sources de notre vie physiologique, en même temps qu'elles avivent notre spiritualité!
> ['Lettre à Gyp sur le printemps à Mirabeau,' *Le Mystère en pleine lumière, Œuvre* XII 241–2]

The nihilistic enchantment Barrès found in the Asiatic and half-animal deities and the world-denying ecstacy of Richard Wagner, and against which *Les Amitiés françaises* played a call to noble action on the 'lyres of all the high places of France' (*Œuvre* V 557), turned into what subsequently sounded to him, in post-Wagnerian music, like positively delinquent sensuality and violence.[30] Faced in his last years

30 *Œuvre* X 400 (R. Strauss); XII 212 (Debussy and Stravinski?)

with the ultimate 'Bolshevism' and 'primitive animalism' of *Le Bal Nègre*,[31] he abandoned altogether the former musical features of his occidental counter-rhetoric:

> – Mes chers amis, dis-je aux jeunes gens qui m'avaient mené là, je vois ce que c'est. Je m'en doutais bien. C'est un des points d'attaque de la maladie. C'est une roséole sur le corps social. Oh! Je ne dis pas que Paris en mourra; tout au contraire, je suis même sûr que Paris en guérira. Il y a dans Paris les églises, le Louvre, les bibliothèques, les maisons des sœurs de charité, la Sorbonne et, tout autour, les profondes campagnes, pleines de paysages. Ah! c'est solide...
> – On a vite fait de traiter de maladie l'élan, la jeunesse.
> – Ah! jeune homme, vous êtes tenté de me traiter de vieille bête! Rien de plus normal. C'est de votre âge. Et l'opinion que vous voulez bien ne pas m'exprimer, je l'ai eue et je l'ai dite ... Oui, il y a là-dedans de l'élan, de la jeunesse ... Mais il y a plus! Je suis sûr d'y voir un élément spécial, le dadaïsme, le bolchevisme, quelque chose qui dit *non* à la civilisation occidentale.
> [*N'Importe où hors du monde, Œuvre* XII 414]

Mediaeval Church music, as opposed to modern music, noted Barrès, after a conversation with Dom Pastourel in 1907, tended to 'exalt' and to 'fortify' the personality (*Mes Cahiers, Œuvre* XV 204, 211). This is partly, he seems to suggest, because the human voice and the organ haven't the 'dissolving force' of modern orchestras (*Œuvre* XV 212; XVI 63–4). But he also learnt how the Church had countered that 'pantheistic' dissolution of human spirit and will in animal vagueness, which was, he believed, the constant danger of 'musical mysticism' (*Œuvre* XV 189, 200), by plain-song less purely non-representational than the mediaeval, by the 'semi-obscure formulae' of the psalms (XV 200, 204–5), and by such non-musical devices as an intermediate 'screen' of angels and saints (XV 186, 189–90), and the clear and practical symbolism of the liturgy and the sacraments. It was a return in 1922 to the grotto, spring, and

31 *Œuvre* XII 413–19

sounding basilica of Lourdes, the complex sanctuary which had released such a spate of vaguely mystical musicality in *Les Amitiés françaises*, two decades earlier, that inspired Barrès's most eloquently affirmative and comprehensive testimony to the genius of the Church, in its 'marvellous ceremonies,' its 'sublime order' of angels and saints, its liturgy, sacraments, and (given due recognition but much less emphasis) moral precepts, for simultaneously both stimulating and regulating what the crude and often dangerous scenic and musical media of instinctive mysticism simply excite:

> Les orgues et les hymnes pressent, supplient, jubilent, gémissent, exultent, se traînent, se creusent, enflent leurs vagues et figurent les mouvements de cet océan, de cette présence envahissante où les fidèles auprès de la grotte se sentaient baigner. La Chrétienté chante ce je ne sais quoi incommunicable qu'elle vient d'éprouver et libère en musique ce qu'elle ne saurait exprimer, tandis qu'une fumée monte de l'encensoir qu'un enfant balance indéfiniment.
>
> O sagesse de l'Église qui sut faire ce beau choix de cérémonies, de cantiques, de processions et de sacrements pour tempérer des états violents et les ramener sous une douce domination! Je connais les effluves des grottes infernales, et quoique je n'aie qu'en passant côtoyé de telles expériences, je mesure leur puissance. Nous risquions d'avoir des gens tout en flammes qui hurlent. Nulle invention, dans aucune science, qui ne débute par un mouvement du cœur, par une intuition, par un coup de chaleur, par une émotion; nul poème qui ne soit dicté, à la suite d'une minute inspirée, sur un rythme qui nous saisit et nous commande à notre insu même; quant à l'amour, il est l'antre des nymphes lui-même, mais n'a de cesse que des sentiments à peine décantés ne s'élèvent de cette fiévreuse obscurité et ne viennent s'ordonner sous un beau front raisonnable: toute la haute civilisation sort des brouillards de la source mystique. Mais son jaillissement est bien trouble et demande à être endigué. Il faut en modérer le côté animal, l'hystérie. L'histoire sait où peuvent mener de telles expériences qui, moitié mystiques et moitiés physiologiques, intéressent tout l'être. Ces eaux souterraines, où le meilleur et le pire jaillissent, l'Église les capte avant qu'elles ne soient devenues le torrent

immonde. Cette source mêlée, elle sait la susciter et la dominer. C'est le but constant et certain de la liturgie, son double but, stimuler et régler.
[*N'Importe où hors du monde, Œuvre* XII 324–5][32]

The scientific view of nature which Barrès had tried so persistently to reconcile with Catholicism during the years between his first and his second visits to Lourdes offered him one of the advantages he perceived in Catholic symbolism: a kind of directional grid, placed between man and his universal environment, which prevents him getting lost in the perilous sea of uncharted pantheism which comes 'flooding' over the individual who is sympathetic to heady music and wild landscape:

Panthéisme. – Il y a une oscillation. Après de grands efforts d'activité déterminée, des contacts, des campagnes électorales, j'ai toujours voulu m'enfoncer dans la rêverie, dans les flots du rythme de Hugo (ses derniers poèmes), dans l'orchestre verbal, ou bien encore dans la nature. Telles après-midi dans les prés au-dessous de Bermont.

Comme je souffrais de voir le cadastre sur la nature!

Puis je reprenais le goût de la discipline, de l'ordre. Je souffrais trop de ne pas dominer, de me dissoudre dans cette nature. C'est alors qu'à Châtelguyon je lisais les œuvres scientifiques de Goethe, je voulais faire de la botanique comme Rousseau. Je découvrais dans la nature classée, interprétée par l'homme un immense jardin de Versailles. *Omnia in mensura et numero et pondere disposuisti.* 'Vous avez réglé toutes choses avec mesure, nombre et poids.' Cette conception scientifique du monde nous dispense de servir ces anges et ces diables et nous sauve du panthéisme. La science fait confesser à l'âme que la nature est ordonnée, comme l'amour divin le lui fait déjà confesser.
[*Mes Cahiers, Œuvre* XV 211][33]

32 Cf. *Œuvre* XI 440–5; XX 15–17.

33 Compare Barrès's use of Pascal – his epitome of science and Christianity, reason and faith, geometry and sentiment reconciled (*see* pp. 75–6,

Taking the 'utility' of Science as much for granted as the practical value of Christian ethics,[34] Barrès concentrated on trying to complete his parallel between *les églises* and *les laboratoires* by presenting the latter as 'centres of enthusiasm,' radiating a kind of genius that is as much in tune with the 'universal harmony' as the tranquil grace of Lourdes and the controlled force of the Konya dancers (*Œuvre* IX 327–30, 377; XI 429–31; XII 325; XX 37). But whereas he found in the liturgical traditions of the Roman Catholic Church, and, to a lesser degree, of Sufi mysticism, an *exemplary* method of persuasion, uniting in a marvellous synthesis the forces of enthusiasm and order, mystery and light, that he was continually trying to combine in his own work, *science*, on the other hand, and such related words as *géométrie* and *pensée*, tend to occur to him simultaneously with, and opposite to *musique*, *rythme*, *harmonie*, and the like, as one only of an antithetical *pair* of terms:

> Je reprends ma thèse sur la musique (le rythme, disais-je dans les cahiers précédents).
>
> J'aime Pascal d'avoir embrassé la raison et la foi, la géométrie et le sentiment. C'est ce que Luther exprimait: 'La musique est la plus belle chose du monde après la théologie.'
>
> [*Mes Cahiers* XIV 133]

> *Ma formation littéraire.* – Comment toute ma vie j'ai été sur une fausse piste par désir de me nourrir l'esprit.
>
> Et puis par le goût de l'harmonie sans pensée.
>
> C'est l'entre-deux qu'il m'eût fallu, l'élan léger.
>
> Les développements trop lourds de Taine et la rhétorique de Hugo sont bien beaux mais à mettre dans les assises de l'édifice. Il faut prendre le vol. Et alors je vais où m'appellent ces signes d'amitié que je reconnais bien.
>
> [*Mes Cahiers, Œuvre* XIII 20][35]

230) – as a counter-agent against 'pantheistic' loss of identity in the landscape of Auvergne (*Œuvre* XV 214, *cit.* Chapter Twelve note 39).

34 *Œuvre* XX 36. *See* above, pp. 201–3.

35 Cf. Chapter Six, note 26.

TRANSPOSITIONS D'ART

Barrès's mythological geography of the Franco-German frontier and his sacred topography of France and the Levant provide appropriate scenes for staging the many private and public ceremonies, pilgrimages in particular, to which his art of persuasion leads. Much of his work as a propagandist and educationalist consisted in advocating, taking part in, and describing live ceremonies of the kind which exploit the visual imagination to the full. Such scenes also gave him abundant material for some of his most successful journalistic, oratorical, and literary *transpositions d'art*. Just as his hero-worship led him to attempt pen-portraits in the style of the *Image d'Épinal*, so his cult of the land which had given his heroes birth – 'Mes cimetières lorrains. (Certains grands hommes dans leur paysage)' (*Œuvre* xv 393) – stimulated his art of rendering in words the landscape spectacle of 'places that are patterns' (*Œuvre* xx 86). A complementary feature of his verbal rhetoric corresponds to the art of music.

The analogical use of musical terms by Barrès to describe not only what is most mysterious in the human condition,[36] but also to stake a claim for words in the poetic border zone that Paul Valéry speaks of, where 'discourse' merges with 'music' in the effort to communicate this mystery,[37] is part of the heritage of Idealism and Symbolism which fell to him as a young man in *fin-de-siècle*, Wagnerian, Paris.[38] The sibyl of Auxerre Cathedral, the Chinese Princess Ling, the whirling dervishes of Konya, the heroines of *La Colline inspirée* and *Un Jardin sur l'Oronte*, a whole aviary of symbolic birds: 'rossignol,' 'rouge-gorge,' 'colombe,' 'aiglon,' 'martin-pêcheur,' 'petit faucon... les ailes battantes et le gosier sonore,'[39] and a French 'vivante,' Anna de Noailles,[40] are so many Barresian avatars of that 'musical' and

36 E.g. *Œuvre* xi 104; xii 62, 134–5; xvi 41; xvii 286

37 P. Valéry, *Pièces sur l'Art* (Paris: Gallimard 1936) 51, *cit.* R. Gibson, *Modern French Poets on Poetry* (Cambridge: Cambridge University Press 1961) 182

38 *See* above, pp. 8–10.

39 *Œuvre* v 555–6, 558–9; vi 354, 477, 498; xi 20–4, 42, 86; xii 183–9, 196–7, 203–23, 242, 277, 471; xix 130

40 *Mes Cahiers*, *Œuvre* xiv 134: 'Mme de Noailles possède au sublime degré la musique. Peut-être quand elle s'oriente vers la science soupçonne-t-elle

'rhythmic' vocation which developed as one of the principal twin coefficients of his mature system of expression:

> *Le style* ... Le style, ça n'est pas les mots ... c'est la tournure, c'est le mouvement de l'âme ... son élan rendu sensible...
> Il y subsiste quelque chose du chant ou de la danse. Je veux dire qu'elle vit de l'instinct rythmique. C'est une incantation. Nul ne peut analyser son charme.
> [*Mes Cahiers, Œuvre* XVI 62–3]

> Des moyens pour contraindre l'esprit, pour obliger l'inspiration à venir! Une mécanique de l'enthousiasme! ... Tout cela nous mènerait à la connaissance de certains rythmes plus capable que d'autres de hâter la naissance de l'extase. Tout cela nous ferait remonter à l'origine des procédés littéraires de cadence, de rime, d'allitération. Nous comprendrions les strophes diverses, le coup de gong du *Never more*, enfin tout le primitivisme de la poésie, de l'art oratoire ...
> [*Une Enquête aux pays du Levant, Œuvre* XI 494–5][41]

But the singer's or the dancer's arts of 'enchantment' and 'prophecy'

des greniers qui lui feraient une autre nourriture également sublime. Mais si elle aime tant les Bergeret, c'est un plan où je la comprends avec indifférence.' Cf. *Le Voyage de Sparte, Œuvre* VII 291–2 and, for Barrès's use of the word *vivante*, I.-M. Frandon, *L'Orient de Maurice Barrès*, 159–64, 289–92.

41 Cf. *Mes Cahiers, Œuvre* XIX 280: 'Sur les moyens mécaniques d'émouvoir: Le coup de gong, Le tercet de Dante, La strophe navigation de Lamartine, L'orchestre de Hugo.' A particular example of incantatory repetition is analysed in *La Colline inspirée* as part of Barrès's account of the heresiarch Léopold Baillard's rapt attention to the singing of his favourite disciple, Sister Thérèse: 'Dans son cantique, un mot entre tous, ce mot de Sion, perpétuellement répété de strophe en strophe, exerçait sur Léopold une action prestigieuse. Sion, c'était pour ce grand imaginatif la Jérusalem terrestre et la Jérusalem céleste; c'était sa montagne, son église et son pèlerinage; c'était plus encore, et, dans ce beau mot, il plaçait le sentiment de l'infini qu'il portait en lui. Lorsque ces magiques syllabes, chargées d'une si riche émotion, se mêlaient au souffle harmonieux de la miraculée, il semblait qu'il subît une incantation' (*Œuvre* VI 334–5). *See* J. Godfrin, *Barrès mystique*, 18–24, 226–7.

correspond to one term only of Barrès's final rhetorical synthesis. He had learned the complementary value of 'a definite theme,' and 'ideas that are clear and in vigorous relief,' features of the doctrinaire, realist, and picturesque traditions of French literature which were as much a part of his early background as Franco-Germanic Idealism and Symbolism. 'Eh bien! l'art pour nous,' he wrote in his preface to the 1904 edition of *Un Homme libre*, 'ce serait d'exciter, d'émouvoir l'être profond par la justesse des cadences, mais en même temps de la persuader par la force de la doctrine. Oui, l'art d'écrire doit contenter ce double besoin de musique et de géométrie que nous portons, à la française, dans une âme bien faite ...' (*Œuvre* I 142). Though he was ready on more than one occasion between 'Chant de confiance dans la vie' (1903) and 'La Musique de perdition' (1921) to yield pride of place in the hierarchy of the arts of expression to music without words,[42] yet his mature position was determinedly literary:

> De l'expérience du poète à l'expérience qu'il s'agit d'émouvoir chez le lecteur, il faut nécessairement un agent de transmission, un messager, un Ariel. Comment le trouver? Dans l'ombre j'écoute, avec moins de fièvre qu'autrefois, mais avec plus de recueillement et de piété, ces bruissements de l'âme. Je voudrais les traduire avec une sincérité plus sérieuse et plus calme. La musique s'offre à me servir, et c'est elle d'abord que nous voudrions employer. Son échec pourtant est certain. Ses sensations trop vagues ne font pas le support pour ce passage de l'état lyrique du poète à l'état lyrique de l'auditeur. Rien ne remplacera le travail intellectuel du poète.

42 E.g. *La Grande pitié des églises de France, Œuvre* VIII 91: 'Et je suis tenté de leur raconter une espèce de petite histoire ... une allégorie en trois points qui ne vaudrait complètement que si les paroles en étaient rayées et remplacées par de la musique...' Cf. *Mes Cahiers, Œuvre* XVI 377, where Barrès has copied the last sentence of the following extract from André Chevrillon's *Nouvelles études anglaises* (Paris: Hachette 1910): 'Si [Ruskin] avait été sensible à la musique, s'il en avait deviné les ensorcelants pouvoirs, s'il avait pu se douter que cet art-là ... est justement celui qui nous enlève le plus à nous-même pour nous exalter jusqu'au divin et nous y absorber, il aurait renversé sa théorie de l'art. Il aurait compris que "au commencement était le rythme" et que l'artiste n'est pas un contemplateur, mais un danseur, et que son art n'est essentiel que par ce qu'il contient de danse et de musique.'

Rien ne me dispensera de me rendre compte de ce que j'ai éprouvé et surtout de me contraindre à l'exprimer. Je ne dispose que de mots trop clairs, trop précis. N'importe, c'est avec ces mots et à l'aide d'un thème concret qu'il faut que je produise sur mes lecteurs une impression voilée analogue à la mienne.
[*Le Mystère en pleine lumière, Œuvre* XII 210]

Cette force inépuisable, cette musique des astres est à ordonner et à distribuer entre les diverses sortes d'art.
'La démarche la plus noble de l'intelligence s'achemine vers la convergence des arts,' dites-vous. Ah! là je cesse d'être votre élève. Dans sa conversation avec Goethe, Napoléon a dit des choses bien raisonnables et comme ces deux grands hommes je crois qu'il faut nous en tenir aux genres tranchés. Nous autres écrivains nous avons pour mission de traduire en idées claires et d'un vigoureux relief, bref de rendre intelligible le mystère qui bourdonne autour des orchestres.
[Preface to A. Cœuroy, *Musique et littérature*
(Paris: Bloud et Gay 1923) vii]

Dante cherche à nous faire voir avec précision toutes les étapes de son voyage ... dans le Paradis, il réussit cette gageure inouïe de vouloir rendre sensible le règne de la vie spirituelle.
... Que l'animal humain atteigne à cette notion de l'amour et de l'intelligence, quelle émouvante grandeur! Et rien de plus vrai! Mais c'est bien difficile de décrire cela par des mots; on touche au domaine de la symphonie; Dante, pourtant, n'abdique pas et il triomphe de la royale difficulté.
[*Les Maîtres, Œuvre* XII 26–7]

Another passage of late reflections on the subject of music and literature, published in an article entitled 'Quelles limites imposer au germanisme intellectuel?', for *La Revue Universelle*, in January 1922, embraces a number of characteristically Barresian national, topographical, and psychological correlatives of musicality and its counteragents, and voices a more explicit reaction against the kindergarten pedagogy of 'hymns and canticles' that he had recommended nineteen years before in *Les Amitiés françaises*, where the then only slightly suspect musical component of his theory of education had featured for the first time:

> Le lied, quand il se rythme si étroitement sur l'inconscient, ne nous fait-il pas retourner par une pente délicieuse vers les dispositions imprécises et troubles, où nous sommes prêts à subir l'effet de toutes les émotions et de tous les désirs?
>
> Sans doute la chanson française se déprend trop aisément de cet élément purement sonore. Les paroles y veulent être pittoresques, dramatiques, sentimentales par elles-mêmes; la musique est serve plutôt que maîtresse, mais ne sommes-nous pas en droit de soupçonner, elle aussi, la volupté où nous invite l'étroit accord des mots et des inflexions musicales? Ce qui nous permet de rester maîtres de nous-mêmes n'est-il pas menacé par une poésie qui ne demande pas à passer par les éléments plus conscients de notre moi? La force d'un rythme, l'hypnotisme d'un refrain, l'alternance des mots martelés et des syllabes atténuées, la valeur suggestive des allitérations, le moulage étroit d'une poussée lyrique sur un balbutiement émotif, tout cela est sans doute délicieux, mais en face de ces alliciances [*sic*][43] de derviche tourneur il y avait, dans un poème de l'antiquité grecque, une part laissée à la réflexion et à la conscience que le lied envoûteur ne possède pas au même degré.
>
> ...Chez nous, nous avons placé le mystère là où il doit être, dans la vie religieuse. Le paysan chantait des romances sans mystère... Il avait dans les cathédrales ses mystères et ses profondeurs. Chez l'Allemand, l'église est partout et, comme elle n'est pas un lieu clos, elle perturbe la vie quotidienne. Le mysticisme n'est pas une faculté inoffensive. Le lied, c'est un appel à l'inconscient. Tout ce qui en appelle à l'inconscient et qui peut paraître nous exalter jusqu'au sublime tend à réveiller l'animalisme ... J'aime le lied;

43 'allitérations'? Cf. *Œuvre* XX 15: 'l'allitération est un procédé analogue à celui des derviches tourneurs.'

> je ne nie pas que nous, trop souvent, nous n'ayons dépassé le point d'équilibre: c'est bien affreux d'entendre un gosse chanter des refrains de café-concert,
>
> *En r'venant de Suresne,*
> *j'avais mon pompon;*
>
> j'aime le lied, mais qu'il soit confiné, ce compagnon inquiétant, dans la région du rêve et de l'abandon; qu'il n'empiète pas plus que la musique, sa voisine, sur notre vie plus forte, sur celle où nous avouons nous reconnaître...
>
> ...Et certainement encore on dira que nous manquons d'impartialité. Il faudrait quelque éducateur chinois, japonais, vérifiant quelle est la sorte d'inconvénient que ces jolis contes peuvent laisser dans les âmes ... des chansons où on met des effets de rythmes indépendants du sens, c'est délicieux pour les uns, c'est inquiétant pour les autres ... Il semble, à voir la manière dont leurs chansons de guerre rentrent dans ces rythmes, que ça peut, à un moment donné, sortir en méchanceté et pure animalité ... Une nourriture d'animal sauvage convient-elle à l'animal entré dans la douce familiarité de la cité? Et pour le lied: est-ce que ces vers que chantent de grands garçons, parce qu'ils les ont chantés étant petits, et dont une part du prestige est presque magique et faite d'allitération, vaut pour le pétrissage des esprits ce que vaudraient des poèmes raisonnés?
>
> Des professeurs américains à qui j'ai posé la question ont dit: 'C'est un problème, ce n'est pas douteux.' *S'il y avait une commission d'éducation constituée pour le monde entier, elle s'inquiéterait de certains aspects de la mythologie, de la musicalité et de la mise en branle de l'inconscient dans l'éducation des* nursery.
> [*Les Grands problèmes du Rhin, Œuvre* x 398–401]

Barrès's allusion to an ideal 'point of balance' between Germanic musicality and *la clarté française* is as typical of his last phase as is the interplay throughout the article between his nationalist doctrine and his theory of persuasion. Near the beginning of this phase, thirteen years before, in his speech of welcome in the French Academy to the poet Jean Richepin, he had used a similar composite analogy from the effects of music and the spirit of places to give public expression for the first time to the principle of unity in equilibrium which is at the heart of his mature traditionalism, and the history of which is the subject of the next, and final, chapter of this book. Between the wild melodies of the Danubian gypsies, 'rois des champs et des prairies, des forêts et des montagnes, des sources et des fleuves,' and the 'monotonous refrain' of a French country town, where does 'perfection' lie?

> Où trouver la perfection? Où nous affermir? ... La règle toute seule et défendue avec superstition mène droit au formalisme stérile; l'indépendance cultivée pour elle-même, c'est la confusion, le caprice, l'incohérence! Heureux celui qui parvient à conquérir son équilibre entre ces tendances ennemies, qui, sans paralyser aucune de ses puissances de désir et sans rien négliger de ces réserves héréditaires, ne fait qu'une seule âme des deux âmes qui nous sollicitent tour à tour, une seule âme, à la fois audacieuse et disciplinée.
> [*Réponse de M. Maurice Barrès au Discours de Réception de M. Jean Richepin. Séance de l'Académie Française du 18 février 1909* (Paris: Juven 1909), *cit.* P. Moreau, *Barrès* (Paris: Desclée de Brouwer 1970) 108–9][44]

44 *See* above, pp. 106–8.

PART IV: CONCLUSION

CHAPTER TWELVE

Barrès's Unity

Barrès's first act of self-determination, as a freshly embarked provincial student of law and apprentice in letters in the Latin Quarter of Paris in the early eighteen-eighties, was to turn his back resolutely on the 'royal road' of nineteenth-century Realism[1] and what he saw as its 'Romantic' degeneration in the school of Zola: 'Romantisme et naturalisme ont même esthétique, le souci perpétuel d'étonner, le virtuousisme, l'outrance et le bavardage qu'on nomme lyrisme ... les vrais Parisiens sont gens mesurés.' ['Figures nouvelles. M. Henry Houssaye,' *La France* 10 March 1886].

Paradoxically, from the standpoint of the young iconoclast, though fittingly for the *ymagier*[2] of French traditionalism he became, Barrès's path to independence and integrity as a writer was about to lead him backwards in time, against the mainstream of modern European literary history, to discover, or rediscover, a sympathy for the literary ideals of Symbolism, Naturalism, Realism, Romanticism, and Classicism, from all of which, in approximately reverse historical order, he would eventually take something for himself, and bring it into the present, for the yet strikingly original synthesis of his mature vocation.

1 'Je veux sortir à tout prix de cette voie qui pour avoir été impériale n'en est pas moins route publique et banale.' Letter to A. Allenet, 5 November 1882, *cit.* H. Mondor, *Maurice Barrès avant le Quartier Latin* (Paris: Ventadour 1956) 142. Cf. *Le Départ pour la vie*, 111.

2 Cf. *Grande Guerre* v 86–7: 'cette paysanne semble un modèle pour les vieux "ymagiers" qui sculptaient des figures de *Stabat* ... À son auditoire de tout âge, elle enseigne qu'il faut accepter le martyre ou s'arranger pour être plus fort que les gens d'outre-Rhin.'

The subjective kind of 'realism' adopted in the first volume of *Le Culte du Moi* ('Voici une courte monographie réaliste. La réalité varie avec chacun de nous, puisqu'elle est l'ensemble de nos habitudes de voir, de sentir et de raisonner' [*Œuvre* I 41]) was an open contradiction of the impersonal variety which had ruled French fiction since the mid-century, but which the author of *Sous l'œil des barbares* confines to the inferior task of interlarding the true pith and marrow of his 'roman de la vie intérieure' with a set of brief, vulgarly realistic 'concordances,' as a contemptuous concession to the 'barbarians' eye view' of things.[3] The heady 'perfume of 1830' had aroused his earlier enthusiasm for such minor Romantics as Borel and Bertrand, but the 'perfection' of Victor Hugo's mature poetry, for instance, at first merely dazzled him:

> certaines pièces de la *Légende des Siècles, le Pape, la Pitié Suprême, Religion et religions* et nombre de pièces des *Contemplations.* C'est beau. – Mais pourquoi? Parce que là s'agitent de grandes questions, parce que cela remue vraiment quelque chose en nous ...Mais dans cette perfection même est l'écueil ... cette grande poésie, je ne la vois pas, c'est-à-dire je ne la comprends point, parce que je ne puis la fixer, elle me fatigue, elle m'éblouit, en un mot elle me dépasse, comme je te le disais, elle est trop forte, je suis trop faible.
> [*Le Départ pour la vie* (letters by Barrès to L. Sorg and S. de Guaita, 1880–7) (Paris: Plon 1961) 45, 65–8]

Next to Hugo and to Leconte de Lisle stand two other masters whom Barrès will remember as the 'gods' of his first years in the capital: Taine and Renan (*Œuvre* I 135). But he was not tempted to imitate the psychology case-book literature of, for instance, his friend Paul Bourget, any more than he aspired to emulate Victor Hugo.[4] On the other hand, Aestheticism, which was the way some recent writers had reacted against the 'wretchedness of reality' as it was shown in the

3 *Œuvre* I 47–8, 58, 71, 89, 100, 110, 121
4 *Le Départ pour la vie,* 109–10; 'Figures nouvelles. M. Henry Houssaye' and *Œuvre* I 25, *cit.* p. 246.

light of science and the Naturalist novel [*Le Départ pour la vie,* 111; 'À propos de *Rosa Mystica,*' *La Minerve* 25 June 1885], seemed too shallow an attitude to life. Like a surfeit of novel-reading, it drove him into what he took to be more intelligent or more responsible company, over the frontier of literature:

> Cette année, je vais travailler, un peu mon fond aussi, pour sortir des sempiternels romans, surtout pour me meubler l'esprit: Soury, Taine, H. Spencer seront mon fond. Je lis en ce moment *la Science des religions,* de E. Burnouf.
> [*Le Départ pour la vie,* 132]

> Personnellement ... je dois vous dire que je ne consacrerais pas volontiers mon existence à ciseler des phrases, à rénover des vocables. J'aimerais mieux lire certaine préface que M. Boutroux a mise à l'*Histoire de la philosophie grecque* de Zeller, – ou les pages de Jules Soury, sur la *Délia de Tibulle* ou les *Rêveries d'un païen mystique,* de Louis Ménard. Il n'y a pas à dire, les gens ayant une intelligence un peu vigoureuse sont tout de même plus intéressants que les 'artistes' attitrés ... Même en art, voyez-vous, il y a intérêt à ne pas être un imbécile.
> [J. Huret, *Enquête sur l'évolution littéraire* (Paris: Charpentier 1891) 20]

Barrès rejected the influence of none of the established novelists, poets, aesthetes, philosophers, and *savants* of his years of apprenticeship out of hand, however. A 'poetic' reading of the great metaphysicians and moralists,[5] an enthusiastic if cloudy vision of 'great questions' in philosophical poetry,[6] an 'ideological' interpretation of the 'most perfect forms of art,'[7] and the discovery, in the documents of laboratory

5 'Chronique Parisienne,' *La Vie Moderne* 8 August 1885: 'nous goûtons à l'égal des plus grands poètes les grands métaphysiciens.' *Mes Cahiers, Œuvre* XIII 264: 'L'Éthique est un poème, non de la science, bien qu'elle soit écrite *modo geometrico.*'

6 *Le Départ pour la vie,* 45, *cit.* above, p. 242.

7 *Le Départ pour la vie,* 132: 'Au Louvre ... tu verras *la Joconde,* le dernier mot de tout ... c'est du bon Baudelaire, c'est du Bourget.' Cf. *Œuvre* I 238

and literary naturalism, in *prose d'idées* from Balzac and Michelet to Taine and Pelletan, and in the Romantic and Parnassian lyric, of the fullest facts and most exciting possibilities of real life,[8] were already beginning to lead him by convergence to an initial 'synthesis,' which is the germ of his vocation, and which he attributed specifically to the influence of 'Baudelaire and his friends,' in the most recent of literary fashions, Symbolism:

> Oui, nous sommes las comme le public entier de l'anecdote détaillée de 400 pages, las du roman machiné, aux identiques péripéties, las de commenter des niaiseries; comme tout ce public nous appelons une forme nouvelle; nous admirons les belles œuvres de hier, mais nous ne voulons point les refaire; après tant d'analyses nous aspirons à une synthèse. Nous croyons entrevoir une forme nouvelle, qui ne sera pas le roman, ni la nouvelle, ni la méditation de Lamartine, de Hugo et des autres; nous goûtons à l'égal des plus hauts poètes les grands métaphysiciens; parmi les hommes de cette heure nous préférons MM. Taine et Renan à M. Zola ... Avouez seulement que le *Prométhée* d'Eschyle, l'Évangile et toute la Bible et les légendes, et pour citer hier, l'œuvre presque entière de Balzac et le satyre de Hugo, auraient pu vous blaser sur les ridicules de l'art symbolique.
> ['Chronique Parisienne,' *La Vie Moderne* 8 August 1885]

> Les symbolistes estiment que tout se mêle en nous. Ce que je pense, disait à propos de l'un d'eux leur ami Jules Tellier, se teinte de ce que je fais et vois. Ce que je fais et vois se transforme au gré de ce que je pense. Si je veux conter ma vie *réelle*, il me faudra trouver des symboles assez compréhensifs pour embrasser toute ma pensée et toute ma vision. Pour le philosophe d'aujourd'hui, il n'y a ni matière ni esprit; simplement des phénomènes. Pour l'artiste de demain, il n'y aura ni des psychologies ni des collections de faits. Il y aura des symboles.

(*cit.* above, p. 8): 'les formes les plus parfaites ne sont que des symboles pour ma curiosité d'idéologue.'

8 *Le Départ pour la vie*, 46; Huret, *Enquête sur l'évolution littérataire*, 17; *Amori et dolori sacrum*, *Œuvre* VII 64

Je ne m'attarderai point à démontrer que cette formule exprime la tendance de l'art entier.
['Jean Moréas, poète symboliste,' *Le Figaro*, 25 December 1890]

Barrès's 'formula' of Symbolism was certainly inspired to some extent by the contemporary school of French poets and by discussion of their work and ideas with such boyhood friends as Stanislas de Guaita and Léon Sorg, and with fellow pillars of the *Vachette* tavern and fellow contributors to *La Revue Indépendante*, *La Vie Moderne*, *La Plume* and *Le Symboliste* such as Wyzewa and Moréas. Some of the terms used in it came straight from Claude Bernard, however, as Zola had recently quoted him in *Le Roman expérimental*,[9] and it was clearly influenced by the relativistic epistemology that the author of *Le Culte du Moi* was simultaneously acquiring from other positivist sources, as well as from historicist and idealist ones.[10] There was in fact a strong positivist bias in his concept of the literary symbol, and this prevented him from understanding fully the originality and the importance of the literary revolution going on round about him:

Baudelaire et ses amis s'imposent comme les interprètes de la sensation. Certes ils ne seraient pas de vrais artistes s'ils ne fécondaient la sensation, en sorte qu'elle suggérât la pensée, pas plus que des penseurs, s'ils n'intéressaient les sens à la pensée, s'ils ne rendaient l'idée sensible.
['La Folie de Charles Baudelaire,' *Les Taches d'encre*, 1er fascicule, 5 November 1884, *Œuvre* I 390]

...Puis-je vous demander si vous êtes symboliste?
...J'ai le goût de faire dire à mes personnages des choses d'un sens plus général que le récit des menus faits de leur existence: dans un sens, je serais donc symboliste. D'ailleurs, c'est là un terme bien vague ... Tous les personnages de Molière et de Shakespeare

9 É. Zola, *Le Roman expérimental* (Paris: Charpentier 1890) 28: '"il n'y a plus ni matérialisme, ni spiritualisme, ni matière brute, ni matière vivante; il n'y a que des phénomènes dont il faut déterminer les conditions...".'
10 *See* above, p. 54ff.

> et de nos auteurs classiques, sont en même temps des cas particuliers, des êtres vivants et des *types* ... Tartuffe, Roméo, Béatrice, par exemple. Il me semble que l'on pourrait écrire des psychologies qui différeraient des études de Bourget, par exemple en ce qu'elles ne s'appliqueraient pas à analyser des cas particuliers, mais chercheraient à exprimer des vérités plus générales, à donner aux idées et aux conceptions modernes des choses et de la vie une expression passionnée. Ce serait faire, en quelque sorte, de la psychologie symbolique.
> [J. Huret, *Enquête sur l'évolution littéraire*, 19]

Like the Symbolist poets, this new novelist of the eighteen-eighties claimed to prefer the inexplicit suggestion of moods to the *pons asinorum* of genetic and environmental 'explanations':

> Que peut-on demander à ces trois livres?
>
> N'y cherchez pas de psychologie, du moins ce ne sera pas celle de MM. Taine ou Bourget. Ceux-ci procèdent selon la méthode des botanistes qui nous font voir comment la feuille est nourrie par la plante, par ses racines, par le sol ou elle se développe, par l'air qui l'entoure. Ces véritables psychologues prétendent remonter la série des causes de tout frisson humain; en outre des cas particuliers et des anecdotes qu'ils nous narrent, ils tirent des lois générales. Tout à l'encontre, ces ouvrages-ci ont été écrits par quelqu'un qui trouve l'*Imitation de Jésus-Christ* ou la *Vita nuova* du Dante infiniment satisfaisantes, et dont la préoccupation d'analyse s'arrête à donner une description minutieuse, émouvante et contagieuse des états d'âme qu'il s'est proposés.
>
> Le principal défaut de cette manière, c'est qu'elle laisse inintelligibles, pour qui ne les partage pas, les sentiments qu'elle décrit. Expliquer que tel caractère exceptionnel d'un personnage fut préparé par les habitudes de ses ancêtres et par les excitations du milieu où il réagit, c'est le pont aux ânes de la psychologie, et c'est par là que les lecteurs les moins préparés parviennent à pénétrer dans les domaines très particuliers où les invite leur auteur. Si un bon psychologue en effet ne nous faisait le pont par quelque commentaire, que comprendrions-nous à tel livre, *l'Imitation*, par

exemple, dont nous ne partageons ni les ardeurs ni les lassitudes? ...

On le voit, je ne me dissimule pas les difficultés de la méthode que j'ai adoptée. Cette obscurité qu'on me reprocha durant quelques années n'est nullement embarras du style, insuffisance de l'idée, c'est manque d'explications psychologiques.

[*Examen des trois romans idéologiques, Œuvre* I 25–8]

But he also declared informative and moralizing purposes which were more in keeping with the aims and practice of Naturalism and the *psychologues*, and with Romantic didacticism, than with what Professor Lehmann calls 'Symbolist anti-positivism':[11]

Ces monographies présentent un triple intérêt:

1° Elles proposent à plusieurs les *formules* précises de sentiments qu'ils éprouvent eux aussi, mais dont ils ne prennent à eux seuls qu'une conscience imparfaite;

2° Elles sont un *renseignement* sur un type de jeune homme déjà fréquent et qui, je le pressens, va devenir plus nombreux encore parmi ceux qui sont aujourd'hui au lycée. Ces livres, s'ils ne sont pas trop délayés et trop forcés par les imitateurs, seront consultés dans la suite comme documents;

3° Mais voici un troisième point qui fait l'objet de ma sollicitude toute spéciale: ces monographies sont *un enseignement*. Quel que soit le danger d'avouer des buts trop hauts, je laisserais le lecteur s'égarer infiniment si je ne l'avouais. Jamais je ne me suis soustrait à l'ambition qu'a exprimé un poète étranger: '*Toute grande poésie est un enseignement, je veux que l'on me considère comme un maître ou rien.*'

Et, par là, j'appelle la discussion sur la théorie qui remplit ces volumes, sur *le culte du moi*.

[*Examen des trois romans idéologiques, Œuvre* I 27]

Romantic also, rather than Symbolist, was the characteristically 'reconciling and mediatory power' of imagination as it appeared,

11 A.G. Lehmann, *The Symbolist Aesthetic in France, 1885–1895* (Oxford: Blackwell 1950) 34–7

fully armed and conscious, 'incorporating the Reason in Images of Sense' (S.T. Coleridge, *The Statesman's Manual*), in the theory of didactic poetry with which Barrès concludes the retrospective *examen* of his first series of 'ideological novels':

> Je ne m'intéresse à mes actes que s'ils sont mêlés d'idéologie, en sorte qu'ils prennent devant mon imagination quelque chose de brillant et de passionné. Des pensées pures, des actes sans plus, sont également insuffisantes. J'envoyai chacun de mes rêves brouter de la réalité dans le champ illimité du monde, en sorte qu'ils devinssent des bêtes vivantes, non plus d'insaisissables chimères, mais des êtres qui désirent et qui souffrent. Ces idées où du sang circule, je les livre non à mes aînés, non à ceux qui viendront plus tard, mais à plusieurs de mes contemporains ...
>
> En suivant ainsi mon instinct, je me conformais à l'esthétique où excellent les Goethe, les Byron, les Heine qui, préoccupés d'intellectualisme, ne manquent jamais cependant de transformer en matière artistique la chose à démontrer.
>
> Or, si j'y avais réussi en quelque sorte, il m'en faudrait reporter tout l'honneur à l'Italie, où je compris les formes.
> [*Examen des trois romans idéologiques, Œuvre* I 40]

When the Boulangist Movement, which had given Barrès a seat in the *Palais Bourbon* at the age of twenty-seven, collapsed suddenly, checking in one direction the 'desire to act' that he and his contemporaries were beginning to feel so strongly,[12] it was natural that he should set himself to apply his successful new literary formula to other, for the moment, more round-about forms of political action, an undertaking for which he now sought an explicitly and emphatically Romantic vindication in the example of such publicly chosen masters as Rousseau, Chateaubriand, Lamartine, and Hugo,[13] and which was furthermore confirmed by his repeated failure, between 1893 and 1906, either

12 *Œuvre* II 387–97 and 'Lettre-Manifeste,' *La Plume* 1 April 1891. *See* M. Décaudin, *La Crise des valeurs symbolistes* (Toulouse: Privat 1960) 20–57 and G. Michaud, *Message poétique du symbolisme* (Paris: Nizet 1947) III 423–6.

13 *See* p. 285.

to secure re-election to parliament or to join others in a credible party of direct action against parliament:

> J'estime le mandat de député comme une petite chose, lors des périodes où une nation se transforme. Je crois qu'un publiciste peut plus sur l'âme de sa patrie qu'un député.
>
> J'entends bien continuer l'œuvre littéraire que j'ai entreprise, et qui est de décrire les états d'âme de ma génération, en en créant de nouveaux.
>
> [Letter published in *Le Matin* 12 October 1889]

As a matter of fact, the fusion of 'Reality' and 'Poetry,' public events and private experience, the 'active' and the 'inward' life, that Barrès claimed rightly to have achieved in the beautifully integrated final volume of *Le Culte du Moi*,[14] was not sustained in his next big work, *Le Roman de l'énergie nationale*, in which he abandoned the experimental forms of the Symbolist novel and joined the mainstream of nineteenth-century fiction, seeking to combine the 'scientific'[15] analysis of human types in their environment, as taught by Taine and turned into literature by Bourget, with the 'popular'[16] thematic and documentary narrative of Hugo and Zola. But this second, and retrograde, stage of Barrès's evolving rhetoric lasted for a comparatively short period – though it was a productive one in terms of pages published and immediate influence achieved. The personal and public crisis of 1898–1901, which was to show him his 'true destiny' as a leader of French nationalist opinion,[17] would also tend to lessen his dependence on the structurally divisive techniques of rational demonstration and

14 *Œuvre* I 379 and J. Huret, *Enquête sur l'évolution littéraire*, 22

15 *Œuvre* I 25, *cit.* above, p. 246 and *Enquête sur l'évolution littéraire*, 18: 'les naturalistes ... avaient fait de minutieuses et pittoresques descriptions des aspects extérieurs et des gestes des passions, des appétits humains. Ceux-là, au contraire, Bourget, par exemple, ont voulu considérer ces appétits comme le ferait un savant d'une plante qu'il étudierait.'

16 *Œuvre* III 5: 'Je travaille à mon grand roman populaire qui de jour en jour devient moins populaire.' Cf. *Mes Cahiers, Œuvre* XIII 277: 'Comme *les Misérables* ont fourni le fumier d'où est née la pensée radicale, républicaine, je voudrais que *les Déracinés...*'

17 *Œuvre* V 21–2. *See* above, pp. 52–4.

realistic reporting that he had borrowed from *Le Régime moderne*, *Les Misérables*, and *Les Rougon-Macquart*, and which for several years, in *Les Déracinés*, *L'Appel au soldat*, *Leurs figures*, and *Scènes et doctrines du nationalisme*, overlaid the more original, and better synthesized vocation of poet-publicist that he had chosen for himself between 1889 and 1892. Thus the preface to *Amori et dolori sacrum* (1903), his first publication after *Le Roman de l'énergie nationale* and *Scènes et doctrines du nationalisme*:

> Bien que ce soit ici un livre de solitude – et je rappelle que les Espagnols donnent le nom de *soledad* à certain petit poème elliptique, – on y recontrera des idées et des images qui nourrissent notre action politique. C'est que l'auteur a vu peu à peu se former en lui une intime union de l'art et de la vie: toutes les réalités où s'appuient nos regrets, nos désirs, nos espérances, nos volontés, se transforment à notre insu en matière poétique. Il en va ainsi de tout homme qui a trouvé, préservé, dégagé sa source, la source vive que chacun porte en soi-même.
>
> Ces pages sont, à vrai dire, un hymne. Je n'ignore pas ce que suppose de romantisme une telle émotivité. Mais précisément nous voulons la régler. Engagés dans la voie que nous fit le dix-neuvième siècle, nous prétendons pourtant redresser notre sens de la vie. J'ai trouvé une discipline dans les cimetières où nos prédécesseurs divaguaient, et c'est grâce peut-être à l'hyperesthésie que nous transmirent ces grands poètes de la rêverie que nous dégagerons des vérités positives situées dans notre profond sous-conscient.
>
> [*Amori et dolori sacrum, Œuvre* VII 9–10]

Barrès's claim to have bridged the 'abyss' so many of his critics (including at times himself) were wont to find between his literary and polical careers,[18] was backed not merely by the 'sense of reality' that the young ideologist and fashionable *littérateur* of the eighteen-eighties and -nineties believed that he had learned in the 'tumults' of Boulan-

18 *Mes Cahiers, Œuvre* XIII 23–5; XIV 414; XV 263, 403; XVII 17–18, 279; XVIII 73–6; XIX 306. *See* below, pp. 260–75.

gism, Panama, and the Dreyfus Affair,[19] but also by the growing conviction of the established *Ligueur*, Parliamentarian, and Academician after 1900 that politics is charged with the most powerful, noble, and true kind of 'poetry' (*Mes Cahiers, Œuvre* XVIII 76), that the leaders of the modern Republic must therefore have as much of the 'musician' as the 'man of action' in them:

> On mène les hommes par l'intérêt, et les assemblées par le sentiment. Aussi, dans notre Gouvernement d'assemblées, il faut que le chef politique soit musicien et homme d'action. Cette rencontre des deux facultés est rare.
> [*Mes Cahiers, Œuvre* XIX 135]

and that his own particular gift was for the 'poetic' rather than the 'reasoned' forms of political insight:

> Quel contraste entre cette chambre vilaine, renfermée, et les immenses plaines solitaires! Comme tout l'être se tend vers mon idéal et comme il souffre, se désespère de s'être donné à cette fange.
> ...
> Il faut que je m'attaque au vice de la politique française qui m'aura été désigné par ma *clairvoyance de poète*, non par des *raisonnements.*
> [*Mes Cahiers, Œuvre* XV 136–7]

Not, of course, that he ceased altogether to reason his case before the Chamber or in the Press, or that the Naturalist technique of *Le Roman de l'énergie nationale*, and the actual 'scenes' and explicit 'doctrines' of French nationalism disappeared from his work after 1902. But the kind of parliamentary action that he was best at, so he came to believe, was one he could associate with what he called 'le plaisir de compléter': now investing technical matters with a degree of idealism, now exposing the bedrock of reality beneath layers of verbiage (*Mes Cahiers, Œuvre* XV 394), while the major contribution of his novels, essays, and articles to the nationalist movement in

19 *Œuvre* V 22. *See* above, p. 16.

France between the Dreyfus Affair and the Great War was to celebrate a similarly imaginative 'marriage' of historical fact and human sensibility, in which the external forms of his *milieu de naissance* became sensuous expressions of his inmost feelings of patriotic solidarity and piety:

> Si je cherche les raisons de ma formation, je les trouve dans mon milieu de naissance, dans ma petite ville, dans les événements de la guerre, dans la conception lorraine. Mon imagination avait été nourrie et orientée par Strasbourg, Sainte-Odile, Sion, le château d'Andlau et je ne cesse pas de construire avec ces beaux éléments une idée dont j'étais à la fois l'auteur et le disciple.
>
> *Mes rapports avec la Lorraine sont d'un mariage, je la crée et je me crée.*
>
> [*Mes Mémoires, Mes Cahiers, Œuvre* XIII 28][20]

An important passage of *Mes Cahiers* dated 1910 describing the mechanism of literary inspiration that was now familiar to him, attests the continued importance, at the height of his powers, of the legacy he had inherited from Romanticism and Symbolism and which he had, in theory, now fully disengaged from the crude 'puppet show' of the Naturalists and the shallow glitter of Aestheticism (*Œuvre* I 135; XVIII 4, 13; XX 172). This was the difficult ideal of a long matured but finally spontaneous sublimation of the writer's raw material (his 'dossiers' of facts, notions, arguments and experiences), into a single, seamless 'equivalent,' to be rendered by words that borrow the painter's expressive colour and form, and approach the threshold of music:

> J'ai dans l'esprit, comme tout le monde, un certain nombre de dossiers, ou si vous voulez de groupes de souvenirs, avec lesquels

20 Cf. *Colette Baudoche, Œuvre* VI 217: 'À défaut d'une affection de naissance, c'était presque un amour de mariage. [Asmus] découvrait, créait, mûrissait en lui une Lorraine par à peu près. Il la composait assez bizarrement d'un amalgame de ses rêves avec les notions que ses logeuses lui fournissaient.'

je m'occupe chaque fois que j'ai un instant de loisir et que j'y suis invité par l'heure et les événements.

Ces dossiers se rapportent à des aventures personnelles ou bien à des personnages attrayants de l'histoire, ils sont le fruit de mes lectures ou de mon expérience propre et du fait même que je continue de respirer et d'être sensible sans aucune intention de ma volonté, ils ne cessent pas d'augmenter en nombre et en importance. Je pense qu'il n'y a là rien que de très banal. Mais il arrive parfois une singulière chose que je crains de ne savoir exprimer.

Il m'arrive que mes dossiers se transforment en images vivantes. Des groupes de faits, voire des groupes de raisonnements précis, oui, des sujets que j'ai étudiés et vécus, que je connais comme des fiches de bibliothèque ou comme des heures déterminées de mon existence disparaissent et à leur place vient se présenter à mon regard quelque tableau équivalent. Mes notions s'amalgament les unes les autres, mes raisonnements cessent de batailler, il se compose en moi, à la place de ces liasses informes, une glace unie, une sorte de miroir profond. Je n'ai plus que faire d'analyser et de discuter, j'oublie comme en un rêve ma propre personnalité, des images se lèvent au fond de ma conscience, des images équivalentes à ce dossier que j'examinais et dont je me délivre. C'est une sorte de tableau, de paysage, voire une suite de scènes lentes qui se proposent et s'imposent à mon âme enchaînée par la sympathie.

Quelques images me demeurent qui me permettent d'anéantir cette fausse et funeste opulence sous laquelle notre esprit finissait par succomber. Cette foule de notions qui m'avaient intéressé ne sont à bien voir que les efforts, les tâtonnements de mon esprit cherchant l'amande, le fruit, l'essentiel. Par une dernière combinaison le problème se résout, ma solution reste et dès lors toutes les fausses combinaisons antérieures doivent disparaître...

Des simplifications savantes réduisent insensiblement à un petit nombre de traits les images les plus intéressantes que j'ai recueillies.

Si j'essaye d'écrire quelqu'une de ces visions, je ne pourrai construire, je m'en doute bien, qu'une sorte de récit très gauche où ceux qui me lisent ne retrouveront à peu près rien, il y manquera les arrière-plans, la profondeur, la sonorité, les lointains

retentissements. Il faudrait que je fusse un musicien. Il faudrait mieux encore que je fusse un des ces peintres que j'aime tant, un Delacroix, qui expriment leur vie intérieure par des ciels orageux, des lueurs argentées et tristes, des couleurs d'une mélancolie lyrique. Car c'est bien un tableau de cette sorte qui le plus souvent se forme sous mon regard intérieur.
[*Mes Cahiers, Œuvre* XVI 342–4]

The subject of this new 'Artist's Confession,' in which, as in Baudelaire's, *moi* and *non-moi*, mingled in the state of *rêverie*, 'think musically and picturesquely, without quibbles, syllogisms, deductions,'[21] is still a frankly useful art (*Œuvre* XVII 278–9) which, like the 'symbolical psychology' of *Le Culte du Moi*, derives its purposes from those of the Romantic poet-preacher, which still inspired Barrès across and against the counter-ideal of the aesthete he had found in the French Symbolist school, and could not assimilate.[22] But the disjunction of content and form implicit in pre-Symbolist positivism[23] remained as foreign to him as the 'imbecile' oversimplification of art for art's sake, which he continued to disavow.[24] So he refused to

21 C. Baudelaire, *Petits poèmes en prose*: 'Le Confitéor de l'artiste.' Cf. *Mes Cahiers, Œuvre* XX 104, *cit.* pp. 273–4: 'sans souci de formules et d'arguments.'

22 *Mes Cahiers, Œuvre* XX 172. Barrès rejected the merely aestheticist interpretation not only of Baudelaire ('Plus que rhétoricien,' he had called him in 'Le Caractère de Baudelaire,' *La Jeune France* (August 1887), and, citing 'L'École païenne,' in *Amori et dolori sacrum* (*Œuvre* VII 104), 'souvent un voisin de Veuillot'; though in a later *cahier* (*Œuvre* XX 90) he regretted his 'despairing' abdication of the poet's mission to 'educate'), but also of Gautier ('Il fournit des images qui sont de nature à perfectionner le lecteur ... s'adressa à des instincts pour les spiritualiser, en tout cas, pour les parer, les entraîner plus haut' (*Œuvre* XII 156), and of the Parnassians: 'L'Hellénisme fut vraiment en ces années .. une école de morale active et sociale' ['Figures nouvelles. M. Henry Houssaye,' *La France* 10 March 1886]).

23 *See* A.G. Lehmann, *The Symbolist Aesthetic in France 1885–1895*, 21–30 and *Le Voyage de Sparte*, *Œuvre* VII 203: 'Ce n'est pas que l'on veuille prétendre que Phidias tailla des statues pour symboliser des idées ...
Il y avait un certain rapport entre la nature et Phidias, et c'était le même qu'entre la nature et Anaxagore.'

24 *See* J. Huret, *Enquête sur l'évolution littéraire*, 20, *cit.* above, p. 243.

'enclose in a formula what he called Lorraine,' convinced that his ideas could be conveyed only in an imaginative 'form', which is 'sensible to the heart' (Pascal's classical art of persuasion),[25] which 'induces much thought yet without the possibility of any definite thought whatever, i.e. *concept*, being adequate to it' (as in the Romantic mode),[26] and within which (as in a Symbolist poem) the thought is not 'apparent' but 'latent':[27]

> Car la Lorraine, je veux le répéter, ce n'est pas essentiellement nos paysages, nos œuvres d'art, nos coutumes, nos meubles, nos plats nationaux, ce n'est même pas notre histoire. Notre province, chaque province de France, c'est une façon spéciale de sentir, c'est un principe de solidarité morale.
>
> Mais ne me demandez pas d'enfermer dans une formule ce que j'appelle Lorraine. Cela ne peut pas s'étreindre dans une définition et quand on y aurait réussi, on ne serait encore arrivé à rien, puisqu'il resterait à le rendre sensible au cœur.
>
> S'il s'agit de faire comprendre ce qui forme l'objet de notre pitié, ce qui est à la source de toutes nos démarches spontanées, on

Also: *L'Appel au soldat, Œuvre* IV 29: 'L'on accorde qu'il y a un élément moral dans le frisson de la beauté et que, pour être tout à fait belles, les choses doivent être bienfaisantes.' *Une Enquête aux pays du Levant, Œuvre* XI 360: 'Mon laurier de Daphné, je le réserve à ceux qui savent hausser et dilater les âmes.' *Les Maîtres, Œuvre* XII 159: 'Produire une croyance, ce qui, disait Carlyle, est le plus grand et en réalité le seul succès littéraire.' *Mes Cahiers, Œuvre* XVI 127: 'J'entends souvent demander ce que c'est un grand écrivain; c'est celui qui hausse la vie, sa qualité.' And XX 115: 'écoutons Platon: "La beauté de la musique consiste dans la beauté même de la vertu qu'elle inspire." '

25 *Cit. Œuvre* XVI 114

26 Kant, *Critique of Judgement, cit.* R.L. Brett, *Fancy and Imagination* (London: Methuen 1969) 47

27 S. Mallarmé, 'Du sens religieux de la poésie,' *cit.* G. Michaud, *La Doctrine Symboliste* (Paris: Nizet 1947) 71: 'Je révère l'opinion de Poe: nul vestige d'une philosophie, l'éthique et la métaphysique, ne transparaîtra; j'ajoute qu'il la faut, incluse et latente.' On Barrès's debt to Leconte de Lisle's opinion: 'que la forme n'est pas une chose distincte du fond, et que bien écrire, ce n'est rien d'autre que bien penser,' *see Amori et dolori sacrum* (*Œuvre* VII 124) and its draft in *Mes Cahiers*, with a reference to Pascal on 'la beauté poétique' (*Œuvre* XIII 106).

arrive tout de suite à la limite de l'exprimable. Pour donner une idée de tout ce qu'enferme pour nous de trésors variés ce mot de Lorraine, il faudrait employer les longs procédés de l'art. Là où n'atteint pas la pensée abstraite, nous sommes capables de parvenir quand nous appelons à notre secours toutes les formes confuses de l'imagination et les riches buées de la rêverie.
['Discours de Maurice Barrès à la réunion du "Courail" de Nancy le 24 juin 1911,' *Mes Cahiers, Œuvre* XVII 74–5]

The whole trend of Barrès's experience and culture, in a world that seemed opaque to reason and brutally hostile to the companionless individual, was towards a community life-support system based on traditional French forms of 'discipline.' It was, he believed, the 'positive' and (to use Baudelaire's exactly appropriate borrowing from the English Romantics[28]) the '*constructive*' function of poetic imagination to 'maintain' and 'develop' this system for the benefit of each new generation of Frenchmen:

La vie n'a pas de sens. Je crois même que chaque jour elle devient plus absurde. Se soumettre à toutes les illusions et les connaître très nettement comme illusoires, voilà notre rôle. Toujours désirer et savoir que notre désir, que tout nourrit, ne s'apaise de rien. Ne vouloir que des possessions éternelles et nous comprendre comme une série d'états successifs!

De quelque point qu'on les considère, l'univers et notre existence sont des tumultes insensés...

Philippe, il faut pourtant nous en accommoder.

...

Pour vaincre la vie et pour triompher du découragement ... il s'agit de concevoir une sage économie de nos forces, d'organiser notre énergie et de sortir d'un désordre barbare pour l'accomplissement de notre destin. De là le choix systématique des images que je propose à un jeune Français.

La France a construit une tradition qu'il faut maintenir et développer ... faite de mœurs, de délicatesses, d'expériences

28 C. Baudelaire, *Œuvres complètes,* 1040. *See* above, p. 293.

préalables les plus propres à nous protéger et à faire digue contre les brutales poussées de la vie, qui est une inventrice, jamais lasse, de douleurs. Dans nos rapports avec l'univers, si nous refusons toute contrainte pour suivre nos impulsions et les circonstances, nous éprouverons plus d'hostilités que d'amitiés. Ce sera tôt fait de notre dégradation. À sortir des sentiments polis que nous préparèrent nos pères, nous rencontrerons les Furies plutôt que les Déesses. L'Honneur, comme dans Corneille, l'Amour, comme dans Racine, la Contemplation, telle que les campagnes françaises la proposent, voilà, selon mon jugement, la noble et la seule féconde discipline qu'il nous faut hardiment élire.
[*Les Amitiés françaises*, *Œuvre* v 559–60]

Il est très naturel qu'un jeune homme exprime d'ardentes aspirations et dise ce qu'il réprouve dans l'univers et décrive les châteaux de nuages qu'il entrevoit sur l'horizon. Mais cet exercice doit déplaire s'il se prolonge ... Et puis un homme avancé dans la vie doit faire de sa puissance un usage positif. Il faut constuire. Il s'agit de donner un sens à sa vie, s'assurer un alibi, un refuge contre la médiocrité de l'univers.

Faire une construction avec des rêves, avec de la poésie où l'on puisse pourtant vivre une vie totale, s'abriter avec ses intérêts, avec ses mœurs de l'époque.

C'est le service que j'ai rendu aux Alsaciens-Lorrains et d'une manière plus générale dans le *Service de l'Allemagne*.
[*Mes Cahiers*, *Œuvre* XVI 213]

Il s'agit de peupler d'images les esprits, de tendre de tapisseries la chambre de l'âme, et ainsi de modifier les volontés profondes, de modifier le sanctuaire intérieur des êtres.

Nous vivons dans un poème. Aux poètes de créer ce poème, de le proposer, de l'imposer par leur génie aux générations qui ont besoin d'un nouveau poème.
[*Mes Cahiers*, *Œuvre* XX 129]

The medium in which Barrès's habitable 'poem' crystallized best was natural and historical landscape – 'la terre de mes morts':

> Les ancêtres que nous prolongeons ne nous transmettent intégralement l'héritage accumulé de leurs âmes que par la permanence de l'action terrienne. C'est en maintenant sous nos yeux l'horizon qui cerna leurs travaux, leurs félicités ou leurs ruines, que nous entendrons le mieux ce qui nous est permis ou défendu. De la campagne, en toute saison, s'élève le chant des morts. Un vent léger le porte et le disperse comme une senteur. Que son appel nous oriente!
> [*Amori et dolori sacrum*, *Œuvre* VII 127–8]

The derisive title: 'littérateur du territoire,' which Barrès's wartime journalism earned him among the 'defeatists' was not only a good description of the 'guide and secretary' of belligerent France,[29] but also the appropriate token of an earlier, more original, and more lasting inspiration:

> Mais la plus belle, la plus sûre, la plus constante des trois déesses qui donnent un sens à la vie, c'est la Nature en France, je veux dire nos paysages formés par l'Histoire. Je leur dois mes meilleurs moments. Devant eux, la grâce toujours descendit sur moi avec même efficace...
> Ces grands états d'émotivité que chacun connut de l'amour, qu'un homme viril reçoit des chefs de sa race, je voudrais que la terre française chargée de tombes les communiquât au promeneur pensif. Il faut qu'autour des lieux classiques de la France Philippe entende cette musique grande, noble, hardie, dont une maîtresse au cœur pur s'enveloppe devant son amant, quand ils surent par une volonté permanente de noblesse créer leur amour comme une œuvre d'art.
> [*Les Amitiés françaises*, *Œuvre* V 556–7][30]

And he accepted it with satisfaction in this sense:

> nous avons bien la persuasion qu'il y a tel coin de terre dont nous avons dégagé et restitué le sens et auquel notre nom et quelques-

29 *Mes Cahiers*, *Œuvre* XVIII 240, 421; *Grande Guerre* IV 39
30 Cf. *Mes Cahiers*, *Œuvre* XIV 211.

unes de nos idées demeurent liées, et là encore ce beau nom de littérateur du territoire est justifié.
[*Mes Cahiers, Œuvre* XVIII 241][31]

As a novelist with characters to portray and a story to tell, as journalist and orator with facts to expose and a thesis to drive home, as critic and biographer with art and lives to explain and appreciate (and Barrès was all these, and usually more than one at a time), he came nearest and most naturally to achieving the 'orderly arrangement of a work of passion' that he had laid down as the formal criterion of nationalist literature in 1902 (*Œuvre* V 22) when, 'applying his senses' to a landscape,[32] and touched by the 'spirit of place,'[33] he could fit characters, story, facts, thesis, art, and biography together in the kind of prose-poetry for 'conjuring up the great dead' from the scene of their exemplary lives[34] that he had first used in the chapters on Lorraine, Venice, and Aigues-Mortes in *Le Culte du Moi* and in the 'psychotherapeutic stations' and Spanish and Italian tours of 1891–7 (*Œuvre* I, II); which he had then applied to nationalist propaganda and education in 'La Vallée de la Moselle,' 'Discours ... pour l'anniversaire de l'"Action française",' 'le 2 novembre en Lorraine,' the 'little pilgrimages' of *Les Amitiés françaises*, and their exotic foil, *Le Voyage de Sparte* (*Œuvre* IV, V, VII); and joined, not very successfully, to the edifying adventures of Paul Ehrmann, the Alsatian medical student who asserts his birthright to a career in Colmar by volunteering for service in the German army, and, rather more so, to the exemplary history of Colette Baudoche, whose patriotism prevents her from accepting a proposal of marriage by an officer of the army

31 Cf. *Œuvre* XIV 32, 85; XVI 158–9 and *Grande Guerre* VIII 95. Mistral, Hugo, and Walt Whitman were among Barrès's principal models of the 'littérateur du territoire' (*Œuvre* IV 77; XIV 151; *Grande Guerre* XIII 383, 392).

32 *Mes Cahiers, Œuvre* XIII 295. The term recalls the Loyolan terminology used in *Un Homme Libre*: 'application des sens' and 'composition de lieu.' *See* above, pp. 22–3 and *Œuvre* I 178–9, 185, 191.

33 *Mes Cahiers, Œuvre* XVIII 226: 'Jamais je ne suis allé dans un pays sans honorer le génie du lieu.'

34 C. Baudelaire, *Fusées, Œuvres complètes,* 125–6: 'De la magie appliquée à l'évocation des grands morts, au rétablissement et au perfectionnement de la santé.' Cf. *Mes Cahiers, Œuvre* XIII 296 and XV 393: 'Mes cimetières lorrains. (Certains grands hommes dans leur paysage.)'

of occupation in Metz, the worthy Frédéric Asmus, who loves her (*Œuvre* VI); before achieving a mature singleness of theme and place in *La Colline inspirée* and many subsequently more fragmentary examples of the *genre*: important passages of *La Grande pitié des églises de France* and *Une Enquête aux pays du Levant*, 'La Sybille d'Auxerre,' 'Lettre à Gyp sur le printemps à Mirabeau,' 'L'Enfance de Jeanne d'Arc,' 'L'Automne à Charmes avec Claude Gelée,' 'Une visite à Lourdes,' 'La Ville enchantée,' 'Une Journée napolitaine' (*Œuvre* VI, VIII XI, XII).[35]

In the particular poetry of France's sacred places and Eastern Bastions Barrès found not only the nucleus of his political doctrine and his public rhetoric but also a congenial unity of style upon which he longed to pattern his life as a whole:

> *Mon journal.* – Mes cultes successifs, mes réactions sous la vie... et puis ce que j'en ai gardé, mes expériences. Ai-je su donner du style à mon être, me créer, me modeler?
> [*Mes Cahiers, Œuvre* XIX 115]

> Une grande affaire, la grande affaire aura été pour moi de trouver ...dans la politique de quoi nourrir mon imagination, ma sensibilité, mon âme. Il ne me suffisait pas de m'y distraire, de m'y employer et dépenser. Il fallait que j'y reçusse quelque chose. J'y parvins par intermittances seulement...
>
> Je désirais sentir ma vie sans contradictions, ne pas être divisé, tiré à quatre chevaux, être *un pour moi.*
> [*Mes Cahiers, Œuvre* XIII 23–4]

> Dans la vie, la grande affaire c'est de s'unifier, de s'employer tout entier dans le même sens, de ne pas se disperser en efforts qui se

35 In 'La Vallée de la Moselle' (*L'Appel au soldat, Œuvre* IV 3–101) evocative landscape poetry is still mixed with a Naturalist's 'scientific' social and historical documentation. *Un Jardin sur l'Oronte*, Barrès's last, post-war novel, also inspired by the spirit of place ('Si j'essaie de mettre dans un récit toute la grâce d'un jardin de Syrie ...' [*Œuvre* XX 94]) tends, on the contrary, towards the literature of pure 'music' (*see* pp. 267–75).

contrarient, s'annulent et nous troublent d'autant plus que nous sommes plus richement doués. Cette coordination est peut-être difficile à notre époque, et surtout à Paris...
['La Vie exemplaire de Paul Bourget,' *La Revue hebdomadaire* 15 December 1923]

In the last year of his life, looking back with little satisfaction over his career as a writer and a politician, for the *Memoirs* he was just beginning to compose for publication, he thought he could make out, beneath the superficial divisions of his time and his employment (which he believed nevertheless had enriched him) and beyond the vain promises of pleasure in notoriety he had perhaps abused his will-power to possess, something that did not ring false: the 'pursuit' and 'expression' of a single 'true note' of personal integrity (*Mes Cahiers, Œuvre* XIII 23–4, 29). This effort of personal integration, which Barrès referred to in his last *cahiers* as 'le problème du salut,' 'l'idée du salut,' and 'faire son salut,'[36] was an act of imaginative self-composition that was closely tied to the realization of his 'integrative' traditionalism in the tangible form of an expressive landscape with figures. Thus, for instance, these home thoughts from Pau in Béarn (to which he retired for a short while in the autumn of 1901 to nurse the wounds of bereavement and political disappointment) painting spontaneously for the mind's eye the image of the idealized province of which he will later claim to be both 'author and disciple' (*Œuvre* XIII 28):

> c'est sur cette terrasse ... qu'en 1890 il advint à notre ami [Charles Maurras] de sentir la nécessité de la soumission pour l'ordre et la beauté du monde. Un paysage agréable où toutes les parties se soumettent les unes aux autres, où celles-ci vivent ensevelies sans se flatter qu'aucun espoir les pousse jamais dehors, tandis que celles-là sont éternellement caressées des feux du Jour et de la Nuit, déterminèrent Charles Maurras à constater allègrement que l'infortune des premières et le bonheur des secondes sont des conditions nécessaires à la qualité de chacune...

36 *See* p. 285.

Ne trouvez-vous pas que la vallée béarnaise prend un beau sens historique si elle fit rêver en 1854 M. Taine, et 36 ans plus tard, un de ses meilleurs fils ? Ses mérites spirituels toutefois, pas plus que ses belles couleurs et ses douces formes, ne sauraient me retenir. Il est des moments où notre pensée s'étend et trouve partour à profiter; d'autres fois elle se replie irrésistiblement sur ses réserves, et c'est encore un hommage à l'ordre, une féconde soumission, d'accepter ces minutes de retraite où peut-être le ressort se bande pour une action importante.

...En vain ici les proportions sont-elles plus vastes et le motif décoratif infiniment multiplié: je vois à Pau la Moselle où je fus élevé, ses grèves, sa prairie, ses côtes boisées, à ma droite l'église de Charmes, et plus loin, à ma gauche, Châtel, le bien situé, c'est-à-dire tous les premiers objets qui me possédèrent et dont je méconnus longtemps ce qu'ils recèlent de discipline. Paysage plus simple que le béarnais, plus court et plus pauvre et qu'enveloppe un ciel plus rude, mais c'est le mien où m'attachent chaque jour des liens que ma raison n'a pas noués...

Mes morts et mon horizon natal m'enveloppent sous ce ciel nouveau et parmi ces étrangers. Ils composent un arrière-fonds à toutes les images que le hasard me propose, et celles-ci ne valent qu'autant qu'elles s'harmonisent avec ma terre et avec mes morts. ['La Semaine des morts,' *Le Gaulois* 2 November 1901][37]

And thus the closing pages of Barrès's twenty-fourth *cahier*, written between the suicide of Charles Demange in August 1909 and the following All Souls' Day, in a similarly grave 'state of recollection':

Voir les fantômes qui soutiennent les créatures, les âmes et donner de la chair et du sang aux fantômes.

Pas des chimères mais des âmes.

Établir une communication entre nos rêves et notre vie réelle; vivre une vie que colorent nos rêves. Supprimer la platitude, réduire les domaines du prosaïsme, transfigurer la réalité.

...

37 Published with some variants in *Amori et dolori sacrum*, *Œuvre* VII 117–19. *See* Barrès's notes for this article in *Mes Cahiers*, *Œuvre* XIII 340, *cit.* below, note 39, pp. 285–6.

Je n'ai pas le temps d'avoir deux vies, de vivre dans deux mondes, mais je veux qu'ils s'accordent et les bâtir l'un sur l'autre.

...

On se lasse de dresser des tentes somptueuses, une sorte de camp du drap d'or au dehors de la ville pour aller y goûter des plaisirs d'art. Mieux vaut orner, embellir la maison familière où nous vivons.

...

Ce sont les faits qui m'ont suggéré mes idées. J'ai examiné les faits lorrains et j'ai fourni la vérité lorraine. Mes matériaux, le les ai publiés.

J'ai été guidé par un sentiment de respect. Je me suis dit que je reconnaissais être devant quelque chose de noble et bon, qu'il ne s'agissait plus de donner une idée de moi-même mais de respecter toutes les formes, tous les aspects de ce qui m'émouvait et que j'honorais. J'ai été le serviteur de mon modèle. J'ai peint Colette et j'ai travaillé pour Colette. Ah! j'avais mes moments de défaillance. Je disais: Est-ce que je vais passer tout mon été avec cette petite bonne.

J'ai voulu que les humbles, que Colette trouvassent dans ce livre des images 'aimables, concrètes et fidèles de leur existence,' et qu'elles fussent fières d'elles-mêmes.

Après cela je pourrai revenir à mes plaisirs. Mais je crois que je n'y reviendrai pas. J'avais un peu la nostalgie de mon Asie intérieure tandis que j'écrivais Colette, mais elle m'a converti sans que je m'en aperçusse et m'a montré que l'on pouvait construire une maison de poésie sur la terre la plus ferme, la plus vraie, au milieu des intérêts humains.

[*Mes Cahiers, Œuvre* XVI 211–13]

Another notebook, *Cahier Pascal*, written at approximately the same date and devoted to the master of imaginative persuasion who was Barrès's very pattern of the great writer,[38] contains a passage attributing the method of creative imitation by which an author identifies himself with a representative type he has conceived for propaganda

38 *Les Maîtres, Œuvre* XII 58–62; *Mes Cahiers, Œuvre* XVI 106, 114, 127–8

purposes (as Barrès had been 'converted' to his model, Colette – 'une vive image de Metz' [*Œuvre* VI 249]), to the author of the *Pensées*:

> *Pascal grand créateur.* – Chacun veut se créer un tombeau.
> Pascal crée un personnage général et éternel dans lequel il entrera. Il se dépose dans un magnifique tombeau spirituel. Les bêtes ont l'instinct de la parure (Edmond Périer). Les femmes. Aux hommes d'un certain degré, il faut mieux. Heredia veut reposer dans un sonnet définitif. C'est mieux de plier une race sur un type et de se déposer au centre. J'ai vu cela en Égypte.
> C'est une âme de poète frémissante et qui va se coucher dans le génie humain tout entier pour s'y perdre, s'y cacher, mais aussi pour le faire frémir comme un personnage de drame.
> [*Mes Cahiers, Œuvre* XVI 121][39]

A critical moment in Pascal's life, his carriage accident at Neuilly bridge in November 1654, helped Barrès to interpret, firstly in a characteristic 'composition of place' published in *L'Écho de Paris* in September 1900, and then, seven years later, in the plan of an autobiographical novel about his conversion to traditionalism (never completed), a similarly crucial stage in his own development: the personal and political crisis of 1898–1901 that had 'shocked' him into recognizing the authority of a mystical Father in the voices of his fatherland:

> Pourtant, si vous tenez à situer dans un décor matériel la pensée de ce grand homme, et s'il vous faut une autre atmosphère que celle qui, se levant de son œuvre même emplit votre cabinet, à deux pas de Paris, vous trouverez le vallon de Port-Royal-des-Champs, et, sur la berge droite de la Seine, à cinquante mètres au-dessous du pont de Neuilly, le point ou Pascal, en carosse, faillit être précipité.
> Lieu sacré, celui-là, qui favorisa la plus admirable folie et ses accents désespérés!...
> ...Sur un tel tempérament, la secousse du pont de Neuilly dut être

39 *See* pp. 285–6.

féconde. Ce n'est point d'une façon incidente que l'on peut aborder cette question, une des plus belles de la haute culture, mais nous sommes autorisés à comprendre que, sous l'influence d'un choc, des parties de nous-mêmes entrent en activité, élaborent des images et des sentiments que nous ne savions pas abriter dans nos replis profonds.
['Faut-il sauver la Maison de Pascal?', *L'Écho de Paris* 18 September 1900][40]

Si je faisais le roman traditionaliste, la première scène montre un individu ayant de grandes passions, eh bien, on ne vit qu'une fois, il faut les épanouir.

Vient un choc. Échec politique. Mort de ma mère. Après de tels chocs, on se rallie à la thèse catholique: il faut dompter, soumettre nos passions. Nous avons vu que nous ne sommes pas maîtres absolus de nous-mêmes; nous acceptons nos fatalismes.

Sous la violence du choc opératoire (la mort d'un être cher, un désastre), crise mystique. Il s'humilie, reconnaît ses misères, les misères de l'homme. Phrase du *Mystère de Jésus*: 'Si Dieu nous donnait des maîtres de sa main, oh! qu'il leur faudrait obéir de bon cœur! La nécessité et les événements en sont infailliblement.'
[*Mes Cahiers, Œuvre* XV 157][41]

Barrès also saw in Pascal's analysis of the limb's love of the body an argument that justified his dissatisfaction after 1901 with the first, secular, form of his nationalism: 'Le numéro 483 de la petite édition

40 Published in *Les Maîtres, Œuvre* XII 85–6 with minor variations. *See* P. Moreau, 'Barrès devant son dernier portrait,' *La Table Ronde*, March 1957, for Barrès's reaction when V. Giraud told him that there was no historical evidence for the legend of Pascal's carriage accident at Neuilly: 'j'ai horreur de la molle théorie des "beaux mensonges," des légendes, etc. Donc s'il n'y a pas de pont de Neuilly, je l'abolis en moi.'

41 Cf. *Œuvre* VII 127; XIII 26: 'État mystique où je me trouvai après la mort de mes parents' (*cit.* above, pp. 53–4), and the less willing parallel Barrès drew between his 'crisis of mysticism' and a stage of Chateaubriand's development: 'Il a la crise mystique consécutive d'un échec et d'un deuil. (À noter, mais sans identité certes, que Chateaubriand interrompit l'*Essai sur la Révolution* [*sic*] et passa au *Génie du christianisme* sur la mort de sa mère)' (*Œuvre* XV 403).

Brunschvicg est un nationalisme qui va à l'universalisme' (*Mes Cahiers, Œuvre* XVI 22). In the same 'unique witness ... whose inner life reproduces, lifts up to the heights, the entire religious crisis of our age ... of the last three centuries, that is to say since the dawn of science' (*Mes Cahiers, Œuvre* XVI 254), he found authority for the way in which the religious traditionalism of his maturity was still growing when he died, that is, outwards from the image of rustic, Catholic France depicted in *La Colline inspirée* and *La Grande pitié des églises de France* towards a broader vision of 'civilisation' defended in the laboratories as well as the churches of a united, and a forward and outward looking saviour of Europe. But the universality which came naturally and immediately to Pascal, as a Christian and as a scientist of the seventeenth century, appears in the context of Barrès's post-Tainian 'passage du local à l'universel'[42] as a 'total synthesis' to be built up progressively from 'diverse elements':

> Mon aspiration à l'unité, satisfaite dans la crypte de Pasteur. C'est là une synthèse totale? Réfléchir encore. Je veux supprimer des barrières qui n'existent pas en moi, les barrières qui séparent le laboratoire et l'Église, les ordres religieux et l'Institut. Puisque tout cela fait ma vie, s'accorde en moi, qu'ont-ils à se nier? Ils ont à exercer une action, tous, et à féconder les êtres. Il faut associer des éléments divers.
> [*Mes Cahiers, Œuvre* XX 134]

Moreover, Barrès was not sufficiently at home in the sphere of speculative reasoning to be able to climb by logical steps over the high barriers that philosophers since Pascal have built up between the Christian and the scientific theories of the universe. He strove hard to explain away the contradictions between the constituents of his traditionalism – patriotism, Catholicism, Science – but where logical argu-

42 *See* above, Chapter Three, pp. 65–77. Regarding Barrès's 'Tainian' and 'Romantic' confusion of Pascal's term, *le cœur* ('chez tous les hommes de même nature ... "une sorte de raisonnement"'), with *sensibilité* ('la sensibilité varie d'individu en individu'), *see* H. Franck, *La Danse devant l'arche*, 189–91 and J. Godfrin, *Barrès mystique*, 165–9, 204–9.

ment fell short, he would turn spontaneously to a more congenial means of arriving at his 'total synthesis' by the imaginative association of their outward forms, such as, in this case, 'the laboratory, the Church, the religious orders and the Institute,' an act of poetic composition normally inspired, as here at the tomb of Pasteur, by the *genius loci* of a sacred place. And it was a kindred feature of Pascal's 'method' that Barrès was able to assimilate best from the 'poet' self-enshrined in the 'magnificent spiritual monument' of the *Pensées* (*Mes Cahiers, Œuvre* XVI 121):[43]

POUR MES MÉMOIRES

Serait-il vrai que dans ma vie ce que je préfère c'est ma tombe? Je ne travaille, je n'existe, à bien voir, que pour la construire. Je n'en ai pas ainsi décidé avec ma raison claire, mais tel est, de fait, l'emploi de mes jours. Prodigieux acharnement surgi du fond de mon cœur. Serait-ce pour ne pas me dissoudre, pour durer par cet expédient. Serait-ce que je m'accorde avec le texte de Pascal: 'C'est une chose horrible de sentir s'écouler tout ce qu'on possède.'

Vue imparfaite. Je vis pour construire mon poème de la vie, une vue chaque jour plus complète, plus riche de l'univers. Et c'est vrai que je regrette qu'elle meure avec moi, je regrette qu'elle ne continue pas de se développer, qu'elle ne devienne pas la vérité totale.

À quarante-huit ans. – Je m'achemine vers la fin du petit poème de ma vie. Les strophes les plus brillantes sont déjà récitées. Combien en reste-t-il à dire? Trois ou quatre. Peut-être une seule. Mais celle-ci, d'un accent plus grave, c'est elle qui donnera tout son prix à l'ensemble et qui pourrait, d'une chanson médiocre, soudain faire un chef-d'œuvre.
[*Mes Cahiers, Œuvre* XVI 336, 339]

The imaginative character of the work Barrès wanted to be remembered by: a 'monument' constructed like a poem from a single 'view

43 *Cit.* above, p. 264.

of the universe' made 'fuller and richer' every day, was thrown into sharp relief by the attack launched in *La Croix* in July 1922 against his only completed post-War work to compare in literary distinction and finish with *La Colline inspirée*, the last, and best, of his pre-War *récits*. *Un Jardin sur l'Oronte* had nothing specifically to do with either church or laboratory, and Barrès explicitly denied that he had any 'edifying' purpose in writing it (*Œuvre* XII 465). The slow genesis of this deeply personal fantasy of love and power in thirteenth-century Syria, marking the resurgence of Barrès's 'inner Asia' from beneath his Lotharingian patriotism, has been traced back to 1903[44] and beyond.[45] Nevertheless, he was prepared to let it stand as an example, if a comparatively unconscious and unmilitant one, of the 'propaganda' for a broadly assimilative French and Catholic outlook by which, at the end of his life, he believed that his 'talent and influence' ought to be judged:

> *La querelle du* Jardin sur l'Oronte. – Je n'écris pas ces réflexions avec mauvaise humeur et dans un esprit de contradiction. Loin de là. Nous sommes d'accord. Un puissant écrivain, à son insu même, collabore à quelque propagande, contribue à l'établissement d'une conception de la vie. Chacun a le droit de lui demander compte de l'emploi qu'il fait de son talent et de son influence. Et la conception que je me fais de la vie, c'est bien la conception catholique, la vie à la française largement accueillante à toutes les notions, qu'elle révise et met au point. Mais qu'est-ce que veulent les critiques catholiques? Suis-je seul enfin? Ai-je seul retenu l'enseignement que j'ai cru recevoir? Est-il incertain, hésitant, équivoque? Ai-je tort de croire que je me suis assimilé Didon, la nymphe Eucharis, Andromaque, Roxane, Phèdre?
> [*Mes Cahiers, Œuvre* XX 78–9][46]

44 I.-M. Frandon, *L'Orient de Maurice Barrès*, 311–51: 'Au bout du rêve: "Un Jardin sur l'Oronte" '

45 Philippe Barrès, note introducinng 'La Musulmane courageuse' (1895) in *N'Importe où hors du monde, Œuvre* XII 352

46 Cf. 'Comment la critique catholique conçoit le rôle de l'artiste,' *L'Écho de Paris* 16 August 1922: 'Il n'est pas de littérature sans âme; il n'y a pas de cloison entre la littérature et la vie supérieure de la pensée;

The 'zeal' and 'science' which, for Barrès, were confusing the young Neo-Thomist contradictors of his heroines, Oriante and Isabelle (*Œuvre* XII 472), drove him back in self-defence to the opposite, 'musical' limit of his theory of the imagination:

> Oriante, ne vous irritez pas, et vous, Isabelle, ne soyez pas inquiète. Ce sont mes amis. Ce sont les critiques catholiques... Certainement ils tiennent à venir saluer des jeunes converties. C'est bien aimable à eux, car ils sont pleins de science, et vous, mes filles, vous n'avez pour vous que la justesse de vos chants.
>
> Je me sers de la puissance expressive des sons. L'harmonie, la mélodie, le rythme produisent une impression qui ennoblit le lecteur. Mozart, quoi qu'il dise, est bon. Il nous élève et épure. [*N'Importe où hors du monde, Œuvre* XII 463–4, 470][47]

and at times, uneasily close to the proposition that beauty is enough to justify a work of art:

> J'ai dit et redit que, le service fait, je me distrayais. J'aime les concerts dans les jardins. L'Oronte en est un. ['Réponse à Robert Vallery-Radot à propos du "Jardin sur l'Oronte",' *La Revue hebdomadaire* 7 October 1922]
>
> Réponse à Valley-Radot. J'ai lu la belle page que vous consacrez à Oriante et à Isabelle.
>
> Où diable avez-vous vu que j'ai l'impertinence de servir l'Église par ce récit? C'est un divertissement; je l'ai dit et redit...
>
> Si l'on veut voir une moralité à cette fable, on peut apprécier qu'elle oriente les imaginations vers les horizons de la victoire,

un puissant écrivain, à son insu même, collabore à quelque doctrine, contribue à l'établissement d'une conception de la vie, fait œuvre de propagandiste.' Henri Massis edulcorates Barrès's consciously committed position by writing 'philosophie' for 'propagandiste' in *Jugements* (Paris: Plon 1923) I 182. *See* H. Massis, *Barrès et nous* (Paris: Plon 1962).

47 The 'musicalization' of the novel was a fashion in France and England after the Great War. *See* M. Raimond, *La Crise du roman*, 403–4.

> comme fait *Le Génie du Rhin*. Mais c'est un poème d'opéra, c'est un oiseau bleu; encore une fois, c'est un plaisir que je me suis donné à moi-même, un *jardin*.
> [*Mes Cahiers, Œuvre* XX 82–3]

This last attempt to have the best of both worlds appears in a less strained form in a letter to Henri Massis (*Œuvre* XII 530), where Barrès presents his novel as a kind of new *Atala*, an episode from *Une Enquête aux pays du Levant* which was then forthcoming, and which might indeed be described as two volumes of his own *Génie du Christianisme*, crossed with a variation on *L'Itinéraire*. Elsewhere among Barrès's reactions to his nationalist and Catholic friends' criticism of his latest novel are several examples of an equally ambiguous but much more natural device for avoiding the charge of aestheticist immorality, the simple apposition of words for beauty, truth, and goodness, e.g. *N'Importe où hors du monde* (*Œuvre* XII 465) : 'l'Église ...laisse l'artiste concevoir comme il veut son œuvre d'art pourvu qu'elle ait de la beauté. Dès qu'il apporte quelque chose de noble, le *sursum corda* vers le beau, vers le bien, on ne le chicane pas, on l'accueille, et on l'interprète au mieux!' [469]: 'Toute bonté et toute beauté collaborent à nous rapprocher de la vérité ...' [470]: 'l'intelligence ... ne nous donne pas le réel, que seules nous donnent les diverses expériences mystiques, sens du beau, sens religieux ...'

But Barrès's last words on the 'dossier de l'Oronte' (*N'Importe où hors du monde*, *Œuvre* XII 471–3; *Mes Cahiers, Œuvre* XX 103–4), confirmed by notes for his memoirs made a few weeks before his death, and published in the first volume of *Mes Cahiers* (*Œuvre* XIII 20), place him nearer to the point of balance he had adopted before the War, between, on the one hand, the fantastic symphonies of the pagan meadow and, on the other, the body of doctrine and city of souls in which the spontaneous experience of the individual is collected, ordered, and preserved, as it were, between the four stout walls of a chapel of stone (*La Colline inspirée, Œuvre* VI 499). From this position, the mission of 'theologians' like Henri Massis appeared as far as ever 'outside' his competence and ambition, but he was also better able to hear their 'insults' as a call to improve both on his latest *jardin* (while protesting, in the name of a score of sensuous beauties such as the Church had traditionally taken into Christian employment by way of art, that his latest heroines should not be singled out for burning) and also on the service he had long given in the very heart of the battle, but which could now, he claimed, be left to others he had helped to inspire (though he permitted himself to doubt whether the restrictive and categorical systems and theories they now appeared to favour would be as effective as the positive results he claimed for his own untrammelled and instinctive grasp of reality) (*N'Importe où hors du monde, Œuvre* XII 462–73).

Whether the literary masterpiece of perfect Christian faith that the author of *Un Jardin sur l'Oronte* challenged his censors to produce might have matured under his own hand, somewhere along the free-ranging pilgrim's progress to which, in taking his leave of them, he dedicated the years that remained to him, remains an open question. He died 'en marche,' without having promised it (*Œuvre* XII 529–30; XIX 123). What he did promise, at least by implication, when the evident disaffection of the post-War generation of French Christians spurred him to contrast his 'vocation' for the last time with that of the doctrinaires now ascendent in the French nationalist and religious revival he had helped to set on foot, was that the 'songs of his winter season' would not be mere 'operatic' music for another Blue-Bird *divertissement* in the style of *Un Jardin sur l'Oronte.* Nor, on the other hand, would they be inspired by dogmatic theology:

> Un rossignol chante sur une branche; un grincheux bougeonne dans la nuit: 'Sale bête, quand donc auras-tu fini de salir mon imagination avec tes rêveries suspectes?' Eh quoi, cette mauvaise humeur modifie-t-elle rien des éclats charmants de l'animal divin? À chacun sa musique...
>
> Mais ils ont raison, mes contradicteurs, de vouloir que je fasse mieux, et après avoir anéanti leurs critiques, je les reprends et je veux qu'elles aient un sens pour m'obliger à mieux faire...
>
> Ce que certains me reprochent aujourd'hui, je note qu'un Jules Michelet s'en faisait un grief à lui-même. Un jour, de passage à Cologne – après s'être posé l'éternel problème du Rhin, – il s'interroge, à la fois, sur sa propre mission et sur la mission de la France, et il écrit sur son carnet intime: 'Nous n'aurons force que

comme simplicité d'idées, rectitude. Exclure tout caprice d'art: *Mala gaudia mentis.*' Voilà trois mots que je comprends. Et pourtant, c'est un grand défaut, l'excès de volonté claire dans la vie spirituelle. Il faut errer, battre le pays, suivre un sentier, l'appel de la lumière, d'un chant, d'une nostalgie, d'un archange, se faire des loisirs. Mes contradicteurs, abusés par leur zèle et leur science, comme par deux œillères qu'ils ont au visage, et emportés par un sentiment préremptoire de leur mission, dédaignent ces espaces magnifiques que nous aménageons à droite et à gauche d'une voie que nous leur avons, pour une part, tracée. [*Œuvre* XII 471–3]

The 'Perfection' that Barrès in 1922 was ambitious to achieve by the self-sufficient and self-regulating efficacy of art was, he believed, beyond his 'blinkered'[48] critics' reach:

Il faut croire que nous sommes de mauvais théologiens et que ces jeunes Messieurs l'entendent mieux. Mais je ne me sens pas entièrement convaincu. Il me semble qu'aujourd'hui on veut trop embrigader, restreindre, classer, couper. Quelle manie de construire des systèmes et des théories! J'aurais peur de paraître infatué, mais de bonne foi, quels résultats obtenez-vous qui dépassent mes expériences propres ... À vous, Messieurs, il faut le garde-fou des systèmes et de la logique. Moi, je suis gardé par un sentiment artistique de la mesure.

Je ne vous condamne pas car je suis une intelligence conciliatrice.

48 Barrès's reference to the 'blinkers' of his critics (*Œuvre* XII 472) contrasts with earlier, bleakly pessimistic references to the value of the 'veil of Isis' and a 'thick bandage over the eyes' as a remedy against nihilism (*Pour la haute intelligence française*, *Œuvre* IX 253 and *Mes Cahiers*, *Œuvre* XVI 178). *See* however his express contempt for the 'sloppy theory' of beautiful life-lies, reported by the late Professor Moreau in 'Barrès devant son dernier portrait' (*cit.* above, note 40), and Jean Cocteau's perceptive *mot*: 'Je parlais d'œillères. Les vôtres sont en verre. C'est ce qui me permet de voir votre œil qui vous dénonce, et c'est ce qui vous permet de jouir, de tirer une amertume riche des spectacles vers quoi votre instinct vous entraîne et que vos théories vous défendent' (*Le Rappel à l'ordre* [Paris: Stock 1926] 162.

Je ne m'occupe pas de théologie. Je ne suis ni au-dessus, ni au-dessous; je suis en dehors, mais certainement au-dessus de toute controverse. Aucune de vos formules ne pourra empêcher mon efficacité. Je crois que j'ai obtenu des résultats positifs qui ne sont pas mauvais, parce que deux ou trois fois, j'ai su atteindre 'le tréfonds enchanté et mystérieux des choses' dont vous parlez. [*N'Importe où hors du monde, Œuvre* XII 470–1]

*La querelle de l'*Oronte. – Ils me reprochent de n'être pas thomiste, et ceci, et cela. Mais n'est-il qu'une voie, est-ce la voie de l'artiste, est-ce ma voie? N'y a-t-il pas le Dieu des philosophes, le Dieu des moralistes, le Dieu des artistes, ou plutôt ne reflètent-ils pas, ces philosophes, ces moralistes, ces artistes, des visages de Dieu? Mozart, Sophocle, Vinci ne manifestent-ils pas Dieu, ne nous approchent-ils pas de lui quand ils nous donnent ces accents surhumains? Ce sont les murmures involontaires d'une foule émue. Indépendamment même de ce que je dis, si ma phrase a un rythme juste, elle m'accorde avec la Perfection.

...

Les Massis disent le mot *Dieu*, mais s'il y a chez les artistes un état que les artistes ne nomment pas? Si les artistes ont vu dans le monde, grâce à leur sens de la beauté, l'étincelle divine, et si elle les extasie et les transfigure, et s'ils la reflètent pour leurs lecteurs?

Croient-ils que je vais subordonner mon imagination et mes désirs à leurs besoins? Ils courent après quelque chose. Grand bien leur fasse! Je ne le leur ai pas promis, je ne me suis pas chargé de les y mener. Je passais, ils m'ont suivi; qu'ils soient là où non, je vais mon chemin, car j'ai ma vocation, que j'écoute en moi-même et non sur aucunes lèvres.

...

Je trouve en moi le fond de la nature française, l'âme collective.

...

Je m'achemine par la vertu de mon sentiment intérieur plus que de la réflexion intellectuelle. Ce qui ne nuit pas à ma lucidité. Cela se fait silencieusement et spontanément à l'intérieur de mon esprit, où je vois clair, et aux heures venues recueille ma vérité toute formée. Elle y repose vivante, agissante, sans souci de formules et d'arguments, élue par une sympathie irrésistible et dans un choix de vie ou de mort.

Il y a dans ton être une force, un élan, une étincelle, une source.

Sache que ce puissant mystère est sacré. Protège-le, écoute-le. Par lui, tu peux plus que tu ne crois.

Pourtant, tu peux en mésuser. Il y a l'expérience accumulée des sages, il y a des disciplines. Quand tu suis ton inspiration, que ce soit sous le portique sacré, sous la voûte toute tapissée des enseignements les plus beaux et qui te rappelle au respect et à l'intelligence du passé!

[*Mes Cahiers, Œuvre* xx 103–4]

By thus declining to 'subordinate his imagination and his desires' to the 'requirements' of Neo-Thomist theory, Barrès confirmed, within little more than a year of his death, his long attachment to that 'Queen of Faculties' he had first found 'enthroned'[49] in the *avant-garde* Symbolist literature of his Parisian apprenticeship, and the practical applications of which, in the wider field of public affairs, he would go on to discover from the great Romantics, from contemporary sociology and psycho-physiology, and for himself amid the successive 'tumults' of Third Republican party politics. For the 'conciliatory intelligence' he cultivated in his last, predominantly religious, phase, imagination as a 'reconciling and mediatory power,' stretched to catch simultaneously, on the frontiers of what he called 'music' and 'science,' and in one movement of 'irresistible sympathy' with the 'collective soul' of the French people, both the 'involuntary murmur of the crowd's emotion' and the 'order' of traditional doctrine and precept inscribed in stone above the heads of the crowd, has become a spontaneous, autonomous, and indispensable means of achieving unity within an essentially poetic 'domain' of inspiration:

De la science à la musique, c'est mon domaine, et sur ces deux limites continuellement je m'efforce de gagner la largeur de deux

49 Cf. M. Gilman, *The Idea of Poetry in France from Houdar de la Motte to Baudelaire* (Cambridge, Mass: Harvard University Press 1958), Chapter Eight, 'Imagination Enthroned.'

doigts. L'ambition, l'attrait du mystère. [J'ai recours] à la science, parce que je crains l'appauvrissement, – à la musique, de crainte de dessèchement, [par besoin de] rafraîchissement.

'La voix mystique qu'on doit entendre au fond de tout poème, laisse à la matière sa légère vibration spirituelle.'
[*Mes Cahiers, Œuvre* XIX 116]

NOTES

FOREWORD

1 'Imagination,' H. Franck, *La Danse devant l'arche* (Paris: Gallimard 1921) 194–7: 'Il faut remarquer d'ailleurs que dans le culte de la terre et des morts, c'est moins le cœur que l'imagination de Barrès qui est satisfaite. Il ne s'agit pas de contester sa sincérité, qui est profonde. Mais ces réalités où il s'appuie, on peut bien le soupçonner de les imaginer. Ce n'est pas la Lorraine qui a créé Maurice Barrès: c'est lui-même qui a créé la Lorraine ... Il est magnifiquement doué pour imaginer les plus nobles attitudes du cœur. Il a adopté de bonne foi celle qu'il a trouvée la plus noble ... Son système ne vaut que pour lui.' C. du Bos, *cit.* R. Lalou, *Maurice Barrès* (Paris: Hachette 1950) 181: 'l'art inégalé de composer toujours pour l'imagination et pour elle seule.' R. Gillouin, *Maurice Barrès* (Paris: E. Sansot 1907) 38: 'Barrès a au plus haut degré la sensibilité *directe* et l'imagination subjective ... l'imagination objective ou intuitive est chez lui relativement très faible.' J. Jary, *Essai sur l'art et la psychologie de Maurice Barrès* (Paris: E. Paul 1912) 65–6: '... c'est par elle [imagination] ... que [Barrès] pénètre l'inconscient, met en lumière des états inadaptés.'
'Image': H. Massis, *La Pensée de Maurice Barrès* (Paris: Mercure de France 1909) 56: 'Sa pensée est tournée en images: il poursuit sans cesse ce qui est propre à traduire sensiblement ce qu'il a senti. Il convertit en figures contagieuses la substance de sa vie intérieure, et c'est comme un flot abondant qui nous emplit d'une incomparable musique.' A. Thibaudet, *La Vie de Maurice Barrès* (Paris: Gallimard 1921) 249: 'Il est naturel qu'une telle sensibilité s'exprime par des images vivantes. M. Barrès est un de nos grands créateurs de belles images. Grâce à cette puissance musicale qui est au centre de son être, il peut par ses vibrations sympathiser avec toutes les vibrations des choses, retrouver dans leurs analogies leur racine musicale commune. Le cœur de son art c'est la puissance de saisir ces analogies, de les nouer d'un geste en une gerbe indissoluble.' J. Madaule, *Le Nationalisme de Maurice Barrès* (Marseille:

Sagittaire 1943) 113: 'Il est intéressant de rechercher maintenant quelle image se faisait Barrès de la France. Ou plutôt quelles images. Ce sont, en effet, ces images, chargées d'émotion, qui sont à l'origine de la plupart de nos comportements. Et, dans le cas de Barrès, nous avons vu que, loin de vouloir se soustraire au pouvoir des images, ou les soumettre au contrôle de la raison, il ne cesse précisément d'en appeler de l'intelligence à l'image.' J. and J. Tharaud, *Pour les fidèles de Barrès* (Paris: Plon 1944) 113: 'Renard me parlant de la littérature de Barrès l'opposait à la sienne ... "Une idée appartient à tout le monde; une image n'appartient qu'à vous." '

'Metaphor': R. Fernandez, *Barrès* (Paris: Éditions du Livre moderne 1943) 152: 'Ce seront des métaphores de lui-même qu'il va chercher à travers les sites et les âmes ... Et peut-être est-ce ainsi, par voie métaphorique, et non point par liaison réelle, qu'il a pu se raccorder à sa terre et à ses morts.'

'Symbol': H. Bremond, *Maurice Barrès: vingt-cinq années de vie littéraire; pages choisies* (Paris: Bloud 1911) lxiv: 'l'aventure du volontaire alsacien est un symbole, tout comme la Lorraine de *l'Appel au soldat*.'

'Myth': J. Jary, *Essai sur l'art et la psychologie de Maurice Barrès*, 104: 'concept et sentiment s'unissent, la pensée revêt une forme mythique. C'est la "manière" de M. Barrès.' J. Madaule, *Le Nationalisme de Maurice Barrès*, 116: 'Le nationalisme de Barrès suppose donc une mythologie.' P. Moreau, *Maurice Barrès* (Paris: Sagittaire 1946) 162: 'Deux mythes ou deux symboles expriment dans ces livres [*La Grande pitié des églises de France*, *La Colline inspirée*] la double religion de Barrès.' C. Maurras, *Réponse à André Gide* (Paris: Éditions de la Seule France 1948) 13: 'ses lectures et relectures du Système de politique positive où je le vis souvent plongé, inspirèrent à Barrès les deux mythes de la Terre et des Morts, prête-noms d'une poésie sublime pour désigner la Patrie et ses Traditions ... Ses mythes faisaient plutôt fonction de portes d'un refuge, colonnades d'un lieu d'asile. Barrès pouvait bien s'y défendre, il n'argumentait ni en eux ni avec eux.'

3 *See*, however, H. Massis, 'Maurice Barrès, ou la génération du relatif' (*Jugements* (Paris: Plon 1923) I 169–252), where due, if hostile, emphasis was first given to the connection between Barrès's relativistic epistemology and his 'poetic' style. But the significance of this connection is blurred by the critic's habit of depriving 'poetry' of all external reference in order to identify it with personal fantasy, voluptuous caprice, sweet dreaming, and beautiful emotions, whereas Barrès was quite determined and well able to use the imaginative forms of poetic discourse descriptively, in 'Ethical, political and religious propositions' (I. Murdoch, *Sartre, Romantic Rationalist* (London: Bowes and Bowes 1953) 29). On the still lingering fascination of the emotive-descriptive alternative, which also, at times, mars the generally more comprehensive and perceptive essay of J. Mercanton, *Poésie et religion dans l'œuvre de Maurice Barrès* (Lausanne: Droz 1940), notably by breaking the unity of his topic into oversimple compartments labelled 'personal emotion,' 'psychological

truth,' 'doctrine,' 'dreams,' 'poet's visions,' 'living faith,' 'poetry of religion,' 'religious poetry,' see Murdoch, *Sartre* and M.H. Abrams, *The Mirror and the Lamp* (New York: W.W. Norton 1958) 151–2.

7 Barrès also, following what was accepted practice in his day, used the word *image* to stand for objects or experiences of sense perception, though rarely without implying some mental or emotional complication of the given percept. *See* below, p. 10, and compare *Mes Cahiers, L'Œuvre de Maurice Barrès* (Paris: Au Club de l'Honnête Homme 1965–8) XVI 44: 'Cet ouvrage qui approche le plus des images que je vois en fermant les yeux aussi bien qu'en les ouvrant et que je voudrais traduire' with H. Bergson, *cit.* A. Lalande, *Vocabulaire technique et critique de la philosophie* (Paris: Alcan 1932) 340: 'Me voici en présence des images, au sens le plus vague où l'on puisse prendre ce mot, images perçues quand j'ouvre les sens, inaperçues quand je les ferme.' Also P. Garcin, 'Les Deux Barrès,' *Critique* (December 1961) 1021: 'Les perceptions optiques ne retentissent en Barrès que s'il peut les rapporter à des notions plus générales qu'elles, plus vagues, où elles demeurent en suspens ... Son regard ne se déplace que dans l'au-delà des images, dans le royaume des choses pensées, pays dépouillé de tout paysage: ce qui frappe les sens est toujours pour lui de l'anecdote.' This is excellent, but for some overstatement towards the end ('tout paysage' ... 'toujours').

CHAPTER ONE

13 *Les Maîtres, Œuvre* XII. At the very beginning of his career Barrès named Michelet, Goethe, and Disraeli as his 'masters' (letter to *Le Matin* 12 October 1889). The influence on Barrès of the British dandy turned statesman was fairly restricted ('Peut-être me faisais-je une idée un peu particulière de ... Disraeli,' he admitted, in a 'Lettre-Manifeste' published in *La Plume* 1 April 1891), but it was definite, and seminal, with respect to his anti-*opportuniste* and anti-Dreyfusard nationalism: 'c'est d'un Disraeli que j'ai reçu peut-être ma vue principale, à savoir que, le jour où les démocrates trahissent les intérêts et la véritable tradition d'un pays, il y a lieu de poursuivre la transformation du parti aristocratique, pour lui confier à la fois l'amélioration sociale et les grandes ambitions nationales.' (*Œuvre* I 140). Goethe's and Michelet's broader influences have been studied by R. Lalou and J.-P. Vaillant respectively, in *Chroniques Barrésiennes*, ed. F. Empaytaz (Paris: Le Rouge et le Noir 1929) II. *See* also F.M. Ross, *Goethe in Modern France* (Urbana: University of Illinois 1937).

CHAPTER TWO

3 Cf. J.G. Fichte, *Doctrine de la science de la connaissance* (Paris: Ladrange 1843) 151: 'Dans le champ pratique l'imagination poursuit

dans l'infini jusqu'à l'idée absolument indéterminable de l'unité suprême.' Barrès referred several times to Fichte's influence on his early thinking, e.g. *Œuvre* I 31: 'Balzac et ... Fichte dans nos chambres étroites, ouvertes sur le grand Paris,' and 241: 'dans l'intrigue de Paris, le soir, je me suis libéré de moi-même parmi les ivresses un peu confuses de Fichte et dans l'orgueil un peu sec de Spinoza.' *See* also his letter to H. Bahr, dated February 1897 *cit.* V. Pica, *Letteratura d'eccezione* (Milan: Baldini, Castoldi 1898) 222: 'ne sais rien de Stirner, de Nietzsche que des études bien médiocres ... Pour Fichte c'est autre chose. Qui aurait pu y échapper?'

CHAPTER THREE

16 Cf. M. Raimond, *La Crise du roman* (Paris: José Corti 1966) 71. It may have been directly inspired (or some personal experience may have been brought into sharper focus) by the *cause célèbre* of Henri Chambige, an intellectual convicted in 1888 of murdering his mistress, and a model of Bourget's *Le Disciple*. 'Une Anecdote d'amour' certainly develops ideas already published by Barrès in his analysis of the murderer's sensibility for the readers of *Le Figaro*, for example: 'la défaillance d'un analyste de vingt-deux ans, qui a été empoigné par sa passion ... C'est une période bien vulgaire, celle où l'on souffre, où l'on jouit vraiment ... Le joli ne commence que dans la mélancolie du souvenir ... Pour présenter quelque agrément, il faut qu'un fait soit transformé en matière de pensée' ('La Sensibilité d'Henri Chambige,' *Le Figaro* 11 November 1888).

26 Cf. H. Clouard, *La Cocarde de Barrès* (Paris: Nouvelle Librairie Nationale 1910) and J. Orville McShine, *Maurice Barrès: Journaliste* (Port-au-Prince: Presses Nationales d'Haïti 1966). Also C. Digeon, *La Crise allemande de la pensée française (1870–1914)* (Paris: PUF 1959) 421: 'Barrès attaquera en cette période confuse de la IIIe République, sur deux fronts: à l'opportunisme bourgeois il opposera le socialisme, à l'idéologie humanitaire, le nationalisme. Et sous son éphémère direction (1894–5), *La Cocarde* ... est singulièrement représentative du chassé-croisé d'idées qui caractérise l'histoire intellectuelle du temps. Barrès y développe son socialisme littéraire, imprégné d'idées aux origines fort diverses. Mais en même temps que les thèmes socialistes apparaît l'idée nationaliste – et cela est nouveau.'

28 *See* in particular the following chapters: 'Déraciné, décapité' (*Œuvre* III 346–55) and 'La liquidation chez Sturel' (*Œuvre* IV 414–31). A common misinterpretation of the novel as a prescriptive rather than a critical study of contemporary French society supposes that it registers approval of the unequal chances of rich and poor in the over-centralized, 'Opportunist' Republic that Barrès is, on the contrary, concerned to expose as viciously wasteful of its young people's potential. *See*, for example, Z. Sternhell, *Maurice Barrès et le nationalisme français* (Paris: Armand Colin 1972) 301, where the fact that 'l'aventure parisienne ne sera fatale qu'à ceux qui proviennent des couches sociales les plus défavorisées,'

whilst 'les ... fils de famille réussissent au moins à moitié,' is alleged to 'illustrate' 'le glissement de Barrès vers un conservatisme bourgeois.'

34 *Œuvre* I 197; III 307; XIII 80, 83, 167–8. *See* also *Œuvre* XIII 297: 'Dans le chapitre de Chateaubriand (*Génie du Christianisme*: des prières pour les morts), il y a une note sur Fontanes: 'Le jour des morts dans une campagne.' On y trouve non seulement les principes du romantisme, l'enchantement de la tristesse, mais la préoccupation de *créer des hommes*.' And E. Renan, *Feuilles détachées* (Paris: Calmann Lévy 1892) 393: 'N'est-il pas remarquable que la fête de la Toussaint, inséparable de la fête des Morts, soit la seule fête que le peuple ait gardée?' These words occur in Renan's articles on Amiel which Barrès said he had 'lived on' in October 1884 (*Œuvre* I 418). And J. Izoulet, *La Cité moderne* (Paris: Alcan 1894) 611: 'Le *culte des morts* et le *culte des héros* sont les deux colonnes du temple de la religion antique et future, de la religion universelle et éternelle.'

62 'Au milieu d'un océan et d'un sombre mystère de vagues qui me pressent, je me tiens à ma conception historique, comme un naufragé à sa barque. Je ne touche pas à l'énigme du commencement des choses, ni à la douloureuse énigme de la fin de toutes choses. Je me cramponne à ma courte solidité. Je me place dans une collectivité un peu plus longue que mon individu; je m'invente une destination un peu plus raisonnable que ma chétive carrière. [*Œuvre* I 141–2] 'Pour un certain nombre de personnes le surnaturel est déchu. Leur pitié qui veut un objet n'en trouve pas dans les cieux. J'ai ramené la mienne du ciel sur la terre, sur la terre de mes morts.' (*Œuvre* V 25) For J. Madaule (*Le Nationalisme de Barrès* [Marseille: Sagittaire 1943] 152–8), this reduction of the supernatural to the earthy was Barrès's final religious position, taking fom Catholicism only what would serve a 'cult of the fatherland,' and fit into a loose religious syncretism. It is true that, for a time, Barrès found that 'la campagne natale nous fait passer de l'absolu au relatif' (*Œuvre* XIII 296); but his subsequent 'passage du local à l'universel' (*Œuvre* XV 239) used the French countryside and its autochthonous nature deities as means and objects of Christian conversion (admittedly 'monotheistic' by Madaule's strict standards), rather than the other way round, as Madaule suggests: 'Barrès ... voyait dans cette religion [Catholicism] le moyen le plus efficace d'élever les hommes de chez nous à cet état de religiosité sur lequel on pouvait fonder le culte de la patrie.'

84 Cf. *Nationalisme*, *Œuvre* V 27, *cit.* below, pp. 125–6. Barrès's traditionalism belongs with the post-Nietzschean philosophies of 'perspectivity' which are grouped and analysed by Señor Claudio Guillén in an article entitled 'On the Concept and Metaphor of Perspective,' published in *Comparatists at Work: Studies in Comparative Literature*, edited by Stephen G. Nichols, Jr and Richard B. Vowles (Waltham, Mass: Blaisdell 1968) and included in the author's collection of essays published three years later: C. Guillén, *Literature as System* (Princeton: Princeton University Press 1971) 328–45. Barrès seems closest to José Ortega y Gasset, and to the American pragmatist George Herbert Mead (1863–1931), whom he does not appear to have read, but who, like him, finds

'the *location* underlying a perspective' to be 'a collective one': the 'social individual is already in a perspective which belongs to the community within which his self has arisen. This involves the assumption of the community attitudes where all speak with one voice in the organization of social conduct' (*cit.* Guillén, 345).

CHAPTER SEVEN

2 E.g. *Œuvre* III 24, 399, 443, 460; IV 86–8, 118, 121, 255, 424, 517; XII 159; XIII 78–9, 111; XV 126; XVI 130, 353; XVII 157–8; XVIII 200; *Grande Guerre*, VI 117. *See* 'Nos Internationalistes,' *Le Figaro* 26 August 1896: 'Que Jaurès me traite de patriotard. Le nationalisme est une réalité et son internationalisme une verbalité, un mot où lui-même est prisonnier.' And Barrès's letter to Henri Vaugeois, from his home at Charmes-sur-Moselle, dated 24 October 1900 (published in J. Caplain, *Maurice Barrès, ami des jeunes*, Paris: Henry Goulet 1924) 16–17: 'si vous veniez me voir ici, je vous montrerais des chapeliers, des tonneliers, des bedaux, des petites gens démocratiques, autoritaires, positifs, antilibéraux, les troupes du Balafré enfin les gens de tous les Césars ... la grossièreté, le réalisme populaire de tout ce monde-là, comme je l'aime! Et que Versailles pue l'idéalisme; on y tua l'ancienne France.'

7 Cf. J. Soury, *cit. Œuvre* XIII 45: 'L'homme surtout s'il est intelligent, est avant tout affectif. C'est-à-dire qu'il se fait une représentation. Elle est là en dedans de nous, elle s'interpose entre moi et le livre que je tiens' (Soury is speaking of the memory of his dead mother). In *Scènes et doctrines du nationalisme*, Barrès hesitates between a general and a more specifically imaginative use of this mechanism of association: 'Certains mots, ainsi les mots *France, Patrie*, éveillent chez certains hommes, dont nous sommes, un si grand nombre d'idées préalablement associées que c'est dans la conscience comme le bruissement créé dans la forêt par un coup de vent' (*Œuvre* V 116). 'Certaines images, et, par exemple, les honteuses figures de la bande à Dreyfus, venant à tomber dans nos âmes, y produisent, – comme un coup de vent dans le feuillage immense d'une forêt, – un bruissement que ne connaîtront jamais les êtres où n'existe pas préalablement notre feuillage d'âme. Ce n'est point affaire d'intelligence; quels que soient leur rapidité et leur affinement, des étrangers ne peuvent rien ressentir de profond qui leur soit commun avec nous' (*Œuvre* V 190–1).

17 E.g. 'la vierge bleue et blanche ... c'est bien l'image sur laquelle se groupent des hommes. Je regrette qu'elle soit fade, mais elle est consacrée, significative' (*Œuvre* XIII 337). 'dans la cathédrale, j'ai reconnu sur ces tapisseries les images de mon histoire sainte d'enfant ... Ici l'art n'est pas une formule ... (*Œuvre* VIII 158). Contrast the following examples of non-representational 'symbols': 'le signe de Svastika, symbole au nom indien... Ces deux branches coudées qui se croisent, ce talisman ... enchante mon esprit' (*Grande Guerre* VI 17–18). 'La cathédrale de Mayence a deux chœurs; cela me parut toujours un symbole; l'un germanique, l'autre

français, veux-je croire, et dont les chants et les vœux doivent un jour s'harmoniser' (*Œuvre* x 297).

20 E.g. 'Ménard ... disait que, si l'on voulait donner au dogme républicain de la fraternité une forme vivante et plastique, on ne pourrait trouver une image plus belle que celle du Juste mourant pour le salut des hommes' (*Œuvre* VII 169). 'Laissez-moi seulement vous conter une simple histoire qui définit assez bien la situation morale de la Prusse et de l'Alsace à la veille de la guerre. C'est l'affaire de Saverne. Cette histoire vraie donne l'impression d'une caricature, tant les traits sont massifs et les couleurs tranchées. En marge de l'exposé abstrait où nous avons dû suivre jusque dans ses pires égarements la folie pangermaniste, elle fera l'effet d'une image durement coloriée, d'une illustration brutale et schématique qui, ébranlant l'imagination, nous aide à comprendre un texte trop aride' (*Grande Guerre* XII 293).

21 E.g. 'Coblence est à cinquante kilomètres de Cochem ... pour cette dernière étape, les deux voyageurs se proposent d'observer mieux que jamais les détails de la route ... ils voudraient amasser le plus possible d'images. C'est sain de sortir d'eux-mêmes, de s'attacher aux réalités ...' (*Œuvre* IV 92). 'Des centaines, des milliers de faits saisissants, criants, attestent la vérité que j'apporte ici ... Nos alliés et tous les peuples savent-ils assez cette situation, voient-ils ces faits ...? Les explications didactiques, les polémiques sont utiles, nécessaires, mais il est indispensable de mettre dans les esprits des faits qui fassent image et qui grandissent d'eux-mêmes après que nous nous sommes tus. Se rappeler le service rendu par *la Case de l'oncle Tom* à la cause antiesclaviste' (*Grande Guerre* x 210).

22 E.g. 'le meilleur symbole du patriotisme' ('Une journée à Flavigny,' *Le Courrier de l'Est* 24 August 1890); 'un merveilleux symbole de l'unité française' ('Au bord des fontaines-fées,' *Le Gaulois* 28 January 1908); 'le plus pur symbole de nos vertus guerrières et pacifiques' (*Grande Guerre* XIV 345); 'J'ai l'idée d'envoyer des images de Jeanne d'Arc dans l'Alsace reconquise ...' (*Grande Guerre* IV 253); '*La statue de Jeanne* ... au bord du Rhin: vous avez là une image féconde' (*Œuvre* XIX 224). Compare especially *Grande Guerre* VIII 218: 'Celle qui vécut trois jours ici, il y a cinq siècles, nous échappe. Sœur chrétienne d'Iphigénie et d'Antigone, Jeanne nous ravit par sa beauté dans le ciel de l'art, ou bien à travers elle nous reconnaissons comme dans un symbole des êtres mêlés à nos préoccupations' with *Grande Guerre* XIV 354: 'Vous rappelez-vous un des innombrables épisodes, de la plus pure beauté, qui composent sa vie? Sur le champ de bataille de Patay, la guerrière transformée en fille de charité soutint dans ses bras la tête d'un blessé ennemi et l'encouragea, l'assista dans son agonie. Quelle image de la France!' Also, in *Une Enquête aux pays du Levant* (*Œuvre* XI 121): 'On sait que les artistes grecs ont interprété les éléments vrais de cette royale figure [Alexander the Great], pour en faire l'image de la destinée interrompue, et qu'ils sont arrivés à créer ainsi le symbole de toutes les nostalgies qu'éveillent la jeunesse et le génie.' The Frenchness of which Joan, and the brief span of which Alexander are 'images' are aspects of their real lives; whereas the fighting

Frenchmen of 1916, symbolized by the Maid, and 'all the nostalgia aroused by youth and genius' by the Conqueror of Asia, are not: the symbol implies a greater degree of abstraction than the image. Compare the use of *signe* and *image* in Barrès's picture of the landscape of occupied Lorraine: 'le signe d'une pensée inexprimable' [i.e. the deep Frenchness of the province] '...une vive image du devoir' [i.e. a way of life characterized by good husbandry] (*Œuvre* VI 187, 215).

CHAPTER NINE

8 *Mes Cahiers, Œuvre* XV 394: 'L'action quasi religieuse d'une assemblée est indiquée p. 300 de Durkheim. Influence fortifiante et quasi religieuse d'une assemblée politique. ... "Quelle différence essentielle y a-t-il entre une assemblée de chrétiens célébrant les principales dates de la vie du Christ et une réunion de citoyens commémorant l'institution d'une nouvelle charte morale ou quelque grand événement de la vie nationale" (Durkheim, 610).' The sociology of festivals also interested two men whose influence on Barrès was early and lasting, though rather diffuse: Comte and Michelet, and a third whom he read up during his campaign for the preservation of France's parish churches, namely Edgar Quinet. See also the reference in *Mes Cahiers, Œuvre* XIV 96, to Montégut on the French genius for 'brilliant spectacles.' Barrès made no reference to E. Drumont's *Les Fêtes nationales à Paris* (Paris: Ludovic Baschet 1879), though he may have known the work.

CHAPTER ELEVEN

23 'Ma chanson heurtée, elliptique, c'est le haut chant de mes profondeurs' (*Œuvre* V 551). *See* 546 ('d'admirables mots latins qu'orchestrait mon imagination'), 547 ('Longues psalmodies intérieures'), 547 ('Les beaux arbres d'automne ne prenaient que la peine de vivre, les vierges, de chanter des plaintes liturgiques, et le gave bruissait dans la verdure'), 548 ('Mes pensées glissaient sur cette belle nature sans plus de secousses qu'une barque au fil de l'eau ... Je suspendais à tous ces arbres mes cantiques journaliers'), 549 ('Ces beaux lieux où l'humanité se dilate le cœur à chanter le *Miserere* ... des transports qui font monter à la surface tous nos secrets et dont la cadence seule attendrit'), 551 ('déchirantes cantilènes d'exilés'), 554 ('l'Amour, l'Honneur et la Nature. Beaux noms et qui suffisent à mettre dans toute âme une musique jaillissante'), 557 ('Une atmosphère enveloppe certains êtres ... La présence de ces personnes rares équivaut à de la musique'), 558 ('Qu'importe si le rossignol chante sur un arbre étranger! C'est en moi que sa chanson, qui montait vers le grand ciel froid, a pénétré pour jusqu'à ma mort').

27 Barrès's chief guide to the psychology, history, and literature of music in the mediaeval monastery was Dom Pastourel, with whom he talked and

corresponded, between 1905 and 1907, on the subject of the biography he proposed to write of Saint Odilon, the eleventh-century monk who, by his cultivation of the 'aesthetic' way to God, was very close to Barrès's own preoccupations during the first decade of the twentieth century. Dom Pastourel pointed out in particular the analogies and distinctions to be made between the monastic 'usage des psaumes,' Pascal's regular meditation of Psalm 118, and the Wagnerian music and theory which had earlier impressed Barrès deeply. He also provided Barrès with a host of references, notably in Migne's *Dictionnaire de Mystique Chrétienne* (*Œuvre* XIX 12). *Mes Cahiers, Œuvre* XV 184–95, 198–201, 211–13, 234, 273, 393, record the conversations and subsequent reflexions on the topics raised, and his further reading, in A. Chide, *L'Idée de rythme* (Digne: Chaspoul 1905) and G. Compayré, *L'Éducation intellectuelle et morale* (Paris: Delaplane 1908). Cf. A. Bazaillas, *Musique et inconscience* (Paris: Alcan 1908) (*Œuvre* XVI 2); H. Collet, *Le Mysticisme musical espagnol* (Paris: Alcan 1913) (XVII 343); and J. Combarieu, *La Musique et la magie* (Paris: Picard 1909) [XVI 379], which examines music 'in the service of religion' and 'in political life,' the 'consequences and survivals in modern society of primitive musical magic,' the 'originally magic character of psalms,' 'music and incantation'; and which contains the Chinese story on which 'La Musique de perdition,' in *Le Mystère en pleine lumière*, is based.

28 *Mes Cahiers, Œuvre* XV 186: 'Panthéisme. Je l'ai senti dans la musique.' *Œuvre* XVIII 14: '*Wagner*. – C'est un de ces hauts sommets où courent les bacchantes. J'ai vu Bayreuth, j'en ai rapporté l'impression d'un monde de déments et de vicieux. Cela manque de pureté. C'est tout l'être qu'il ébranle, il ne choisit pas, il ne décante pas.' XX 89: 'La danse est un rythme ...Si l'on danse en commun, quelque chose de panthéistique.' XX 165 (notes for Barrès's preface to André Cœuroy, *Musique et littérature*, Paris: Bloud et Gay 1923): 'La musique n'est-elle pas un des moyens les plus puissants pour rapprocher les âmes de leur patrie originaire? Un chant sublime nous élève dans les régions de la sympathie et nous rapproche du Cœur du Monde! l'expression n'est pas claire, mais comment nommer ce pays de la joie, de la souffrance, du mystère, de la lumière, où soudain une force inconnue se met à nous dicter ce que nous ignorions savoir. La musique fait monter à la surface de notre conscience de profondes mélodies que nous sentons bien n'être qu'une note du concert universel.' Cf. Compayvé, *cit. Œuvre* XV 215: '*Action physique de la musique* ... Elle n'enseigne pas telle ou telle catégorie de la vertu, comme fait une leçon de morale ou un sermon. Elle agit plutôt en remuant le fonds commun à toutes les vertus, la force vive de l'âme. "Cette action, a dit Pécaut, est à la fois physiologique et psychologique, en sorte qu'elle touche et ébranle l'être à cette profondeur vague et mystérieuse où la vie physique et la vie morale ont leurs racines communes."' Cf. also A. Bazaillas, *Musique et inconscience*, 165–6: 'au cours de l'expérience musicale ... Nous voyons peu à peu ce moi se fondre et s'abîmer devant nous ... c'est un repos dans l'inconscient'; and 297–8: 'L'art entendu dans un sens émotionnel, et notamment l'art musical, nous apparaît comme le refuge ou la sauvegarde de la sensibilité profonde.'

CHAPTER TWELVE

13 'Chateaubriand ... Lamartine ... Hugo ... ont servi leurs partis de haut et de loin, mieux que ne firent les plus ambitieux politiciens de l'agitation au jour le jour... Ils font émouvantes les idées. Ils créent un état d'âme ... Ils n'ont pas à se mêler à l'intrigue quotidienne. Ils se prêtent, ils ne se donnent pas.' ['Se prêter, non se donner,' *Le Journal* 10 August 1894]. 'C'est une idée maîtresse de M. Izoulet, que, n'en déplaise aux politiques, le monde est mené par les poètes, car ils éveillent et déterminent les états d'âme d'où naissent les mœurs et les lois. Par une action de tous les instants, les savants modifient notre façon de concevoir le monde, et les poètes notre façon de sentir la vie. Nous nous entendons, n'est-ce pas, sur le mot poète? Il ne s'agit pas de versificateurs. Quelques-uns des plus grands poètes français furent des prosateurs, mais ils avaient l'esprit poétique, c'est-à-dire qu'ils étaient des voyants, des annociateurs, des forces de lumière. Et le premier de ces écrivains sociaux qu'Izoulet a commencé d'étudier ... c'est J.-J. Rousseau, dont l'imagination est un des grands ressorts de la vie européenne depuis plus de cent ans' ('Izoulet au Collège de France,' *Le Journal* 1 January 1898).

36 The word *salut* retains its Catholic associations for Barrès (e.g. *Mes Cahiers, Œuvre* XIX 150 ; XX 5), but the sense he gives it is predominantly secular, e.g. 'Il faut connaître son but, sa voie propre, sa vérité, son devoir' (XIX 123). 'Toujours le problème du salut. Devons-nous être fidèle au personnage de notre imagination ou à notre nature propre? La réponse n'est pas si aisée. Se perfectionner, c'est réaliser sa meilleure imagination. Être fidèle à sa nature, c'est l'accepter. On voit, ici et là, des inconvénients' (XIX 291). Cf. Barrès's earlier secularization of Loyola's Spiritual Exercises and of the Christian rite of pilgrimage, and compare the dictum of 'Mes Mémoires': 'être *un pour moi*' (*Œuvre* XIII 24 *cit.* above, p. 260) with Baudelaire's 'Être un grand homme et un saint *pour soi-même*, voilà l'unique chose importante.' (*Mon Cœur mis à nu, Œuvres complètes,* 1289) and 'L'homme de génie veut être un, donc solitaire. La gloire, c'est de rester *un*, et se prostituer d'une manière particulière' (*ibid.*, 1294).

39 The counterpart in nature of the mimetic aspect of this method, together with Nietzsche's comment on the 'problem of the actor' ('Avant d'avoir "pensé" il faut déjà avoir "imaginé"' [*Œuvre* XIV 83, 418]) had intrigued Barrès for years. *See* his reference to 'mon papillon': *Mes Cahiers, Œuvre* XIII 108, 210, 388; XIV 83, 418; XIX 230; and XIII 340: 'En face d'un paysage, impossibilité de le saisir, vide. Faute de méthode. Analyser ses motifs décoratifs. Comprendre comment j'ai réagi. Ma chanson spontanée. Mon papillon; mimétisme. De quelle pensée humaine est-il chargé ...' Barrès's sense of identification with certain landscapes appears to owe something also to Bergson. In 1907, after reading, or dipping into 'Introduction à la métaphysique' [*Œuvre* XV 214], he noted a personal experience of what Bergson had called 'cette espèce de sympathie intellectuelle par laquelle on se transporte à l'intérieur d'un objet pour coïncider avec ce qu'il a d'unique et par conséquent d'inexprimable' (*Revue de métaphysique et de morale* January 1903, 3 published with

some modifications in H. Bergson, *La Pensée et le mouvant* [Paris: PUF 1962] 181): 'Chaque année en Auvergne je pense à cette terre en panthéiste; je m'y abandonne; je vais au centre d'elle; sa pierre noire, ses noyers, sa chaîne des Dômes ... de tout cela surgit Pascal. La figure humaine sanctifie ce paysage où je me perdais ... C'est une opération de sympathie intellectuelle (Bergson, *Introduction à la Métaphysique*). De Pascal, je passe à Saint Odilon. Je coïncide de mieux en mieux avec ce pays.'

BIBLIOGRAPHY

LIST OF WORKS CITED

BOOKS AND MANUSCRIPTS BY BARRÈS

L'Œuvre de Maurice Barrès (with notes by Philippe Barrès and prefaces by various hands) 20 volumes. Paris: Au Club de l'Honnête Homme 1965–8 [*Œuvre*]

Réponse ... au Discours de Réception de M. Jean Richepin Paris: Juven 1909

Chronique de la Grande Guerre 14 volumes. 2nd ed., Paris: Plon 1931–9 [*Grande Guerre*]

En Provence Paris: Cadran 1930

Un Homme libre Bibliothèque Nationale. Manuscrits, Nouvelles Acquisitions Françaises, no. 11728

Les Amitiés françaises Bibliothèque Nationale. Manuscrits, Nouvelles Acquisitions Françaises, no. 22967

La Colline inspirée (critical edition by Joseph Barbier) Nancy: Berger-Levrault 1962

PREFACES BY BARRÈS

Beaubourg, M. *Contes pour les assassins* Paris: Perrin 1890

Beyle, H. *Correspondance de Stendhal 1800–1842* Paris: C. Bosse 1908

Coeuroy, A. *Musique et littérature* Paris: Bloud et Gay 1923

Madelin, L. *Croquis lorrains* Paris: Berger-Levrault 1907

Meunier, G. *En lisant l'histoire de Jeanne d'Arc* Paris: Delagrave 1913

Nousanne, H. de *Des Faits, des hommes, des idées* Paris: Plon-Nourrit 1907

Oliphant, Mrs *La Ville enchantée* (translated by Henri Bremond) Paris: Émile-Paul 1911

Perrout, R. *Autour de mon clocher* Paris, Épinal: Huguenin, 1905

– *Les Images d'Épinal* Paris: Ollendorf 1912

BOOKS AND ARTICLES ABOUT BARRÈS

Actes du Colloque Maurice Barrès organisé par la Faculté des lettres et des sciences humaines de l'Université de Nancy (Nancy, 22–5 octobre 1962) Nancy: Annales de l'Est, Mémoire no. 24, 1963

Audibert 'Idéologies et paysages passionnés' *La Table Ronde* March 1957

Blanche, J.-E. 'Maurice Barrès' *Le Gaulois* Paris 22 February 1913

Bremond, H. *Maurice Barrès: vingt-cinq années de vie littéraire; pages choisies* Paris: Bloud 1911

Byvanck, W.G.-C. *Un Hollandais à Paris en 1891* Paris: Didier 1892, 277

Caplain, J. *Maurice Barrès, ami des jeunes* Paris: Henry Goulet 1924

Carrassus, E. *Barrès et sa fortune littéraire* Paris: Ducros 1970

Clouard, H. *La Cocarde de Barrès* Paris: Nouvelle Librairie Nationale 1910

– *Histoire de la littérature française du Symbolisme à nos jours* Paris: Albin Michel 1947 I 315–23

Cocteau, J. *Le Rappel à l'ordre* Paris: Stock 1926

Domenach, J.-M. *Barrès par lui-même* Paris: Aux Éditions du Seuil 1954

Dufay, P. 'Maurice Barrès au Quartier Latin' *Mercure de France* 1 January 1924

Duhourcau, F. *La Voix intérieure de Maurice Barrès* Paris: Grasset 1929

Empaytaz, F., ed. *Chroniques Barrésiennes* Paris: Le Rouge et le Noir 1929
Fernandez, R. *Barrès* Paris: Éditions du Livre Moderne 1943
Franck, H. *La Danse devant l'arche* Paris: Gallimard 1921
Frandon, I.-M. *'Assassins' et 'Danseurs mystiques' dans 'Une Enquête aux pays du Levant' de Maurice Barrès* Geneva: Droz 1954
– *L'Orient de Maurice Barrès* Geneva: Droz 1952
Garcin, P. 'Les Deux Barrès' *Critique* Paris, December 1961
– 'Barrès,' *Dizionario critico della letteratura francese* Turin: Unione Eipografico torinese 1972
Gillouin, R. *Maurice Barrès* Paris: E. Sansot 1907
Godfrin, J. *Barrès mystique* Neuchâtel: À la Baconnière 1962
Huret, J. *Enquête sur l'évolution littéraire* Paris: Charpentier 1891
Jary, J. *Essai sur l'art et la psychologie de Maurice Barrès* Paris: E. Paul 1912
Jeanès, J.E.S. *D'Après nature* Besançon: Granvelle 1946
Lalou, R. *Maurice Barrès* Paris: Hachette 1950
Launay, R. 'Maurice Barrès à "L'Action Française"' *Mercure de France* Paris 1 February 1924
Lucas-Dubreton, J. 'Notes sur Maurice Barrès' *La Table Ronde* Paris, March 1957
Madaule, J. *Le Nationalisme de Maurice Barrès* Marseille: Sagittaire 1943
Massis, H. *Barrés et nous* [suivi d'une correspondance inédite, 1906–23] Paris: Plon 1962
– *Jugements* I Paris: Plon 1923
– *La Pensée de Maurice Barrès* Paris: Mercure de France 1909
Maurras, C. *Pour un jeune Français* Paris: Amiot-Dumont 1949, 234
– *Réponse à André Gide* Paris: Éditions de la seule France 1948
McShine, J.O. *Maurice Barrès: journaliste* Port-au-Prince: Presses Nationales de Haïti 1966
Mercanton, J. *Poésie et religion dans l'œuvre de Maurice Barrès* Lausanne: Rouge, Geneva: Droz 1940
Miéville, H.-L. *La Pensée de Maurice Barrès* Paris: Éditions de la Nouvelle Revue Critique 1934

Mondor, H. *Maurice Barrès avant le Quartier Latin* Paris: Ventadour 1956
Moreau, P. *Maurice Barrès* Paris: Sagittaire 1946
– *Barrès* Paris: Desclée de Brouwer 1970
– 'Barrès devant son dernier portrait' *La Table Ronde* Paris, March 1957
Pica, V. *Letteratura d'eccezione* Milan: Baldini 1898
Pottecher, M. 'Maurice Barrès' *Le Monde Français* Paris, October 1947
Rachilde *Portraits d'hommes* Paris: Mercure de France 1930 41–2
Ross, F.M. *Goethe in modern France, with special reference to Maurice Barrès, Paul Bourget and André Gide* Urbana: University of Illinois 1937
Sartre, J.-P. *Situations* Paris: Gallimard 1948, II 209–10
Sternhell, Z. *Maurice Barrès et le nationalisme français* Paris: Armand Colin 1972
Tharaud, J. and J. *Mes années chez Barrès* Paris: Plon 1928
– *Pour les fidèles de Barrès* Paris: Plon 1944
– *Le Roman d'Aïssé* Paris: SEIF 1946
– *Sons nouveaux: Maurice Barrès* Paris: Conferencia 1933
Thibaudet, A. *La Vie de Maurice Barrès* Paris: Gallimard 1921
Vettard, C. 'Jules Soury et Maurice Barrès' *Mercure de France* Paris 15 November 1924
Zarach, A. *Bibliographie barrésienne* Paris: PUF 1951

A comprehensive, accurate, and well-indexed account of some 300 books, prefaces, and *pages choisies* and of more than two thousand articles by Barrès, listing also many of his letters and *inédits* and adding a complete record of his speeches and proposals to Parliament; a final section numbers 1737 titles of theses, books, and articles about Barrès.

This work quite supersedes the previously published bibliographical studies of Barrès's life and work, but should be supplemented by the bibliographies appended to I.-M. Frandon, 'Barrès' and *L'Orient de Maurice Barrès cit.* above and E. Carassus, *Barrès et sa fortune littéraire*. *See* also the catalogue of the exhibition in 1962 at the Bibliothèque Nationale: *Maurice Barrès, 1862–1923*.

NB Two articles I have cited do not appear in *Bibliographie barrésienne*, namely:
'Les Grandes figures de France' *La Grande Revue de Paris et de St-Pétersbourg* 15 September 1888
'Le livre seule richesse normale essentielle' *Le Livre à travers les âges. Numéro unique résumant l'Histoire du Livre depuis les Origines de l'Écriture*, publié sous la direction de Charles Mendel par Georges Brunel, Paris: Charles Mendel 1894

CORRESPONDENCE

Barrès, M. [S. de Guaita and L. Sorg] *Le Départ pour la vie* Paris: Plon 1961
Barrès, M. and Maurras, C. *La République ou le Roi* Paris: Plon 1970
Barrès, M. Letter to H. Bahr, *cit.* Pica, V. *Letteratura d'eccezione* Milan: Baldini 1898
Barrès, M. Letter to P. Campaux, *cit. La Revue hebdomadaire* Paris 8 January 1927
Barrès, M. Letter to R. Launay, *cit.* 'Maurice Barrès à "L'Action Française"' *Mercure de France* Paris, 1 February 1924
Barrès, M. Letter to H. Vaugeois, *cit.* J. Caplain *Maurice Barrès, ami des jeunes* Paris: Henry Goulet 1924
Barrès, M. Letter to É. Zola, *cit. Mercure de France* Paris 15 October 1931, 459–61
Massis, H. *Barrès et nous* [suivi d'une correspondance inédite, 1906–23] Paris: Plon 1962

SOURCES AND RELATED WORKS

Balzac, H. de *La Comédie humaine* Paris: Pléiade 1965
Baudelaire, C. *Œuvres complètes* Paris: Pleíade 1961
Bazaillas, A. *Musique et inconscience* Paris: Alcan 1908
Bergson, H. 'Introduction à la métaphysique' *Revue de métaphysique et de morale* Paris, January 1903

– *La Pensée et le mouvant* Paris: PUF 1962
Blondel, M. *Histoire et dogme* La Chapelle-Montligeon: Imprimerie-Librairie de Montligeon 1904
Bourget, P. *Le Disciple* Paris: Plon 1901
– *Essais de psychologie contemporaine* Paris: Plon 1901
Boutroux, E. *Science et religion dans la philosophie contemporaine* Paris: Flammarion 1908
Bremond, H. *L'Enfant et la vie* Paris: Victor Retaux 1902
Chateaubriand, F.-R. de *Le Génie du Christianisme* Paris: Lefèvre, Ladvocat 1830
Chevrillon, A. *Nouvelles études anglaises* Paris: Hachette 1910
Chide, A. *L'Idée de rythme* Digne: Chaspoul 1905
Collet, H. *Le Mysticisme musical espagnol au* XVIe *siècle* Paris: Alcan 1913
Combarieu, J. *La Musique et la magie* Paris: A. Picard et fils 1909
Compayré, G. *L'Éducation intellectuelle et morale* Paris: P. Delaplane 1908
Comte, A. *Système de politique positive* Paris: Dunoud 1880–3
Cyon, E. de *Dieu et Science* Paris: Alcan 1909
Darmsteter, J. *Essais de littérature anglaise* Paris: Delagrave 1883
Demolins, E. *L'Éducation nouvelle: L'École des Roches* Paris: Firmin-Didot 1898
Drumont, E. *Les Fêtes nationales à Paris* Paris: Ludovic Baschet 1879
Durkheim, E. *Les Formes élémentaires de la vie religieuse* Paris: Alcan 1912
Fichte, J.G. *Doctrine de la science de la connaissance* Paris: Ladrange 1843
Gide, A. *Si le grain ne meurt, Œuvres complètes* Paris: Nouvelle Revue Française, x 1936
Guaita, S. de *Essais de sciences maudites.* I *Au seuil du mystère* Paris: Carré 1886
Guyau, J.-M. *Esquisse d'une morale sans obligation ni sanction* Paris: Alcan 1885
– *L'Irréligion de l'avenir* Paris: Alcan 1887
Hegel, J.F.G. *Cours d'esthétique* (trs. Ch. Bénard) Paris: Joubert 1843
Hébert, M. *Le Pragmatisme* Paris: Librairie critique 1909

Izoulet, J. *L'Âme française et les universités nouvelles selon l'esprit de la Révolution* Paris: Colin 1892
– *La Cité moderne* Paris: Alcan 1894
Lange, F. *Histoire du matérialisme* Paris: Reinwald 1877–9
Le Bon, G. *Psychologie de l'éducation* Paris: Flammarion 1902
– *Psychologie des foules.* Paris: Alcan 1895 and 40th ed., Paris: Alcan 1937
Ménard, L. *Rêveries d'un païen mystique* Paris: Durel 1909
Mentré, F. *Cournot et la renaissance du probabilisme* Paris: Rivière 1908
Michelet, J. *L'Étudiant* Paris: Calmann Lévy 1899
– *Le Peuple* Paris: Calmann Lévy 1877
– *Tableau de la France. Œuvres complètes. Histoire de France* Paris: Flammarion 1893
Migne, L'Abbé J.-P. *Dictionnaire de mystique chrétienne* Paris: J.-P. Migne 1858
Moore, G. *Confessions of a young man* London: Heinemann 1917
Moréas, J. *Le Symboliste* Paris 7 October 1886
Pascal, B. *Pensées et opuscules* (ed. Brunschvicq) Paris: Hachette 1909
Renan, E. *L'Avenir de la science* Paris: Calmann Lévy 1890
– *Dialogues et fragments philosophiques* Paris: Calmann Lévy 1876
– *Drames philosophiques* Paris: Calmann Lévy 1888
– *Feuilles détachées* Paris: Calmann Lévy 1892
– *Questions contemporaines* Paris: Michel Lévy Frères 1868
Sand, G. *Impressions et souvenirs* Paris: Michel Lévy Frères 1873
Soury, J. *Bréviaire de l'histoire du matérialisme* Paris: Charpentier 1881
– *Les Fonctions du cerveau* Paris: Bureaux du Progrès Médical 1891
– *Science et religion* Paris: L'Action Française 1901
Stendhal *Histoire de la peinture en Italie* Paris: Michel Lévy Frères 1854
Taine, H. *Essais de critique et d'histoire* Paris: Hachette 1874
– *Histoire de la littérature anglaise* Paris: Hachette 1863
– *Les Origines de la France contemporaine. Le Régime moderne* Paris: Hachette 1926

– *Les Philosophes classiques du* XIXe *siècle en France* Paris: Hachette 1876
Wilson, R.A. *The pre-war biographies of Romain Rolland* Oxford: Humphrey Milford 1939
Wyzewa, T. de *Nos Maîtres* Paris: Perrin 1895
Zola, É. *Le Roman expérimental* Paris: Charpentier 1890

WORKS OF GENERAL INTEREST

Abrams, M.H. *The mirror and the lamp* New York: Norton 1958
Bartlett, F.C. *Political propaganda* Cambridge: CUP 1940
Brett, R.L. *Fancy and imagination* London: Methuen 1969
Chapman, G. *The Third Republic of France. The first phase 1871–1894* London: Macmillan 1962
Décaudin, M. *La Crise des valeurs symbolistes* Toulouse: Privat 1960
Digeon, C. *La Crise allemande de la pensée française (1870–1914)* Paris: PUF 1959
Domenach, J.-M. *La Propagande politique* Paris: PUF 1955
Doob, L.W. *Public opinion and propaganda* London: The Cresset Press 1949
Drever, J. *A dictionary of psychology* London, Penguin Books 1952
Frye, N. *Anatomy of criticism* Princeton: Princeton University Press 1957
Germain, A. *Les Croisés modernes de Bloy à Bernanos* Paris: Nouvelles Éditions Latines 1958
Gibson, R. *Modern French poets on poetry* Cambridge: CUP 1961
Gilman, M. *The Idea of poetry in France from Houdar de la Motte to Baudelaire* Cambridge, Mass.: Harvard University Press 1958
Guillén, C. *Literature as system* Princeton: Princeton University Press 1971
Gusdorf, G. 'Mythe et philosophie' *La Revue de métaphysique et de morale* Paris, April–June 1951
Hoffmann, S., ed. *France: change and tradition* London: Victor Gollancz 1963
Lalande, A. *Vocabulaire technique et critique de la philosophie* Paris: Alcan 1932

Leakey, F.W. 'Baudelaire's metaphor in *Les Fleurs du Mal:* an essay in interpretation' PHD thesis (typescript) University of London 1951
Lehmann, A.G. *The Symbolist aesthetic in France 1885–1895* Oxford: Blackwell 1950
McKellar, P. *Imagination and thinking: a psychological analysis* London: Cohen and West 1957
Merleau-Ponty, M. *Humanisme et terreur* Paris: Gallimard 1947
Michaud, G. *La Doctrine symboliste* Paris: Nizet 1947
– *Message poétique du Symbolisme* Paris: Nizet 1947
Morris, C. *Signs, language and behaviour* New York: Prentice-Hall 1946
Murdoch, I. *Sartre, Romantic rationalist* London: Bowes and Bowes 1953
Peyre, H. *Connaissance de Baudelaire* Paris: José Corti 1951
Raimond, M. *La Crise du roman* Paris: José Corti 1966
Roudiez, L.S. *'Maurras jusqu'à "L'Action Française".'* Paris. André Bonne 1957
Ruyer, R. 'Perception, croyance, monde symbolique' *Revue de métaphysique et de morale* Paris, January–March 1962
Saint-Exupéry, A. de *Œuvres* Paris: Pléiade 1953
Sartre, J.-P. *L'Imagination* Paris: PUF 1950
– *Psychology of imagination* London: Rider 1950
Thibaudet, A. *La République des professeurs* Paris: Grasset 1928
Valéry, P. *Pièces sur l'art* Paris: Gallimard 1936
Wellek, R. and A. Warren *Theory of literature* London: Jonathan Cape 1961 and Peregrine Books 1963

INDEX

abstraction xi, 8–10, 12–14, 24, 60, 62, 83–4, 129, 132, 134, 203, 245, 256, 283; in education 201, 206–9, 211–13, 220, 222; in politics 9, 11, 56, 124, 127–9, 137, 154, 282; 'unconscious' 8, 11, 26, 28, 31–2, 213–14
absurd 67, 74, 94, 97, 108, 116, 215–16, 256–8
Ackermann, L. 57
Action Française 68–70, 111–12, 124, 133, 137, 146–7, 153, 158, 165, 173n, 176, 179, 259, 281
Adam, P. 64, 111n
aestheticism 75, 242–3, 252, 254, 263, 269–70
Aigues-Mortes 11n, 39–40, 51, 172, 174, 177n, 191, 259
Alexander the Great 282–3
allegory 16, 35, 39, 40, 46, 50, 220–1, 233n
Alsace 11, 77, 95n, 128, 132, 163, 165, 167n, 181, 184–7, 192, 199, 216, 217, 231, 252, 257–60, 282
America 138n, 145, 167n, 280
Amiel, H.-F. 31, 55, 89n, 96, 280
analogy 39, 63–4, 93n, 95, 96n, 97, 100, 190, 224, 231, 237, 277
anarchism 48, 52, 67, 138, 201
anarchy 106, 112, 142, 181, 256
Anaxagora 254n
ancestors, cult of x, 52–4, 62–5, 139, 166n, 170, 180, 196, 213, 216–17, 224, 258–9, 262, 264, 280; and religion 70, 74–5, 82, 97, 280
animality 27, 37–9, 42, 48, 157, 189, 200, 225–8, 234, 236
Antigone 151, 282
anti-semitism *see* Jews
Antoine 151n
architecture 25, 160, 161, 169, 174, 198
Ariosto, L. 218–19
Aristophanes 151
Armenia 146, 172
art 9, 233–4, 259; effects of 45, 169, 227, 282; and education 47, 219–21; and ideas 243, 245, 248; and life 250, 259; and morals 169, 268–75; and nationalism 125–6, 147, 179–80, 183, 227, 256, 259, 268–70; and reality 150–1, 271–3; and religion 75–6, 82–4, 99, 112–17, 267–73, 281; and science 105, 233, 244, 272; and the unconscious 187, 253, 267, 273–4, 284; the visual arts 8n, 25n, 160, 220–1, 248; *see also* architecture, iconography, painting, sculpture
Asia 12–13, 39, 109, 169, 172–3,

187, 225, 226, 230, 231, 263, 268, 283
association: psychological x, 57–64, 126, 213, 221, 266–7, 281; sociological 63–5, 126
Atlantic Union 167n
Auvergne 180–1, 285
Auxerre, and the sibyl 86–7, 108, 113, 196–7, 231, 260

Baillard, L. 6, 106, 196, 232n
Balzac, H. de 20, 21, 85–6, 147, 244, 279
Barrès, C.A. (Maurice Barrès's mother) 52–4, 71, 264–5
Barrès, J.-B. (Maurice Barrès's grandfather) 147
Barrès, J.-A. (Maurice Barrès's father) 53–4, 71, 264–5
Barrès, P. (Maurice Barrès's son) 71, 179, 211, 217–19
Bashkirtseff, M. 5, 11n, 31, 37, 138, 171, 194n
Baudelaire, C. 5, 24, 25, 28, 33n, 37, 139, 243n, 259n; and 'bohemianism' 31, 194n–5; and the 'constructive' imagination 256, 274n; and 'la gloire ... de rester *un*' 285; poetics of 112, 117, 245, 254
Bazaillas, A. 284
Bergson, H. 101–2, 117, 199, 285–6
Bernadette Soubirous, Saint 72, 196
Bernard, C. 61n, 102, 112, 245
Berthelot, A. 59n, 64n
Berthelot, P. 82n
Bertrand, L. 242
Bible 137, 244
Bismarck, O. von 156
Bloch, G. 181
Blondel, M. 86, 101, 103n, 104, 199
Blum, L. 137
bohemianism 31, 171, 194n–5, 237
Bolshevism 227
Bonapartism *see* Napoleon Bonaparte
Borel, P. 242
Bossuet 3
Boulanger, G., General: Boulangism xi, 6, 15, 19, 32–3, 44, 46, 48–50, 67, 131, 140, 144–5, 148, 159, 165, 172, 211, 248, 250–1
Bourget, P. 31, 55, 69, 242, 243n, 246, 249, 261, 279
Boutroux, E. 104, 114–15, 243
Bremond, Abbé H. 84, 109, 223
Brazza, P.S. 161
Brisson, H. 127
Brittany 77, 97–8, 206
Burdeau, A. 17, 81, 207n
Burke, E. 55, 85–6
Burnouf, E. 81, 243
Byron, Lord 59, 248

Cabanis, G. 23
Caesarism 45, 49–50, 52, 68, 141, 142n, 147–50, 170, 210–11, 281
capitalism 127, 199–202
Carlyle, T. 83, 136
Catherine of Siena, Saint 22
Catholicism *see* Roman Catholic Church
Celts 108, 153
centralization *see* decentralization, Paris
ceremonial xii, 21, 164–8, 172; drama as 152; and landscape 231; Napoleon and 147n; patriotic 135n, 144, 164–5, 169–70, 177–8, 182–3, 184; purificatory 200; religious 71, 82, 113–16, 164–6, 168, 228–9, 280; sociology of 283; *see also* pilgrimage, Roman Catholic Church
Chamber of Deputies *see* Parliament
Chambige, H. 279
Charmes-sur-Moselle 106, 151, 161, 182, 185, 191, 260, 262, 281
Chateaubriand, F.-R. de 36, 75, 215n, 248, 265n, 270, 280, 285
Chesterton, G.K. 84
Chevrillon, A. 84, 233n
Chide, A. 284
Christ 35, 74n, 101, 109, 111, 135n, 282, 283; *Imitation of Christ* 246–7

Christianity 38, 71–2, 84, 86–96, 133, 137n, 215, 265–75, 280, 285; 'aesthetic' 75–6, 269–75, 281, 284; forms of worship 43, 75–6, 82, 109, 112–16, 164–6, 225–30, 280, 283–4, 285; and nationalism 15, 17, 71–2, 87–92, 98, 104–5, 110–12, 150, 152–4, 265–9, 280, 283; and paganism 18, 44, 70, 91, 102, 104, 108–10, 113, 116, 131, 133, 138, 153–4, 165–6, 182, 186, 191, 196–9, 228–30, 270, 280; and science 70–1, 75–6, 82–3, 87–9, 92, 94–100, 102–7, 110, 112–13, 225, 228–330, 266–9, 272; and socialism 52, 70, 282; *see also* God, Protestantism, Roman Catholic Church
classicism 63, 95n, 170, 241, 246, 255, 268
Claude *see* Gelée, Claude
Clemenceau, G. 142, 145–6
La Cocarde 45, 59, 136, 138–40, 205, 279
Cocteau, J. 272n
Cœuroy, A. 284
cognition 7–8, 58–62, 75–6, 85–7, 100, 113, 207–8, 213n, 245, 250, 278–9, 281
Coleridge, S.T. 248
collectivity, collectivism *see* groups, socialism
Collet, H. 284
'la colline inspirée' *see* Sion-Vaudémont
Combarieu, J. 284
Compayré, J. 284
composition of place, *compositio loci* *see* Loyola, Saint Ignatius de
Corneille, P. 150n, 216n, 257
Corot, J.-B. 125
corporativism 72, 77, 200, 203
cosmopolitanism 11n, 31, 67, 74–5, 138, 139, 171, 173n, 182, 188, 199, 281
Cournot, A.-A. 100
crowd 33, 48, 52, 64n, 127, 129, 144, 165–6, 169, 178, 273
'crystallization' 28–9, 112, 144n, 148–9, 218
'culte des morts' *see* ancestors
'culte du moi' *see* egotism
Cyon, E. de 99–100

dadaïsm 227
Dante 5, 43, 96n, 232n, 234, 246
Danton 9n, 128
Darmesteter, A. 84
Darwin, C. 93–4
Daudet, L. 3n
death 52–3, 71, 97, 116, 157, 166, 186
Debussy, C. 226n
decentralization 46–8, 209–14, 279–80
De Gaulle, C. 159
Delacroix, E. 225, 254
Demange, C. 71, 116, 262
democracy 5, 6, 32, 40, 42–3, 48, 50, 52n, 64, 141, 153, 155, 158, 184, 199, 200, 201, 281, 282
Demolins, E. 212n, 214n
Déroulède, P. 3–4, 141, 142–5, 147n, 164
Descartes, R. 40, 95
determinism 33, 53–4, 61–3, 66, 77, 137, 213–14, 221–2, 265, 281
dialogue 15, 50, 73, 114, 123, 181
dilettantism xi, 22, 29, 32–3, 44, 46, 82, 214
direction *see* propaganda
Disraeli, B. 278
Djelal-Eddin Roumi *see* Jalal Ad-Din Rumi
Domremy 152–3, 179, 183–4, 191, 216, 223
drama 151–2, 194, 198–9, 264
Dreyfus, Alfred; Dreyfus Affair ix, xi, 82, 251; aftermath of 77, 98, 111, 152, 179, 211, 251–2; and nationalism 15, 49–50, 52, 60–3, 67, 69, 73–4, 77, 126, 173, 198–9, 214, 278; and racialism 65, 77; as a symbol 52

Drumont, E. 283
Duparc, H. 225n
Durkheim, E. 89–90, 102, 103, 165, 199, 283

education: *collège* and *lycée* 38, 40, 47–8, 77, 112, 204–12; elementary 77–8, 99, 153, 198–201, 211, 224, 234–6; German 47, 210, 236; and heredity 65, 77–8, 213, 215–16; and hero-worship 140–1, 209–10, 224n; and individualism 78, 224; and instinct 38, 40–3; musical 223–4, 234–6, 284; nationalist 68–9, 72, 77–8, 122, 137n, 140–1, 178, 198–201, 203–20, 224, 259; philosophical 47–8, 60–2, 207–10, 212; and poetry 247–8, 254; and propaganda 121–2, 204; and reason 48, 205–8, 213n, 216–17; and reflexes 63, 213; and regions 77–8, 210–14, 217; and religion 87–90, 105, 153; and science 202–3; and *scientisme* 105; and the state 87, 99, 105, 204–10; and tradition 77–8, 90, 224; and the unconscious mind 213, 214, 236; visual 220–3; *see also* university
egotism 5, 6, 15–54; and commitment 16, 30, 32, 40–54, 77–8, 111, 191, 256, 263; and cosmopolitanism 31, 138, 171–3, 182; and dilettantism 22, 29, 32–3, 44, 46, 214; and education 19, 34–5, 38, 43, 46–8, 205, 213–14, 220–1, 247–9; expression of 16, 18–54, 243–9; and *genius loci* 177, 259; and German metaphysics 20, 27, 29n, 36, 55n, 157n, 186–7, 194, 208–10; and hero-worship 19, 25, 52, 136–7, 154; and instinct 32, 34, 36–43, 48, 194; and madness 15–17, 19, 129; and religion 15–17, 19–20, 26–7, 30, 50–4, 66–8, 71, 102, 157n, 167–73, 177, 285; techniques of 19–45, 77, 137–9, 154, 167, 170–3, 177, 213–14, 221, 259; and women 27–9, 33–4, 36–43, 48
Egypt 113, 173, 197n, 264
Emerson, R.W. 83, 136, 145
empiricism *see also* experience 88, 215
energy, and direction 124n, 204; human 139, 167–8; of the masses 33, 200; multiplication of 22, 26, 33, 163, 167–8, 170–1, 176, 183, 208–9; national 33, 40–9, 140, 148, 170, 178, 188, 203, 204; organization of 256; personal 18, 55n, 67, 183, 208–9
England 83–6, 167n, 176, 256
enthusiasm *see also* energy; mechanics of 22, 163, 167–8, 170–1, 176, 232; and order 230; and privilege 48; religious 91, 106, 108, 109, 116, 191, 194, 217; and science 114n, 201–3, 230
Épinal cartoons *see* imagery, popular
epistemology, *see also* cognition xi, 54, 59–63, 71–2, 75–6, 87, 92, 100, 125, 207–8, 245
exemplar xi, 3–6, 11n, 52, 135, 137, 142–5, 147, 160–1, 168, 203, 259, 263–4
experience, collective 11, 102–4, 165–6, 174, 195, 256–7, 274; individual 71, 87, 88, 91, 138, 205, 223, 249; and reason 87, 89, 106, 262, 267, 272–3; religious 87–91, 98, 102–10, 115–17, 165–6, 195, 270, 272–4; and science 87, 98, 102–6, 174, 274–5
experiment 75, 87–8, 103, 174

fable: and politics 138, 146, 269; and truth 83; *see also* fiction
Fabre, J. 152
fancy, fantasy 6, 11–13, 83, 95n, 106, 108, 151n, 201, 218, 220, 268, 270, 277, 278
Fénelon, Archbishop 86
festival *see* ceremonial

Fichte, J.G. 20, 50n, 55, 83n, 85, 93, 96n, 278–9
fiction, useful 89n, 94–5, 100, 105, 135, 262; *see also* fable, life-lie, novel
Flaubert, G. 112
Fonesgrive, G.-L. 212
Fontanes, L. de 280
formula xii, 37, 110–13, 130–2, 135, 172, 183, 194, 202, 214, 223n, 245, 247–8, 254n, 255, 274, 281; magic 112, 127, 225; political 8n, 78, 110–12, 126–9, 158; religious 71–2, 74, 76, 100, 110–13, 115n, 117, 227, 274
Fourier, C. 35
Fourier, P. 5
France, A. 31, 35, 152, 231n
France réelle, La see realism
François de Sales, Saint 13
Frazer, Sir J. 102, 151, 199
Fustel de Coulanges, N.-D. 55

Gambetta, L., Gambettism 9, 128
garden, *hortus conclusus* 32, 34, 39–40, 43, 63, 139, 171, 219, 229, 260n, 269–70
Gautier, T. 112, 254n
Gelée, Claude 4, 260
genius loci, see landscape
Gerbéviller 165
Germany: and France 143, 157–8, 161–2, 166, 167n, 172, 176, 181–2, 184–8, 195, 219, 231, 259–60, 281–2; and the Rhineland 114n, 131–2, 155–8, 185–7; and Rome 128, 146, 182, 186; and German literature 152, 235–6; occupation of Alsace-Lorraine 91, 128, 184, 192–3; philosophy 20, 27, 29n, 35, 36, 55–6, 58n, 186–7, 207–12, 233, 234–6; universities 47, 54, 56, 210; pangermanic myth 146, 156–8
Gide, A. 16, 102, 194
Gillouin, R. 154, 158
Giorgione 219
Gluck, C.W. 225n
God 75, 81, 96–7, 107, 194, 265; of artists 273; and individual 15, 17, 20–1, 25–7, 101, 116–17, 168, 233n; and nation, race 25; and science 75, 99–101, 103
gods 95n, 169, 174–5, 193; 280; *see also* landscape: *genius loci*
Goebbels, J. 157
Goethe, J.W. von 25n, 55, 95, 114, 116, 117, 147n, 151, 229, 234, 248, 278
Great Britain 83, 167n, 176, 278
Greece 151–2, 173, 174, 176, 178–80, 186, 191, 197n, 235, 254n, 259, 268, 282
Grimm, J. 146, 156–7
groups: control of 166n; formation of 144, 148, 150, 169, 210; and individuals 25–6, 46, 64, 66, 210, 256, 281; as models 25–6, 43, 46, 103, 169, 273; peer group 206; political 14, 142, 144, 251; psychology of 40, 48, 77, 103, 155n, 169, 174, 251, 283; *see also* crowd, corporativism, unanimism
Guaita, S. de 31, 82n, 93, 112, 177, 191, 245
Gusdorf, G. 184

Hartmann, C.R.E. von 64, 102
Hasan 4
Havard de la Montagne, R. 154, 158
Hébert, M. 95–6, 101n, 103n
Hegel, G.F., Hegelianism 25, 29n, 55–6, 96n, 97
Heine, H. 248
Hennebicq, L. 212n
Heredia, J.-M. de 264
hero, hero-worship 136–59, 160–1, 163, 168–70, 174, 178, 180, 202, 209–10, 224n, 225–6, 231, 258, 280; hero and leader 140–3, 145–6, 158, 180, 258; *see also* egotism, intercessors
historicism 55–6, 245

Homer 161
Hugo, V. 4, 48, 61, 85–6, 137n, 144–5, 151, 161, 165, 169–70, 177–8, 197n, 209, 214, 229–30, 232n, 242, 244, 248–50, 259n, 285
humanism 3, 61, 110, 158, 173, 198, 205, 211, 266–7, 279, 282
hypothesis xi, 12, 69, 74, 76, 92–7, 100, 110–12

iconography 8, 10, 51, 135, 160–3, 172, 218, 220–1, 281–2
idealism, philosophical 8, 9n, 20–2, 27–30, 36–7, 54–6, 71–2, 85, 186, 205, 231, 233, 245, 278–9; political 124, 154, 158, 206, 261, 281
ideals 70, 83, 98, 137, 154, 251
image, and abstraction 10, 69, 134, 214, 276–8; exemplary 51, 135, 160–2, 169, 171, 178, 184, 195, 209–10, 214, 216–20, 256–7, 263–4, 281–3; of France 72, 159, 176–203, 205, 214; and historiography 137; and intuition 117; and memory 67, 222, 265, 281; and percept 10, 62, 127, 135, 221, 278, 281; persuasive xii, 11–12, 43, 129, 132–5, 144, 160–3, 165, 168, 172, 203, 214–23, 250, 253, 254n, 256–7, 261–5, 276–7, 281–3; pictorial 134n, 160–2, 217–18, 220–3, 281–3; poetic 5, 96n, 248, 250, 253, 254, 276; and reality 59, 62, 137, 253, 281; religious 76, 115n, 134n, 135, 281–3; of the self 40, 55n; symbolic 10, 59, 115n, 134n, 135, 281–3; *see also* imagery, popular
imagery, popular 144, 160–2, 220–1, 231, 241n, 282
imprinting 216, 222
incantation 112, 226, 232, 284; *see also* music
individualism *see* egotism
instinct 17, 26–8, 30, 32–45, 48, 51, 62, 100, 102, 104, 111, 128, 135n, 139, 144, 153, 188, 194, 195, 196, 228, 248, 254n, 271, 272n
intellect, intellectuals, intellectualism 32, 35–9, 41, 46, 47, 48, 54, 56, 73, 83, 117, 129, 173, 203, 233–4, 248, 254, 255, 266, 271–3, 279, 281
intercessors 24–6, 28–9, 35, 47, 138–40, 153, 174–5, 181, 202, 227, 229
intuition 37, 41, 83–6, 96n, 102, 117, 174, 222, 276
Ireland 146
irony 19, 21, 30–1, 74, 141, 171
Italy 25, 35, 39n, 155, 160, 171–2, 174, 177n, 178, 189, 218–20, 221n, 248, 259, 260
Izoulet, J. 63–5, 83, 101, 123, 124n, 126, 136, 280, 285

Jalal Ad-Din Rumi 2, 225
Jamblicus 86
James, W. 102, 104, 109, 165, 199
Jammes, F. 88
Jansenius 24
Jaurès, J. 3–4, 9, 15, 86, 105, 108, 128, 200, 281
Jews 38, 65, 77, 101, 127
Joan of Arc 4, 72, 87, 108, 132, 135, 150–5, 157–8, 163, 165, 167, 179, 184, 191, 196, 218, 260, 282; *see also* Domremy
John of the Cross, Saint 86

Kant, E., Kantism 54–5, 60–1, 95, 207–8, 212n
Konya dervishes 4, 13, 86, 166–8, 225, 230–1, 235

Laforgue, J. 23
Lamartine, A. de 5, 82n, 86, 137, 232n, 244, 248, 285
landscape 10, 39–40, 125, 129, 135, 152, 159, 177–80, 217–20, 253–4, 257–60, 278, 280, 283; art of 159, 177–80, 203, 214n, 220, 231, 253–4, 257–60, 278, 280; *genius loci* 95n, 106–10, 153–4, 156,

168–82, 184–93, 196, 231, 237, 259, 260n, 264, 267, 280, 285–6; and music 67, 180, 189, 225–9, 237, 254, 258, 285–6; 'properties' 106–7, 190–203, 225, 285; and self-composition 53, 129, 213, 219, 221, 257–8, 261–3, 270, 286; symbolic 10, 11n, 18, 39–40, 106–7, 180, 184, 189, 193, 203, 212–14, 253–4, 261–2, 277, 283, 285–6
Lange, F. 95
language 11n, 37, 60, 83–4, 85, 91–2, 96, 126, 129, 148, 157
Lassalle, F. 35
Latinity, Latin civilization *see* Rome
Lavisse, E. 181
Lebanon *see* Levant
Le Bon, G. 64n, 127n, 212n, 213n
Le Cardonnel, L. 88
Leçon de choses, *see* object lesson
Leconte de Lisle, C. 82n, 242, 255
legend xii, 5, 8n, 39n, 51, 65, 135, 137–9, 142, 144–50, 152, 155–8, 160, 161, 171, 172, 174, 178, 188, 244, 265n
Lehmann, A.G. 247
Leonardo da Vinci 35, 273
Le Play, F. 47, 212n
Levant 108–9, 115–16, 135n, 165–9, 173, 188–9, 193–4, 231, 260n, 268–70
Le Verrier, U.-J.-J. 94–5
life-lie 108, 256, 262, 265n, 272n
limit, limit-situation 8–10, 12–14, 22–6, 32, 50, 73, 76, 89n, 219, 269, 274–5
Littré, E. 67, 81, 163
liturgy *see* Roman Catholic Church
Loisy, A. 100–1
Lorraine: art of 160, 172; Barrès's 'marriage' with 10–11, 129, 252; countryside 21, 24–5, 31–3, 34, 47, 72, 107–8, 124–5, 129, 172, 174, 177, 179–88, 190–3, 200, 202, 212–13, 216–19, 223, 229, 259–60, 262, 280; and France 11, 47–8, 128, 165, 179–88, 208, 212–13, 219; and Germany 128, 132, 167n, 181–8, 212–13, 217, 219; German-occupied 91, 128, 184, 259–60; imaginary 10–11, 174; and industrial development 124, 174, 200; legends of 155, 174; 'mes cimetières lorrains' 174, 212–13, 259; mythical 277; and regionalism 77, 211–12; significance of 10, 111, 125, 129, 179–88, 191–3, 213, 216–17, 223, 255, 260, 262–3, 268; symbolic 10, 106–7, 180–1, 186–8, 192–3, 195, 212–13, 255–6, 261–2, 277–8, 283
Louis IX of France, Saint 110, 148
Lourdes 66–7, 166n, 179, 191, 217, 223, 228–30, 260
love 6, 10, 18, 20, 21, 27–9, 31, 33–4, 36–43, 48, 148, 157, 180, 228, 234, 257–8, 268, 279, 283; *see also* crystallization
Loyola, Saint Ignatius de 4, 12–13, 22–3, 170–1, 177, 186, 221, 259n, 285
Luis de Leon 86
Luther, M. 230
Lyautey, L.-H.-G., Marshal 142n

Madaule, J. 70, 277, 280
Maistre, J. de 55, 97
Malebranche, N. de 84, 222–3
Mallarmé, S. xi, 255n
Marchand, J.-B., Commandant 142, 145
Marx, K., Marxism 35, 50n, 138, 161
Massis, H. 268n, 270, 273
materialism 13, 23, 55, 61, 244–5
Mauriac, F. 70
Maurras, C. 3–4, 52, 64, 68–70, 88–9, 111, 146–8, 176, 261–2, 277
Mead, G.M. 280–1
Méhul, E. 225n
Ménard, L. 81–3, 89n, 93n, 109, 111n, 177, 243, 282
metaphor ix, 132, 135, 174, 186, 190, 191, 203, 212, 214, 277, 280

Metz 135n, 162n, 165, 184, 259–60, 264
Michelangelo 22–3, 26, 117
Michelet, J. 12, 38, 61, 66n, 68n, 137, 151n, 162, 177, 207n, 208n, 221, 222, 244, 271–2, 278, 283
Midi, le 181–2, 200, 206; *see also* Provence
Mieckiewicz, A. 136
Migne, Abbé 86, 284
mimesis 263, 285
Mirabeau, H.-G., Marquis de 3, 9n, 128
Mistral, F. 3–4, 47, 73, 163, 210, 221, 259n
Molière 245–6
monarchism *see Action Française*
Montégut, E. 283
Moore, G. 16
Moréas, J. 55, 245
Moreau, G. 36
Morès, Marquis de 142, 145
Moselle 124, 174, 178, 180, 185, 213, 214n, 222, 259, 260n, 262
Mozart, W.A. 225n, 269, 273
Mun, A., Comte de 200n
music xii, 9, 114, 130–1, 205, 219, 237, 274–5; in education 219–20, 223–4, 234–6, 284; and emotion 9, 187, 223–7, 251, 283; and government 225, 227, 251, 284; and landscape 67, 180, 225–9, 235–7, 253–4, 260n, 283; and literature 9, 130–1, 219, 224–7, 230–7, 252–4, 260n, 269–75, 277, 283; and magic 225–6, 232, 284; and the mechanics of persuasion xii, 165–6, 168, 225, 230, 232–3, 235–7, 251, 284; and mysticism 227–8, 231, 234–5, 284; and politics 7, 9, 78, 165, 227, 284; and religion 6, 9, 68, 78, 82, 113–14, 168, 181, 225–30, 269–75, 283–4; *see also* science
mysticism 22, 53, 71, 86, 109, 116, 127, 181, 193, 227–8, 230, 235, 264–5, 270, 275
myth ix, xii, 6, 11n, 84, 88–9, 95n, 116, 138, 146, 151n, 156–7, 159, 184–90, 193, 226, 231, 236, 277

Nancy 17n, 46, 56, 184, 205–7, 212
Napoleon Bonaparte, Bonapartism 4, 34n, 137, 147–50, 156–8, 161, 165, 172, 179, 205, 218, 234
nationalism 15, 30, 43–78, 110, 121–6, 128, 132, 160–7, 172–88, 203, 236, 248–52, 258–9; commitment to 46, 49–54, 181, 248–52, 256–7, 265–6, 271–2; and the cult of heroes 136–59, 168–70, 178, 225; and determinism 33, 52–4, 61–3, 66, 77, 213–14, 221–2, 265, 281; and education 68–9, 72, 77–8, 122, 137n, 140–1, 173, 178, 198–201, 203–24; and legend 137–40, 144–50, 155–60; and the novel 45–9, 210–15, 249–50, 259–60; and poetry 146, 256–7, 259; and political realism 10, 16, 72, 90–1, 124–5, 128, 136, 141, 147, 201, 209, 212–15, 219, 250–1, 277–8, 281; and reason 125, 157, 188, 216–17, 251, 256; and relativism 54–65, 73–8, 125–6; and Roman Catholicism 53, 66–78, 87–92, 98–9, 109–12, 150, 152–5, 182–3, 186, 195, 197, 203, 216–17, 225, 235, 265–6, 268, 271, 280–3; and socialism 3, 45–9, 52n, 157, 279, 281; *see also Action Française*, Caesarism, corporativism, race
nature 85, 174–5, 185, 220, 225–6; cult of 32–3, 39–40, 42, 44, 106, 109–10, 179–80, 229, 251, 258, 280, 283; personification of 11n, 39–40, 42, 51, 135n; protection of 200; and science 229; and technological development 35, 42, 200; *see also* animality, instinct, landscape
Naturalisme 17, 151n, 180, 241, 243, 245, 247, 251, 252, 260n

Newman, Cardinal J.H. 84, 101, 103n, 222–3
Nietzsche, F. 95, 225, 279, 280, 285
nihilism 157, 187, 215, 226, 272n; *see also* absurd
Noailles, Anna, Comtesse de 3–4, 71n, 87, 231
novel xi, 6, 16–17, 22, 28, 36, 45–9, 64, 130–1, 133, 209–15, 242–50, 259–60, 268–75

object, objectivity 11n, 16, 21, 24, 31–2, 34, 37, 41–2, 46, 52, 55n, 73, 96, 103, 125, 130, 137, 148, 174, 180, 212, 218, 279, 285
object lesson xii, 41, 124–6, 130, 135, 142, 174, 179, 180, 211–12, 214, 215, 219
Odilon, Saint 181, 225, 284, 286
order 114n, 116–17, 168–9, 187, 189, 195, 200, 206, 225–6, 229–30, 237, 250, 256, 261–2; and art and literature 116, 259, 272; political 6, 72, 91, 141; and religion 82, 89–91, 100, 108, 116, 272
Orient *see* Asia
Ortega y Gasset, J. 280
Ottilienberg *see* Saint-Odile

paganism 18, 44, 70, 91, 95n, 102, 104–10, 113, 116, 131, 133, 138, 153–4, 165–6, 169, 174–5, 182, 186, 191, 193, 196–9, 228–30, 231, 269–70, 280, 284
painting 5, 9, 35, 125, 160, 162n, 219–20, 243n, 252–4
Panama Scandal xi, 15, 46, 48–9, 67, 200, 251
pantheism 181, 197n, 225, 227, 229, 284, 285
Paris: ceremonial in 144, 164–5, 169–70, 177–8; the crowd in 144, 169–70, 178; Latin Quarter 27, 47, 85, 169–70; literary xi, 16, 18, 19–21, 27, 44–9, 57, 171, 199, 227, 231, 241–2, 245, 274, 279; political 19, 45–9, 144, 164, 172, 177–8, 200, 206–7; and provinces 47, 206–7, 212, 227, 279–80; provincials in 19–21, 39, 46–9, 162, 205–7, 209, 279–80; society 18, 26–7, 34, 39, 199, 200, 227, 279
Parliament 3, 6, 7, 15, 16, 33, 45–6, 48–9, 70, 87–92, 99, 127, 131, 141–5, 151n, 152–3, 158, 183, 198, 229, 248–51, 278, 279
Parnasse, Le, Parnassian literature 18, 177, 244, 254n
Pascal, B. 5, 53, 58, 59, 61, 75, 76, 95, 100, 178, 181, 229n, 230, 255, 263–7, 284, 286
Pasteur, L. 95, 161, 202, 266
Pastourel, Dom 227, 283–4
paternalism 51–4, 264
Pau 261–2
Paul, Saint 225
Péguy, C. 111n, 151
Pelletan, E. 244
Perspective, perspectivism, point of view 16–17, 56, 59, 62–3, 73, 76, 77, 125–6, 138, 178, 180, 212, 242, 267–8, 280–1
Phidias 254n
pilgrimage 164, 167–75, 178, 184, 188, 191, 217, 223, 231, 259, 285
Pitts, J.R. 206
Plato 50n, 96n, 151
Plutarch 143
poet, function of 4, 5, 13, 43, 64, 81–2, 144, 146, 161, 168, 173, 233–4, 247, 250–1, 254, 257, 267, 278, 285
poetry 112, 168–9, 217–20, 228, 231–2, 235, 242–9, 255, 259, 260–4, 267–8, 270, 274–5; didactic 247–8, 264n, 277; habitable 116n, 257–64, 267–8; and philosophy 93, 94, 96, 243, 277; and politics 10n, 43, 70, 94, 137n, 147n, 184, 219, 250–7, 277, 285; and religion 6, 81–7, 96, 99–100, 105, 109, 112–13, 115–17, 168, 270, 277–9
Poland 146
Pomairols, C. de 88

positivism 60, 87, 91, 95, 106, 245, 247, 250, 254, 278
pragmatism 48, 84, 89, 93, 95–6, 101n, 103n
Pressensé, F. 105
propaganda xii, 43, 121–2, 136–8, 140–59, 182, 185–6, 201, 203, 205, 231, 249–50, 258–60, 263–4, 268; direction and stimulus 123–6, 129, 132, 140, 144, 162, 166n, 178, 188, 204, 220, 223–4, 228–9; mechanics of 13, 132–4, 138, 154, 160–3, 166–9, 173n, 177–8, 184, 198, 217, 225, 232–3, 282; in Nazi Germany 157
Protestantism 183
Proudhon, P.-J. 55
Proust, M. 28, 33
Provence 5, 35, 39, 44, 51, 73, 108, 160, 162, 172, 189, 191, 220–1, 226, 260
Puvis de Chavannes 36, 162n

race 25, 32, 40, 42, 64–5, 66, 77–8, 139–40, 145, 169, 178, 187n, 193, 195, 203, 209, 222, 264
Racine, J. 109, 151, 257, 268
radical-socialism 82, 99, 124, 249n
Rashid Ad-Din Sinan 4, 167–9
rationalism *see* reason
realism: in education 211–14, 218–19, 222, 223n; literary 9, 233, 241–7, 249–50; political 7, 9n, 10, 16, 69, 72, 90–1, 103, 124–5, 128, 136, 141, 147, 158, 161, 174, 201–3, 209, 212–15, 219, 250–1, 277–8, 281; *La France réelle* 69, 125, 211–12, 218–19, 277, 281; subjective 242
reason: cult of 135n, 153; in education 48, 205–8, 213n, 216–17; and experience 87, 89, 106, 242, 262, 267, 272–3; and experiment 94n, 102; and the individual 208, 280; and instinct 43, 111–12; isolates 46, 48, 206; and myth 138, 188–9; and nation 125, 153, 157, 187, 188, 216–17; and observation 93n, 214, 242; and order 116, 228; and poetry 236, 248, 251, 266–7; and politics 138, 251, 281; practical reason 95–6; and reality 189, 216, 242, 255–6; and reflex action 12, 61–3, 213, 281; and religion 82, 84, 87, 89, 117, 153, 188, 229n, 230; and sensation 12, 129, 253
récit xii, 50n, 130, 172, 245, 253, 268–9
reflex, conditioned 12, 61–3, 213, 281
relativism 64–78, 81, 100, 102, 125–6, 130, 212, 245, 254n, 277, 280
Renan, E. 5, 9n, 28, 31, 35, 50, 55–6, 61, 82n, 89, 96–8, 101, 104, 114, 137, 144n, 177, 203–4, 212n, 242, 244, 280
Renard, J. 277
Revolution, French 3, 69, 70, 135n, 153, 158, 167, 212n
Richepin, J. 237
Rhine, Rhineland 4, 86, 114n, 131–2, 134, 155–8, 162, 165, 167, 185, 187, 212–13, 241n, 270, 271, 282
Rhône valley, development of 35
rhythm *see* music
Rio, A.-F. 82n
ritual *see* ceremonial
Rolland, Romain 158–9
Romanticism 335–7, 47, 78, 84–5, 137, 173, 177, 204, 218, 241–4, 247–8, 250, 252–6, 266n, 274, 280
Roman Catholic Church: and art 75–7, 115–17, 150–2, 267–75, 281–2; and disestablishment 87–92, 99, 110, 133–4, 197–200; and egotism 19, 26–7, 71–2, 170–1, 177, 246–7, 285; and language 91–2; liturgy 75, 82, 112–16, 164–6, 170–1, 225–30, 283–4; modernism 100–1; and morals 87–91, 99, 164, 197–8, 201–3, 225–9, 235–6, 285; and

nationalism 30, 53, 66–8, 70–8, 87–92, 98, 99, 109–12, 150, 152–5, 182–3, 186, 195, 197–203, 216–17, 225, 235, 265–6, 268–71, 280–3; and paganism 70, 91, 102, 104–10, 113, 116, 131, 133, 153, 166, 182, 186, 191, 196–9, 228–30, 231, 269–70, 280; parish churches 15, 17, 72, 131, 195–203, 283; pilgrimages 170–3, 177; and science xi, 70–1, 75–6, 82–3, 87–110, 112–14, 201–3, 225, 228–30, 266–9, 272; and the Sorbonne 89–90, 199, 225
Rome, Roman Empire, Latin civilization 8, 11n, 44, 91, 95n, 100, 128, 132, 146, 153, 167n, 171, 181–7
Rostand, E. 151
Rouen 150n
Rousseau, J.-J. 5n, 9, 88, 229, 248, 285
royalism *see Action Française*
Rude, F. 166
Rumania 146
Ruskin, J. 84, 233n
Russia 172
Russian novel 64

Saint-Odile 11, 95n, 128, 180–2, 252
Saint-Simon, C.H. de Rouvroy, Comte de 35
Sand, G. 15–18, 81, 83
scepticism 46, 54, 207, 216
Schelling, F.-C.-J. 93
Schiller, F. 151
Schopenhauer, A. 18, 27, 28, 55
science 12, 48, 57–62, 72, 75, 93–110, 137, 189, 214n, 225–6, 228–30, 243–4, 269, 272; and literature 174, 246, 249, 260n, 274–5; and music 14, 114, 205, 225–6, 229–30, 231n, 233, 269–75; and religion xi, 70–1, 75–6, 82–3, 87–110, 112–14, 197, 225–6, 228–30, 266–9, 272; and society 64, 121, 188, 201–3, 225–6, 229–30, 285
scientisme 92, 105–6, 201
Scott, W., Sir 151
sculpture 5, 160, 166, 254n
Ségur, L.-P., Comte de 147
Sembat, M. 105
Seneca 44–5, 50–1, 54
sensation: and abstraction xi, 8–10, 11–14, 20, 96n, 129, 168, 214, 245; 'application des sens' 23, 259; and existence 44, 256; and image ix, 134–5, 277, 278; and relativism 59, 61–3, 75–6; and religion 74–6, 91, 96n, 97, 166, 168, 226; 'rendre l'idée sensible' 7, 11n, 12, 23, 62, 65, 75n, 91, 107, 125, 127, 138, 168, 171–80, 214, 221–2, 234, 245, 252–4, 262, 277; 'sensible au cœur' 75, 255; sensuality 34, 39–40
Shakespeare, W. 85–6, 142, 151, 245–6
Simon, O.J. 85
Sion-Vaudémont ('la colline inspirée') 11, 53, 106–8, 131, 165, 174, 179, 180–3, 190, 195, 202, 216–18, 223, 232n, 252
slogan 110, 127–8
socialism 3, 35–6, 45, 49–50, 52n, 70, 93–4, 124, 279
sociology 63–4, 89, 126, 206, 274, 283
solipsism 9–11, 29, 55, 210
Sorbonne, La see university
Sorg, L. 245
Soury, J. 56–63, 65, 99–100, 123, 126–7, 199, 214, 221, 243, 281
Spain 135n, 155, 160, 171, 174, 177n, 178, 250, 259, 284
Sparta *see* Greece
Spencer, H. 243
Spinoza, B. 93, 243n
Stendhal 8n, 23, 28, 221
stimulus *see* propaganda
Stirner, M. 279
Strauss, R. 226n

Stravinski, I. 226n
subjectivism 5, 9–10, 55, 242
Sufi *see* Konya dervishes
symbol, symbolism ix, xii, 5–6, 8, 10–11, 59–60, 131, 134–5, 137, 151–2, 160n, 171, 172, 213, 254n, 281–3; inhabited 60; in politics 6, 10–11, 52, 137, 145, 150–3, 156, 165, 180–1, 193, 198–202, 213, 277; in religion 82, 96, 112, 114–15, 151, 164–8, 193, 198–200, 227–9, 277; in science 59–60, 96, 98, 103n
Le Symbolisme 9, 16, 18, 55, 151, 231, 233, 241, 244–7, 249, 252, 254, 255, 274
sympathy 38, 82–3, 85, 107, 109, 117, 134, 174, 180, 225, 253, 274, 277, 284, 285–6
syncretism 69–71, 89–92, 97–117, 150–3, 195, 198–9, 228, 280
syndicalism *see* trade unions
Syria *see* Levant
Sophocles 273

Taine, H. 12, 15, 17, 25, 47, 54–6, 61, 71, 81, 83, 84n, 89, 95, 104, 161, 174, 177, 210, 221, 230, 242–4, 246, 249, 262, 266
Tasso, T. 86
technocracy 35, 42, 200, 202
Tellier, J. 244
Teresa of Avila, Saint 5, 22, 109, 135n, 225
Tharaud, J. and J. 27
Thévenin, M. 55–6
Thibaudet, A. 206–8, 216n, 276
Thomas Aquinas, Saint, Thomism 112, 269–74
Tiepolo, G.B. 35
trade unions 72, 200
type 5, 40, 42, 43, 142, 155n, 160, 169, 188, 246, 247, 249, 263–4

unanimism 64, 144, 157, 165; *see also* crowd, groups
unconscious, the 5, 6, 42–5, 64, 102–3, 174, 187, 188–9, 190, 212, 213n, 214, 250, 253, 267, 273–4, 284
unity: Atlantic 167n; European 266; French 72, 110, 137, 150, 266; of literary form 130, 230, 244, 252–60, 274–5; personal 34, 39, 73, 78, 178, 237, 241–4, 250–2, 260–3, 266, 274–5, 285; regional 39; universal 20n, 73, 78, 279
university 47, 54–6, 61, 89–90, 92, 96, 101, 131, 155, 169–70, 199, 204–5, 210, 211, 212n, 222, 227
utilitarianism 91, 208, 230, 254

Valéry, P. 231
Vaugeois, H. 125, 179, 281
Venice 8, 10, 25–9, 31–5, 171, 191, 213, 221n, 259
Verlaine, P. 36
Versailles 58, 281
Veuillot, L. 254
Vidal de la Blache, P. 181
Villiers de l'Isle-Adam, A. de 27, 36, 55
Viviani, R. 92n
Vogüé, C.-M. de 101
Vosges 182, 186

Wagner, R. 8–9, 26, 55, 82, 151, 156–7, 172, 194, 226, 231, 284
War, Franco-Prussian (1870) 72, 143, 156, 161–2, 173, 177, 184, 217, 252
War, World (1914–18) ix, 3, 142, 143, 145, 153–9, 162, 164–7, 173, 179, 184–8, 199, 201–3, 258, 269–71, 282–3
Whitman, W. 259n
Wordsworth, W. 84
Wyzewa, T. de 55, 245

Zola, E. xi, 16, 45, 61n, 94n, 150n, 241, 244, 245, 249–50

UNIVERSITY OF TORONTO ROMANCE SERIES

---

1 *Guido Cavalcanti's Theory of Love*
J.E. SHAW

2 *Aspects of Racinian Tragedy*
JOHN C. LAPP

3 *The Idea of Decadence in French Literature, 1830–1900*
A.E. CARTER

4 *Le* Roman de Renart *dans la littérature française et dans les littératures étrangères au moyen âge*
JOHN FLINN

5 *Henry Céard: Idéaliste détrompé*
RONALD FRAZEE

6 *La Chronique de Robert de Clari: Etude de la langue et du style*
P.F. DEMBOWSKI

7 *Zola before the* Rougon-Macquart
JOHN C. LAPP

8 *The Idea of Arts as Propaganda in France, 1750–1759: A Study in the History of Ideas*
J.A. LEITH

9 *Marivaux*
E.J.H. GREENE

10 *Sondages, 1830–1848: romanciers français secondaires*
JOHN S. WOOD

11 *The Sixth Sense: Individualism in French Poetry, 1686–1760*
ROBERT FINCH

12 *The Long Journey: Literary Themes of French Canada*
JACK WARWICK

13 *The Narreme in the Medieval Romance Epic: An Introduction to Narrative Structures*
EUGENE DORFMAN

14 *Verlaine: A Study in Parallels*
A.E. CARTER

15 *An Index of Proper Names in French Arthurian Verse Romances, 1150–1300*
G.D. WEST

16 *Emery Bigot: Seventeenth-Century French Humanist*
LEONARD E. DOUCETTE

17 *Diderot the Satirist. An Analysis of* Le Neveu de Rameau *and Related Works*
DONAL O'GORMAN

18 *'Naturalisme pas mort': Lettres inédites de Paul Alexis à Emile Zola, 1871–1900*
B.H. BAKKER

19 *Crispin Ier: La Vie et l'œuvre de Raymond Poisson, comédien-poète du* XVIIe *siècle*
A. ROSS CURTIS

20 *Tuscan and Etruscan: The Problem of Linguistic Substratum Influence in Central Italy*
HERBERT J. IZZO

21 Fécondité *d'Emile Zola: Roman à thèse, évangile, mythe*
DAVID BAGULEY

22 Charles Baudelaire *Edgar Allan Poe: Sa Vic et ses ouvrages*
W.T. BANDY

23 *Paul Claudel's* Le Soulier de Satin: *A Stylistic, Structuralist, and Psychoanalytic Interpretation*
JOAN FREILICH

24 *Balzac's Recurring Characters*
ANTHONY R. PUGH

25 *Morality and Social Class in Eighteenth-Century French Literature and Painting*
WARREN ROBERTS

26 *The Imagination of Maurice Barrès*
PHILIP OUSTON

This book

was designed by

ANTJE LINGNER

under the direction of

ALLAN FLEMING

and was printed by

University of

Toronto

Press